FROZEN & FABULOUS

A DELICIOUSLY FRESH APPROACH TO FREEZER & MAKE-AHEAD MEALS

BY GAIL KURPGEWEIT

All brands used within the text are registered trademarks of their respective owners.

Montreal Steak Seasoning (McCormick® brand)
"Better Than Bouillon® Beef Base
Montreal® steak seasoning
Guinness®
Shan® and MDH® brands
Avery®
Frank's Red Hot Sauce (Original)®
Microsoft®, Boeing®
Amazon®
FoodSaver®
Ziploc®
INSTAPOT®

Author is the owner of the Frozen & Fabulous brand of meal prep containers and associated products.

At the time of publication, no affiliate fees, royalties, commissions or other fees were earned, paid or promised to the Author for other brand-named products recommended throughout this book.

Specific products and brand recommendations are solely based upon the opinion of the Author.

Member's Only Website at
www.FrozenandFabulous.com

VIDEO TUTORIALS, NEW RECIPES, AND MORE!
SCAN THIS QR CODE FOR A 1-YEAR FREE MEMBERSHIP
FOR PURCHASERS OF THIS COOKBOOK

*If you have questions or need help accessing the Member's Only site,
please send an email to info@frozenandfabulous.com*

Chef Gail Kurpgeweit is Professionally Represented by:
Alan Morell and Tim Troke

amorell@creativemanagementpartners.com
ttroke@creativemanagementpartners.com
Creative Management Partners, LLC (CMP)
BEVERLY HILLS GARDENS BUILDING
9440 Santa Monica Blvd, Suite 301
Beverly Hills, CA 90210
Direct Dial: 508-292-7900

Brick Tower Press
Manhanset House
Dering Harbor, New York 11965-0342

bricktower@aol.com

All rights reserved under the International and Pan-American Copyright Conventions. No part of this publication may be reproduced, stored in a retrieval system, or transmitted in any form or by any means, electronic, or otherwise, without the prior written permission of the copyright holder. The Brick Tower Press colophon is a registered trademark of J. T. Colby & Company, Inc.
www.IngramContent.com
For sales in the UK and Europe, stef@gazellebooks.co.uk

Library of Congress Cataloging-in-Publication Data
Kurpgeweit, Gail
Frozen & Fabulous
p. cm.
Includes biographical references and footnotes
ISBN 978-1-899694-89-1, hardcover edition
ISBN 978-1-899694-99-0, trade paper edition

1. COOKING / Comfort Food 2. COOKING / Individual Chefs & Restaurants 3. COOKING / Methods / Professional

Copyright © 2021 by Gail Kurpgeweit

First Printing, November 2021

Cover recipe: Tuscan-Style Horseradish-Crusted Beef Roulade with Roasted Red Peppers & Provolone, page 66
Cover photograph by Kyle Ledeboer, Copyright @2021 Gail Kurpgeweit
The Frozen & Fabulous colophon is a trademark of Taste of Amazing, a division of Purple Cloth Hospitality, Inc.
Cover food styling by Joanna Meyer
All photographs contained in this book and on cover, Copyright @2021 Gail Kurpgeweit

I am sure my friends and family – especially my kids - are breathing a sigh of relief that this is a cookbook and not a tell-all. All I can say is this is my "first" book... so I'm not making any promises about the content of my next one. ;)

Seriously, I am so grateful to so many for support and encouragement over the five-year journey that went into getting this cookbook done. It was (mostly) a labor of love.

Thank you to my writing coach, Martha Murphy, who was the key to completing the proposal for this book and referred me to my uber agent, Alan Morell. Alan saw my potential early on and without him, this book would not be. Also, a big thank you to my Publisher, John T. Colby, of J. Boylston & Company, who brought my heart for cooking to life on these pages.

I also want to thank friends and family for their tremendous support while I was growing my business and creating the recipes that I'm sharing here. My pastor and dear friend, Dr. Paul Dean, of Soma Eastside Church in Issaquah, Washington, not only was the recipient of good, bad and terrible dishes that I served him on recipe testing days, but he was my absolute rock for the highs and lows of my business and personal life. I could write a book on the countless ways this man has impacted my life, my family, my cooking, and my relationship with God.

And dear friends DeAnna (Percival) Gatrel, Kelly Morrison, Ellie Deets and Kay Conley who supported me and my business and, on many occasions, worked with me side-by-side to cook and package food to make delivery deadlines. They are all amazing, admirable women and I really miss our days (and nights) in the kitchen creating delicious food.

But most of all, and with my whole heart, I dedicate this cookbook to my incredible family! My amazing, beautiful daughters Ashley, Kaitlyn, and Madelyn, my handsome son-in-law, Nick, and my gorgeous grandchildren, Parker, Oliver, and Harriet, are the inspiration behind everything I do. There are no words for how much I love, adore and appreciate them!

To everyone who buys, reads and cooks from this cookbook, I wish you tremendous blessing and joy in the process!

Chef Gail

TABLE OF CONTENTS

Introduction 3

Chapter 1: "Need to Know" 5

Chapter 2: From Planning to Plate 13

Chapter 3: Packaging Options & Recommendations 19

Chapter 4: Life Expectancy of a Freezer Meal 25

Chapter 5: Cooking for Fitness 27

Chapter 6: Cooking for Giving 29

Chapter 7: Grab & Go Lunch Recipes 31
    Chicken Cacciatore with Basmati Rice 32
    Latin Flank Steak with Spanish Rice & Bell Peppers in Chipotle Crema Sauce 36
    Teriyaki Chicken with Rice & Broccoli 42
    Blood Orange- Roasted Chicken 48
    Firecracker Salmon 52
    Just Add Mayo Curry Chicken Salad 56

Chapter 8: Main Dish Dinner Recipes 61
    Cantonese Braised Beef 62
    Horseradish-Crusted Beef Roulade Tuscan-Style with Roasted Red Peppers & Provolone . . 66
    Coffee-Rubbed Steak with Coffee Butter 72
    Peanut Butter, Bourbon & Bacon Burgers 76
    Prosciutto-Stuffed Chicken Breasts with Fig & Honey Sauce 81
    Butter Chicken (a/k/a Indian Chicken Makhani) 87
    Chicken Ballotine with Rosemary Beurre Blanc Sauce 91
    Spinach & Feta Stuffed Chicken with Pesto & Mediterranean Salsa . . 97
    Southern-Fried Bacon-Wrapped Chicken & Waffles 102
    Cilantro-Grilled Chicken with Mango Salsa 107
    Oven-Baked Parmesan Chicken 111
    Lamb Cutlets with Mint Orange Cointreau Sauce 115
    Chipotle Roasted Leg of Lamb 119
    Cherry-Stuffed Pork Loin with Black Cherry Chutney 126
    Pork Tenderloin with Bourbon Pear Sauce 131
    Bourbon BBQ Babyback Ribs 135
    Seafood-Stuffed Portobello Mushrooms 141
    Macadamia Nut-Crusted Halibut with Raspberry Sauce 145
    Glazed Salmon (multiple varieties) 149

Drunk Irishman's Shepherd's Pie 153
Roasted Vegetable Lasagna (Vegetarian) 158
Chicken Enchiladas 162
Habanero, Turkey & Sausage Meatballs 167
Swedish Meatballs with White Gravy 170
Spicy Italian Meatballs with Marinara 175

Chapter 9: Drop & Go Slow Cooker Recipes **181**
Chunky Chicken & Corn Chili 183
Guinness Pot Roast with Gravy 187
Carolina-Style BBQ Pulled Pork 192
Andouille Sausage & Shrimp Cajun Jambalaya 196

Chapter 10: Spice Blends **197**
Chef Gail's BBQ Dry Rub 204
Chef Gail's Chipotle Dry Rub 204
Chef Gail's Coffee Rub 205
Chef Gail's Creole Seasoning Spice Blend 206
Chef Gail's Indian Butter Chicken Spice Blend 206
Chef Gail's Mexican Spice Blend 207
Chef Gail's Southern Spice Blend 207

Chapter 11: Meat Brines **209**
Quick Brine for Chicken Breast 210
Overnight Brine for Pork 211

Chapter 12: Troubleshooting **213**

Chapter 13: Quick Guide to Online Tools **215**

Chapter 14: Resources **219**

INTRODUCTION

Traditional freezer meals have *earned* their bad reputation! Exhaustive shopping trips, hours of prep work, eating the same meal repeatedly for several weeks (primarily soups and casseroles), and ending up with meals with no texture or freshness left after months in the freezer.

This book is about to change all those assumptions and show you *innovative ways* to prepare freezer-ready make-ahead meals that **taste delicious**, have **great texture**, and preserve the same **freshness** after six months in the freezer as they had the day you created them. Plus, we'll leave old-school "soups and casseroles" behind as we make **flavorful, premium meals** that you and your family will truly enjoy eating.

Even better, in this book I share how to create delicious, gourmet freezer meals using my favorite time-saving technique, **"eat some, freeze some!"** which allows you to make freezer-friendly make-ahead meals 'on the fly' as you prepare the day's meal. No extra shopping, prep, cleaning or fuss – plus you'll end up with a **great variety** of meal options in your freezer.

The secret behind creating amazing freezer meals is all about *process and packaging* – and I'm sharing with you the **professional "secrets"** I have learned and utilized after years of manufacturing commercial frozen prepared meals for sale online and in grocery stores across the United States.

I am **Chef Gail Kurpgeweit** and I have been in the food business since 2009, sharing my passion for **palate-pleasing, full-flavor foods that entertain and nourish**. I started my business selling cupcakes out of my home, then went to Le Cordon Bleu College of Culinary Arts and expanded my business to include catering. After a year, we had outgrown our commercial kitchen so I acquired a frozen foods manufacturing facility and immediately plunged into a whole new world of food preparation on a massive scale. In catering, it's all about making delicious, aromatic, beautiful food for guests to enjoy. In the frozen foods business, it was that and more: We had to package and freeze the food so it would taste just as fresh, flavorful and hold a variety of textures as it did the day we made it.

When I branched into this new division I had to quickly learn the complex requirements of premium-quality frozen food preparation and preservation, only possible because I was surrounded by mentors and associates with tremendous expertise. But that was only the jumping-off point. My team and I learned and tested new processes, techniques, and packaging designs; and embraced *innovation* to solve previously unsolvable problems.

Over the last decade, while building my 5-star catering business, I created custom-designed, gourmet frozen "grab & go" meals for Microsoft, Boeing, hospitals and universities through the greater Pacific Northwest area. We have also taken our frozen meals to a broader, national market; and many of my commercial recipes for baked goods, prepared meals and powdered formulas are manufactured and sold across the U.S. under various brand names.

And now I'm sharing my best with you. In this book, you will learn how to create **catering-quality, gourmet meals made heat-and-serve convenient.** You can enjoy all the benefits of freezer meal cooking – time and cost savings, convenience, and shareability – while also genuinely enjoying the food you've prepared.

Why? **Because getting families around the table is essential**. Most of us live super busy lives between work, school, kids' activities, family responsibilities and social lives. **As simple as it sounds, an enjoyable meal around the table - talking, listening, sharing stories and delicious food - are the things that make family and friends feel connected.**

When my middle daughter, Kaitlyn, was in high school, she would frequently bring friends home for dinner who she knew weren't headed home to a hot meal. It wasn't unusual for us to have five to six extra kids, skateboards stacked up by the front door, folding chairs squeezed together, as we all gathered around the table. These kids became part of the fabric of our family.

Typically, I was so busy with work and the responsibilities of being a single mom our meals were nothing more than noodles, beef or chicken, and a doctored-up, off-the-shelf canned sauce to pull it together. Other times, I would listen to the kids share their favorite foods and I'd make meals I knew would make them feel special. Such a simple thing it would seem - gathering around a hot meal, sharing the highs and lows of the day. **But in this simplicity, strangers became friends, friends became family, and these relationships continue to bless my life years later.**

I have three amazing daughters – Ashley, Kaitlyn and Madelyn – and even during their most difficult teenage years, when it was often challenging even to know where they were at times, I could get us all back to the table with a hot meal. **We had more laughs around the table than we ever did sitting around the television or running carpool.** It's where we connected, and those bonds are still there today as they've grown older and become incredible young women, one with a family of her own. It is pure joy to see Ashley and her husband, Nick, and my gorgeous grandchildren, Parker, Oliver and new baby Harriet, sharing regular family meals around their own table.

My heart and love of food, cooking and people are in each recipe I've shared in this cookbook, and I hope you enjoy every delicious bite of your own unique creations inspired by it. Please connect with me on social media and share your stories – I can't wait to see how you put your own special touches on these dishes to make them your own.

Meet you in the kitchen!

Chef Gail

Instagram @askchefgail
Facebook @frozenandfabulous.freezermealprep | @tasteofamazing.catering
Websites frozenandfabulous.com | tasteofamazing.com

Chapter 1:
"NEED TO KNOW"
The Essentials of Freezer Meal Cooking

LET'S START WITH "WHAT NOT TO DO!"

There are a few foods to avoid when making freezer meals, as they simply won't perform well after thawing:

- **Mayonnaise** – Real mayonnaise will separate after freezing and becomes oily, watery and very unappetizing. The only exception to this is baking: When using mayonnaise in fully cooked cakes, muffins or pastries, freezing isn't a problem. For savory dishes, however, the best way to prepare recipes that call for mayonnaise is to put together all the other ingredients, package them, then include "add mayonnaise" in the proper quantity to your label instructions. You will see this technique demonstrated in our ***"Just Add Mayo: Curry Chicken Salad"*** recipe in this book. Another option (if you like the taste) is to substitute Miracle Whip for the mayonnaise, which will recover from frozen if thawed in the refrigerator.

- **Leafy, Water-rich Vegetables**, such as lettuce, kale, whole celery, cucumbers and other high-water content vegetables do not freeze well. Many, however, can be par- or fully cooked and then frozen. Sliced or diced celery will hold up nicely when incorporated into a dish. Cucumbers are best when added fresh just before serving.

- **Fresh, Whole Tomatoes:** Uncooked, whole tomatoes will become quite soggy and slimy after freezing, so it's best to cook tomatoes before freezing.

- **Pre-frozen Meats:** When making freezer meals, it is best to start with fresh meats and avoid pre-frozen. The meat will lose moisture during the freezing/thawing process, so putting it through that process twice can lead to dry, tasteless meat. If you must work with frozen meats, it's best to stick with braises, soups or other slow-cooking, high liquid content cooking methods.

- **Pre-frozen Fish & Seafood:** When working with pre-frozen seafood, it is best to keep it frozen until ready to serve, if possible. Cleaned, frozen shrimp, for example, can easily be incorporated into ***"Jambalaya"*** or other high-liquid dishes after the cooked dish has cooled, prior to packaging, and then finish cooking quickly at the time of service. No need to thaw – just add to the dish frozen and it will cook during the reheating process. Salmon can be kept frozen – just prepare the sauce or other recipe ingredients, package separately, and combine at time of service. However, if you must thaw frozen fish or seafood and plan to refreeze it, you'll achieve the best taste and texture if you incorporate it into a saucy, high-liquid dish and avoid overcooking.

FOODS REQUIRING "SPECIAL HANDLING"

- **Potatoes:** Yukon Gold, Russet and other white and yellow potatoes require special handling to freeze successfully, although sweet potatoes and yams are more forgiving. While working with white/yellow potatoes, you'll want to keep peeled potatoes or cut pieces submerged in cold water to avoid exposure to air; otherwise, they will turn dark and unpalatable. When freezing, if other high-liquid ingredients fully cover the potatoes they will perform well, but exposed potatoes need to be par- or pre-cooked to avoid darkening during storage. Raw, peeled potatoes (sliced, diced or whole) can be frozen and will retain their color and texture ONLY if stored in vacuum-sealed packaging and then placed in cold water, or cooked, immediately after breaking the seal.

- **Cheese:** Hard cheeses will freeze safely, but the texture will change. It is best if pre-frozen hard cheeses are used only for cooking after thawing. It is also helpful to shred hard cheeses before freezing to make them easier to work with, as block cheese can become crumbly after freezing. Soft cheeses like brie, cream or cottage cheese will freeze well if they have been transformed by incorporating into a recipe; however, they won't hold up to freezing in their original state.

- **Eggs:** Never freeze a whole egg in the shell, as it poses a food safety risk. However, raw whole eggs outside the shell, egg whites, and egg yolks transferred to a freezer-safe container can be frozen and will perform well if thawed overnight in the refrigerator. Hard-boiled or fried eggs should not be frozen, although there are some techniques where baked or scrambled eggs can work.

- **Milk, Creams & Yogurts:** Milk can be frozen (technically) but the structure will change, making it challenging to consume. Also, milk or cream used in an emulsion (like a sauce) can easily break down after freezing, creating a watery dish that is less than appetizing. Sour cream and yogurt will also separate unless transformed into a dish properly. For cream-based sauces that will hold well and retain a creamy, silky texture, use the specific separation-preventing techniques you will find detailed in recipes throughout this cookbook. It's essential to pay close attention to the processes used and the binding ingredients recommended based on the style of the dish.

- **Mushrooms:** Raw mushrooms should never be frozen – they will not hold up to the process and you'll end up with rubbery mush. However, you can freeze cooked mushrooms and they'll hold up remarkably well when appropriately packaged. It is best to use a tightly sealed freezer-safe container, a resealable zippered bag with all air removed, or a vacuum-sealable bag. Air is the enemy when it comes to freezing cooked mushrooms, so getting a proper seal is key.

- **Rice & Pasta:** This surprises many people because they have seen a considerable variety of rice and pasta dishes on our frozen food menus, and there are many in this cookbook. But to create a flavorful pasta or rice-based dish that will hold up well to freezing, **technique is the key**. One technique is to undercook the pasta or rice before packaging to finish cooking when the dish is reheated. However, this technique requires a specific amount of liquid in the dish to make sure the pasta or rice has enough to absorb to finish cooking, but not too much so it becomes soggy. The pasta or rice will also absorb excess moisture created by water releasing from other ingredients in the dish (like frozen broccoli or other vegetables) so ratios matter.

- Another technique is to add rice or pasta to a frozen, prepared dish on the day of service. This strategy works well for meals at home but presents a challenge if you want to make meals to deliver to a loved one or the convenience of heat and eat. We test all recipes in this cookbook and on our Member's Only website at www.frozenandfabulous.com to ensure a proper balance of liquids so your finished dish will have fluffy rice or *al dente* pasta when prepared according to the instructions.

- **Fried Foods:** Crispy fried foods can become soggy and limp after being stored in the freezer if not handled correctly. The key for successfully freezing and reheating fried foods is all in the technique, which is generally a combination of par-cooking and baking or quick-frying at time of service. For a great tutorial on working with fried foods, check out **Taste of Amazing's Southern Fried Chicken & Waffles**, a wildly popular Chef Gail signature dish.

FOOD SAFETY: COOLING & HEATING FOOD PROPERLY

Before you begin cooking, make sure to have **adequate refrigerator and freezer space available** to handle cooling processes. When working on larger batches or having a group cooking session, fill a large cooler with ice to hold prepped ingredients so the refrigerator is available for cooling finished dishes.

Also, **check your freezer's temperature** to ensure it consistently runs at 0°F (-18°C) or below to provide the best environment for preserving food without causing any damage or breakdown in quality. Your **refrigerator temperature** should be running at 40°F (4°C) or below.

You will also want to have a **reliable, calibrated stem thermometer** available for taking food temperatures. To calibrate a stem thermometer, fill a small glass with ice, then add cold water to the ice's halfway point. Place the stem thermometer into the center of the ice water and read the temperature after 15 seconds. It should read 32°F (0°C). If it doesn't, then adjust the thermometer until it is reading temperatures correctly.

COOLING ESSENTIALS

The most important thing to remember when cooling hot foods is never to **put covered hot or warm food in the refrigerator or freezer.** Covered hot foods are the perfect environment for dangerous bacteria to grow, so it is **critical** that you leave hot or warm foods uncovered when you place them in the refrigerator or freezer. Once fully cooled the dish can then be covered, sealed and stored safely.

The best way to cool foods properly is to place them in a shallow container, approximately 2" (5cm) in height or less, and put them uncovered in the refrigerator. This will allow the food to cool quickly and completely so it can then be packaged for longer-term storage.

Avoid cooling foods in deep vessels or dishes, such as canning jars or deep bowls. With larger volumes, the food will cool more slowly in the center, allowing microorganisms to grow that could permeate the entire dish. Using a shallow pan or dish to cool is the ideal way to ensure food cools quickly and all the way through before transferring to a plastic freezer-safe bag or freezable container.

If you don't have a 2" (5cm) deep container in which to hold and cool foods, here are a few other suggestions for getting food cooled quickly and safely:

- Separate into smaller portions to allow faster cooling.
- Stir loose foods, such as soups or sauces, frequently during the cooling process.
- Place container in an ice bath. To make an ice bath, place a larger container than the one holding the food on the counter, fill it with ice, then place the container holding food into the ice so the ice surrounds the container as high up the sides as possible. Carefully monitor and stir often to make sure the food is cooling quickly.

HIGH-RISK FOODS

High-risk foods are those that provide the best conditions for harmful bacteria growth. These include ingredients that are low in acid, high in starch or protein, and high in moisture, such as:

1. Meat and meat products
2. Milk and dairy products
3. Cut, fresh fruit (tomatoes are fruit)
4. Unpasteurized, raw eggs (outside the shell)
5. Cooked Rice

The best ways to ensure food safety with high-risk foods are:

- Cooking thoroughly to the appropriate temperature;
- Managing temperatures during food preparation, cooling and storage; and
- Thawing frozen foods in the refrigerator or under continuously running cold water.

The "danger zone" for high-risk foods is between 41°F to 135°F (5°C to 57°C), so never leave foods in this temperature range for more than two hours. Cool and maintain high-risk foods to temperatures under 40°F (4°C) or above 136°F (58°C).

Also important: When you add a high-risk ingredient to a dish containing non-high-risk foods, the entire dish now becomes "high risk" and temperatures must be carefully and properly controlled.

FREEZER BURN & HOW TO PREVENT IT

Freezer burn occurs when frozen foods are exposed to air or temperature fluctuations, causing the item to lose moisture. Freezer burn appears as a white or grey-colored area on the surface of the food, or the food can become dry and crumbly around the edges.

Food that shows signs of freezer burn is usually still safe to consume if you cut out freezer burnt areas and preserve the remainder of the dish; however, the taste, texture and nutritional content will most likely be affected.

To prevent freezer burn:

- Avoid temperature fluctuations in the freezer
  - **Shut the door!** I think I've yelled this to my children about a million times. Don't allow the freezer door to stand open for extended periods

"NEED TO KNOW" THE ESSENTIALS OF FREEZER MEAL COOKING

or temperature fluctuations will occur, leading to freezer burnt food.
- Keep a freezer thermometer on a middle shelf inside the freezer and verify it consistently runs at 0°F (-18°C) or below.
- Store foods in airtight containers.
- Wrap the outside of freezer-safe containers in plastic wrap to provide additional protection.
- If using resealable freezer bags, ensure all the air has been removed from the bag. (See more on techniques to remove air in *Chapter 3: Packaging Options & Recommendations*.)
- Avoid wrapping frozen foods in aluminum foil or thin layers of plastic wrap.
- Meats and grocery store items packed in foam or light plastic wrap should be re-packaged into air-tight containers or vessels. Vacuum-sealed bags are very effective at keeping ingredients fresh and air-tight.

THAWING FROZEN FOODS

Many foods can be "cooked from frozen" and do not require advanced thawing. In this cookbook, you will find specific instructions for cooking or heating from frozen whenever possible to do so and still retain the integrity of the dish, as this is generally the most convenient way to enjoy prepared meals from the freezer.

Raw, Par- or Fully-Cooked Meat. It is always best to pre-thaw meat (chicken breast, pork loin, steak, etc.) prior to cooking so the meat will retain its moisture and not overcook during the reheating or final cooking process. The only exception is if you are using a *sous vide* cooking technique, which will ensure the meat will cook evenly from frozen. To learn more about this cooking process see *Chapter 2: From Planning to Plate*.

The best way to thaw raw, par- or fully-cooked meat is to place in the refrigerator overnight with paper towels, a tray or container underneath to contain excess moisture. Large cuts of meat (like roasts, full loins or whole poultry) may require 1-2 days to thaw all the way to the center.

Casseroles, sauces and all other frozen foods can also be placed in the refrigerator to thaw overnight. Keep covered to avoid drying out of the top layers.

In a hurry? Try these "quick-thaw" techniques:

Cold Running Water Method: This technique works well to quickly thaw meats, seafood or other food items packaged in an air-tight container, resealable bag or vacuum-sealed packaging. Place the item - with its container or packaging fully intact - into the sink. Run cold water over the top to allow cold water to continuously cover the majority of the item and drain into the sink below. Avoid water accumulating – the water should be continuously flowing, not standing.

For shellfish (like shrimp), you can remove them from the bag, place in a colander and allow cold water to run over the top directly onto the shellfish so it can drain underneath.

Cold Bath Method: If your food is packaged in a vacuum-sealed bag or airtight resealable bag, this technique will work pretty quickly to thaw the item. Place the fully-sealed item in a bowl of cold water so it is completely covered. Most food items will be fully thawed within 15 to 20 minutes using this method. If the item is not fully thawed after 20 minutes, replace the water with fresh cold water. Replace water at least every 30 minutes until thawed – water should stay cold to the touch to be most effective.

Never use hot or warm water with these quick-thawing techniques. The water must be cold to ensure food safety and thaw the items to the center.

COOKING INSTRUCTIONS – WHEN TO FOLLOW/WHEN TO FLEX

In sharing these recipes, I have written detailed instructions so you can enjoy the same dish I would create if I were standing with you in the kitchen. It is my hope you will benefit from the techniques and strategies I've shared to extract a **full palate experience** from these recipes, and use these strategies as tools in other areas of cooking.

When it comes to technique, I encourage you to follow the instructions as written. Anyone can throw ingredients together in a pan and cook or freeze it. What makes delicious food happen is in the techniques employed to develop flavor, create balance, and preserve texture and richness. This is especially important if you want these qualities to survive a day, month or year or more in the freezer.

When it comes to flavor profiles, I encourage you to flex! As you create these recipes, you'll find "the sweet spot" for your personal taste preferences; and may even want to take some shortcuts to make the cooking process easier.

Spice blends are a great example: You can purchase **Chef Gail's Spice Blends** on our website at www.frozenandfabulous.com; you can make your own using the recipes provided; or you can use your own favorite spice blend concoction. The same goes for sauces: If you don't have time to make a sauce from scratch, use a bottled version of your favorite.

Cooking delicious food doesn't have to be complicated – have confidence knowing almost every mistake can be corrected and still result in a tasty meal. (*See Chapter 12: Troubleshooting – How to Correct Mistakes.*)

Meat portion sizes are flexible. When you see a recipe indicating a 2 LB (912g) roast, but your roast is 1.5 LB or 3 LB (684g or 1368g) – but not quite to the size shown in the next up or down batch size - it's okay to flex a little. Just know that cooking times may be more or less, or your final portions might be slightly more or less, so adjust your expectations accordingly.

Mostly I hope you will "flex" your cooking muscles with every new recipe you use from this cookbook. Consider these a starting point for your own creativity to make something incredible!

KITCHEN TOOLS, EQUIPMENT & SUPPLIES

As a professional Chef, I appreciate intelligent, reliable tools that save time, money and provide a better quality of finished dish. Here are a few of the tools I recommend that are of particular relevance to freezer meal cooking:

- **Oven-safe, microwave-safe, freezer-safe plastic containers.** This is such an essential tool for freezer meal prep, I have developed my own line of kitchenware products. You can find more information about these containers on my website at www.frozenandfabulous.com, along with a direct link to my product pages on Amazon. Our containers are available in several sizes, are BPA-free, reusable and/or recyclable, and come with handy storage lids.

    We also have a microwave-safe "grab & go" bowl product with a tight-fitting, vented lid that is perfect for making single-serving lunches or meals on the run. These particular containers aren't oven-safe but will work perfectly in the microwave directly from the freezer.

    Although it's typically a challenge to find quality oven-safe, freezable plastic containers, there are many microwave-safe food prep products on the market. The key is to find a non-glass, non-aluminum product that will protect your food in the freezer, is easy to use when it comes time to serve, and accommodates your personal reheating preferences (oven, microwave, *sous vide*, crockpot, etc). Learn more about meal prep containers in *Chapter 3: Packaging Options & Recommendations*.

- **Vacuum-seal packaging system** with sealable bags. The brand I use at home is FoodSaver and I highly recommend its reliability and ease of use. You can easily find vacuum-seal bags and supplies locally or online, and most models will accommodate both dry and high-liquid foods. I also like the convenience of FoodSaver packaging rolls so you can customize the size of the bag to what you need. There are, however, other brands of vacuum-seal packaging systems available that also work well – the key is to have a system that is accessible and convenient so you'll consistently use it.

    Foods stored in quality vacuum-sealed packaging will last longer in the freezer, generally do not suffer freezer burn, and you will have more options when it comes to thawing, reheating and cooking. The *sous vide* techniques discussed in *Chapter 2: From Planning to Plate* are best used with vacuum-sealed packaging versus resealable bags, for reasons that will be spelled out in more detail in *Chapter 2*.

    Vacuum-sealing systems also prove helpful when buying ingredients in large quantities. Depending on the food item, you will get 1-2 weeks longer shelf-life in the refrigerator, or a year or more in the freezer when you package smaller amounts until ready for use. Even dry storage items, like nuts, will hold texture and freshness longer when stored in vacuum-sealed bags. It's a great way to save money on food costs and preserve freshness.

- ***Sous Vide* Immersion Circulator** – A *sous vide* immersion circulator device is designed to sit on the side of a container or pot and hold the temperature to a precise degree. This level of temperature control prevents overcooking, and newer models can be controlled by an app so you can set and adjust time and temperature even if you're away from home. There are many brands to choose from, as these items become more popular for home cooks.

An immersion circulator is not required for *sous vide* cooking at home, but it does make it much more manageable.

- **Crockpot or Slow Cooker** – Crockpots and slow cookers allow you to cook food slowly over several hours. They are particularly useful for working families who want to set the food before leaving for the day and come home to a ready meal. I have dedicated an entire chapter in this cookbook to recipes that work well in a crockpot – see *Chapter 9: Drop & Go Slow Cooker Recipes*.

- **Instant Pot or Pressure Cooker** – An Instant Pot can slow-cook like a crockpot, but it can also cook food quickly when used as an electric pressure cooker. Some Instant Pot models can also be used to sauté or brown foods and steam-cook vegetables and rice.

    When used as a Pressure Cooker, food will cook faster than by any other method. High pressure is created by forcing liquid and moisture into the food, which also tenderizes tough meat cuts.

> **CHEF NOTE:** You won't find crockpots, slow cookers or instant pots in most professional chef kitchens. Controlling cooking times and liquid absorption rates using these tools is less precise, so we rely on ovens, fire, pressure cookers or other controllable heat sources. However, among home cooks these types of units are popular and can be great tools when convenience is important, which is why I have included them in this cookbook.

- **Quality Chef Knife and Ceramic Sharpening Steel.** If you only invest in one good knife, I recommend that it be a high-quality Chef knife in a size that fits well with the size of your hand. It's the one tool you will use repeatedly and it can handle almost any cutting task in the kitchen. Cheap knives will dull quickly, making it tougher to cut through meats, fruits and vegetables; and a dull knife is frequently the cause of injury because they are difficult to control. If you buy a good, quality Chef knife and a ceramic sharpening stone, you'll be able to keep your quality knife sharp and effective. The Chef's knife should be sharpened every 60 minutes or so during heavy cooking times.

    To learn more about properly sharpening a Chef knife using a ceramic sharpening stone, watch our online video, *"How to Sharpen a Chef Knife"* at www.frozenandfabulous.com.

- **Food Processor** – I love a food processor for making salsas, pestos, sauces, and speeding up the process of chopping and slicing. A good food processor will allow you to control the size of your chop so you can keep it chunky, or develop a smooth puree, depending on the dish.

- **Immersion Hand Blender** – An immersion blender – or stick blender – is handy when making sauces or soups. It allows you to blend directly in the pot or pan rather than transferring large quantities to a food processor or blender.

- **Potato Ricer** – A potato ricer is a tool that pushes soft foods through tiny holes. Using this tool with more firm foods will result in pieces the size of a grain of rice (great for making riced cauliflower). When used with softer foods, like cooked potatoes, the food will come out with a smooth, velvety texture.

    It is important not to overwork mashed potatoes, as the starches will build up and become "gummy" in texture. This is a common problem for home cooks who use hand or stand mixers to make mashed potatoes. On the other hand, using a manual potato masher will typically yield "smashed potatoes," as it is nearly impossible to get a smooth, fluffy texture using a hand tool.

    A good quality potato ricer is the "chef secret" behind fluffy, silky mashed potatoes. In my opinion, I wouldn't make mashed potatoes if I didn't have this tool on hand as it makes such a significant difference to the texture. Without this tool, I would instead make "rustic" smashed potatoes that don't require over-working.

    You can also use a potato ricer to make silky smooth guacamole, celery root puree, riced or pureed cauliflower, and more.

- **Mandoline** – A mandoline is a cutting tool that will save time when performing slicing tasks. I particularly like to use a mandoline when making *"Potatoes Au Gratin with Celery Root & Gruyere" (find this recipe at www.frozenandfabulous.com)* because it delivers consistency in size which facilitates even cooking throughout the dish. When hand slicing, it is easy to get some slices thicker and thinner than others – this will result in some slices getting overcooked, others undercooked, and a less enjoyable finished dish. The mandoline solves this problem and can be used to slice almost any vegetable quickly. I also use it to slice hard cheeses and Italian meats to make beautiful *charcuterie* displays when entertaining.

- **Stand Mixer** – It is typical to use a stand mixer to make cookie doughs, cake batter, frostings, and baked goods, but I also like to use it to make meatballs, meat loaf, hash, and "pulling" or shredding cooked pork or beef. A good quality stand mixer is a "must-have" for incorporating ingredients, whether savory or sweet.

- **Hand Mixer** – If you don't have a stand mixer, a hand mixer is the next best thing. It will allow you to mix softer foods, make whipped cream, meringues, and soft batters for cookies, cakes and cheesecakes.

- **Stockpot** – A large, heavy-bottomed stockpot is essential when creating large batches of soups, stocks, and sauces. Lightweight aluminum pans will cause foods to burn quickly, so look for stockpots with heavy, thick bottoms to get the best results.

- **Kitchen Scale** – A small kitchen scale that will weigh out ounces, grams and pounds will make your life so much easier! From weighing out ingredients for a recipe to separating meat purchased in bulk, using a scale will make the process faster, more efficient, and accurate.

- **Stainless Steel Mixing Bowls** – I would recommend having several large, wide-mouth stainless steel mixing bowls on hand for preparing large batches. They are easy to clean, hold large quantities of food, and make mixing faster and easier.

Chapter 2:
FROM PLANNING TO PLATE

Whether you're preparing several recipes in a batch cooking session to fill the freezer, or taking it one meal at a time, a good meal prep plan will bring it all together with the least amount of effort. In this chapter, I'll lay out the best ways to approach meal prep planning so you can enjoy the process.

WHAT'S FOR DINNER? EAT SOME, FREEZE SOME!

This is my favorite method of filling the freezer with a variety of family-favorite frozen meals: **Make today's meal plus a little extra for the freezer.** It's a super-efficient method and doesn't require a lot of advance planning or heavy shopping.

All recipes in this cookbook include "make it now" instructions so you can enjoy the dish the same day you prepare it. These instructions are usually different from those for a make-ahead meal, as the freezer meal instructions are specifically designed to preserve freshness, taste and texture, and extend freezer shelf life.

Keep it simple: Follow the recipe instructions, and when it comes to the "make it a freezer meal" instruction, separate the portions you want to freeze. Then continue to the "Make it Now!" instructions with the remaining amounts to finish preparing today's meal. These recipes have been designed for this exact process so you'll find it easy to create delicious meals for today, next week and next month, all in one efficient cooking session.

It's also an option to make the entire batch according to the "Make it Now!" instructions and then cool and freeze leftovers. However, this method will not generally give you the best taste and texture results with the frozen portions. To improve performance, choose packaging that will allow you to reheat in the least amount of time possible to avoid overcooking.

ADVANCE MEAL PREP PLANNING

The easiest way to begin meal planning is to visit www.frozenandfabulous.com and use our handy "**Meal Planning Wizard**" Tool (available exclusively to our Members). Our tool will walk you through a few questions, help you choose the perfect recipe or recipes, and you'll be able to print:

- Recipes with detailed instructions and packaging recommendations;
- A handy shopping guide; and
- A detailed Meal Prep Plan if you are planning a bulk cooking session.

MEAL PLANNING – MANUAL METHOD

If you prefer to make your own plan, here are some key questions to ask yourself before getting started:

- **Who am I cooking for?** Deciding this in advance will help you choose relevant recipes and the best packaging option for how and when it will be served. For example: If you are cooking for a family of four and an elderly parent, you could package quantities of 4-servings together plus single servings to deliver to your elderly parent. Cooking for kids? Choose dishes they are excited to eat and that you find nutritionally fulfilling.

- **How will it be served?** Will it be enjoyed the same day you prepare it, or is it a make-ahead meal to go in the freezer? Will it be cooked or reheated in the microwave, oven, stovetop, instant pot, crockpot, via the *sous vide* method or on the grill? This decision provides the roadmap of which recipe instructions to follow and the packaging choices to make so final heat-and-serve is super easy. (See also *"Chapter*

3: Packaging Options & Recommendations" for help choosing the right type of packaging.)

- **Making an entire meal or just a side, entrée, "meal starter" or dessert?** When planning a complete meal preparation, side dish recommendations are provided with each entrée recipe to make it easy to choose successful combinations. If you're only planning to make main dishes, I recommend choosing a good variety of meats and dish styles to make "eating from the freezer" a super enjoyable experience. You can also decide if you want to package an entire meal together, or keep all the components separate, as this will affect your packaging options. Deciding in advance the style of dish you want will help bring focus to your recipe selections.

- **Do I want to control portions, calories, or a nutritional element of the dish?** Knowing this will help you choose recipes, and modifications to recipes, to achieve your portion size and dietary targets. It's also good to decide this in advance so you can choose packaging that will allow you to control portion sizes for your preferred method of heat and serve.

- **Am I trying to reduce costs or stay within a specific budget?** If so, choose recipes with low-cost ingredients or look for multiple dishes that share the same items. For example, chicken can be used across several recipes allowing you to benefit from bulk-buy cost savings and still enjoy lots of variety through different flavor profiles. For help choosing recipes that cross-utilize items, see *Chapter 14: Resources* for an Index of Ingredients AND our handy Index of Mix & Match Components. It's also helpful to "shop your own cupboards" to use up spices and less frequently used pantry items.

- **Am I cooking for everyday meals or a special occasion?** Deciding on purpose or function will also help narrow down your recipe selections.

Once you've answered these questions, meal prep planning becomes simple and focused:

- Choose your recipe or recipes.
- Choose packaging style or styles.
- Create a shopping guide based on the ingredients and packaging chosen (See *Chapter 13: Quick Guide to Online Tools* to access our customized **Shopping Guides** on our members-only website at *www.frozenandfabulous.com*.
- Purchase the ingredients (*make life easier and get your groceries delivered!*)
- Turn up the music, pour a glass of wine, and follow the recipes.
- Package the food and store it in the freezer (*reserve some to serve today*).
- Recruit the kids, spouse or a friend to help with the dishes.
- RELAX! And next time you're hungry, head to the freezer to **heat, serve and enjoy!**

BATCH COOKING

Setting aside a few hours to do "batch cooking" is undoubtedly the most efficient way to fill the freezer with a large selection of prepared meals. However, it does require more advanced planning; and, depending on the number of recipes, more space in your fridge and freezer for ingredients and prep process.

But if you're ready to schedule a cooking day, the key to a successful prep session is in the **Batch Cooking Production Plan.** This step-by-step plan breaks out prep steps (like cleaning, dicing, slicing) from the cooking and packaging steps. For example: If three of your recipes call for diced onions, chop all the onions you'll need for all three recipes, then separate the cut onions according to the amount needed for each recipe. The same goes for all other common ingredients amongst the recipes you'll be preparing, making the preparation process quick and efficient. See *Chapter 13: Quick Guide to Online Tools* to access our customized Production Plans and Production Plan Wizard Tool.

When batch cooking, it's essential to prepare your space *before* you do any heavy shopping. You'll want to make sure your fridge and freezer are clean and have plenty of room to store ingredients. In addition to holding finished, packaged meals, your freezer will also be helpful during the prep process to speed up cooling times and to quick-freeze individual portions, when applicable. Having several shelves clear will be very useful. The same is true for your refrigerator: You'll need shelves empty to hold foods for cooling before packaging.

When menu planning for a batch cooking session, choose recipes that have complementary cooking processes so you can keep things moving. For example, if all your recipes require stovetop cooking, that could create a production bottleneck. But if some of your recipes can be cooking in the oven while you're finishing other elements on the stovetop, while another recipe requires no advanced cooking at all, you'll end up with a great variety of finished meals from a much shorter cooking session.

Careful menu planning will also allow you to choose ingredients that can be cross-utilized across multiple dishes, allowing you to save time and money and avoid waste. You will also find a helpful index of ingredients at the end of this book, making it fast and easy to choose dishes that prep well together.

> **GO TEARLESS:** When cutting onions, try chilling in the refrigerator first. Colder onions will reduce or eliminate tears.

GROUP COOKING

All the same rules of Batch Cooking apply to Group Cooking, except organizing a Group Cooking session can be a lot more fun. It also helps spread the work and costs around to get more food prepared in less time at the lowest price.

Creating a Production Plan for a group cooking session is made substantially more manageable with the **Group Cooking Production Planning Tool**, which you'll find in the Member's Only section of the www.frozenandfabulous.com website. Like the Batch Cooking Production Plan, this guide will break out the prep steps according to the overall ingredients used across multiple recipes.

The difference is, you can print these tasks as **Individual Prep Lists** so each person in your group will know what they should be doing. Imagine: Each person shows up to cook, you hand them their individualized **Prep List**, and everyone can work together without crossing over or duplicating tasks. See *Chapter 13: Quick Guide to Online Tools* to access our Group Production Plan and Individual Prep Lists Online Tool.

When preparing for a group cooking event, it's important to include plans for the following:

- **Shopping.** It's a good idea to have a couple of people do the group's shopping together rather than multiple people shopping individually. By purchasing ingredients in large quantities, you'll save money and ensure consistency of quality and style.

- **Splitting Costs.** One of my favorite ways to share costs fairly for group cooking events is to divide the expenses and finished dishes equally among all the participants. For example, if you have six people prepping, follow the recipes to create portions that are divisible by six (6, 12, 18, 24, etc.) to ensure everyone can take the same number of finished meals home. Then divide the total costs for food and packaging by six so everyone pays the same and receives the same value.

- **Extra Cold Storage Space.** Bring in large coolers with ice to hold extra refrigerated ingredients. This will allow you to keep the refrigerator shelves open for faster cooling of prepared foods prior to packaging.

> **QUICK TIP:** If each person in the group brings their own cooler, the coolers can be used to store ingredients during prep, then used to hold finished, packaged meals to take home.

- **Work Stations.** Create comfortable workspaces for everyone in the group.
  - Starting with a clean, sanitized sink, create a **washing station** for fruits and vegetables, with access to a produce washing product and colanders for drying. (*For info on my favorite produce-washing products, visit www.FrozenandFabulous.com.*)
  - **Prep stations** should have a cutting board, knife, peeler, a mandolin for slicing (if available), scales for weighing ingredients (if available) and a bowl for waste.
  - The **stovetop cooking station** needs a cleared space adjacent to the stove for prepping and handling the food, along with access to pots, pans, utensils and a thermometer.
  - Once the prep is done, clean up and convert Prep Stations to **Packaging Stations**. If you're using a vacuum sealer, form an assembly line process where the food gets portioned and placed in bags, then another person seals and labels. Use the same assembly-line process for meals packaged in zip-lock bags and containers: One person fills the container or bag with the correct portion of food,

another person attaches the lids and labels, and another person places in the freezer or individual coolers.

- **Recipe Selections.** A good strategy for choosing recipes for group cooking sessions is to select recipes that:
  - Use the same ingredients across multiple recipes;
  - Incorporate a variety of prep and cooking techniques so not everyone will need to be working in the same station at the same time;
  - Address allergen or special dietary restrictions for one or more people in the group.

  To make it easier to choose recipes, visit www.frozenandfabulous.com to use our handy **Recipe Selection Tool**. This tool will act as a "wizard" to help you find and select recipes that will make the group cooking process easier and more rewarding for everyone. See *Chapter 13: Quick Guide to Online Tools*.

- **Large Scale Group Cooking Events.** If you have a larger group who want to cook together, it's a great idea to **rent a commissary-style kitchen space**. These are typically available for public rental in larger church buildings, but you could also conduct an online search for "commissary kitchens," "shared-use kitchens," "ghost kitchens," or "cloud kitchens" in your area that offer day rentals.

- **The most important ingredient for Group Cooking: The First Aid Kit**. Light injuries, such as minor cuts or burns, are quite common in the kitchen, but bringing together a group of people cooking in a small space can substantially increase the risk of injury. It is essential to have a first aid kit readily available so injuries can be quickly managed and contained. You can also find our "Kitchen Essentials First Aid Kit" on our website at www.frozenandfabulous.com.

PLANNING FOR PACKAGING

How you package your prepared meals is even more important than choosing your ingredients. The proper packaging will provide a long shelf life (up to 2 years in the freezer) and make reheating or cooking very convenient. On the other hand, the wrong packaging can make reheating a colossal pain in the neck.

Because it's so important, I have dedicated an entire chapter to the topic of packaging. (*See Chapter 3: Packaging Options & Recommendations.*) I encourage you to read through that information before making final plans for your meal prep session.

I have also included recommendations with each recipe in this cookbook as to which packaging option I recommend to make all phases of the process easier, and to preserve the life of your delicious creations.

PAR-COOKED OR FULLY COOKED

Many of my recipes will instruct you to partially cook (also known as *par-cook*) all or part of the dish. Par-cooking is a method that I frequently use for freezer meals to preserve freshness and provide a much tastier experience when it's time to serve the food.

For example: If you were to sear and fully cook a pork tenderloin, freeze, then thaw and reheat it, you would have very over-cooked, dry pork. Instead, it is better to get a hard sear on the meat (*to get the beautiful caramelization flavor*) and then cool and place it in vacuum-sealed packaging. It will stay in the freezer for up to two years, and when you're ready to eat simply thaw, finish cooking in the oven, and have a fantastic dining experience. Using this method, the meat or seafood is cooked to a safe temperature without overcooking, and your taste buds will never know it was previously frozen.

The same goes for pasta. If you par-cook, then freeze, the pasta will finish cooking during the reheating process and you'll enjoy a wonderful texture. It's essential to get the liquid ratios right so the pasta can finish cooking, so recipes that use this method will include these measurements and instructions.

Chicken is another good example: If you are working with chicken breasts marinated or rubbed with flavorful spices, it is *sometimes* better to par-cook. Chicken overcooks very easily, so using this method will preserve moisture and prevent overcooking. However, not all chicken recipes will work for this method, especially if you plan to reheat in the microwave. It is important to read the recipe instructions carefully – if par-cooking is the right option for the specific recipe, it will be detailed for you in the instructions.

ADJUSTING FOR ALLERGENS AND DIETARY RESTRICTIONS

If you need to adjust these recipes to accommodate allergies or dietary restrictions, it's important to read beyond the recipe and check the actual product labels of every ingredient you plan to use. Sauces, spice blends, and special flavoring ingredients may contain ingredients that are not immediately obvious. For example, many condiments contain soy or gluten, bouillon may contain gluten, traditional soy sauce contains soy and gluten, pesto typically contains dairy, and many oil blends contain peanut oil. For someone who is deathly allergic to a particular ingredient, even small amounts can cause big problems. The only way to be absolutely sure your finished dish is free from a specific element is to read product labels carefully.

I have specialized in developing gluten-free products for my clients for over a decade, so I've learned a few tricks to making gluten-free foods taste just as good as the original versions. I'm sharing my gluten-free "tips" and best practices by incorporating a **"Make it Gluten-Free"** section for each recipe in this cookbook. Here you will find ingredients in the dish that typically contain gluten along with recommendations on how to replace them.

ORGANIZING FREEZER SPACE FOR QUICK FREEZING

Before you begin an extensive meal prep session, it's important to clear out a few shelves in your freezer, which will allow you to use the food storage technique called "IQF."

What is IQF? IQF stands for **Individually Quick Frozen**. IQF is a technique where an individual portion of food is frozen completely before being packaged together with multiple servings of the same item. You've seen this technique used if you have ever purchased a bag of chicken nuggets, meatballs or frozen vegetables. If you were to put all those items together in a bag, thawed, and stick it in the freezer, you'd end up with a big frozen ball that would take days to thaw and separate.

Using the IQF method, you can quickly freeze individual pieces before packaging all the portions together, making it much easier to heat, serve, and maximize storage space.

It is also helpful to put some hot foods in the freezer to quickly cool the item down prior to packaging. In Chapter 1, under the Section *"Food Safety: Cooling & Heating Food Properly,"* I discuss how **critically important it is to fully cool foods before storing them**. If you have shelf space available in your freezer during food prep, you can use the freezer to expedite cooling so the items can be packaged sooner.

One more handy tip is to place a baking sheet or other flat pan in your freezer during food prep, then place foods packaged in resealable or vacuum-sealed bags on the flat surface for quick freezing. Once the bagged items are frozen flat, they can be stored vertically to maximize freezer space.

WHAT IS SOUS VIDE?

You will see the term *"sous vide"* used frequently throughout this cookbook. *Sous Vide* means "under pressure" and refers to the process of packaging food in vacuum-sealed bags where all air has been removed (*see Chapter 3: Packaging Options & Recommendations*).

From there, the food is thawed, reheated or cooked in a temperature-controlled water bath while the food is still inside the vacuum-sealed packaging. You can create the temperature-controlled water bath using a pot of water on the stovetop and an accurate thermometer; or a *sous vide* immersion circulator (*see Chapter 1: "Need to Know:" The Essentials of Freezer Meal Cooking*). For more information, you can visit our website at www.frozenandfabulous.com for reviews and recommendations on *sous vide* immersion circulators.

Vacuum-sealed packaging is far and away my preferred method when it comes to packaging meat. It gives you greater protection from air, control over temperature during thawing, reheating or cooking, and it is the best way to preserve moisture. I also love the convenience and food quality that comes from *sous vide*-style cooking and reheating. For that reason, you'll find instructions for this packaging method included throughout this book.

SOUS VIDE AND THE "KILL STEP"

One interesting thing to know about the *sous vide* cooking process is how it differs from traditional cooking methods with regard to **targeted cooking temperatures**.

In the food industry, we call reaching the safe cooking temperature for meat the "kill step" or "lethality step" because reaching that target ensures dangerous bacteria are killed (or in other words, the lethality risk is eliminated). For example, you probably know to cook chicken to 165°F (74°C) so it will be safe to eat.

However, there are <u>two ways to achieve the kill step</u>. One is through <u>immediate heat</u> (hitting the target temperature at least once) as described above. The other is through <u>time and heat</u> (hitting a lower target temperature but staying in that lower temperature range for a longer period of time).

What *sous vide* cooking allows you to do is cook meat to a safe temperature without over-cooking it to a point where the meat begins to lose moisture and texture. By using lower temperature and a slower cooking time you achieve much tastier results: Tender, juicy meat, perfectly crisp vegetables, and an overall much richer dining experience.

If you package your dishes in vacuum-sealed packaging, you'll be ready to go for *sous vide* cooking and re-heating.

For more information, you can visit our website at www.frozenandfabulous.com.

TIME TO EAT!

Once you've frozen your delicious meals, there are several ways to quickly and easily get the food on the table when you're ready to serve.

In this cookbook, every recipe includes recommendations on whether cooking or reheating the meal directly from frozen is best, or if pre-thawing would improve the quality of the finished dish. **Sometimes these recommendations are included on the Freezer Meal Label itself, rather than within the text of the recipe.** Freezer meal labels are available online and via email, as they are too voluminous to print within the pages of this book. See *Chapter 13: Quick Guide to Online Tools*.

When pre-thawing, you have several options. Please review the recommendations under **Thawing Frozen Foods** in *Chapter 1: "Need to Know:" The Essentials of Freezer Meal Cooking*.

Many dishes can be cooked or reheated directly from frozen which is perfect if you sometimes forget to plan ahead.

If you need help finding recipes that finish cooking or reheating in a particular way, visit our Member's Only website at www.frozenandfabulous.com and use the Meal Planning Wizard. It will allow you to choose the re-heating method first, then choose applicable recipes from there.

Chapter 3: PACKAGING OPTIONS & RECOMMENDATIONS

Determining which packaging style to use to hold and store your frozen prepared meals is as important as choosing quality ingredients. The packaging you choose will determine whether your food will maintain flavor and texture; or if it will become damaged by freezer burn. The packaging will also make it super easy – or hugely annoying – to thaw, reheat or finish cooking the food when you're ready to eat.

PACKAGING METHODS

CHEF GAIL'S FROZEN & FABULOUS BRAND MEAL PREP CONTAINERS

I typically recommend *Frozen & Fabulous* meal prep containers because they have been specifically designed for perfect storage, preservation and service when used correctly.

Our **oven-safe containers** can go from the freezer to the microwave or oven, then to the table. They're made of BPA-free recyclable/reusable plastic so you never have to worry about broken glass in your freezer, or an aluminum taste transferring to your food, and they come in a variety of sizes to fit your family's needs.

To use our oven-safe containers properly, it is important to always place the container on a baking sheet before using it in the oven. I also recommend that once your food is in the container and the lid is secured, you wrap the entire container and lid in plastic wrap. The plastic wrap will provide further protection from freezer burn, is easily removed when you're ready to reheat or cook and will prevent the lid from being dislodged if bumped in the freezer or dropped.

Although our oven-safe containers are dishwasher-proof, the lids are not, so it's important to hand-wash the storage lids only.

For **on-the-go single-serve microwaveable meals**, we have a very popular microwaveable bowl with a tight-fitting, vented lid that allows the air to circulate and heat the food more evenly. These containers <u>do not go in the oven</u>, but they are excellent for taking frozen meals straight from the freezer and into the microwave. The vented lid allows air to circulate evenly and releases excess moisture to avoid soggy food. We use this container and cover for our premium frozen manufactured meals and it has proven to be a winner!

You can find more information regarding our *Frozen & Fabulous* meal prep containers on our website at www.frozenandfabulous.com, along with a direct link to our Amazon product pages.

OTHER MEAL PREP PACKAGING OPTIONS

Frozen & Fabulous meal prep containers are not your only option when it comes to choosing affordable, reliable packaging for your delicious meals.

The first step is to decide how you will want to reheat or finish cooking the food, then choose the appropriate container. The reheating method is typically driven by the recipe, type of food, and whether it is fully- or partially cooked, so packaging in a container style that works for the corresponding method is key.

Air is the enemy. Whichever packaging option you choose, make sure you release as much air as possible to reduce freezer burn and extend the shelf life of your finished foods.

The following is a handy chart to help you determine which packaging option is best once you have selected the reheating or cooking method you want to use:

OVEN OR MICROWAVE	OVEN ONLY	MICROWAVE ONLY	STOVE TOP | IMMERSION CIRCULATOR | CROCKPOT
FROZEN & FABULOUS OVEN-SAFE CONTAINERS - can be used in oven or microwave - food can be thawed or frozen when placed in oven or microwave - no thawing required - stackable to maximize freezer space - eco-friendly and great for sharing food - containers are disposable, recyclable or re-usable - BPA free **OVEN-SAFE PAPER CONTAINERS** - can be used in both oven or microwave - food can be thawed or frozen when placed in oven or microwave - no thawing required - good for sharing food - containers are disposable and recycleable. RISKS: - offers little protection against freezer burn. If using, wrap in plastic wrap for more protection. - bottoms can become soggy and break during reheat **GLASS DISHWARE** - can be used in oven or microwave RISKS: - if glass breaks in freezer, clear shards are difficult to detect. - meal must be pre-thawed before going into oven or microwave. Frozen glass under high temperature breaks easily. **CERAMIC DISHWARE** - most can be used in both oven and microwave - see manufacturer instructions RISKS: - pre-thawing is usually required to prevent breakage	**ALUMINUM CONTAINERS** - food can be thawed or frozen when placed in oven - no thawing required - stackable to maximize freezer space - great for sharing food - containers are disposable and recyclable RISKS: - limited to oven-use only - food can take on a metallic taste if stored too long in the freezer - aluminum containers and aluminum foil lids can easily get punctured or come loose in the freezer - it's always best to wrap the entire aluminum container and its' covering in plastic wrap prior to placing in freezer. Just remove the plastic before placing in oven.	**FROZEN & FABULOUS MICROWAVE-SAFE CONTAINERS** - safe for microwave use - perfect for "Grab & Go" meals - food can be thawed or frozen when placed in microwave - no thawing required - vented lid allows for even heating and prevents excess moisture accumulation - stackable to maximize freezer space - eco-friendly and great for sharing food - containers are disposable, recyclable or re-usable - BPA-free RISK: - reheating or cooking options limited to microwave only. - Not suitable for most par-cooking techniques **MICROWAVEABLE MEAL PREP CONTAINERS** - safe for microwave use - many affordable options and sizes available, either online or in local grocery stores - most are stackable to maximize freezer space - easy to share - most are disposable, recyclable or re-usable - always look for BPA-free plastics for safety RISK: - reheating or cooking options limited to microwave only. - not suitable for most par-cooking techniques	**VACUUM-SEALED PACKAGING** - extended shelf life in freezer / prevents freezer burn **FULLY SEALED PACKAGING** - reheat or finish cooking using stovetop or immersion circulator sous vide methods - can be thawed under running water **PARTIALLY SEALED PACKAGING** - cut an opening in the corner of the packaging to reheat in the microwave **RESEALABLE ZIPPERED BAGS** - easily transfer contents to another dish for heating or cooking by microwave, oven or crockpot - affordable - freeze flat, then stack vertically to maximize freezer space - if property sealed and all air removed, can be used with sous vide methods RISKS: - reduced shelf life - high risk for freezer burn. - to maximize shelf life, use heavy-duty bags, double-bag and make sure all air is removed. - food must be transferred to another vessel for heating or cooking.

PACKAGING OPTIONS & RECOMMENDATIONS

PACKAGING FOR SOUS VIDE PREPARATIONS

The easiest and most reliable way to package food for *sous vide* preparation is to use a **vacuum-sealing system**. The system I use at home is the FoodSaver but there are many high-quality brands available. The key to choosing a good system is finding one that will allow you to package both dense and liquid foods, remove all the air from the bag, and create a tight seal. Choosing high-quality bags is equally important as selecting the right sealing machine.

To use a vacuum-sealing system, simply place the food in a sealable bag, place the filled bag into the machine, and let it do all the work of removing the air and creating a tight seal.

Don't have a vacuum-sealing machine? Resealable, zippered bags (like Ziploc) can also be used for *sous vide* preparations.

Method 1:

1. Fill a pot, tub or sink with water. The water level needs to be about as deep as the size of your resealable bag.
2. Place the food in the resealable bag, leaving the top of the bag partially open.
3. Place the bag into the pot, tub or sink of water, being careful not to expose the open end of the bag to the water.
4. As the resealable bag of food is lowered into the water, the water pressure will cause the air to push up.
5. Seal the bag, remove it from the water, and test the seal again to ensure it is locked and well-sealed.

Method 2:

1. Place the food in the resealable bag.
2. Push out as much air as possible – the more air that remains in the bag, the less likely sous vide methods will be successful.
3. Seal the bag.

Both methods will create a sealed bag that will then be suitable for reheating or cooking the food in a hot water bath, either using the thermometer method or an immersion circulator to control temperature.

PACKING FOR THE FREEZER-TO-CROCKPOT (OR INSTAPOT) COOKING METHOD

Resealable, zippered bags (like Ziploc) are very useful when cooking food for the crockpot or InstaPot. One of my favorites is the "form it and freeze it" method:

1. Open the resealable bag and spray the inside with non-stick spray.
2. Place the cooled food into the bag and seal, removing as much air as possible.
3. Place the filled bag into a bowl that is the same size, or slightly smaller, than your crockpot.
   a. If you don't have a bowl of the right size, place the filled bag on a baking sheet and place items (bag of frozen peas, for example) around it to hold its shape.
   b. Shape it in a size that will fit into your crockpot.
4. Place in the freezer for 30 to 60 minutes or until the food begins to hold its shape.
5. Remove the bowl or "holding" items so the filled bag can then be stored in your freezer while retaining its shape.
6. Keep the top part of the food flattened so the finished frozen bags will be stackable.
7. When it comes time to reheat, simply remove the contents from the sealed bag and place directly into your crockpot or InstaPot.
   a. The non-stick spray will make the frozen food release from the bag easily.
   b. If there is any trouble removing the food from the bag, place the sealed bag in a dish of cold water for 5 minutes to thaw the edges. At that point it should remove easily.
8. Cook or reheat according to your recipe instructions.

This method sounds like a bit more work (and it is), but when it comes time to throw it in the cooker and dash out the door, you'll be thankful for the few extra minutes spent during meal prep.

A FEW TIPS ABOUT ALUMINUM FOIL

If you are using aluminum foil to cover your container for storage in the freezer, always add a final plastic wrap around the entire container (and its' foil wrap) to maximize freshness and prevent freezer burn. Aluminum can easily come loose in the freezer or get holes in it when jostled or punctured by another item, so it is *not* a great solution on its own. The final layer of plastic wrap will typically solve or reduce this problem.

But there is a valuable little *"chef's secret"* about using aluminum foil that surprises most home cooks - and I'm going to share with you.

In catering and restaurants, you will frequently see chefs apply plastic wrap to a baking vessel, then cover it in aluminum foil. The first reaction to most people seeing plastic wrap headed for the oven is, "Oh no! It'll melt!" But it is entirely safe to use this method if the aluminum foil completely covers the plastic wrap.

Why do chefs do this? The plastic wrap will seal the baking pan better than aluminum foil, allowing steam to accumulate and keep moisture in the food while cooking.

If you want to use this method when preparing your freezer meals, simply cover the top of your oven-safe container with plastic wrap and tuck it in under the lip of the container. Then apply aluminum foil over the top to completely cover the plastic wrap and then wrap the entire container in a final wrap of plastic. Now it's ready for storage. When you're ready to reheat, simply remove the outer layer of plastic and heat in the oven as usual. After cooking, be careful when removing the cover because the accumulated steam will be HOT!

PACKAGING SIZES

When choosing containers, choose ones that will hold the number of servings you want without over-filling the container. Food packed too tightly won't reheat or finish cooking evenly.

When searching for containers online, you'll frequently see the size indicated in "ounces" or "mL." This almost always refers to *fluid ounces or fluid mL*, not density ounces or grams, and is not a measure of how many ounces or grams of actual food the container will hold. A pound of liquid does not fit into the same size of container as a pound of food.

Although it always varies by the type of food to be packaged, a good "rule of thumb" is HALF. If a container holds 16 fluid ounces (473mL), it will generally hold 8 ounces (227g) (or approximately 1 cup) of prepared food. If it holds 32 fluid ounces (946mL), it should hold around 1 pound (16 oz (456g)) of food.

When packaging meals for a family, here is a handy reference tool for knowing how much food to pack for a single meal **per person for the main meal of the day**. Keep in mind that the weights shown are for **finished, cooked weights**. When you cook meats, for example, there will be shrink. A raw 8 oz (227g) chicken breast will yield approximately 5 to 6 oz (142g to 170g) of finished, cooked meat, depending on the cooking method. **When packaging foods for lunch or breakfast, reduce portions by 3 to 4 oz (85g to 113g).**

TYPE OF FOOD	LIGHT APPETITE & CHILDREN-SIZED PORTIONS	AVERAGE-SIZED PORTIONS (ADULTS)	LARGER PORTIONS (HEARTY APPETITES)
Main Entrée	8 oz (227g) or (1 cup)	12 oz (340g) or (1-½ cups)	14 to 16 oz (397g to 456g) or (2 cups)
Meat or Protein (if not part of a larger main entrée)	4 oz (113g) or (½ cup)	6 oz (170g) or (¾ cup)	8 to 10 oz (227g to 283g) or (approx. 1 cup)
Side of Vegetables	2 oz (57g) or (¼ cup)	3 oz (85g) or (⅓ cup)	4 to 6 oz (113g to 170g) or (approx. ½ cup)
Side of Starch (rice, pasta, etc.)	3 oz (85g) or (⅓ cup)	6 oz (170g) or (¾ cup)	6 to 8 oz (170g to 227g) or (approx. 1 cup)

PACKAGING OPTIONS & RECOMMENDATIONS

> **Important Note:** The measurements shown in the previous table are not based on USDA or other national dietary standards, and are not meant to be a nutritional guide. Instead, these measurements are based on my **real-world experience** as a caterer, prepared meals manufacturer, and a mom cooking for my family.

PACKAGING COMPONENTS

When a recipe calls for multiple components (meat, sauce, toppings, etc.), it is frequently best to package each element separately. This will allow you to reheat or finish cooking each component to the appropriate time and temperature and will keep textures alive in your finished dish.

You can package these elements in resealable, zippered bags (or small containers), lay them on top of your other components (heaviest items on the bottom), then wrap all the recipe's items together in plastic wrap or place in a larger resealable bag. This will make it easy to find all the pieces to your meal when ready to serve.

LABELING FREEZER MEALS

Labeling your foods properly with the dish's name, date prepared, and reheating or cooking instructions is very important. Once food has frozen, it is almost impossible to remember or identify what is inside the packaging and the best way to heat or finish cooking to maintain the integrity of the dish (flavor, texture, doneness).

Also, including the "date packaged" on your label will allow you to pull the oldest to the newest items to maximize shelf life for each dish. In the food industry, this is called the "FIFO" method (first in, first out).

For more information on labeling your freezer meals, please see *Chapter 13: Quick Guide to Online Tools*.

FROZEN & FABULOUS

Chapter 4:
LIFE EXPECTANCY OF A FREEZER MEAL

Your delicious, prepared meal is now tucked safely into the freezer – but how long will it last? The "life expectancy" of your frozen, prepared meals and ingredients is primarily determined by the packaging used and the ability to maintain even temperature levels in your freezer. *(See Chapter 3: Packaging Options & Recommendations and see Chapter 1: "Need to Know:" The Essentials of Freezer Meal Cooking, specifically the section "Freezer Burn & How to Prevent It.")*

SHELF LIFE OF PREPARED MEALS (PAR- AND FULLY-COOKED

TYPE OF PACKAGING	CONTAINER WITH LID OR COVERING	CONTAINER & LID WRAPPED IN OUTER LAYER OF PLASTIC WRAP
Frozen & Fabulous Oven-Safe Containers	9 to 12 months	18 to 24 months
Frozen & Fabulous Microwave-Safe Containers	9 to 12 months	18 to 24 months
Ceramic Dishware	5 to 6 months	6 to 9 months
Glass Dishware	5 to 6 months	6 to 9 months
Microwaveable Meal Prep Containers	9 to 12 months *(depending on the brand)*	12 to 18 months *(depending on the brand)*
Resealable Zippered Bag (air removed)	3 to 6 months	6 to 9 months
Vacuum-Sealed Packaging	12 to 24 months	24 to 36 months
Plastic Wrap Only	1 to 3 weeks	1 month to 6 weeks
Aluminum Foil Only	1 to 2 weeks	1 month to 6 weeks

SHELF LIFE OF PURCHASED FROZEN INGREDIENTS

If you purchase ingredients in bulk and store them in the freezer, the shelf life depends on the manufacturer's type of packaging.

TYPE OF FOOD	MANUFACTURER'S STANDARD PACKAGING	HOW TO EXTEND SHELF LIFE
Baked Goods & Desserts	See "Best By" date on packaging	Wrap in a layer of plastic wrap - add 3 months to "Best By" date on packaging
Frozen Prepared Meals (aka TV dinners)	See "Best By" date on packaging	Wrap in a layer of plastic wrap - add 3 months to "Best By" date on packaging
Fruit & Vegetables	3 to 6 months	Transfer contents of bag to vacuum-sealed packaging – add 12 to 18 months
Raw Meats	1 to 3 months	Wrap in a layer of butcher paper, then wrap that in plastic wrap. Ensure all air is removed from packaging touching the meat – add 3 to 6 months.

Chapter 5:
COOKING FOR FITNESS

Meal prepping can be a tremendous asset for those looking to lose weight, eat more healthfully, or adhere to a special diet or eating plan.

"MAKE IT FIT-FRIENDLY" COOKING INSTRUCTIONS

Each recipe in this cookbook provides recommendations on reducing calories and/or carbs to make the dish more "fit friendly" by swapping ingredients. Just look for the "Make it Fit-Friendly" section at the end of each recipe's instructions.

NUTRITIONAL PANELS

Along with each recipe, you will find nutritional information detailing calories, fat, carbohydrates and other dietary factors for the completed dish. The nutritional information provided with each recipe is based on the main recipe made exactly as specified, then weighed to the specified portion size. The portion size is included so you can strictly adhere to that amount when packaging your dietary-focused meals.

PORTION CONTROL

The easiest way to ensure portion sizes align with your calorie targets is to weigh portions using a **kitchen scale**.

Place your empty container or packaging on the scale, then "tare it out" (or reset it to zero). Make sure it is set to weigh in ounces or grams, whichever is applicable. Then fill the container or packaging with food until it reaches the desired weight.

If you do not have a kitchen scale, then the chart in *Chapter 3: Packaging Options & Recommendations*, specifically the section called *"Packaging Sizes,"* can be used as an approximate reference for use with measuring cups.

Chapter 6:
COOKING FOR GIVING
Sharing your Freezer Meals

My love language is most definitely food. It gives me tremendous joy to gather friends, family and strangers around my table to share a delicious meal, talk about our lives, and bond over the everyday act of eating, which becomes so uncommon and extraordinary simply by experiencing it with others.

Sometimes the best way to shower love on others is by sharing a prepared meal – fresh or frozen – when they need a reprieve from day-to-day meal prep.

MEAL SHARING FOR FAMILIES, FRIENDS, AND ELDERLY LOVED ONES

Whether celebrating the birth of a new baby, managing illness or injury, or mourning a loss, it can be tremendously helpful to receive a meal in these moments. When using a meal-sharing scheduling app, or coordinating delivery directly with the family, here are a few tips to consider:

- **Allergies.** Always find out if anyone in the family has an allergy or food sensitivity and make sure your dishes do not contain any trace. Gluten is a common allergen and can be hidden in sauces and thickening agents, so it's important to check labels before sharing any food that could contain it. Nuts and soy are other common and frequently hidden allergens – and the only way to avoid these allergens entirely is to check your ingredient labels carefully.
  - When using the recipes in this cookbook, see *"Make it Gluten-Free"* at the end of the instructions.

- **Ingredient Preferences.** Ask about food preferences. Do they eat strictly vegan or vegetarian? Do they avoid pork or alcohol? Do they hate mushrooms? Do they like spicy food?
  - When using the recipes in this cookbook, see *"Make it Vegetarian"* at the end of the instructions.

- **Meal Preferences.** If you are feeding a family with children, keep in mind what types of foods would appeal to kids (macaroni & cheese, lasagna, pasta dishes). If creating meals for adults, they will likely prefer more sophisticated meals.

  When cooking for the elderly, make meals that are softer and don't require excessive chewing. Salt can also be an issue for the elderly, so reducing salt and swapping for low-sodium ingredients in the recipe can be helpful.

- **Mobility and Physical Limitations.** If you are cooking for an older adult or someone recovering from surgery, provide meals that can easily accommodate their level of mobility. Heat-and-serve from the microwave would be far easier for them to manage than a meal that may require stove-top or oven cooking, or multiple trips to the kitchen for final preparation.

- **Moving-Time Meals.** When someone is moving, meals can help keep everyone fed while packing, loading, and unloading. But keep it simple! Meals that can be heated and served in a disposable container, no dishwasher required, will be gratefully received.

- **Fresh or Frozen? Important Rules for Packaging:** If the meal will be enjoyed the same day of delivery, then providing fresh or thawed food is, of course, the right choice. However, if making meals for an aging parent or those dealing with long-term illness, it's frequently preferable to deliver fresh but easily freezable meals so they can store, heat and serve as needed.

Either way, I always recommend following these basic rules for packaging:

1. Use packaging so the food can easily be served now or frozen for later, in the same container; and
2. Have a no-need-to-return policy on your containers. When someone is going through a difficult situation, and several people are preparing their meals, it can be stressful and frustrating to keep track of who owns which dish and figuring out how to return them all.
3. Always include the instruction label and date so the recipient can enjoy the meal the way you intended.

FOOD AS A GIFT

It is really common to give homemade cookies, candy and baked goods to friends, family and neighbors during the holidays. It's one of my favorite gifts to receive because it shows the heart of the person who created them.

But consider giving your delicious frozen prepared meals as a gift, too. Having ready-to-eat food in the freezer – food made with heart and passion and love – is something to be treasured. Put your meals in premium packaging, add a festive bow, include a heartfelt message with your reheating instructions and you'll have a gift that will be genuinely appreciated and enjoyed by college students, single adults, busy families and food lovers.

Chapter 7:
GRAB & GO LUNCH RECIPES

A tall stack of delicious, microwaveable heat-and-eat single-serve meals in the freezer is the perfect solution to busy lunchtime schedules. Whether it's a healthy alternative to school lunch for the kids or a sophisticated, fuel-rich meal for a working lunch at the office, grab-and-go freezer meals are the perfect solution.

First up is a selection of "flavor bowls" – combination meals with protein, starch and vegetable components. These complete meals-in-a-bowl are satisfying, heat-and-eat convenient, and can be easily measured to achieve calorie or portion-control targets. It's also really easy to make your own "flavor bowls" using leftovers from your favorite dinner recipes.

Need the perfect container for your "flavor bowl" or grab-and-go freezer meal? Visit our website at www.frozenandfabulous.com for our microwaveable bowls with a vented lid. The vented lid allows for perfect air circulation in the microwave to hold moisture and retain flavor. Plus, these bowls are disposable/recycle or can be washed and reused several times.

FLAVOR BOWLS
(MULTI-COMPONENT ALL-IN-ONE MEALS)

Chicken Cacciatore
with Basmati Rice

Sweet diced tomatoes slow-cooked in a flavorful stew of chicken, bell peppers, onion, garlic and fresh Italian herbs make this one of my favorite go-to comfort foods. It's so fresh and light, it's perfect for summer but also warm and cozy on a chilly autumn evening.

This was one of the most popular dishes I served at my first restaurant, which I opened back in 1991. Because of that, it will always hold a special place in my heart.

Since then, I modernized the recipe when I developed an exclusive line of grab-and-go meals for sale in Microsoft cafés under my brand name, Taste of Amazing. This particular dish included basmati rice, sauce, and chicken in one microwaveable container and was enormously popular. It has been a long-time 'fan favorite' and I'm so excited for you to try it.

From the freezer, this dish heats up quickly in the microwave without losing any of its freshness or texture, and the flavor grows even more intense over time.

Leftovers make an incredible soup! Just heat together chicken stock, carrots, celery, black beans and potatoes or rice, and when they're done cooking add in the leftover cacciatore sauce and chicken. Delizioso!

Make a large batch, then enjoy some now and package the rest for easy meals you'll love all year long!

GRAB & GO LUNCH RECIPES | FLAVOR BOWLS

INGREDIENTS:

# of Servings		4 qty | msmt (weight)	6 qty | msmt (weight)	10 qty | msmt (weight)	14 qty | msmt (weight)
CHICKEN CACCIATORE					
1 ½ LB (684g)	Boneless Chicken Thighs		2 ¼ LB (1026g)	3 ¾ LB (1701g)	5 ¼ LB (2394g)
1 tsp (7g)	Salt, divided		1 ½ tsp (11g)	2 ½ tsp (18g)	1 TBSP (25g)
1 tsp (2g)	Black Pepper (divided)		1 ½ tsp (3g)	2 ½ tsp (5g)	1 TBSP (7g)
2 TBSP (30mL)	Olive Oil		3 TBSP (45mL)	5 TBSP (75mL)	7 TBSP (105mL)
¾ each (170g)	Medium Yellow Onion, chopped into small squares (small dice cut)		1 ⅛ each (254g)	2 each (424g)	2 ½ each (593g)
¾ each (80g)	Green Bell Peppers, de-seeded and sliced into thin strips		1 each (119g)	2 each (199g)	2 ½ each (278g)
1 cup (65g)	Small White or Cremini Mushrooms, sliced thinly		1 ½ cups (98g)	2 ½ cups (163g)	3 ½ cups (228g)
3 each (8g)	Garlic Cloves, minced		4 each (13g)	6 each (21g)	8 each (29g)
½ cup (14mL)	Red Wine		¾ cup (21mL)	1 ¼ cups (35mL)	1 ¾ cups (49mL)
1 (14.5-oz cans) (411g)	Fire-Roasted Diced Tomatoes, with juice		1 ½ (14.5-oz cans) (617g)	3 (14.5-oz cans) (1028g)	4 (14.5-oz cans) (1439g)
½ cup (119mL)	Chicken Stock or Broth		¾ cup (178mL)	1 ¼ cups (296mL)	1 ¾ cups (415mL)
½ tsp (3g)	Sugar		¾ tsp (4g)	1 ¼ tsp (6g)	1 ¾ tsp (9g)
1 tsp (3g)	Italian Seasoning		1 ½ tsp (4g)	2 ½ tsp (7g)	1 TBSP (9g)
⅛ tsp (1g)	Crushed Red Pepper Flakes		¼ tsp (1g)	⅓ tsp (1g)	½ tsp (2g)
½ tsp (3g)	Chicken Base (*Chef Gail recommends "Better Than Bouillon Chicken Base"*)		¾ tsp (5g)	1 ¼ tsp (8g)	1 ¾ tsp (11g)
3 TBSP (48g)	Tomato Paste		4 ½ TBSP (72g)	½ cup (120g)	¾ cup (168g)
1 TBSP (1g)	Fresh Flat-Leaf Italian Parsley, finely chopped (for garnish)		1 ½ TBSP (1g)	2 ½ TBSP (2g)	3 ½ TBSP (2g)
4 each (<1g)	Fresh Basil Leaves, cut into ribbons (chiffonade style) (for garnish)		6 each (<1g)	10 each (1g)	14 each (1g)
BASMATI RICE					
1 cup (180g)	Basmati Rice		1 ½ cups (270g)	2 ½ cups (450g)	3 ½ cups (630g)
1 TBSP (14g)	Butter (Salted)		1 ½ TBSP (21g)	2 ½ TBSP (35g)	3 ½ TBSP (49g)
½ tsp (3mL)	Olive Oil		¾ tsp (5mL)	1 ¼ tsp (8mL)	1 ¾ tsp (11mL)
14 fl oz (444mL)	Cold Water		21 fl oz (665mL)	35 fl oz (1109mL)	49 fl oz (1553mL)
¼ tsp (1g)	Salt, Kosher		⅓ tsp (2g)	½ tsp (3g)	1 tsp (4g)

NUTRITION FACTS:

Serving Size 8 oz   **Calories** 380   **Total Fat** 11g   **Total Carbohydrates** 40g   **Protein** 31g

The portion size shown is based on industry dietary standards and may be smaller than the portion size allowed for in recipe.

INSTRUCTIONS:

Prepare Chicken.
Sprinkle both sides of each **chicken thigh** with HALF of the **salt** and **black pepper**. Add HALF of the **olive oil** to a skillet over HIGH heat. Add the chicken to **SEAR ONLY** on both sides – about 1 to 2 minutes per side. Do not fully cook at this stage. Remove chicken from pan and set aside, leaving behind excess oil and liquid in the pan.

Reduce heat to MEDIUM. In the same pan (*once the chicken is removed*), add the remaining **olive oil** and chopped **onions**. Stir over MEDIUM heat for 1 to 2 minutes, then add **bell pepper** strips. Continue cooking over MEDIUM heat until onions are translucent (*bell peppers should still be firm*). Toss in **mushrooms** and sauté for about 1 minute, then add in chopped **garlic**. Toss lightly until garlic is soft (about 1 minute) and the ingredients are starting to stick to the pan. Add in **red wine** and stir to deglaze.

Allow red wine to reduce by half, then add in **fire-roasted diced tomatoes and juice**, **chicken stock**, **sugar**, **Italian seasoning**, **crushed red pepper flakes**, **chicken base** and **tomato paste**. Stir together and bring to a boil. Continue stirring to make sure tomato paste is fully blended in, then add **partially cooked chicken thighs** back into the pan.

Reduce heat to MEDIUM and cook for 2 minutes, then reduce heat to LOW and simmer for 45 minutes or until chicken is very tender.

> **NOTE:** While sauce is simmering, prepare rice.

After 45 minutes, check sauce for taste.

- If the taste is bitter or acidic, add a little more sugar, continue cooking for 1 to 2 minutes, and then taste again.
- If the taste is most prominent toward the front of your palate but seems to be missing from the back of your palate, add a half teaspoon of Chicken Bouillon Base, stir it in, and continue cooking for 2 to 3 minutes and taste again.
- If the taste is missing from the "finish" or back of your palate, add a little more heat with crushed red peppers or a pinch of cayenne pepper.
- If desired, add more salt and black pepper according to your taste preference.

MIS EN PLACE

1. Cut onions into small squares (dice cut)
2. Chop garlic into small pieces (minced size)
3. Clean (de-seed) and cut green bell peppers into thin strips.
4. Slice mushrooms.
5. Assemble remaining ingredients on list for Cacciatore and Basmati Rice.

CHEF NOTES

If you use Chicken Breasts instead of thighs, pre-brine the breasts in Quick Brine for Chicken (see recipe Chapter 16: Meat Brines).

When preparing mushrooms, clean with a paper towel before slicing. Do not use water or mushrooms will become overly soggy.

If you find this dish too spicy, reduce the amount of Crushed Red Pepper Flakes.

CHEF NOTES

Add **fresh herbs** to this dish near the end of cooking time (fresh parsley, basil, oregano) for an added boost of flavor.

When the sauce is finished to your taste, check the internal temperature of the chicken to make sure it has reached 165°F (74°C). If not, continue cooking on simmer until meat is fully cooked.

Remove from heat.

Prepare Basmati Rice.
Option 1: Prepare rice according to package directions.
Option 2: Rinse the **Basmati rice** well by placing in a mesh strainer and running under cold water until the water runs clear. Set aside.

Heat **butter** over medium heat until melted and starting to brown (should be a golden color). Then add in **olive oil** and the rinsed/drained Basmati rice. Stir

GRAB & GO LUNCH RECIPES | FLAVOR BOWLS

until fragrant (it should have a nutty smell – usually takes about 2 to 3 minutes). Pour in the **cold water**, add the **salt**, stir well and bring to a boil. Stir once more, then immediately cover tightly and turn heat to LOW. Cook for 15 minutes or until the water is absorbed and rice is fluffy and tender.

Remove pan from heat, then allow to sit covered for another 5 minutes, then fluff with a fork.

MAKE IT NOW!

Platter the rice, then pour the Chicken Cacciatore (meat and sauce) over the top. Garnish with freshly chopped **parsley** and fresh **basil**, cut chiffonade style.

MAKE IT A FREEZER MEAL:

Prepare Flavor Bowls.
In freezable, microwaveable bowls, assemble:
- 3 oz (85g) Basmati Rice (pushed to on one side of the bowl)
- 6 oz (170g) Chicken Cacciatore (at least one whole chicken thigh per bowl plus sauce) – pushed to the opposite side of the bowl as the rice.

When each ingredient is completely cooled, cover each bowl tightly and apply label titled "Cacciatore Chicken & Rice Bowl." **Do not seal or fully cover the bowl until all components are cooled to 41°F (5°C) or lower.** When ready to serve, follow reheating instructions on the label.

CHEF NOTES

If you plan to serve this dish on the same day it is made, I recommend using bone-in chicken thighs. Cooking chicken on the bone brings tremendous flavor to the dish.

However, when making this into a grab-and-go flavor bowl, the bone isn't easy to manage when it's time to enjoy. In that case, I recommend using boneless chicken.

FREEZER LABELS

Find and print freezer meal labels for this dish at www.frozenandfabulous.com. (See also *Chapter 13: Quick Guide to Online Tools*.")

ONLINE RESOURCES

Scan this QR code for a direct link to an instructional cooking video for this recipe on www.frozenandfabulous.com, "along with these helpful "How It's Done" videos."

- How to Sear Meat
- How to Clean Mushrooms

VARIATIONS

MAKE IT GLUTEN-FREE

All the ingredients in this dish are naturally gluten-free; however, check the label on the chicken base and chicken stock you choose, as some brands contain gluten.

MAKE IT VEGETARIAN

Swap the chicken thighs for firm tofu cut into 1" (2.5cm) squares and swap the chicken base and chicken stock for vegetarian versions.

MAKE IT "FIT-FRIENDLY"

Use chicken breasts instead of thighs. Then reduce the amount of chicken and comparatively increase the number of bell peppers in the dish. Also, exchange long-grain brown rice or riced cauliflower for the Basmati rice to reduce the glycemic index for the dish.

MAKE IT BUDGET-FRIENDLY

To reduce cost, omit the Chicken Bouillon Base and choose short-grain white rice instead of Basmati.

FLAVOR BOWLS
(MULTI-COMPONENT ALL-IN-ONE MEALS)

Latin Flank Steak
with Spanish Rice & Bell Peppers in Chipotle Crema Sauce

It's a fiesta in a bowl! Premium flank steak is marinated in a lively sauce of chiles, jalapeno peppers and bright spices, then cooked to tender perfection. Served with Spanish Rice, lightly sautéed green bell peppers and a spicy chipotle crema sauce, this dish is big on flavor and perfect for hearty appetites.

If flank steak isn't handy, skirt steak makes a nice alternative. The key is to choose a good quality cut of beef and fresh, crisp, bright green bell peppers. Why green? Because they look soooo pretty next to the red steak and Spanish rice. We do eat with our eyes first, right?

I like to sear this steak over hot coals during grilling season and serve it with Mexican Street Corn. The Chipotle Crema Sauce included in this recipe makes a quick-and-easy "street corn" sauce, especially with a bit of Cotija cheese crumbled on top for texture and flavor. Simple and delicious!

On its own, the Latin Flank Steak is also a great "Salad Starter" – just slice thinly and add to mixed greens along with a few spicy bell peppers for a hearty, healthy meal. I try to keep some in the fridge, too – it's a yummy high-protein snack (hot or cold) and is a quick add-in to rice or pasta for meals in a hurry.

Enjoy every festive bite!

GRAB & GO LUNCH RECIPES | FLAVOR BOWLS

INGREDIENTS:

# of Servings					
4 qty | msmt (weight)		Ingredient	**6** qty | msmt (weight)	**10** qty | msmt (weight)	**14** qty | msmt (weight)
LATIN FLANK STEAK & MARINADE					
2 LB (912g)		Flank Steak, trimmed	3 LB (1368g)	5 LB (2280g)	7 LB (3192g)
1 TBSP (15mL)		Soy Sauce	1 ½ TBSP (22mL)	2 ½ TBSP (37mL)	3 ½ TBSP (52mL)
½ cup (118mL)		Lime Juice	¾ cup (177mL)	1 ¼ cup (296mL)	1 ¾ cups (414mL)
¼ cup (2g)		Sugar	½ cup (3g)	¾ cup (5g)	1 cup (7g)
¾ cup (170mL)		Olive Oil	1 ¼ cups (255mL)	2 cups (425mL)	2 ½ cups (595mL)
2 TBSP (18g)		**Chef Gail's Mexican Spice Blend** (see Recipe in *Chapter 10: Spice Blends*)	3 TBSP (27g)	5 TBSP (45g)	7 TBSP (63g)
1 cup (79g)		Fresh Cilantro Leaves, finely chopped *(1 avg bunch =1 cup (79g) chopped)	1 ½ cups (119g)	2 ½ cups (198g)	3 ½ cups (277g)
4 each (11g)		Garlic Cloves, peeled & smashed	6 each (17g)	10 each (28g)	14 each (39g)
2 each (40g)		Jalapeno Peppers, de-seeded and sliced thinly	3 each (60g)	5 each (100g)	7 each (140g)
¼ tsp (2g)		Salt	½ tsp (3g)	¾ tsp (4g)	1 tsp (6g)
¼ tsp (1g)		Black Pepper	½ tsp (1g)	¾ tsp (1g)	1 tsp (2g)
SPANISH RICE					
2 tsp (10mL)		Olive Oil	3 tsp (15mL)	5 tsp (25mL)	2 ⅓ TBSP (35mL)
½ each (113g)		Medium White Onion, chopped into small squares (small dice cut)	¾ each (170g)	1 ¼ each (283g)	1 ¾ each (396g)
2 each (6g)		Garlic Cloves, minced	3 each (8g)	5 each (14g)	7 each (20g)
1 (4.5 oz can) (127g)		Green Chiles (canned)	1 ½ (4.5 oz can) (191g)	2 ½ (4.5 oz can) (318g)	3 ½ (4.5 oz can) (445g)
1 tsp (3g)		**Chef Gail's Mexican Spice Blend** (see Recipe in *Chapter 10: Spice Blends*)	1 ½ tsp (5g)	2 ½ tsp (8g)	3 ½ tsp (11g)
1 cup (192g)		Basmati Rice	1 ½ cups (288g)	2 ⅔ cups (480g)	3 ¾ cups (672g)
½ cup (124g)		Tomato Sauce	¾ cup (186g)	1 ¼ cups (310g)	1 ¾ cups (434g)
16 fl oz (473mL)		Chicken Stock or Broth	24 fl oz (710mL)	40 fl oz (1183mL)	56 fl oz (1656mL)
1 TBSP (14g)		Butter (Salted)	2 TBSP (21g)	3 TBSP (35g)	4 TBSP (49g)
½ tsp (4g)		Salt	¾ tsp (5g)	1 ¼ tsp (9g)	1 ¾ tsp (12g)
SAUTÉED BELL PEPPERS					
1 TBSP (15mL)		Olive Oil	1 ½ TBSP (23mL)	2 ½ TBSP (38mL)	3 ½ TBSP (53mL)
2 ½ each (265g)		Green Bell Peppers, medium-sized, de-seeded and sliced into thin strips	4 each (398g)	6 each (663g)	8 ½ each (928g)
1 pinch (<1g)		Salt	⅛ tsp (1g)	¼ tsp (1g)	½ tsp (2g)
1 pinch (<1g)		Black Pepper	1 ½ pinches (<1g)	2 ½ pinches (1g)	3 ½ pinches (1g)
CHIPOTLE CREMA SAUCE					
½ cup (118mL)		Mexican Crema	¾ cup (177mL)	1 ¼ cups (296mL)	1 ¾ cups (414mL)
½ TBSP (8g)		Chipotle Chiles in Adobo Sauce (canned), cut into small pieces	¾ TBSP (12g)	1 ¼ TBSP (19g)	1 ¾ TBSP (27g)

GRAB & GO LUNCH RECIPES | FLAVOR BOWLS

NUTRITION FACTS:

Serving Size 8 oz　　**Calories** 330　　**Total Fat** 21g　　**Total Carbohydrates** 18g　　**Protein** 18g

The portion size shown is based on industry dietary standards and may be smaller than the portion size allowed for in recipe.

INSTRUCTIONS:

Prepare Flank Steak.
"Clean" the **flank steak** by removing the silver skin and muscle band before seasoning and cooking. (For step-by-step instructions, please see our online video *"How to Clean and Prepare Flank Steak for Cooking."*)

Prepare Marinade.
Whisk together the following ingredients until sugar is dissolved:

- Soy Sauce
- Lime Juice
- Sugar

Once sugar is dissolved (it will no longer feel gritty when rubbed between your fingers), slowly add in the **Olive Oil** by drizzling it into the mixture while whisking to emulsify. Then whisk in the following ingredients:

- Chef Gail's Mexican Spice Blend
- Cilantro

Mix well, then add in:

- **Garlic Cloves**, peeled and smashed
- **Jalapeno Peppers**, de-seeded and sliced thinly

Place flank steak and **Marinade** in a vacuum-sealable bag or tightly covered container. Allow steak to marinate for 8 hours or overnight.

Remove flank steak from **Marinade**, brush off excess, and air dry about 15 minutes before cooking. Preheat oven to 375°F (190°C).

Sprinkle both sides generously with **salt** and **black pepper**.

In a cast-iron pan or on the grill on HIGH heat, sear the flank steak on both sides, then transfer to a baking sheet. Bake in 375°F (190°C) oven until internal temperature reaches 120°F (49°C) (approximately 8-10 minutes for a whole flank steak).

If planning to freeze, the internal temperature for this flank steak should be Rare 120°F (49°C). This is because the meat will finish cooking when you microwave it at time of service. If you overcook the meat at this stage, it will be dry and flavorless when it's time to enjoy your meal. To achieve perfectly rare, pull from the oven when internal temperature reaches 115°F (46°C) and allow to come to 120°F (49°C) during the rest period.

> **Note:** If you aren't planning to make a "flavor bowl" and instead want to use this flank as an entrée later, sear the meat ONLY, then package the full flank (seared, raw in the middle) in a vacuum-sealed or resealable, zippered bag. Then, when ready to serve, thaw in the refrigerator, let sit on the counter for 30 minutes, then finish in the oven as directed above.

Once the meat has rested, place on a cutting board so the meat's grain is running horizontally to you. Then slice thinly into ¼" (.6cm) wide strips, slicing against the grain. This is very important. Flank and skirt steaks are tougher cuts of meat, so slicing against the grain yields a more fork-tender bite. For detailed, step-by-step instructions on the proper way to cut flank steak, please refer to the online video "Cutting and Slicing Flank Steak" in the Resources section of our website.

Prepare Spanish Rice.

- Heat **olive oil** over MEDIUM heat, then sweat **onions** until translucent. Add in **garlic, canned green chiles**, and **Chef Gail's Mexican Spice Blend** and toss for 1-2 minutes or until spices are very fragrant.
- Rinse **Basmati rice** through a sieve under cold running water and drain thoroughly.
- Add rinsed, drained rice to onion/garlic/spice mixture and sauté lightly for 1-2 minutes over MEDIUM heat until rice begins to smell "nutty."
- Add in **tomato sauce, chicken stock or broth, butter** and **salt**. Bring to a boil, then reduce heat to LOW and cover tightly. Continue cooking for 15 minutes. Rice is done when water is absorbed and rice is fluffy.

MIS EN PLACE

1. Assemble Chef Gail's **Mexican Spice Blend** if it is not already on hand. Place in sealed container for use in this and other recipes.
2. Clean flank steak (see video instructions)
3. Squeeze limes for juice
4. Garlic Cloves: Peel & smash garlic cloves for the **Steak Marinade**, and chop into minced size for the **Spanish Rice**
5. De-seed and slice jalapeno peppers for **Steak Marinade** and the bell peppers for the **Sauteed Bell Peppers**
6. Chop fresh cilantro for the **Steak Marinade**, plus a little extra for garnish on the finished dish

For Spanish Rice

7. Chop onions into small diced size

CHEF NOTES

If you don't have Mexican Crema on hand, you can substitute sour cream mixed with milk to a consistency similar to heavy whipping cream.

To spice things up a bit, add some of the canned Chipotle Peppers (from the can used in the **Crema Sauce** recipe) into the **Steak Marinade** and **Spanish Rice**. Just a little will add a big kick!

RESERVE the leftover Steak Marinade. Just remove the steak, transfer the marinade to a clean, resealable bag, seal tightly, label and freeze. Can be used twice.

Note: If rice is too crunchy, add more water or chicken stock/broth, cover with lid, and continue cooking until desired consistency is reached. Elevation can affect the amount of water needed for cooking rice, so adjustments may be needed. Finished rice should be *al dente* and not mushy.

Prepare Bell Peppers.

- In skillet, heat **olive oil** over MEDIUM heat. Add **bell peppers** and sauté lightly for 1-2 minutes or until peppers are just tender. Do not overcook – peppers should be tender but still crisp.

Note: *To spice things up, add a pinch or two of Chef Gail's Mexican Spice Blend to the Bell Peppers mixture to amp up the flavor.*

- Remove from heat and season with **salt** and **black pepper**.

Prepare Chipotle Crema Sauce

- Place **Mexican Crema** into a small dish or bowl suitable for mixing.
- Remove **chipotle chiles in Adobo sauce** from the can, being careful to keep some of the sauce with the chiles.
- Chop the chiles into small pieces, then scoop the pieces and sauce and mix into the Mexican Crema.
- For a spicier sauce, add more chipotle peppers and Adobo sauce until the desired heat level is reached.
- Mix well and set aside.

MAKE IT NOW!

If the above instructions have been followed, all items are ready to serve. If you prefer your meat more well done, here is a temperature guide for cooking it longer. Cooking flank steak beyond rare is **not recommended** for freezer or make-ahead meal preparation.

GRAB & GO LUNCH RECIPES | FLAVOR BOWLS

120°F (49°C)	130°F (54°C)	140°F (60°C)	150°F (65°C)	160°F (71°C)
Rare		Medium		Well Done

MAKE IT A FREEZER MEAL:

Prepare Flavor Bowls.
In freezable, microwaveable bowls, assemble:

- 4 oz (113g) Spanish Rice
- 4 oz (113g) Flank Steak, sliced thinly against the grain
- 2 oz (57g) Sautéed Green Bell Peppers
- Top Green Bell Peppers with 2 TBSP (32g) of the Chipotle Crema Sauce

When each ingredient is completely cooled, cover each bowl tightly and apply label titled *"Latin Flank Steak Flavor Bowl."* **Do not seal or fully cover the bowl until all components are cooled to 41°F (5°C) or lower.** When ready to serve, follow reheating instructions on the label.

FREEZER LABELS

Find and print freezer meal labels for this dish at www.frozenandfabulous.com. (See also *"Chapter 13: Quick Guide to Online Tools."*)

ONLINE RESOURCES

Scan this QR code for a direct link to an instructional cooking video for this recipe on www.frozenandfabulous.com, along with these helpful "How It's Done" videos.

- How to Clean and Prepare Flank Steak for Cooking
- Cutting and Slicing Flank Steak
- How to Sear Meat

VARIATIONS

MAKE IT GLUTEN-FREE

The Spanish Rice, Bell Peppers and Chipotle-Crema Sauce are all naturally gluten-free when made with gluten-free stock or broth. For the steak, replace the soy sauce with a gluten-free version.

MAKE IT VEGETARIAN

This marinade is delicious when made with a variety of grilled or sautéed vegetables. Replace the steak with Eggplant "steaks" or a medley of squash and tofu.

MAKE IT "FIT-FRIENDLY"

Increase the amount of meat and bell peppers, reduce the amount of chipotle-crema sauce and Spanish Rice to reduce carbs and calories. For the Basmati Rice, you can substitute riced cauliflower or long-grain brown rice.

MAKE IT BUDGET-FRIENDLY

Flank steak can be expensive, depending on your location and the time of year. Skirt steak is an easy swap, but this marinade is also delicious on other, less expensive cuts of beef.

FLAVOR BOWLS
(MULTI-COMPONENT ALL-IN-ONE MEALS)

Teriyaki Chicken
with Rice & Broccoli

In Japan, the word teriyaki means "shiny grilled meat" - and when you enjoy this delicious flavor bowl, it'll put a shine on your whole day! Served with white or brown rice and broccoli, this is a delicious, hearty meal in a bowl – and kids love it, too!

This recipe was inspired by my very talented chef friend, Kay Conley. I made a few minor tweaks to her gluten-free version but kept the highlights. This ginger-forward soy sauce carries just the right balance of sweet and savory when married with tender chicken and is so yummy you can enjoy it several times a month (so make lots!).

The Teriyaki Chicken on its own is also a great appetizer if you like to entertain. Just place the chicken strips on skewers before grilling and brush generously with sauce. Voilá! Easy, delicious and super popular with party guests.

Need a quick dinner solution? Throw it in a wok, add fresh or frozen veggies and enjoy a flavorful stir fry.

The possibilities are endless so grab some chopsticks and shine on, my friend!

GRAB & GO LUNCH RECIPES | FLAVOR BOWLS

INGREDIENTS:

No of Servings				
4		**6**	**10**	**14**
qty | msmt (weight)		qty | msmt (weight)	qty | msmt (weight)	qty | msmt (weight)
TERIYAKI CHICKEN & MARINADE/SAUCE				
½ cup (118mL)	Soy Sauce	¾ cup (177mL)	1 ¼ cups (296mL)	1 ¾ cups (414mL)
½ TBSP (7mL)	Rice Vinegar	¾ TBSP (11mL)	1 ¼ TBSP (18mL)	1 ¾ TBSP (26mL)
1 TBSP (14g)	Sugar	1 ½ TBSP (21g)	2 ½ TBSP (35g)	3 ½ TBSP (50g)
1 TBSP (14g)	Brown Sugar	1 ½ TBSP (21g)	2 ½ TBSP (35g)	3 ½ TBSP (50g)
5 each (14g)	Garlic Cloves, minced	8 each (21g)	13 each (35g)	15 each (49g)
2 tsp (7g)	Fresh Ginger Root, peeled and grated or minced	3 tsp (11g)	5 tsp (18g)	7 tsp (25g)
3 TBSP (443mL)	Sesame Oil	4 ½ TBSP (664mL)	½ cup (1106mL)	2/3 cup (1549mL)
2 LB (912g)	Boneless Chicken Thighs	3 LB (1368g)	5 LB (2280g)	7 LB (3192g)
½ tsp (4g)	Salt, divided	¾ tsp (5g)	1 ¼ tsp (9g)	1 ¾ tsp (12g)
½ tsp (1g)	Black Pepper, divided	¾ tsp (2g)	1 ¼ tsp (3g)	1 ¾ tsp (4g)
½ TBSP (5g)	Corn Starch	¾ TBSP (7g)	1 ¼ TBSP (11g)	1 ¾ TBSP (16g)
1 TBSP (15mL)	Water	1 ½ TBSP (22mL)	2 ½ TBSP (37mL)	3 ½ TBSP (52mL)
RICE				
1 cup (181g)	Basmati Rice	1 ½ cups (272g)	2 ½ cups (454g)	3 ½ cups (635g)
2 cups (473mL)	Water or Chicken Stock or Chicken Broth	3 cups (710mL)	5 cups (1183mL)	7 cups (1656mL)
1 tsp (5g)	Butter (Salted)	1 ½ tsp (8g)	2 ½ tsp (13g)	3 ½ tsp (18g)
½ tsp (4g)	Salt	¾ tsp (5g)	1 ¼ tsp (9g)	1 ¾ tsp (12g)
BROCCOLI				
1 tsp (7g)	Salt	1 ½ tsp (11g)	2 ½ tsp (18g)	3 ½ tsp (25g)
2 LB (912g)	Broccoli Florets	3 LB (1368g)	5 LB (2280g)	7 LB (3192g)
⅛ tsp (1g)	Black Pepper	¼ tsp (1g)	½ tsp (1g)	¾ tsp (2g)
GARNISH (OPTIONAL)				
1 tsp (5g)	Scallions (Green Onions), sliced thinly	1 ½ tsp (7g)	2 ½ tsp (12g)	3 ½ tsp (17g)
1 tsp (3g)	Toasted Sesame Seeds	1 ½ tsp (5g)	2 ½ tsp (8g)	3 ½ tsp (11g)

NUTRITION FACTS:

Serving Size 8 oz **Calories** 290 **Total Fat** 11g **Total Carbohydrates** 15g **Protein** 31g

The portion size shown is based on industry dietary standards and may be smaller than the portion size allowed for in recipe.

INSTRUCTIONS:

Prepare Teriyaki Chicken.
Whisk together:

- **soy sauce**
- **rice vinegar**
- **white and brown sugars**

Whisk until sugar dissolves (*is no longer grainy-feeling when rubbed between your fingers*), then add in:

- minced **garlic**
- minced **ginger**
- **sesame oil** poured in a steady stream while continuing to whisk.

Trim **chicken thighs** to remove unwanted fat, then place in marinade for at least 8 hours or overnight.

Remove chicken and **reserve the marinade**. Sprinkle both sides of chicken pieces with HALF of the **salt** and **black pepper**.

Preheat oven to 375°F (190°C).

In a cast-iron pan or on grill sprayed with non-stick pan spray, sear the chicken pieces over MEDIUM-HIGH heat until grill marks form, then transfer to a baking sheet.

Bake in 375°F (190°C) oven, uncovered, until internal temperature reaches 165°F (73°C) (approximately 5 minutes). Do not overcook.

> **Note:** It's possible to finish baking the chicken pieces on the grill – it's just very important to monitor closely to avoid overcooking. The "grill mark then finish in the oven" technique is typically used by professional Chefs to retain control over temperature.

Once chicken is fully cooked, allow to rest for 5 minutes, then slice into strips.

While chicken is cooking, transfer **reserved marinade** to a saucepan and heat over MEDIUM heat. Bring to a boil, then reduce heat and continue simmering uncovered until sauce is reduced by 20%.

Make a slurry with the **corn starch**, **water** and remainder of the **salt** and **black pepper**, stirring the corn starch quickly into the water with a fork to break up chunks. While sauce is boiling, whisk the slurry into the sauce. Continue cooking until sauce thickens and coats the back of a spoon (approximately 5-8 minutes).

MIS EN PLACE

1. Peel & grate the fresh ginger root.
2. Mince fresh garlic.
3. Trim chicken thighs to remove unwanted fat.
4. Optional: Toast sesame seeds and slice scallions for garnish.

CHEF NOTES

When working with **fresh ginger root**, peel off the outer skin with a spoon. Then you can either grate or chop the fresh ginger into the desired size.

When making a **corn starch slurry**, pour into the sauce through a mesh sieve to avoid getting lumps into your finished sauce.

Why rinse rice? Raw rice products contain a large amount of starch. If you don't rinse the rice well, it will become gummy instead of light and fluffy. Parboiled and some other kinds of rice do not need to be rinsed, so watch recipe notes carefully to know when rinsing is recommended.

Prepare Rice.
Rinse **Basmati rice** through a sieve under cold running water. Add rinsed rice to measured **water**, **butter** and **salt** in a saucepan. Bring to a boil, then reduce heat to low and cover tightly. Continue cooking for 15 minutes. Rice is done with all water is absorbed and rice is fluffy.

Prepare Broccoli.
Bring a pot of water to boil (*enough water to fully cover broccoli*) and add **salt** to the cooking water. Add in **broccoli**, reduce heat, and allow to cook for 4 minutes only.

Prepare an "ice bath" by filling a bowl with water and ice.

GRAB & GO LUNCH RECIPES | FLAVOR BOWLS

After 4 minutes of cooking time, immediately remove broccoli from boiling water and place it in an ice bath. Allow to sit in the ice bath for 3-4 minutes or until broccoli is completely cooled. Strain well, pat dry with a paper towel and sprinkle with **black pepper**. Taste and add more salt, if needed.

MAKE IT NOW!

If the above instructions have been followed, all items are ready to serve. Broccoli may need to be reheated before serving. Garnish with sliced **scallions** (green onions) and **toasted sesame seeds**.

MAKE IT A FREEZER MEAL:

Prepare Flavor Bowls.
In single-serving sized freezable, microwavable bowls assemble:

- 3 oz (85g) Rice
- 4 oz (113g) Teriyaki Chicken pieces
- 2 oz (57g) Teriyaki Sauce (pour over chicken)
- 3 oz (85g) Broccoli

Garnish with sliced scallions or green onions and toasted sesame seeds.

When each ingredient is completely cooled, cover each bowl tightly and apply label titled *"Teriyaki Chicken Flavor Bowl."* **Do not seal or fully cover the bowl until all components are cooled.**

FREEZER LABELS

Find and print freezer meal labels for this dish at www.frozenandfabulous.com. (See also *"Chapter 13: Quick Guide to Online Tools."*)

ONLINE RESOURCES

Scan this QR code for a direct link to an instructional cooking video for this recipe on www.frozenandfabulous.com, along with these helpful "How It's Done" videos."

- How to Sear Meat
- How to Work with Fresh Ginger Root

VARIATIONS

MAKE IT GLUTEN-FREE

Replace the Soy Sauce with a gluten-free version.

MAKE IT VEGETARIAN

Replace chicken with firm tofu or portobello mushrooms. Reduce marinating time to 1 hour.

MAKE IT "FIT-FRIENDLY"

Use brown long-grain rice and reduce the sugar by 10-15%. You can also exchange the rice for riced cauliflower or spiraled steamed vegetables. Swapping chicken breasts for the thighs will also reduce calories, but make sure you pre-brine the breasts to maximize moisture retention (see Quick Brine for Chicken Breasts recipe in Chapter 11: Meat Brines).

MAKE IT BUDGET-FRIENDLY

This dish is budget-friendly as is, costing approximately $1.50 per serving.

Chapter 7: (Cont.)

GRAB & GO SALAD STARTERS

The recipes in this section are perfect for pulling delicious proteins from the freezer, giving a quick heat-up in the microwave, and adding to a heaping bowl of fresh, seasonal greens!

They are also delicious as "stand-alone" entrees or easy lunch options. The Firecracker Salmon and Blood Orange-Roasted Chicken work as a delicious entree for dinner, and the Curry Chicken Salad makes the most amazing sandwiches when paired with freshly baked bread or as a dip for crackers. It is one of our most requested menu items for our corporate lunch caterings and BYO sandwich buffets.

So enjoy! The options are endless with these quick and easy recipes.

SALAD STARTERS
MAKE IT FRESH FROM THE FREEZER!

Blood Orange
Roasted Chicken

This decadent, silky blood orange sauce glazed over tender roasted chicken breast provides the perfect start to a delicious Italian salad. Add slices of this flavorful chicken to a bowl of fresh, seasonal greens, blood orange supremes, Italian salami, thinly sliced red onion, and your favorite zesty Italian dressing. Garnish with shaved parmesan and toasted pine nuts, and voila! Enjoy a delicious, satisfying salad made "fresh from the freezer!"

What I also love about this dish is the ease and simplicity of making the glaze. Since the fruit, vegetables and aromatics are discarded after reduction, you can quickly "rough chop" everything, throw it into the pan, let the sauce reduce, and then strain for a lovely, satiny glaze. Easy peasy!

But save a few blood orange supremes along the way... they are a gorgeous addition to the plate (and the pop of intense, juicy sweetness is just divine)!

INGREDIENTS

No of Servings				
4 qty | msmt (weight)		**6** qty | msmt (weight)	**10** qty | msmt (weight)	**14** qty | msmt (weight)
ROASTED CHICKEN				
1 ¼ LB (570g)	Boneless Chicken Breasts	2 LB (855g)	3 LB (1425g)	4 LB (1995g)
	* Pre-brine with **Quick Brine for Chicken Breasts** (see *Chapter 11: Meat Brines*)			
2 TBSP (30mL)	Olive Oil	3 TBSP (45mL)	⅓ cup (75mL)	½ cup (105mL)
⅛ tsp (1g)	Salt	¼ tsp (1g)	⅓ tsp (2g)	½ tsp (3g)
⅛ tsp (<1g)	Black Pepper	¼ tsp (<1g)	⅓ tsp (1g)	½ tsp (1g)
BLOOD ORANGE GLAZE				
2 tsp (3mL)	Olive Oil	1 TBSP (4mL)	1 ¼ TBSP (6mL)	2 TBSP (9mL)
½ each (113g)	Red Onion, cut into slices (rough cut)	¾ each (170g)	1 ¼ each (283g)	1 ¾ each (396g)
2 each (6g)	Garlic Cloves, peeled & smashed	3 each (8g)	5 each (14g)	7 each (20g)
3 TBSP (2mL)	White Wine	¼ cup (2mL)	½ cup (4mL)	¾ cup (5mL)
3 oranges (375g)	Zest, Juice and Pulp of Blood Oranges (remove pith)	4 oranges (563g)	7 oranges (938g)	10 oranges (1313g)
10 supremes (100g)	Supremes of Blood Oranges (Avg 8-10 supremes per orange)	15 supremes (150g)	25 supremes (250g)	35 supremes (350g)
8 fl oz (237mL)	Chicken Stock	12 fl oz (355mL)	20 fl oz (591mL)	28 fl oz (828mL)
4 sprigs (2g)	Fresh Thyme, whole sprigs	6 sprigs (3g)	10 sprigs (5g)	14 sprigs (7g)
1 TBSP (21g)	Honey	2 TBSP (32g)	3 TBSP (53g)	4 TBSP (74g)
½ tsp (3g)	Chicken Base (*Chef Gail recommends "Better Than Bouillon Chicken Base"*)	¾ tsp (5g)	1 ¼ tsp (8g)	1 ¾ tsp (11g)
1 TBSP (9g)	Corn Starch	1 ½ TBSP (5g)	2 ½ TBSP (8g)	3 ½ TBSP (11g)
2 fl oz (59mL)	Cold Water	3 fl oz (89mL)	5 fl oz (148mL)	7 fl oz (207mL)
⅛ tsp (1g)	Salt	¼ tsp (1g)	⅓ tsp (2g)	½ tsp (3g)
⅛ tsp (<1g)	Black Pepper	¼ tsp (<1g)	⅓ tsp (1g)	½ tsp (1g)
1 TBSP (14g)	Butter (Salted), cut into ½" (1.3cm) size pieces	2 TBSP (21g)	3 TBSP (35g)	4 TBSP (49g)

NUTRITION FACTS:

Serving Size 6 oz   **Calories** 170   **Total Fat** 7g   **Total Carbohydrates** 11g   **Protein** 16g

The portion size shown is based on industry dietary standards and may be smaller than the portion size allowed for in recipe.

INSTRUCTIONS

Prepare Chicken
Preheat oven to 375°F (190°C).

Place **chicken breasts** in **Quick Brine for Chicken Breasts** for 15 minutes. Remove from brine and place on a rack to dry.

Optional: Split **chicken breasts** in half. Place chicken breast on cutting board, place palm firmly on top to hold in place, then cut horizontally through the middle. (*See our online video, "How to Split a Chicken Breast."*) Cover with plastic wrap, pound with a mallet until the pieces are tenderized, being careful not to tear the meat. This will yield a more tender piece of chicken that will cook more quickly than a full breast and is easily sliced for a salad. If planning to serve this as an Entrée, keep the breast whole.

Sear the Chicken Breast.
Once dry, brush both sides of each breast with **olive oil** and sprinkle with **salt** and **black pepper**.

Heat grill or cast-iron skillet to MEDIUM-HIGH heat. Add **olive oil**. When hot (but not smoking), place chicken breasts into pan. Do not overcrowd the pan. Allow breasts to sear (1 to 2 minutes per side), then remove from pan and place on baking sheet. (The breasts will not be fully cooked – just grill-marked or seared on the outside.)

Prepare Blood Orange Glaze
Heat olive oil in skillet over MEDIUM heat. Add in sliced **red onions** and toss in oil until softened, then add in smashed **garlic** cloves.

When garlic and onions begin to brown and stick to the pan, add **white wine**, then whisk to clear all the "bits" off the bottom of the pan. Continue until the wine is reduced and the pan is almost dry (*au sec*).

Add in the **blood orange zest, juice, pulp** and **supremes, chicken stock**, fresh **thyme** sprigs, **honey** and **chicken base**. Whisk together, then reduce heat to MEDIUM-LOW and allow to simmer until reduced by two-thirds.

Note: Visit www.frozenandfabulous.com for a tutorial video on *"How to Supreme an Orange"* for cooking or beautiful plating.

MIS EN PLACE

1. Place chicken breasts in Quick Brine for 15 minutes.
2. Cut chicken breasts in half horizontally (optional).
3. Rough-chop red onion and garlic cloves.
4. Zest and juice first measurement of blood oranges, then discard the white pith. Set aside.
5. Peel and supreme (remove pieces) of second measurement of blood oranges. Set aside.
6. Assemble remaining ingredients.

CHEF NOTES

To grill-mark or sear meat properly, the meat should be dry before placing onto the oiled grill or hot pan.

Then **do not disturb**. If the meat is sticking to the pan, it means it isn't done yet. When it is properly seared, it will release from the pan and you can remove without tearing the meat or losing the golden crisp sear or dark grill marks.

If you have too much liquid in your pan or if the temperature is too low, it will not sear properly.

For more tips on how to create a beautiful grill-mark or sear on your meats, see our "how it's done" video - *Chapter 18: Quick Guide to Online Tools*.

STRAIN sauce through a fine-mesh strainer into another dish, clean any remaining bits from the skillet with a paper towel, then strain sauce again through a fine-mesh sieve back into the cleaned skillet. Increase heat to MEDIUM.

With a fork, whisk **corn starch** into the **cold water** to create a slurry. Once the sauce returns to a boil, whisk in the corn starch slurry. Continue whisking over MEDIUM heat for 3 minutes or until the corn starch taste is gone. Sauce should have a syrup-like consistency. Add in **salt** and **black pepper** to taste.

GRAB & GO LUNCH RECIPES | SALAD STARTERS

> **Note:** If the sauce is not thick enough, repeat the slurry process by adding more corn starch to cold water. It's important to add slurry only when the sauce is boiling, and let the sauce cook another 3 to 5 minutes after adding the slurry to remove any chalky taste. If slurry creates lumps, strain sauce again through a mesh strainer before continuing.

Reduce heat to LOW, then place **butter pieces** on top and swirl the pan lightly until the butter melts and incorporates into the sauce. Remove from heat and set aside.

MAKE IT NOW!

Brush **Blood Orange Glaze** on each chicken piece, then place in preheated 375°F (190°C) oven. After 5 minutes (for thinly sliced breast or 10 minutes for full breast pieces), remove pan from the oven and apply more glaze to each of the pieces. Return to oven. Bake another 5 to 10 minutes or until internal temperature reaches 165°F (74°C) using a stem thermometer into the thickest area of the chicken breast. Remove from oven and allow to rest 5 minutes before slicing.

To serve, slice into thin strips for a salad or serve whole as an entrée. Chicken may be served cold or warm. Reserve extra unused glaze to serve as a sauce with the chicken.

MAKE IT A FREEZER-READY SALAD STARTER

Brush **Blood Orange Glaze** on each chicken piece, then place in preheated 375°F (190°C) oven. After 10 minutes, remove from the oven. Turn each piece over, apply more glaze and return to the oven. Bake another 10 minutes or until internal temperature reaches 165°F (74°C) using a stem thermometer into the thickest area of the chicken breast. Remove from oven and allow to cool completely.

Once cooled, cut chicken into ½" (1.27cm) wide strips. Brush each piece with remaining **Blood Orange Glaze** and package fully-cooled chicken into a small freezable container, vacuum-sealable bag or resealable zippered bag. Seal tightly and remove all excess air. Apply label "*Blood Orange Roasted Chicken.*"

> **Note:** *If you have excess sauce, you can pour it over the packaged chicken before sealing or store and freeze the sauce separately to use as a dipping sauce.*

FREEZER LABELS

Find and print freezer meal labels for this dish at www.frozenandfabulous.com. (See also "*Chapter 13: Quick Guide to Online Tools.*")

ONLINE RESOURCES

Scan this QR code for a direct link to an instructional cooking video for this recipe on www.frozenandfabulous.com, along with these helpful "How It's Done" videos.

- How to Split a Chicken Breast
- How to Grill-Mark Meat
- How to Sear Meat
- How to Supreme an Orange

VARIATIONS

MAKE IT GLUTEN-FREE	**MAKE IT VEGETARIAN**	**MAKE IT "FIT-FRIENDLY"**	**MAKE IT BUDGET-FRIENDLY**
Use gluten-free chicken stock and chicken base. All other ingredients in this recipe are naturally gluten-free.	Brush this glaze on sliced portobellos or eggplant, then roast in the oven.	Since the sugars in this dish come from natural fruit and honey, it is a healthier option than off-the-shelf orange sauces that are typically full of added sugar. To reduce calories, reduce the amount of glaze used on the chicken pieces.	Purchase chicken breast in bulk and blood oranges in season, and reduce portion sizes, to lower cost.

SALAD STARTERS
MAKE IT FRESH FROM THE FREEZER!

Firecracker Salmon

Firecracker marinade delivers an explosion of flavor – it is the perfect way to make lunch or dinner a more exciting experience!

Choose fresh, wild-caught salmon to marinate with the umami notes of soy sauce, red chiles and lively spices. (Frozen wild-caught salmon works, too.) Want more or less heat? It's as easy as adding more or less of the crushed red peppers and cayenne pepper. The level of heat shown in this recipe is what has been most popular with my catering and prepared-meal clients over the years, but my personal preference is to make it a bit hotter.

To use this dish as a salad starter simply marinate, fully cook, separate into 4 oz (113g) portions, and freeze in a microwave-friendly bowl, vacuum-sealed bag or resealable zippered bag.

If you want this as a frozen entrée, simply marinate, freeze raw in full-size portions and bake in the oven when you're ready to serve.

Best of all? Make it for dinner! Once the salmon has marinated it'll finish in the oven in 8-10 minutes. Chop up a green and red bell pepper, toss with a bit of the Firecracker Marinade, and sauté for 3 to 4 minutes or until softened but still crunchy. Serve with buttery Orzo and you have an incredibly easy yet flavorful meal!

This marinade was another inspiration from my chef friend, Kay Conley. I added a few tweaks here and there, but I always loved her creation and am so happy I now get to share it with you!

Bon appetit!

GRAB & GO LUNCH RECIPES | SALAD STARTERS

INGREDIENTS:

No of Servings				
8 Salad Starter or 4 Entrée Portions qty | msmt (weight)		**12 Salad Starter or 6 Entrée Portions** qty | msmt (weight)	**20 Salad Starter or 10 Entrée Portions** qty | msmt (weight)	**28 Salad Starter or 14 Entrée Portions** qty | msmt (weight)
FIRECRACKER MARINADE				
3 fl oz (71mL)	Vegetable or Canola Oil (*do not use Olive Oil*)	5 fl oz (107mL)	8 fl oz (178mL)	11 fl oz (249mL)
1 TBSP (15mL)	Sesame Oil	2 TBSP (23mL)	3 TBSP (38mL)	4 TBSP (53mL)
3 fl oz (227mL)	Soy Sauce	5 fl oz (341mL)	8 fl oz (568mL)	11 fl oz (795mL)
5 fl oz (148mL)	Balsamic Vinegar	8 fl oz (222mL)	13 fl oz (370mL)	18 fl oz (518mL)
1 ½ TBSP (24g)	Brown Sugar, packed	2 ½ TBSP (36g)	¼ cup (60g)	½ cup (84g)
4 each (22g)	Garlic Cloves, minced	6 each (33g)	10 each (55g)	14 each (77g)
1 ¼ inch root (11g)	Fresh Ginger Root, peeled and grated or minced	2 inch root (17g)	3 inch root (28g)	4 ¼ inch root (39g)
1 pinch (<1g)	Cayenne Pepper *	2 pinches (1g)	⅛ tsp (2g)	¼ tsp (3g)
1 TBSP (15g)	Sea Salt (fine)	1 ½ TBSP (22g)	2 ½ TBSP (37g)	3 ½ TBSP (51g)
1 tsp (23g)	Crushed Red Pepper Flakes * *Adjust "spicy heat" level by increasing or reducing these ingredients.	1 ½ tsp (35g)	2 ½ tsp (58g)	3 ½ tsp (81g)
FIRECRACKER GLAZE/SAUCE				
¼ cup (59mL)	*Reserved **Firecracker Marinade**	½ cup (89mL)	¾ cup (148mL)	1 cup (207mL)
1 tsp (3g)	Corn Starch	2 tsp (5g)	2 ½ tsp (8g)	3 ½ tsp (11g)
1 ¼ TBSP (18mL)	Cold Water	2 TBSP (28mL)	3 ¼ TBSP (46mL)	4 ½ TBSP (65mL)
2 each (25g)	Scallions (Green Onions), sliced thinly	3 each (38g)	5 each (63g)	7 each (88g)
SALMON				
2 LB (456g)	Wild Caught Salmon, skin off, cut into 6 oz (170g) or 8 oz (226g) portions	3 LB (684g)	5 LB (1140g)	7 LB (1596g)

NUTRITION FACTS:

Serving Size 6 oz   **Calories** 310   **Total Fat** 13g   **Total Carbohydrates** 1g   **Protein** 46g

The portion size shown is based on industry dietary standards and may be smaller than the portion size allowed for in recipe.

INSTRUCTIONS

Prepare Firecracker Marinade.
Whisk together all ingredients listed.

Remove the portion of marinade needed for the glaze/sauce (see **Firecracker Glaze/Sauce** measurements). This is the reserved portion mentioned on the ingredients list.

Marinate Salmon.
Place **salmon** portions in a shallow container and fully cover with **Firecracker Marinade**. Allow to marinate in the refrigerator for 6 hours (not more than 12 hours).

Prepare Firecracker Glaze/Sauce.
Place reserved portion of the **Firecracker Marinade** into a small saucepan over MEDIUM heat.

In a separate cup, stir together **corn starch** and **cold water** until blended to make a slurry.

When sauce comes to a boil, reduce heat and quickly whisk in the corn starch/water slurry, making sure to break up any lumps.

Continue cooking over MEDIUM-LOW heat for 5 minutes or until the taste of corn starch is gone and the sauce is lightly thickened. Remove from heat. Add in HALF of the sliced scallions. Set aside.

MAKE IT NOW!

- Preheat oven to 400°F (204°C). Allow marinated salmon to come to room temperature (set on the counter for 15 to 20 minutes).

- Spray baking sheet with non-stick spray. Place salmon portions on the baking sheet (if using skin-on, place skin-side down). Brush the tops of all salmon pieces with **Firecracker Glaze/Sauce**.

- Place in pre-heated oven for 5 minutes. Brush with more **Firecracker Glaze/Sauce**. Continue baking 2 to 5 minutes more or until salmon is opaque and flakes easily with a fork. Confirm that internal temperature reaches 145°F (63°C). DO NOT OVERCOOK. Salmon temperature will rise about 5° once removed from the oven and allowed to sit on the baking sheet.

- Serve with remaining warmed **Firecracker Glaze/Sauce** as a stand-alone sauce or drizzled lightly over a mixed greens salad.

MIS EN PLACE

1. Chop garlic cloves, fresh ginger root and scallions.
2. Measure out remaining ingredients.

FIRECRACKER VINAIGRETTE SALAD DRESSING

To make a **Firecracker Vinaigrette Salad Dressing** using extra Firecracker Glaze/Sauce, **after** boiling and reducing by half, but *before* adding corn starch slurry remove about ¼ cup of the sauce, then allow to cool in refrigerator uncovered.

Once cool, drizzle in 1 to 2 TBSP of olive oil while whisking constantly. Keep refrigerated until ready to serve.

MAKE IT A FREEZER-READY ENTREE

Remove full-size Salmon portions from **Firecracker Marinade** and place into a vacuum-sealable or resealable zippered bag. Add in the remaining HALF of the sliced scallions. Seal tightly and remove all excess air. Apply label *"Salmon for: Marinated Firecracker Salmon."*

Note: If using frozen salmon, keep the frozen salmon pieces in the manufacturer's packaging (keep frozen), then package the Firecracker Marinade and sliced scallions in a resealable bag. When ready to serve, remove frozen salmon portions from their packaging, place in the marinade for 6 hours, and then finish the glazing/cooking process.

GRAB & GO LUNCH RECIPES | SALAD STARTERS

Package cooked and fully-cooled **Firecracker Glaze/Sauce** into a small freezable container, vacuum-sealable bag or resealable zippered bag. Seal tightly and remove all excess air. Apply label *"Firecracker Glaze."*

Place both into a resealable zippered bag and place in the freezer. Follow cooking instructions at the time of service.

MAKE IT A FREEZER-READY GRAB & GO SALAD STARTER

1. Preheat oven to 400°F (204°C). Spray baking sheet with non-stick spray. Place thawed salmon portions on the baking sheet (*if using skin-on, place skin-side down*). Brush the tops of all salmon pieces with **Firecracker Glaze/Sauce**.

   Place in pre-heated oven for 5 minutes. Brush with more **Firecracker Glaze/Sauce**. Continue baking 2 to 5 minutes more or until salmon is opaque and flakes easily with a fork. Confirm that internal temperature reaches 145°F (63°C). DO NOT OVERCOOK. Salmon temperature will rise about 5° once removed from the oven and allowed to sit on the baking sheet.

2. Allow cooked **Firecracker Salmon** and **Firecracker Glaze/Sauce** and to cool completely in the refrigerator.

3. Package fully-cooled **Firecracker Salmon** into a small freezable container, vacuum-sealable bag or resealable zippered bag. Seal tightly and remove all excess air. Apply label *"Firecracker Salmon Salad Starter."*

4. Package fully-cooled **Firecracker Glaze/Sauce** into a small freezable container, vacuum-sealable bag or resealable zippered bag. Seal tightly and remove all excess air. Apply label *"Firecracker Sauce."*

5. Place both into a resealable zippered bag and place in the freezer. Follow reheating instructions at the time of service.

FREEZER LABELS

Find and print freezer meal labels for this dish at www.frozenandfabulous.com. (See also *"Chapter 13: Quick Guide to Online Tools."*)

ONLINE RESOURCES

Scan this QR code for a direct link to an instructional cooking video for this recipe on www.frozenandfabulous.com.

VARIATIONS

MAKE IT GLUTEN-FREE

This dish is usually gluten-free prepared as is, but check the ingredients label on your soy sauce just to be sure.

MAKE IT VEGETARIAN

This marinade would be delicious married with jackfruit but reduce the marinade time to one hour.

MAKE IT "FIT-FRIENDLY"

Reduce the amount of brown sugar used in the marinade by half and choose a low-sodium soy sauce. If reducing the brown sugar, add a bit of honey or agave for sweetness as needed.

MAKE IT BUDGET-FRIENDLY

The best way to reduce the cost for this recipe is to find good quality fresh salmon on sale, then buy in bulk to freeze. Another option is to choose other recipes to make ahead that will use some of these same ingredients so you can cross-utilize and get more meals for the same cost.

SALAD STARTERS
MAKE IT FRESH FROM THE FREEZER!

Just Add Mayo

Curry Chicken Salad

My daughter, Madelyn, finds this Curry Chicken Salad mighty addictive! When she was little and I was making this dish for a catering event, I always made extra knowing she'd be all over it! Now that she's off to college, I try to keep this one stocked for visits home plus a little extra to send back with her. There's something sweet in knowing there's a little bit of home in her far-away freezer.

What makes this dish so craveable is its' vibrant curry heat married with the sweetness of carrots and raisins, plus the crunch of roasted cashews. It makes an amazing dip for crackers, wrap fillings, stuffing for sea salt-kissed artichoke bottoms, or nestled between two hearty pieces of freshly baked French bread.

And yes... it makes an incredible salad topper, too! Serve over fresh, peppery arugula or seasonal mixed greens for a light, satisfying meal.

Mayonnaise isn't freezable (it turns pretty nasty) so to make this for freezing just assemble all the ingredients except mayo, then when you're ready to eat just thaw, add mayo and enjoy every delicious bite!

GRAB & GO LUNCH RECIPES | SALAD STARTERS

INGREDIENTS

No of Servings		4	6	10	14
		qty | msmt (weight)	qty | msmt (weight)	qty | msmt (weight)	qty | msmt (weight)
CHICKEN BREAST					
	Boneless Chicken Breasts	1 ¼ LB (570g)	2 LB (855g)	3 LB (1425g)	4 LB (1995g)
	*Pre-brine with **Quick Brine for Chicken Breasts** (see *Chapter 11: Meat Brines*)				
	Mirin Sweet Rice Cooking Wine	¼ cup (59mL)	½ cup (89mL)	¾ cup (148mL)	1 cup (207mL)
	Salt	⅛ tsp (1g)	¼ tsp (1g)	⅓ tsp (2g)	½ tsp (3g)
	Black Pepper	⅛ tsp (<1g)	¼ tsp (<1g)	⅓ tsp (1g)	½ tsp (1g)
CURRY SALAD INGREDIENTS					
	Chicken Stock or Broth, divided	2 fl oz (59mL)	3 fl oz (89mL)	5 fl oz (148mL)	7 fl oz (207mL)
	Black Raisins	¼ cup (38g)	½ cup (56g)	¾ cup (94g)	1 cup (131g)
	Red Onion, cut into small squares (small dice cut)	¼ each (57g)	½ each (85g)	¾ each (141g)	1 each (198g)
	Garlic Cloves, minced	2 each (15g)	3 each (23g)	5 each (38g)	7 each (53g)
	Celery, sliced into ¼" (.6cm) pieces	1 rib (51g)	1 ½ ribs (77g)	2 ½ ribs (128g)	3 ½ ribs (179g)
	Carrots, medium-sized (shredded)	1 each (68g)	1 ½ each (102g)	2 ½ each (170g)	3 ½ each (238g)
	Curry Powder	1 ½ TBSP (9g)	2 ¼ TBSP (14g)	3 ¾ TBSP (24g)	5 ¼ TBSP (33g)
	Cashews, chopped	⅛ cup (19g)	¼ cup (28g)	⅓ cup (47g)	½ cup (66g)
	Cayenne Pepper	⅛ tsp (<1g)	¼ tsp (<1g)	⅓ tsp (1g)	½ tsp (1g)
	Lemon Zest, fresh (*Zest of 1 lemon = 1 TBSP*)	¼ TBSP (2g)	½ TBSP (2g)	¾ TBSP (4g)	1 TBSP (6g)
	Salt	¾ tsp (5g)	1 ¼ tsp (8g)	2 tsp (13g)	2 ½ tsp (18g)
	Black Pepper	½ tsp (1g)	¾ tsp (2g)	1 ¼ tsp (3g)	1 ¾ tsp (4g)
MAYONNAISE *DO NOT FREEZE*					
	Mayonnaise	¾ cup (165g)	1 cup (247g)	2 cups (412g)	2 ½ cups (577g)

NUTRITION FACTS:

Serving Size 6.5 oz **Calories** 340 **Total Fat** 22g **Total Carbohydrates** 13g **Protein** 22g

The portion size shown is based on industry dietary standards and may be smaller than the portion size allowed for in recipe.

INSTRUCTIONS

Prepare Chicken & Raisins
Preheat oven to 375°F (190°C).

Place **chicken breasts** in **Quick Brine for Chicken Breasts** for 15 minutes.

While chicken is brining:

- Heat **Mirin Sweet Rice Cooking Wine** in a saucepan over MEDIUM heat. Bring to a boil, reduce heat and continue cooking until the liquid is reduced by HALF.

- Place **raisins** in bowl and pour **Chicken Stock or Broth** over the top so they are fully submerged. Allow to soak for about 30 minutes.

Remove chicken pieces from the brine and place on a baking rack to dry.

Optional: Split **chicken breasts** in half. Place chicken breast on cutting board, place palm firmly on top to hold in place, then cut horizontally through the middle. (*See our online video, "How to Split a Chicken Breast."*) Cover with plastic wrap, pound with a mallet until the pieces are tenderized, being careful not to tear the meat. This will yield a more tender piece of chicken that will cook more quickly than a full breast and is easily sliced for a salad.

Once dry, brush the top and bottom of each chicken piece with the reduced Mirin Sweet Rice Cooking Wine, then sprinkle both sides with **salt** and **black pepper**.

Spray baking sheet with non-stick spray, then place chicken breasts on the baking sheet.

Bake at 375°F (190°C) for 12-15 minutes (for split breasts) or 15-20 minutes (for whole breasts), or until internal temperature reaches 165°F (74°C) using a stem thermometer into the thickest area of the chicken breast. Remove from oven and allow to cool completely.

Once cooled, cut chicken breasts into thin slices. Set aside.

After raisins have been in chicken stock/broth for 30 minutes to an hour, drain raisins and discard leftover chicken stock/broth.

Prepare Salad Ingredients
Mix together **all remaining salad ingredients (except mayonnaise)**.

MIS EN PLACE

1. Brine chicken breasts, then cut in half (optional).
2. Make Mirin wine reduction.
3. Soak raisins.
4. Chop red onion, garlic cloves, celery, carrots and cashews.
5. Zest and juice fresh lemon.
6. Toast or roast the cashews.
7. Assemble remaining ingredients (except mayo if freezing).

Note: For added flavor, roast the cashews before adding to the mixture. Simply toss in a dry pan over MEDIUM-LOW heat until fragrant and darker in color.

Add cooked, cooled and sliced chicken breast and drained raisins. Mix well.

MAKE IT NOW!

Add **mayonnaise** to the mixed chicken, raisins and salad ingredients. Mix well, adjust salt and pepper to taste, and then enjoy as a sandwich filling or over fresh mixed greens (*arugula is a good match for this dish*).

MAKE IT FREEZER-READY

Package mixed salad ingredients into a freezable container, vacuum-sealed or resealable zippered bag, removing as much air as possible. Apply label "*Curry Chicken Salad (just add mayo)*." On the label, write the correct amount of mayonnaise to add to the recipe based on the batch size made.

When ready to serve, follow instructions for thawing and mixing.

FREEZER LABELS

Find and print freezer meal labels for this dish at www.frozenandfabulous.com. (See also "*Chapter 13: Quick Guide to Online Tools.*")

GRAB & GO LUNCH RECIPES | SALAD STARTERS

ONLINE RESOURCES

Scan this QR code for a direct link to an instructional cooking video for this recipe on www.frozenandfabulous.com, plus this helpful "How It's Done" video.

- How to Split a Chicken Breast

VARIATIONS

MAKE IT GLUTEN-FREE	**MAKE IT VEGETARIAN**	**MAKE IT "FIT-FRIENDLY"**	**MAKE IT BUDGET-FRIENDLY**
Use gluten-free chicken stock or broth.	Replace the chicken with thick slices of turnip, rutabaga or jicama. Adjust the amount of mayo used to taste, as less may be needed if chicken is omitted.	Use reduced-calorie mayonnaise, reduce the amount of chicken, and increase the quantity of carrots and celery.	To reduce cost, use pre-cooked deli rotisserie chicken in place of raw chicken breasts.

Chapter 8:
MAIN DISH DINNER RECIPES

When schedules are full and appetites are ravenous, getting dinner on the table can feel like an overwhelming task. Too often, we sacrifice the joy and comfort that comes with conversation over a meal of good hearty food, with whatever we can get our hands on quickly just to satisfy our need for fuel.

In addition to being delicious and convenient make-ahead meals, the dinner recipes included in this chapter are downright sexy! Full of exciting flavor and textures, when you pull these meals from the freezer, reheat in the oven or microwave, and serve after a long, busy day, you'll savor every ooh, aaah, and "OMG, this is delicious!"

Originally created for my catering company, Taste of Amazing, these meals have entertained clients and their guests during the most special of occasions. I hope to share a little of the joy of the catering experience with you as you make these dishes at home. It is so rewarding to prepare food and watch guests experience the meal – to savor a perfect bite, share tastes with each other, and return to the buffet line for seconds and thirds. It gives me goosebumps sometimes – the awe of it – the privilege of feeding and entertaining people with delicious food.

So now I'm sharing a few of my favorite recipes with you to enjoy cooking, sharing, and experiencing. I hope you'll "make it your own" as you get comfortable with the recipes and add your unique style and taste to each dish.

I raise my glass… to joyful cooking, gathering round the table, and loving each other with amazing food.

Cheers!

BEEF

Cantonese Braised Beef

I originally enjoyed this dish at a tiny Chinese restaurant in downtown Seattle and fell in love! The restaurant's menu was mostly in Chinese with just a few words of English thrown in, so it was impossible to know what to order. Instead, I just pointed to another guest's dish and that's what they brought to our table.

It was divine! I spoke to the chef-owner and he happily shared a few tips on making the dish, but his instructions were in Chinese and I couldn't understand a word. Immediately upon returning home I began my quest to recreate this recipe. I spent days watching Chinese cooking videos, using Translator to figure out what they were saying, and then headed into the kitchen to test the various techniques I observed.

This recipe is the loving result, and I hope you will savor it as much as I do! Every time I make it, I get rave reviews and the aroma from its' cooking will bring the family running. Generous chunks of tender beef and crunchy Daikon radish stewed in rich aromatics create this sweet, garlicky flavor experience that is at once as comforting as it is decadent.

Making this recipe requires a visit to your neighborhood or online Asian grocery store, but once there the ingredients are easy to find. If you prefer not to buy all the items, refer to the "budget-friendly" version that requires fewer specialty purchases.

Just a note: If you're cooking for kids or picky eaters, you may want to go with potatoes instead of the Daikon radish or turnips. My kids don't care for radish or turnips, so I always make the swap when making this at home.

So take your time and enjoy the process. You'll love how the aroma will fill your house with the anticipation of savoring this incredible dish!

MAIN DISH DINNER RECIPES | BEEF

INGREDIENTS

No of Servings		4	6	10	14
		qty | msmt (weight)	qty | msmt (weight)	qty | msmt (weight)	qty | msmt (weight)
CHEESECLOTH BAG FOR AROMATICS					
1 TBSP (6g)	Star Anise		2 TBSP (9g)	3 TBSP (15g)	4 TBSP (21g)
1 TBSP (6g)	Dried Orange or Tangerine Peel *1 TBSP of dried orange peel is equal to zest of 1 medium fresh orange. Dried works best for this recipe.		2 TBSP (9g)	3 TBSP (15g)	4 TBSP (21g)
2 pods (6g)	Cardamom Seeds, whole, or Cardamom Pods (black or green)		3 pods (9g)	5 pods (15g)	7 pods (21g)
1 each (<1g)	Bay Leaves		2 each (<1g)	3 each (<1g)	4 each (<1g)
1 each (3g)	Cinnamon Sticks		2 each (5g)	3 each (8g)	4 each (11g)
1 each (3g)	Cassia Bark Sticks		2 each (5g)	3 each (8g)	4 each (11g)
½ TBSP (4g)	White Peppercorn		¾ TBSP (6g)	1 ¼ TBSP (10g)	1 ¾ TBSP (14g)
½ TBSP (4g)	Szechuan Peppercorn		¾ TBSP (6g)	1 ¼ TBSP (10g)	1 ¾ TBSP (14g)
BEEF BRISKET & BRAISING INGREDIENTS					
1 ½ LB (912g)	Beef Brisket - cut into 1" (2.5cm) cubes		2 ¼ LB (1368g)	3 ¾ LB (2280g)	5 ¼ LB (3192g)
2 TBSP (20g)	All-Purpose Flour		3 TBSP (30g)	5 TBSP (50g)	7 TBSP (70g)
1 fl oz (30mL)	Vegetable or Canola Oil (do not use Olive Oil), divided		1 ½ fl oz (44g)	2 ½ fl oz (74g)	3 ½ fl oz (104g)
1 each (28g)	Medium Shallot, sliced thinly		1 ½ each (43g)	2 ½ each (71g)	3 ½ each (99g)
1 inch (9g)	Fresh Ginger Root, peeled and sliced thinly		1 ½ inch (14g)	2 ½ inch (23g)	3 ½ inch (32g)
3 each (17g)	Garlic Cloves, minced		4 ½ each (25g)	7 ½ each (41g)	10 ½ each (58g)
¼ tsp (1g)	Chinese Five Spice		½ tsp (2g)	¾ tsp (3g)	1 tsp (4g)
¼ cup (59mL)	Shaozing Wine (Chinese Wine) or Yellow Rice Wine		½ cup (89g)	¾ cup (148g)	1 cup (207g)
1 ½ TBSP (23g)	Chu Hou Paste		2 ¼ TBSP (34g)	3 ¾ TBSP (56g)	5 ¼ TBSP (79g)
¾ TBSP (14g)	Hoisin Sauce		1 TBSP (21g)	2 TBSP (36g)	2 ¾ TBSP (50g)
¾ TBSP (11mL)	Oyster Sauce		1 TBSP (17g)	2 TBSP (28g)	2 ¾ TBSP (39g)
8 fl oz (237mL)	Water (may need more or less)		12 fl oz (355g)	20 fl oz (591g)	28 fl oz (828mL)
FINISHING INGREDIENTS					
¾ LB (342g)	Daikon Radish or Turnips or Russet Potatoes, peeled and cut into 1" (2.5cm) cubes		1 LB (513g)	2 LB (855g)	2 ¾ LB (1197g)
1 ½ TBSP (23mL)	Soy Sauce		2 ¼ TBSP (34g)	3 ¾ TBSP (56g)	5 ¼ TBSP (79mL)
¾ TBSP (11mL)	Dark Soy Sauce		1 TBSP (17g)	2 TBSP (28g)	2 ¾ TBSP (39mL)
6 fl oz (177mL)	Beef Stock or Broth		9 fl oz (266g)	15 fl oz (444g)	21 fl oz (621mL)
¾ TBSP (10g)	Rock Sugar (or Raw/Turbinado Sugar)		1 TBSP (15g)	2 TBSP (24g)	2 ¾ TBSP (34mL)
1 tsp (7g)	Salt		1 ½ tsp (11g)	2 ½ tsp (18g)	3 ½ tsp (25mL)
¼ tsp (<1g)	Black Pepper		½ tsp (<1g)	¾ tsp (1g)	1 tsp (1g)
1 each (11g)	Scallions (Green Onions), sliced thinly (for garnish)		1 ½ each (17g)	2 ½ each (28g)	3 ½ each (39mL)

NUTRITION FACTS:

Serving Size 8 oz   **Calories** 300   **Total Fat** 15g   **Total Carbohydrates** 15g   **Protein** 30g

The portion size shown is based on industry dietary standards and may be smaller than the portion size allowed for in recipe.

INSTRUCTIONS

Bring a pot of water to boil with enough water to hold and cover the beef brisket. While water is coming to a boil, prepare the aromatics and beef.

Prepare Cheesecloth Cooking Bag for Aromatics.
In a dry skillet over MEDIUM heat, toss the aromatics listed under **"Cheesecloth Bag for Aromatics"** for 2 to 3 minutes or until the aroma begins to release and they become very fragrant.

Lay out a double layer of cheesecloth flat on the counter. Place the warmed aromatics in the center, then pull up all four corners of the cheesecloth to create a bag. Tie into a secure knot or tie off with kitchen twine.

Prepare Beef
Cut away large areas of fat, then cut the **beef brisket** into 1-2" (2.5-5cm) cubes, then add to boiling water. Blanch for 8-10 minutes in boiling water, then remove beef and rinse under cold water. Pat the beef pieces dry with a paper towel.

Dredge dried brisket pieces in **flour** and shake off any excess.

Heat HALF the **vegetable oil** in a skillet on MEDIUM-HIGH heat, then sear meat pieces on all sides (about 2-3 minutes per side).

> **Note:** Layer the pieces in a single layer with plenty of room between them so each piece can brown on each side. An over-filled or over-oiled skillet will cause moisture build-up and steaming of the meat. Add additional oil if needed but use caution. Meat is browned correctly when it easily removes from the pan. If it is sticking, it needs to sear longer or lower the heat to prevent the flour from burning.

When each piece is seared/browned on each side, remove from pan and set aside.

Heat remaining HALF of **vegetable oil** in skillet over MEDIUM heat. Add **shallots** and **ginger**, then toss until shallots become clear (approximately 1 minute). Add **garlic** and **Chinese Five Spice** and continue to stir until garlic is softened (approximately 1 minute). Add **Shaoxing Wine** and stir another 1 to 2 minutes until slightly reduced.

Add **Chu Hou Paste** and seared beef pieces, then stir to coat the meat with the pan ingredients.

> **MIS EN PLACE**
> 1. Cut beef into cubes.
> 2. Slice shallot, ginger and mince garlic.
> 3. Cut Daikon radish (or turnips or potatoes, depending on your selection). For radish or turnips, cover with a damp paper towel and hold in refrigerator until ready to use. For potatoes, place in a bowl of cold water until ready to use.
> 4. Slice scallions for garnish.
> 5. Assemble remaining ingredients.

Add the following items: **Cheesecloth bag of aromatics**, **hoisin sauce** and **oyster sauce**.

Stir well, then add just enough **water** to cover the ingredients, but only to the point where they are just barely covered. Bring to a boil, then reduce heat to LOW and simmer for 2-½ hours or until meat is tender.

After 2-½ hours, check that the meat is pull-apart tender. If not, continue cooking for another 20 to 30 minutes.

When the meat is pull-apart tender, add the **Daikon radish** (**or turnips or potatoes**, depending on your selection). Stir in the **soy sauce**, **dark soy sauce**, **beef stock**, **rock sugar** (or raw/turbinado sugar) and **salt**.

> **Note:** If the liquids in the dish do not cover the Daikon radish, add a bit more water just to cover.

Return to a boil, then reduce heat, cover and simmer until the radish (or turnips or potatoes) are fork-tender but firm (15-20 minutes). **Do not over-cook.** Remove from heat, then add **salt** and **black pepper** to taste.

MAIN DISH DINNER RECIPES | BEEF

MAKE IT NOW!

- Remove cheesecloth bag of aromatics. Stir well, then taste. Add additional salt if needed.
- Allow to rest for 5 minutes before serving.
- Garnish with fresh, sliced **scallions**.

MAKE IT A FREEZER MEAL

- Remove cheesecloth bag of aromatics. Stir well, then taste. Add additional salt if needed.
- Pour into a shallow container so the stew is no more than 2" (5cm) deep. Set in refrigerator to cool, approximately 1 hour.
- Once the beef stew has completely cooled, remove from the refrigerator and pour the number of servings needed into resealable zippered or vacuum-sealable bags or a microwave-safe freezer meal container.
- Seal tightly, removing all air. Apply label titled *"Cantonese Braised Beef Brisket."*
- When ready to serve, follow reheating instructions on the label.

FREEZER LABELS

Find and print freezer meal labels for this dish at www.frozenandfabulous.com. (See also *"Chapter 13: Quick Guide to Online Tools."*)

SUGGESTED PAIRINGS

SIDE DISH PAIRINGS

- Rice Noodles
- White or brown rice

WINE AND/OR ALCOHOL PAIRINGS

- Kabinett-style German Reisling Wine
- Beer (dark or IPA)

ONLINE RESOURCES

Scan this QR code for a direct link to an instructional cooking video for this recipe on www.frozenandfabulous.com, along with these helpful "How It's Done" videos."

- How to Sear Meat
- How to Work with Fresh Ginger Root

VARIATIONS

MAKE IT GLUTEN-FREE

Replace the following ingredients with gluten-free versions: Soy Sauce, Hoisin Sauce & Beef Stock.

MAKE IT VEGETARIAN

Replace beef brisket with seitan and reduce cooking time by 1-½ hours. Replace beef stock with vegetarian stock. Omit oyster sauce.

MAKE IT "FIT-FRIENDLY"

Reduce portion size or replace the Daikon radish with cauliflower florets.

MAKE IT BUDGET-FRIENDLY

This dish is budget-friendly as is, costing approximately $.70 per serving when made in large quantities. However, to avoid the expense of purchasing bottled items you may not use often, use regular soy sauce for both types of soy sauce called for in the recipe and look for an Asian market where you can buy small quantities of the sauces and aromatics.

BEEF

Horseradish-Crusted Beef Roulade

Tuscan-Style with Roasted Red Peppers & Provolone

This is one of those dishes I like to keep on hand in the freezer for special occasions. It is gorgeous to look at and heavenly when served with a rich demi-glace made from pan drippings and red wine.

Although the traditional Beef Roulade or Rouladen dish was of German origin, this version takes on Mediterranean flavors and French cooking techniques for a new spin on the classic.

I start with a vibrant marinade, then fill thin, tenderized beef with layers of rich flavor. Creamy horseradish, bright roasted red peppers, mushrooms, fresh spinach and herbs marry together with the Tuscan-style beef.

The outer crust gives this dish its' "wow!" factor, with incredible texture and a spicy kick. When rolled into a roulade, cut into rounds, and served with rich, silky demi-glace sauce, it delivers an amazing taste and presentation experience.

The Tuscan Marinade used for the beef is also a great stand-alone recipe. I use this marinade frequently for flank steak – simply marinate for 4 to 5 hours or overnight, then remove and pat dry, sear on both sides and finish in the oven. I also have several videos on our website demonstrating how to prepare, cook and serve flank steak correctly. When properly prepared, it can be a very tender, flavorful style of meat. No need to wait for a special occasion to make this dish. You deserve to eat delicious, beautiful food every day of the week!

Bon appetit!

MAIN DISH DINNER RECIPES | BEEF

INGREDIENTS:

No of Servings				
4		**6**	**10**	**14**
qty | msmt (weight)		qty | msmt (weight)	qty | msmt (weight)	qty | msmt (weight)
TUSCAN-STYLE MARINATED BEEF				
2 LB (912g)	Top Round Beef Roast (cut to ¼" (.6cm) thickness) or 4 boneless round steaks (cut to ¼" (.6cm) thickness)	3 LB (1368g)	5 LB (2280g)	7 LB (3192g)
MARINADE				
4 fl oz (118mL)	Balsamic Vinegar	6 fl oz (177mL)	10 fl oz (296mL)	14 fl oz (414mL)
4 fl oz (118mL)	Olive Oil	6 fl oz (177mL)	10 fl oz (296mL)	14 fl oz (414mL)
8 each (22g)	Garlic Cloves, peeled & smashed	12 each (34g)	20 each (56g)	28 each (78g)
2 tsp (9g)	Kosher Salt	1 TBSP (13g)	1 ½ TBSP (22g)	2 TBSP (30g)
2 sprigs (2g)	Fresh Rosemary, whole sprigs	3 sprigs (3g)	5 sprigs (5g)	7 sprigs (7g)
2 sprigs (1g)	Fresh Thyme, whole sprigs	3 sprigs (2g)	5 sprigs (3g)	7 sprigs (4g)
2 tsp (10g)	Sun-Dried Tomatoes	1 TBSP (15g)	1 ½ TBSP (25g)	2 TBSP (35g)
ROULADE FILLING				
2 each (213g)	Red Bell Peppers, de-seeded and sliced into thin strips	3 each (319g)	5 each (532g)	7 each (744g)
2 tsp (10mL)	Olive Oil	1 TBSP (15mL)	1 ½ TBSP (25mL)	2 TBSP (35mL)
3 TBSP (42g)	Cream Cheese, softened	4 ½ TBSP (63g)	⅓ cup (105g)	½ cup (148g)
3 TBSP (45g)	Sour Cream	4 ½ TBSP (68g)	⅓ cup (113g)	½ cup (158g)
2 tsp (11g)	Dijon Mustard	3 tsp (17g)	5 tsp (28g)	7 tsp (40g)
3 TBSP (45g)	Prepared Horseradish *add more or less according to taste and heat-level preference	4 ½ TBSP (68g)	½ cup (113g)	2/3 cup (158g)
ROULADE FILLING LAYERING INGREDIENTS				
2 tsp (9g)	Kosher Salt	1 TBSP (13g)	1 ½ TBSP (22g)	2 TBSP (30g)
2 tsp (4g)	Black Pepper	1 TBSP (6g)	1 ½ TBSP (10g)	2 TBSP (14g)
1 cup (30g)	Fresh Spinach Leaves, whole, stem removed	1 ½ cups (45g)	2 ½ cups (75g)	3 ½ cups (105g)
½ cup (33g)	Small White or Cremini Mushrooms, sliced thinly	¾ cup (49g)	1 ¼ cups (82g)	1 ¾ cups (114g)
2 tsp (10g)	Sun-Dried Tomatoes, julienne-cut, drained and chopped	1 TBSP (15g)	1 ½ TBSP (25g)	2 TBSP (35g)
2 each (11g)	Garlic Cloves, minced	3 each (17g)	5 each (28g)	7 each (39g)
2 tsp (2g)	Fresh Rosemary Leaves, finely chopped	1 TBSP (4g)	1 ½ TBSP (6g)	2 TBSP (8g)
2 tsp (2g)	Fresh Thyme Leaves, finely chopped	1 TBSP (2g)	1 ½ TBSP (4g)	2 TBSP (6g)
2 tsp (<1g)	Fresh Flat-Leaf Italian Parsley, finely chopped	1 TBSP (1g)	1 ½ TBSP (1g)	2 TBSP (2g)
½ LB (228g)	Provolone Cheese, sliced thin	¾ LB (342g)	1 ¼ LB (570g)	1 ¾ LB (798g)
HORSERADISH CRUST				
1 cup (136g)	Panko Bread Crumbs	1 ½ cups (204g)	2 ½ cups (340g)	3 ½ cups (476g)
1 TBSP (10g)	All-Purpose Flour	1 ½ TBSP (15g)	2 ½ TBSP (25g)	3 ½ TBSP (35g)
1 TBSP (5g)	Prepared Horseradish *add more or less according to taste and heat-level preference	1 ½ TBSP (8g)	2 ½ TBSP (13g)	3 ½ TBSP (18g)

1 tsp (1g)	Fresh Rosemary Leaves, finely chopped	1 ½ tsp (2g)	2 ½ tsp (3g)	3 ½ tsp (4g)
1 tsp (1g)	Fresh Thyme Leaves, finely chopped	1 ½ tsp (1g)	2 ½ tsp (2g)	3 ½ tsp (3g)
1 tsp (<1g)	Fresh Flat-Leaf Italian Parsley, finely chopped	1 ½ tsp (<1g)	2 ½ tsp (1g)	3 ½ tsp (1g)
2 fl oz (30mL)	Olive Oil, divided	3 fl oz (45mL)	5 fl oz (75mL)	7 fl oz (105mL)
1 TBSP (14mL)	Butter (Salted), melted	1 ½ TBSP (21mL)	2 ½ TBSP (35mL)	3 ½ TBSP (49mL)
½ tsp (4g)	Salt	¾ tsp (5g)	1 ¼ tsp (9g)	1 ¾ tsp (12g)
¼ tsp (1g)	Black Pepper	½ tsp (1g)	¾ tsp (1g)	1 tsp (2g)

RED WINE DEMI-GLACE

1 TBSP (15mL)	Olive Oil	1 ½ TBSP (23mL)	2 ½ TBSP (38mL)	3 ½ TBSP (53mL)
½ each (14g)	Medium Shallot, whole, peeled and rough-chopped	1 each (21g)	1 ½ each (35g)	2 each (50g)
2 each (6g)	Garlic Cloves, peeled & smashed	3 each (8g)	5 each (14g)	7 each (20g)
8 fl oz (237mL)	Red Wine	12 fl oz (355mL)	20 fl oz (591mL)	28 fl oz (828mL)
16 fl oz (473mL)	Beef Stock or Broth	24 fl oz (710mL)	40 fl oz (1183mL)	56 fl oz (1656mL)
1 TBSP (18g)	Beef Base (Chef Gail recommends "Better Than Bouillon Beef Base")	1 ½ TBSP (27g)	2 ½ TBSP (45g)	3 ½ TBSP (63g)
1 sprig (1g)	Fresh Rosemary, whole sprigs	2 sprigs (1g)	3 sprigs (2g)	4 sprigs (3g)
1 sprig (1g)	Fresh Thyme, whole sprigs	2 sprigs (1g)	3 sprigs (2g)	4 sprigs (2g)
1 pinch (<1g)	Cayenne Pepper	2 pinches (<1g)	⅛ tsp (<1g)	¼ tsp (1g)
1 pinch (<1g)	Salt	2 pinches (<1g)	⅛ tsp (1g)	¼ tsp (1g)
1 pinch (<1g)	Black Pepper	2 pinches (<1g)	⅛ tsp (1g)	¼ tsp (1g)
1 TBSP (9g)	Corn Starch *optional	1 ½ TBSP (14g)	2 ½ TBSP (23g)	3 ½ TBSP (32g)
2 fl oz (59mL)	Cold Water *optional	3 fl oz (89mL)	5 fl oz (148mL)	7 fl oz (207mL)
1 TBSP (1g)	Fresh Flat-Leaf Italian Parsley, finely chopped (for garnish)	1 ½ TBSP (1g)	2 ½ TBSP (2g)	3 ½ TBSP (2g)

NUTRITION FACTS:

Serving Size 8.5 oz   **Calories** 440   **Total Fat** 28g   **Total Carbohydrates** 20g   **Protein** 25g

The portion size shown is based on industry dietary standards and may be smaller than the portion size allowed for in recipe.

INSTRUCTION:

Prepare Beef.
Prepare **beef** for roulade by slicing it horizontally to ¼" (.63cm) thickness.

Lay the beef out flat, then pound with a mallet so it is of a consistent thickness and tenderized, without tearing the meat.

Place meat into a vacuum-sealable bag or container large enough to hold the beef covered in marinade.

Prepare Marinade.
Whisk together the **marinade ingredients,** then pour over the beef. If using a vacuum-sealable bag, make sure the meat is flattened inside the bag so the marinade can be evenly disbursed after sealing. If using a container, make sure the meat is fully submerged in the marinade and turn the meat over halfway through the marinating time.

Place beef and marinade in the refrigerator and marinate for 4 to 6 hours (not more than 8 hours).

> **NOTE:** You can ask your butcher to cut the meat to ¼" (.63cm) thickness, or you can purchase a roast and cut it yourself. See our "How It's Done" video called "Preparing Top Round Beef Roast for Roulade" - Chapter 13: Quick Guide to Online Tools.

MAIN DISH DINNER RECIPES | BEEF

Roast Red Bell Peppers.
Brush or toss whole or sliced **red bell peppers** with **olive oil**.

If using whole peppers, make sure most of the oil has dripped away, then place bell peppers over the flame of a gas stove or grill. Cook over the direct flame, turning until all sides of the bell pepper are blackened. Immediately transfer to a resealable zippered bag, seal tightly, and allow to cool. Once cooled, release the seal on the bag. From the outside of the bag, rub the peppers inside the bag to remove most of the black char. Then remove the peppers from the bag and slice into thin strips, removing seeds and stem.

If using sliced peppers, place oiled slices onto a baking sheet and roast under a broiler for 1 to 2 minutes or until softened and starting to color golden brown.

Create Creamy Horseradish Mixture.
In a small bowl, mix together the softened **cream cheese**, **sour cream**, **Dijon mustard** and prepared **horseradish**. Taste and add more horseradish if additional heat is desired. Set aside.

Assemble remaining **Roulade Filling Layers ingredients**. Set aside.

Prepare Horseradish Crust.
In a small bowl, mix together the **ingredients for Horseradish Crust**, using only ¾ of the olive oil measurement shown. Set aside.

Prepare Roulade.
Remove beef from marinade and place on a rack to dry. Allow to sit for 5 minutes, then turn over and allow to sit another 5 minutes. Pat away any remaining moisture from the beef with a paper towel.

Sprinkle both sides of meat generously with **kosher salt** and **black pepper**, then lay the meat out flat on a working surface. If there are any tears or gaps in the meat surface, place those closest to you to contain the contents during the rolling-up process.

> **IMPORTANT:** When you roll up the meat, you will need to roll WITH the grain so that when you cut into medallions you will be cutting AGAINST the grain. This step is really important to ensure the meat will be as tender as possible.

MIS EN PLACE

1. Prepare garlic - rough-chopped for marinade and demi glace, minced for filling.
2. Roast red bell peppers, then slice into thin strips.
3. Remove stems from spinach leaves.
4. Thinly slice mushrooms.
5. Chop drained sun-dried tomatoes for filling.
6. Chop fresh herbs for filling, crust and garnish.
7. Rough chop shallot for demi glace.
8. Assemble remaining ingredients.

CHEF NOTES

If you are one of those people who keep bacon or duck fat in your pantry (like me), here's a tip:

Once your marinated beef is laid out flat, dried and you're ready to start adding the filling ingredients, brush the meat with a light layer of bacon or duck fat. Then salt, pepper and assemble as instructed.

This will bring moisture and a "next level" of flavor to the meat that you'll really love.

Assemble the Layers
Layer the **cream cheese/horseradish mixture** evenly across the surface of the meat, being careful not to go all the way to the edge (leave about ¼" (.6cm) clear around the edge of the meat). Apply generously, as this layer will add an essential creaminess to the dish.

Place an even layer of **spinach leaves** across the surface, then top with sliced, **roasted red bell peppers**, **sliced mushrooms** and **sun-dried tomatoes**.

Sprinkle minced **garlic** and chopped **rosemary**, **thyme** and **parsley** evenly across the surface.

Place round slices of **Provolone cheese** on top, covering all the other layered ingredients. Press down on the cheese layer firmly to make sure all ingredients adhere to each other.

Roll Up the Roulade (Rolled Steak).
Double-check that you are rolling the meat WITH the grain so when it's time to slice into medallions, you will cut AGAINST the grain.

Starting at the end closest to you, begin rolling up with beef and fillings. Keep a tight pressure to ensure all the fillings stay evenly disbursed and the meat forms into an evenly-sized, tightly compacted roll.

> **CHEF NOTES**
>
> Another way to amp up the flavor for this dish is to reserve some of the marinade used for the beef, then place the sliced, roasted red bell peppers in the marinade for 30 minutes. Remove from the marinade, drain, and follow the instructions for the roulade filling.
>
> Want a complementary side dish? Toss sliced, fresh bell peppers or green beans in a skillet over MEDIUM heat, then add in a bit of the reserved marinade. Cook until softened and serve. So delicious!
>
> **IMPORTANT:** If you use any of the marinade that was previously used for the beef, it must be fully cooked before serving to prevent any cross-contamination from the raw beef.

Apply Horseradish Crust.
Pat all sides of the rolled beef dry – if the beef is wet, the **Horseradish Crust** will come off during cooking or slicing.

Lay out a large piece of parchment paper or plastic wrap, just slightly larger than the size of the meat before it was rolled.

Layer the **Horseradish Crust** evenly across the parchment paper or plastic wrap.

Brush the **Beef Roulade** evenly with the remaining ¼ of the measurement of **olive oil**, then place on one end of the laid-out **Horseradish Crust**. Begin to roll so the crust will stick to the outside of the **Roulade**. Use the parchment paper or plastic wrap to apply pressure so the crust applies evenly. Continue rolling to cover the entire **Roulade** in the **Horseradish Crust**. By hand, apply leftover crust to the ends of the Roulade and any bare areas.

Wrap tightly to make sure the roulade is holding its' shape, then place in the freezer for 15 minutes to "seize" ingredients into place. Remove from freezer, hand-press wrapped roulade to keep it rolled together tightly and ensure it retains its perfectly rounded shape.

If serving now, place the wrapped roll in the refrigerator. If making a freezer meal, keep it in the freezer until ready to package.

Make Red Wine Demi-Glace Sauce
In a skillet, heat **olive oil** over MEDIUM heat, then add in chopped **shallots**. Stir together until shallots are softened, then add minced **garlic**. Toss for 1 minute (be careful not to burn the garlic), then add in **red wine**. Reduce heat, then continue cooking until red wine has reduced by half.

Add in **beef stock**, **beef base**, and **fresh herbs**. Bring to a boil, then reduce heat to simmer. Continue cooking until reduced by 75%.

Once reduced, the sauce should be silky and coat the back of a spoon. Add **cayenne pepper**, **salt** and **black pepper**, taste and add more seasoning if needed.

If the sauce is not thick enough, make a slurry of **corn starch** and cold water. Bring sauce to a boil, then whisk in the slurry and continue cooking for 4 to 5 minutes.

Strain finished sauce through a fine-mesh strainer three times. The first time is to remove the shallots, garlic and herbs. The second and third times will remove any remaining pieces and facilitate a silky, luxurious sauce.

MAKE IT NOW!

Preheat oven to 425°F (218°C).

Spray a baking sheet or roasting pan with non-stick spray, then transfer the Crusted Roulade to the center of the sheet or pan. It is best to transfer the roulade to the pan when it is chilled so it will hold its' shape; however, let it sit on the counter for 30 minutes before placing in oven. Meat needs to be close to room temperature before cooking.

Roast in the oven for 20-25 minutes, or until internal temperature reaches 125°F (52°C). Allow to rest for 15 minutes. The temperature will rise during resting time to hit perfect Medium-Rare of 130°F (54°C).

MAIN DISH DINNER RECIPES | BEEF

120°F (49°C)	130°F (54°C)	140°F (60°C)	150°F (65°C)	160°F (71°C)
Rare		Medium		Well Done

After resting, cut into ¾" to 1" (1.9cm to 2.5cm) thick medallions and serve with warmed Red Wine Demi-Glace sauce. Garnish with freshly chopped **Italian flat-leaf parsley**.

MAKE IT A FREEZER MEAL:

Spray a large piece of plastic wrap with non-stick spray, then wrap tightly around the partially frozen or chilled Crusted Roulade with the sprayed side of the plastic facing the crust. Once covered, wrap the entire piece with a second piece of plastic wrap, then add an outside layer of aluminum foil. For longer shelf life, place in a resealable zippered bag or vacuum-sealable bag, remove all excess air and seal. Apply label *"Tuscan-Style Horseradish-Crusted Beef Roulade"* and follow thawing and cooking instructions when ready to serve.

Once the sauce is fully cooled, place in a freezable, sealable container or a resealable zippered bag and remove all excess air. Apply label *"Red Wine Demi Glacé for: Tuscan-Style Horseradish-Crusted Beef Roulade."* Following cooking instructions when ready to serve.

FREEZER LABELS

Find and print freezer meal labels for this dish at www.frozenandfabulous.com. (See also *"Chapter 13: Quick Guide to Online Tools."*)

SUGGESTED PAIRINGS

SIDE DISH PAIRINGS
- Celery Root Purée
- Mashed or Rustic Smashed Potatoes
- Puréed Cauliflower
- Roasted Root Vegetables
- Rice Pilaf

WINE AND/OR ALCOHOL PAIRINGS
- Medium to low-tannin red wines
- Barbera
- Aglianico
- Montepulciano d'Abruzzo
- Chianti Classico

ONLINE RESOURCES

Scan this QR code for a direct link to an instructional cooking video for this recipe on www.frozenandfabulous.com, along with these helpful "How It's Done" videos.

- Preparing Top Round Beef Roast for Roulade
- How to Clean and Prepare Flank Steak for Cooking

VARIATIONS

MAKE IT GLUTEN-FREE

Use gluten-free versions of beef stock, beef base and Panko bread crumbs, and replace all-purpose flour with white rice flour.

MAKE IT VEGETARIAN

The marinade used for the beef would be lovely paired with eggplant steaks, cauliflower steaks, portobello mushrooms or a variety of root vegetables, such as squash or turnips. To create the roulade effect, use long strips of thinly sliced squash. Replace beef stock and beef base with vegetarian versions.

MAKE IT "FIT-FRIENDLY"

Omit the crust – the beef roulade will still be delicious served with the sauce. You can also reduce calories by reducing or omitting the cream cheese/sour cream mixture and instead brushing the beef with plain horseradish.

MAKE IT BUDGET-FRIENDLY

Choose lower-cost cuts of beef or buy it in bulk when on sale. Also, choose an inexpensive red wine and omit the beef base if you don't already have it on hand.

BEEF

Coffee-Rubbed Steak
with Coffee Butter

Get ready for the heat! Upon first biting into this tender, juicy steak you'll notice the bold, assertive taste and texture of the crust running across your palate. The coffee brings a sharp, earthy richness, then fades to let the flavor of the steak shine through, followed by the heat of chile on the finish. Every bite is a journey of rich flavors, exploding one by one with perfect timing, leading up to a lingering, satisfying finale.

This recipe works well with any cut of steak, but my particular favorites are Porterhouse, Rib-Eye, Flat Iron or Strip, and I choose bone-in cuts whenever possible. These steaks marry well with the flavors in this rub and stay amazingly tender when seared on a flaming hot grill or cast-iron skillet. Choose big fat steaks – at least 1" (2.5cm) thick – to allow a strong char on the outside and perfect pink on the inside, and after cooking let the meat rest 10 minutes before slicing. It also pairs deliciously with steak topped with bacon.

One of my favorite ways to cook this steak is directly on hot coals, adding another dimension of flavor and enhanced crust. Just scan the QR code for a video with step-by-step instructions for cooking with this method.

This rub is also delicious on flank or skirt steak. The cooking technique is the same – sear hot and finish cooking to rare or medium-rare under reduced heat. However, when cooking flank or skirt, the most important thing to remember is to let the meat rest, then slice against the grain into very thin strips – about ¼" (.6cm) – to keep the meat tender.

And one little tip about this Coffee Dry Rub: It goes well with chicken, pork and even vegetables so I recommend making a large batch and storing extra in the freezer. It's safe to store in your spice cupboard, too, if you plan to use it within a few months. To make it even easier, I have included the weights for each ingredient for quicker assembly. If you haven't used a kitchen scale before, you can see this method demonstrated by viewing our instructional video – see the "How It's Done" section in Chapter 13: Quick Guide to Online Tools.

Leftovers make an excellent energy-fueled breakfast, too! My daughter, Kaitlyn, loves it when I put this steak in her scrambled eggs or omelet in the morning. The coffee rub provides a caffeinated "kick-start" of energy, while the steak and eggs provide a massive shot of protein that keeps her going all day.

MAIN DISH DINNER RECIPES | BEEF

INGREDIENTS:

No of Servings				
4 qty | msmt (weight)		**6** qty | msmt (weight)	**10** qty | msmt (weight)	**14** qty | msmt (weight)
COFFEE-RUBBED STEAK				
1 ⅓ cup (186g)	**Chef Gail's Coffee Dry Rub** (see Recipe in *Chapter 10: Spice Blends*)	2 cups (279g)	3 ⅓ cups (466g)	4 ⅔ cups (652g)
2 TBSP (30mL)	Olive Oil	3 TBSP (45mL)	5 TBSP (75mL)	7 TBSP (105mL)
4 each (1132g)	Beef Steaks, 1" to 2" (2.5cm to 5cm) thick, approximately 10 oz (283g) each	6 each (1698g)	10 each (2830g)	14 each (3962g)
1 tsp (7g)	Salt	1 ½ tsp (11g)	2 ½ tsp (18g)	3 ½ tsp (25g)
½ tsp (1g)	Black Pepper	¾ tsp (2g)	1 ¼ tsp (3g)	1 ¾ tsp (4g)
COFFEE BUTTER				
4 TBSP (56g)	Butter (Salted), softened	6 TBSP (84g)	10 TBSP (140g)	14 TBSP (196g)
½ tsp (2g)	**Chef Gail's Coffee Dry Rub** (see Recipe in *Chapter 10: Spice Blends*)	¾ tsp (2g)	1 ¼ tsp (4g)	1 ¾ tsp (5g)

NUTRITION FACTS:

Serving Size 6 oz **Calories** 420 **Total Fat** 30g **Total Carbohydrates** 2g **Protein** 38g

The portion size shown is based on industry dietary standards and may be smaller than the portion size allowed for in recipe.

INSTRUCTIONS:

Prepare Steaks.
If not already on hand, measure and assemble ingredients for **Chef Gail's Coffee Dry Rub** and set aside.

Brush approximately ½ TBSP (7mL) olive oil on both sides of each **steak**.

> **Note:** If cooking immediately, lightly season the steak with salt & pepper before applying oil. If creating a freezer meal, do not perform this step – storing salted steak in the freezer will cause it to lose moisture and flavor.

Apply **Rub** mixture to both sides of each steak (approximately 1 to 1-½ TBSP (14g to 42g) of Rub per steak).

MIS EN PLACE
1. Pull butter from refrigerator to soften.
2. Make Chef Gail's Coffee Dry Rub, if not already on hand
3. Assemble remaining ingredients.

Place rubbed steaks on a wire rack inside a baking sheet and refrigerate 4 to 6 hours, uncovered, to allow the rub seasonings to penetrate the meat.

Prepare Coffee Butter Logs.
Place softened, salted **butter** in a mixing bowl, then add **Chef Gail's Coffee Dry Rub**. Mix well to combine the seasonings evenly. It will be slightly lumpy.

Spread out a piece of plastic wrap, then approximately 2" from the edge of the plastic wrap form the mixed butter into a log shape. Then take the edge of the plastic, pull it over the butter log, tuck it in firmly, then roll the log of butter across the plastic wrap until it is completely wrapped. Swirl the plastic on each end of the butter log to tighten and seal, then tuck the ends back over the log and tape into place. Place wrapped log of butter in the refrigerator to chill. (For help with making butter logs, see our "how it's done" video referenced at the end of this chapter.)

CHEF NOTES: BUTTER LOGS

If you are creating multiple freezer meals, create logs of butter according to the number of servings at each meal (1 TBSP (14g) per steak) so it can be stored with the other components.

If you are unfamiliar with this rolled flavored butter technique, you can see this method demonstrated by viewing our instructional video online. See the "How It's Done" section in Chapter 13: Quick Guide to Online Tools.

MAKE IT NOW!

One hour before cooking, remove steaks and prepared **Coffee Butter** from the refrigerator and allow to reach room temperature. (*This is important. If you try to cook a cold steak or it will be overdone and unevenly cooked.*)

GRILLING METHOD

- Prepare grill so one side is set to very high heat while the other side is open for lower temp cooking.
- Sear steaks on HIGH until a crust forms (approximately 2 to 3 minutes per side), then move to the cooler side of the grill.
- Continue cooking at the lower temperature for 5 to 8 minutes or until done. See the temperature chart below.
- Place 1 TBSP (14g) of Coffee Butter on each steak (it will melt), then allow steak to rest for 10 minutes before serving.

STOVETOP & OVEN METHOD

- Preheat oven to 375°F (190°C). Heat olive oil and an equal amount of butter in an oven-safe skillet (cast-iron is preferred).
- Once hot, place steaks in an oven-safe skillet (do not overcrowd the pan) and SEAR. It will take approximately 1 to 3 minutes for the first side.
- Flip the steak over, cook for one minute more, then remove from heat and place pan in the oven.
- Cook in oven for 8 to 10 minutes or until medium-rare. Duration of cooking time will depend on the length of searing time, steak's thickness, and preferred level of doneness.

Note: If cooking multiple steaks that do not fit in one skillet, transfer steaks to a baking sheet after searing on both sides. Then all steaks can go into the oven on one baking sheet.

- Remove from oven and place 1 TBSP (14g) of Coffee Butter on each steak (it will melt), then allow steaks to rest for 10 minutes before serving.

TEMPERATURE GUIDE FOR STEAKS

I strongly recommend that you cook your steaks to 120°F (49°C) (using an internal stem thermometer) and then pull them off heat to rest. The temperature will rise during during the rest period to a perfect medium-rare doneness. Cooking beyond that temperature will create tough, dry meat.

However, for those of you who prefer another level of doneness, here is a handy guide:

120°F (49°C)	130°F (54°C)	140°F (60°C)	150°F (65°C)	160°F (71°C)
Rare		**Medium**		**Well Done**

MAIN DISH DINNER RECIPES | BEEF

MAKE IT A FREEZER MEAL:

If using resealable zippered freezer bags:
Wrap each steak individually in butcher paper, then place wrapped steaks in a zippered freezer bag along with the log of butter. Remove as much air as possible before sealing.

If using vacuum-sealed bags:
For best quality, seal each steak individually, then place the sealed portions in a zippered freezer bag along with the log of butter. This will be your best option if you want to reheat using the *sous vide* method, which is the superior option.

Apply label titled *"Coffee-Rubbed Steak with Coffee Butter"* to the outside of bag and place in freezer. When ready to serve, follow the cooking instructions on the label.

FREEZER LABELS

Find and print freezer meal labels for this dish at www.frozenandfabulous.com. (See also *"Chapter 13: Quick Guide to Online Tools."*)

SUGGESTED PAIRINGS

SIDE DISH PAIRINGS

- Rice Pilaf with Porcini, Spinach & Walnuts
- Wild Mushroom Risotto
- Charred Corn with Jalapeno & Red Pepper Crema
- Haricot Vert with Caramelized Pearl Onions & Roasted Red Peppers
- Grilled Asparagus or New Potatoes
- Roasted Fingerling Potatoes with Bourbon Butter

WINE AND/OR ALCOHOL PAIRINGS

- Cabernet Sauvignon
- Cabernet Blends or Bordeaux-style Blends
- Bordeaux
- Casa de Illana Tresdecinco 2004 (Spain)
- Malbec

ONLINE RESOURCES

Scan this QR code for a direct link to an instructional cooking video for this recipe on www.frozenandfabulous.com, along with these helpful "How It's Done" videos.

- How to Grill Directly on Coals
- How to Speed Up Production with a Kitchen Scale
- How to Make Flavored Butters & Logs
- How to Sear Meat
- How to Grill-Mark Meat

VARIATIONS

MAKE IT GLUTEN-FREE

This dish is naturally gluten-free. No changes are required.

MAKE IT VEGETARIAN

This rub and butter would be delicious on portobello mushrooms, which hold up well to grilling. Just apply oil and Coffee Dry Rub to the portobello cap, grill and enjoy with a drizzle of Coffee Butter.

MAKE IT "FIT-FRIENDLY"

To save calories with this dish reduce the amount of butter. Choose a lean cut of steak, a smaller portion (nutritional information provided for this recipe is based on a 4 oz (113g) portion of steak), or exchange the steak for chicken breast.

MAKE IT BUDGET-FRIENDLY

To save money, choose a less expensive cut of beef or a smaller portion. Flank or skirt steaks are typically less costly options – just follow the cooking tips for these cuts as outlined at the top of this recipe.

CHEF GAIL KURPGEWEIT @ASKCHEFGAIL

BEEF

Burgers
Peanut Butter, Bourbon & Bacon

I had a client refer to these once as "flavor beasts!" They are amazing, for sure, so I had to agree the name really fits.

Smoky with a hint of sweetness, elevated with a creamy peanut butter sauce made with Bourbon and jalapeno, these burgers are my "most requested" summer BBQ dish. Whether it's a catering client, family member or friend, if someone has the grill going they want these burgers on it! Happily, they're quick and easy to make, especially if I have a few stocked in the freezer for last-minute get-togethers.

Not in the mood for peanut butter? This burger patty is delicious as a "stand-alone" recipe. Will you pair it with sautéed mushrooms and Swiss? Or grilled pineapple, cream cheese and Dijon aioli? If you have a favorite flavor combination, this burger patty is the perfect vehicle for all your ideas. For a less smoky flavor, just reduce the amount of bacon and replace it with sausage or lamb.

And most importantly, with this recipe I'm sharing some "game-changing" tips for making amazing burgers. Scan the QR code at the end of this recipe to watch the complete video on how it's done, including the "thumbprint" technique and how to use temperature changes to improve the quality of your burgers.

So when you're ready to unleash this beast I'll meet you at the grill!

MAIN DISH DINNER RECIPES | BEEF

INGREDIENTS:

No of Servings				
4 qty | msmt (weight)		**6** qty | msmt (weight)	**10** qty | msmt (weight)	**14** qty | msmt (weight)
BACON BURGER PATTIES				
2/3 LB (304g)	Bacon, frozen and finely chopped to match consistency of ground beef	1 LB (456g)	1 2/3 LB (760g)	2 1/3 LB (1064g)
2/3 LB (304g)	Angus Ground Beef (90/10 lean beef/fat ratio)	1 LB (456g)	1 2/3 LB (760g)	2 1/3 LB (1064g)
2 TBSP (44g)	Sweet White Onion, shredded, with juice	3 TBSP (66g)	1/3 cup (110g)	1/2 cup (154g)
2 tsp (10mL)	Heavy Whipping Cream	1 TBSP (15mL)	1 2/3 TBSP (25mL)	2 1/3 TBSP (35mL)
1 1/3 TBSP (7mL)	Worcestershire Sauce	2 TBSP (10mL)	3 1/3 TBSP (16mL)	4 2/3 TBSP (23mL)
1 tsp (5mL)	Soy Sauce	1 1/2 tsp (7mL)	2 1/2 tsp (12mL)	1 1/4 TBSP (17mL)
1 tsp (5mL)	Fish Sauce	1 1/2 tsp (7mL)	2 1/2 tsp (12mL)	3 1/2 tsp (17mL)
1 each (43g)	Eggs	2 each (65g)	3 each (108g)	4 each (151g)
1 each (3g)	Garlic Cloves, minced	2 each (6)	3 each (8g)	5 each (14g)
1 sprig (1g)	Fresh Rosemary Leaves, finely chopped	2 sprigs (2g)	3 sprigs (3g)	4 sprigs (4g)
1 1/3 TBSP (7mL)	Maple-Flavored Bourbon Whiskey (may be substituted with regular Bourbon)	2 TBSP (10mL)	3 1/3 TBSP (16mL)	4 2/3 TBSP (23mL)
1 pinch (1g)	Cayenne Pepper	1/8 tsp (1g)	1/4 tsp (2g)	1/2 tsp (2g)
1 tsp (7g)	Salt	1 1/2 tsp (11g)	2 1/2 tsp (18g)	3 1/2 tsp (25g)
2/3 tsp (1g)	Black Pepper	1 tsp (2g)	1 2/3 tsp (3g)	2 1/3 tsp (5g)
4 slices (3g)	Optional: Medium-Sharp Cheddar Cheese, sliced thinly	6 slices (5g)	10 slices (8g)	14 slices (11g)
PEANUT BUTTER, BOURBON & JALAPENO SAUCE				
2 2/3 TBSP (32g)	Creamy Peanut Butter (Crunchy Peanut Butter is an acceptable substitute for an added element of texture)	1/4 cup (48g)	1/2 cup (80g)	3/4 cup (112g)
2 TBSP (38g)	Green Jalapeno Jelly	3 TBSP (57g)	1/3 cup (95g)	1/2 cup (133g)
2 TBSP (30mL)	Heavy Whipping Cream	3 TBSP (44mL)	1/3 cup (74mL)	1/2 cup (104mL)
2 tsp (10mL)	Pure Maple Syrup	1 TBSP (15mL)	1 2/3 TBSP (25mL)	2 1/3 TBSP (35mL)
2 TBSP (10mL)	Maple-Flavored Bourbon Whiskey (may be substituted with regular Bourbon)	3 TBSP (15mL)	1/3 cup (25mL)	1/2 cup (35mL)

NUTRITION FACTS:

Serving Size 8.5 oz   **Calories** 850   **Total Fat** 44g   **Total Carbohydrates** 9g   **Protein** 29g

The portion size shown is based on industry dietary standards and may be smaller than the portion size allowed for in recipe.

INSTRUCTIONS FOR BACON BURGER PATTIES:

Cut **frozen bacon** into 1 to 2" (2.5cm to 5cm) chunks and place in a food processor. Process until bacon becomes finely ground and of a similar consistency to ground beef.

> **Note:** You will want to use frozen bacon for this step because thawed bacon will leave fibrous strings throughout the pureed meat. Freezing the bacon will allow it to break up more cleanly, and the final burgers will have a more enjoyable mouthfeel.
>
> Running frozen bacon in a food processor will be very loud and can cause some food processors to shake around on the counter. Place one hand firmly on the top of your machine before turning it on.

Combine the **pureed bacon, Angus ground beef,** and **remaining ingredients (except cheese)** in a bowl and combine well with your hands or stand mixer.

Once mixed, take a small amount of the meat mixture (approximately 1 TBSP) and fry it in a pan. Once cooked through, taste, and add more salt and pepper to the meat mixture if needed according to your preference.

Create patties from the meat mixture.
- Standard burgers: 6 oz (170g) patties
- Jumbo burgers: 8 oz (227g) patties
- Slider-size burgers: 3 to 4 oz (85g to 113g) patties

Thumbprint Technique: For standard and jumbo-sized burgers, form the patty, then create an indent in the center with your thumb. This will thin out the middle so the patty will cook through evenly without being overdone on the outside or underdone in the center.

> **Note:** See the thumbprint technique demonstrated by watching the video referenced at the end of this chapter.

Place formed patties in the refrigerator for at least 30 minutes to allow flavors to meld together.

While patties are chilling, make **Peanut Butter, Bourbon & Jalapeno Sauce**.

MIS EN PLACE

1. Freeze, then chop bacon.
2. Shred onion.
3. Mince garlic and chop fresh rosemary leaves.
4. Assemble remaining ingredients.

INSTRUCTIONS FOR PEANUT BUTTER, BOURBON & JALAPENO SAUCE:

In a small bowl, mix **peanut butter, green jalapeno jelly, heavy whipping cream, maple syrup** and **maple-flavored Bourbon whiskey.**

Mix until well blended. Consistency should be thick, smooth and silky, and when tasted it should *not* stick to the roof of your mouth. If necessary, add more cream until the mixture is satiny and easy to spread, but not runny.

> **CAUTION: PEANUT ALLERGIES**
>
> If someone with a peanut allergy will be enjoying this dish, swap a different type of nut butter or eliminate the Peanut Butter Bourbon Sauce from this recipe preparation.

MAKE IT NOW!

OVEN & GRILL OR STOVETOP METHOD

- Remove patties from refrigerator and allow to reach room temperature before cooking. This usually takes about 30 minutes if set on the counter.
- Preheat oven to 375°F (190°C).
- Bring grill or skillet to HIGH heat and lightly brush or spray with pan spray, olive oil, or a mixture of half olive oil, half butter.
- Sear burger patties over HIGH heat until grill marks form or patties are golden brown. This should take 1 to 2 minutes per side.

MAIN DISH DINNER RECIPES | BEEF

- Transfer seared patties to baking sheet and place in oven.
- Bake 4 to 6 minutes, or until meat reaches an internal temperature of 160°F (71°C) using a stem thermometer.
- For cheeseburgers, place one slice of **cheddar cheese** on each patty 3 minutes before the end of cooking time.
- Remove from oven, then spread 1 to 2 TBSP (14g to 28g) of **peanut butter, Bourbon** and **jalapeno sauce** on each patty.
- Allow burgers to rest 5 minutes, lightly covered with foil, before serving or cutting.

GRILL-ONLY METHOD

- Prepare grill so one side is set to very HIGH heat while the other side is open for lower temp cooking.
- Sear burger patties on HIGH until grill marks and crust forms (approximately 1 to 2 minutes per side), then move to the cooler side of the grill.
- Continue cooking at the lower temperature for 4 to 6 minutes or until the burger reaches an internal temperature of 160°F (71°C) using a stem thermometer.
- For cheeseburgers, place one slice of **cheddar cheese** on each patty 2-3 minutes before the end of cooking time.
- Remove from heat, then spread 1 to 2 TBSP (14g to 28g) of **Peanut Butter, Bourbon & Jalapeno Sauce** on each patty.
- Allow burgers to rest 5 minutes, lightly covered with foil, before serving or cutting.

MAKE IT A FREEZER MEAL:

Preparing Peanut Butter, Bourbon & Jalapeno Sauce for freezer:
Package **Peanut Butter, Bourbon & Jalapeno Sauce** in a freezable container and apply label titled *"Peanut Butter Sauce for Peanut Butter Bacon Burgers."* If packaging sauce for multiple meals, package 2 TBSP (28g) of sauce for each regular or jumbo-sized burger patty, and 1 TBSP (14g) for each slider-sized patty.

Preparing burger patties for freezer:

Option 1 - Freeze Raw:

- Lay patties on a baking sheet or other tray that will fit in your freezer, making sure patties do not touch. Place in the freezer for 30 to 40 minutes, or until patties start to freeze individually.
- Remove from the freezer and place a piece of parchment or patty paper between each burger patty. Place the number of burgers you want to serve at each meal in a vacuum-sealed bag or resealable freezer bag, removing as much air as possible before sealing.
- Apply label titled *"Peanut Butter & Bacon Burgers-Uncooked"* to outside of bag and place in freezer.

Option 2 – Partial Cook: You can pre-sear the burger patties, freeze, then finish cooking in the oven from frozen.

- Remove patties from refrigerator and allow to reach room temperature before cooking. This usually takes about 30 minutes if set on the counter.
- Bring grill or skillet to HIGH heat and lightly brush or spray with pan spray, olive oil, or a mixture of half olive oil, half butter.
- Sear burger patties over HIGH heat until grill marks form or patties are golden brown. This should take 1 to 2 minutes per side.
- Remove from heat, place patties on a baking sheet or other tray that will fit in your freezer. Place tray in the freezer for 30 to 40 minutes, or until seared patties are starting to freeze individually.
- Remove from the freezer and place a piece of parchment or patty paper between each burger patty. Place the number of burgers you want to serve at each meal in a vacuum-sealed bag or resealable freezer bag, removing as much air as possible before sealing.
- Apply label titled *"Peanut Butter & Bacon Burgers-Partially Cooked"* to outside of bag and place in freezer.
- When ready to serve, follow the cooking instructions on the label.

FREEZER LABELS

Find and print freezer meal labels for this dish at www.frozenandfabulous.com. (See also *Chapter 13: Quick Guide to Online Tools."*)

SUGGESTED BURGER TOPPINGS

- Toasted Ciabatta Roll with Dijon-Aioli
- Cheddar, Swiss or Provolone Cheese (avoid smoky cheeses)
- Fresh green or red-leaf lettuce
- Fresh, thinly sliced red onions
- Sliced, fresh tomatoes
- Grilled jalapenos, thinly sliced

SUGGESTED PAIRINGS

SIDE DISH PAIRINGS

- Roasted Brussel Sprouts with Garlic
- Grilled Corn
- Sweet Potato French Fries
- Grilled Romaine Caesar Salad
- Potato Salad
- Grilled Watermelon, Peaches or Pineapple

WINE AND/OR ALCOHOL PAIRINGS

- Bourbon
- Well-balanced oaked wines, such as Syrah, Petite Sirah or Red Zinfandel
- Lightly sweet wines, such as an Australian pinot noir
- Beer (golden ale)
- Chocolate wine

ONLINE RESOURCES

Scan this QR code for a direct link to an instructional cooking video for this recipe on www.frozenandfabulous.com, along with these helpful "How It's Done" videos.

- Chef Gail's Secrets for Amazing Burgers
- How to Speed Up Production with a Kitchen Scale

VARIATIONS

MAKE IT GLUTEN-FREE

Use gluten-free versions of Worcestershire and Soy Sauce and serve with a gluten-free bread roll.

MAKE IT VEGETARIAN

Substitute a pre-made Garden Burger patty for the Bacon Burger and apply the Peanut Butter, Bourbon & Jalapeno Sauce as instructed.

MAKE IT "FIT-FRIENDLY"

To save calories with this dish:
- Reduce or omit the bacon, and exchange for ground turkey sausage.
- Exchange ground beef for ground turkey.
- Exchange milk for the heavy cream
- Reduce the amount of Peanut Sauce placed on each patty.

MAKE IT BUDGET-FRIENDLY

To save money in preparing this dish, exchange some or all the bacon for ground beef, and choose a higher fat to lean meat ratio, such as 80/20. You could also eliminate the fish and soy sauces if you don't already have these items on hand.

CHICKEN

Prosciutto-Stuffed Chicken Breasts
with Fig & Honey Sauce

"Uptown girl looking for a downtown man..."

This dish marries culinary sophistication with down to earth style, especially when prepared on the grill. The smokiness adds a depth of flavor that brings a delicious edginess to the fig, chevre, honey and fresh herbs. It is one of my favorite dishes to prepare and serve.

When entertaining and this dish is on the menu, I like to prepare a gorgeous charcuterie board with Italian meats, cheeses, fruits, jams and crostini. It is the perfect "starter" to the vibrant flavors of this roulade-style chicken and rich, decadent sauce. You can also turn this into an appetizer by slicing the roulades into ½" (1.27cm) thick pinwheels, then drizzling with a bit of **Fig & Honey Sauce** and garnishing with fresh parsley. Depending on your presentation style, it works for either a highly formal or more casual event.

When figs are in season, there is no better dish to share with good friends and close family. It is as entertaining to behold with the beautiful color and freshness of the fig, as it is delicious to enjoy. But don't let the seasons stop you – dried figs will make this a favorite go-to all year long.

I hope you enjoy this colorful, flavorful dish as much as I've enjoyed creating it.

Bon appetit!

MAIN DISH DINNER RECIPES | CHICKEN

INGREDIENTS:

No of Servings

4		6	10	14
qty | msmt (weight)		qty | msmt (weight)	qty | msmt (weight)	qty | msmt (weight)
CHICKEN BREASTS				
4 each (340g)	Boneless Whole Chicken Breasts, approx 6 oz (170g) each	6 each (510g)	10 each (851g)	14 each (1191g)
	* Pre-brine with **Quick Brine for Chicken Breasts** (see *Chapter 11: Meat Brines*)			
1 each (1g)	Fresh Rosemary, whole sprigs	1 ½ each (1g)	2 ½ each (2g)	3 ½ each (3g)
1 TBSP (15mL)	Olive Oil	1 ½ TBSP (23mL)	2 ½ TBSP (38mL)	3 ½ TBSP (53mL)
1 tsp (7g)	Salt, divided	1 ½ tsp (11g)	2 ½ tsp (18g)	3 ½ tsp (25g)
1 tsp (2g)	Black Pepper, divided	1 ½ tsp (3g)	2 ½ tsp (5g)	3 ½ tsp (7g)
PROSCIUTTO STUFFING				
2 TBSP (19g)	Dried Figs, chopped into thin pieces	3 TBSP (28g)	⅓ cups (47g)	½ cups (66g)
2 fl oz (59mL)	Balsamic Vinegar	3 fl oz (89mL)	5 fl oz (148mL)	7 fl oz (207g)
4 tsp (23g)	Dijon Mustard (1 tsp (5.5g) per breast)	2 TBSP (34g)	3 ⅓ TBSP (57g)	4 ⅔ TBSP (79g)
½ cup (118g)	Chevre Cheese (or goat cheese) (2 TBSP (14.79g) per breast)	¾ cup (177g)	1 ¼ cups (295g)	1 ¾ cups (413g)
⅓ cup (107g)	Fig Jam (1-¼ TBSP (25g) per breast)	½ cup (160g)	1 cup (267g)	1 ¼ cups (373g)
8 each (112g)	Prosciutto, thinly sliced *(there are approximately 30 slices of prosciutto per pound)	12 each (168g)	20 each (280g)	28 each (392g)
1 TBSP (21g)	Honey	1 ½ TBSP (32g)	2 ½ TBSP (53g)	3 ½ TBSP (74g)
1 cup (30g)	Fresh Spinach Leaves, whole, stem removed	1 ½ cups (45g)	2 ½ cups (75g)	3 ½ cups (105g)
1 cup (30g)	Fresh Basil Leaves, whole, stems removed	1 ½ cups (45g)	2 ½ cups (75g)	3 ½ cups (105g)
2 TBSP (14g)	Walnuts, finely chopped	3 TBSP (21g)	⅓ cup (35g)	½ cup (49g)
2 TBSP (30mL)	Olive Oil	3 TBSP (45mL)	⅓ cup (75mL)	½ cup (105mL)
1 TBSP (14g)	Butter (Salted)	2 TBSP (21g)	3 TBSP (35g)	4 TBSP (49g)
FIG & HONEY SAUCE				
2 TBSP (30mL)	Olive Oil	3 TBSP (45mL)	⅓ cup (75mL)	½ cup (105mL)
4 TBSP (56g)	Butter (Salted), divided	6 TBSP (84g)	10 TBSP (140g)	1 cup (196g)
1 each (28g)	Medium Shallot, whole, peeled and rough-chopped	1 ½ each (43g)	2 ½ each (71g)	3 ½ each (99g)
2 each (11g)	Garlic Cloves, peeled & smashed	3 each (17g)	5 each (28g)	7 each (39g)
1 each (1g)	Fresh Rosemary, whole sprigs, leaves removed	1 ½ each (1g)	2 ½ each (2g)	3 ½ each (3g)
1 tsp (6g)	Dijon Mustard	1 ½ tsp (9g)	2 ½ tsp (14g)	3 ½ tsp (20g)
3 TBSP (60g)	Fig Jam	4 ½ TBSP (90g)	½ cup (150g)	⅔ cup (210g)
1 TBSP (9g)	Dried Figs, chopped into thin pieces	1 ½ TBSP (14g)	2 ½ TBSP (23g)	3 ½ TBSP (33g)
3 each (150g)	Fresh Figs, cut in half	4 ½ each (225g)	7 ½ each (375g)	10 ½ each (525g)
3 each (42g)	Prosciutto, thinly sliced, cut into small pieces *(there are approximately 30 slices of prosciutto per pound)	4 ½ each (63g)	7 ½ each (105g)	10 ½ each (147g)
8 fl oz (237mL)	White Wine	12 fl oz (355mL)	20 fl oz (591mL)	28 fl oz (828mL)
12 fl oz (355mL)	Chicken Stock or Broth	18 fl oz (532mL)	30 fl oz (887mL)	42 fl oz (1242mL)
4 fl oz (118mL)	Balsamic Vinegar, divided	6 fl oz (177mL)	10 fl oz (296mL)	14 fl oz (414mL)
2 TBSP (20g)	All-Purpose Flour	3 TBSP (30g)	⅓ cup (50g)	½ cup (70g)
2 TBSP (43g)	Honey	3 TBSP (64g)	⅓ cup (106g)	½ cup (149g)
½ tsp (4g)	Salt	¾ tsp (5g)	1 ¼ tsp (9g)	1 ¾ tsp (12g)
¼ tsp (1g)	Black Pepper	½ tsp (1g)	¾ tsp (1g)	1 tsp (2g)
1 TBSP (1g)	Fresh Flat-Leaf Italian Parsley, finely chopped, for garnish	1 ½ TBSP (1g)	2 ½ TBSP (2g)	3 ½ TBSP (2g)

NUTRITION FACTS:

Serving Size 8.5 oz **Calories** 250 **Total Fat** 10g **Total Carbohydrates** 22g **Protein** 18g

The portion size shown is based on industry dietary standards and may be smaller than the portion size allowed for in recipe.

INSTRUCTIONS:

Prepare Chicken.
Place **chicken breasts** in **Quick Brine for Chicken Breasts** along with the **rosemary** sprig for 15 minutes, then remove, pat dry with a paper towel and lay out on a cutting board or work area with the breast opened and cut side facing up. Discard the used rosemary.

Butterfly chicken breasts by cutting the shorter side horizontally just past the center of the breast. Do not cut all the way through. Once cut, you should be able to open the breast like a book, with both sides lying flat in the shape of a butterfly.

Cover open chicken breasts with plastic wrap and pound with a mallet until the entire piece is of even size and approximately ¼" (.6cm) thick, being careful not to tear the meat. Repeat for all breasts, then remove plastic wrap.

Brush both sides of each butterflied chicken breast with **olive oil** and sprinkle with **salt** and **black pepper**, then lay flat on the work surface, cut side facing up.

Stuff Chicken Breasts.
Place **dried figs** in a small dish and cover with HALF the **balsamic vinegar**, then set aside.

Layer in the fillings, being careful to keep a ¼" (.6cm) margin around the edge of each breast, as follows:

- Spread a thin layer of **Dijon mustard** on the open breast (approximately 1 tsp (5.5g) each).
- Spread a thick layer of **Chevre goat cheese** on each breast over the mustard (approximate 2 TBSP (15g) each).
- Next, spread a thick layer of **fig jam** on each breast over the goat cheese (approximately 1-¼ TBSP (25g) each).
- Layer 2 slices of **prosciutto** over the fig jam. Prosciutto should be in two layers and covering the entire breast except for a small margin around the edge.
- Lightly drizzle **honey** over the prosciutto (approximate ¼ tsp (7g) per breast)
- Lay fresh **spinach leaves** in a single layer on top of honeyed prosciutto and top with a layer of fresh **basil leaves**.
- Remove **dried figs** from balsamic vinegar (reserve the balsamic vinegar) and distribute the pieces evenly on each chicken breast.
- Drizzle **reserved balsamic vinegar** (approximately ½ tsp (9mL) per breast) over fig, spinach & basil leaves.
- Sprinkle chopped **walnuts** over the top (approximately 1 tsp (2g) per breast).

MIS EN PLACE

1. Place chicken in quick brine with fresh rosemary, then perform butterfly cut on each piece.
2. Chop dried figs, shallot, garlic, fresh figs, prosciutto and walnuts for filling and sauce.
3. Remove stems from spinach and basil.
4. Chop fresh parsley for garnish.
5. Assemble remaining ingredients

CHEF NOTE

For help with preparing chicken, see the butterfly technique demonstrated in our online video *"How to Butterfly-Cut a Chicken Breast."* See the *"How It's Done" section in Chapter 13: Quick Guide to Online Tools."*

When all the fillings are layered on, start on the short side of the butterflied breast and roll up the chicken, being careful to keep all the fillings evenly distributed. Tuck in any loose end pieces, then tie up the breast with kitchen twine. Repeat for remaining breasts. These rolled chicken breasts are called "roulades."

Sear Chicken Roulades.
Whichever searing method is used, the searing process will not fully cook the chicken. Final cooking instructions are different for the "make it now!" method versus the "make it a freezer meal" option, so please continue to the appropriate instructions after searing the meat.

SEARING STOVETOP/OVEN METHOD:
Heat skillet (preferably cast-iron) over MEDIUM-HIGH heat. Add **olive oil** and **butter** to the skillet and swirl until the pan is hot, the butter is melted, and the fats are shimmering. Place roulades into the pan, then cook until golden brown on all sides (approximately 1 to 2 minutes per side). Transfer roulades to baking sheet, but do not clean the skillet as it will be used to make the sauce.

SEARING GRILLING METHOD:
Prepare grill so one side is set for very HIGH heat while the other side is open for lower temp cooking. Sear roulades on HIGH heat until hash-tag grill-marked on two sides (top & bottom), then remove (if making a freezer meal) or move to the cooler side of the grill (if making it now).

Make the Fig & Honey Sauce.
Heat cast-iron skillet (the same pan used for searing the chicken) over MEDIUM heat (either on stove-top or grill).

Add **olive oil** and HALF of the **butter**. Once the butter is melted, add **shallots** and **garlic**. Sauté 1 to 2 minutes or until shallots are transparent and garlic is softened, then add in fresh **rosemary leaves**, **Dijon mustard**, **fig jam**, **figs** (both dried & fresh) and **prosciutto**.

Continue stirring until the items begin to brown and caramelize in the pan. When the pan is nearly dry, add **white wine** and whisk to deglaze the pan. Continue cooking until wine is mostly gone (to the *au sec* stage). Only about a tablespoon of liquid should remain.

Add in **chicken stock or broth** and HALF of the **balsamic vinegar** and bring to a boil, then reduce heat to LOW and continue cooking until reduced by 1/3 (about 10 minutes).

Run sauce through a chinois or fine mesh colander and reserve strained sauce.

Wipe out skillet with a paper towel, increase heat to MEDIUM, then add remaining HALF of the **butter**. Allow it to melt, then whisk in **flour**, stirring briskly until mixture begins to brown and smell nutty. Return the reserved, strained sauce to the pan and continue to whisk together until the sauce is smooth.

Add **honey**, remaining HALF of the **balsamic vinegar**, **salt** and **pepper**. Taste and adjust salt, if needed, and add more honey if additional sweetness is desired. Reduce heat and continue cooking until sauce is thickened and coats the back of a spoon (may take up to 5 minutes). Remove from heat.

MAKE IT NOW!

STOVETOP/OVEN METHOD:
Preheat oven to 400°F (204°C).

Place baking sheet of roulades in preheated oven. Bake 8 to 12 minutes, or until the chicken reaches an internal temperature of 165°F (74°C) using a stem thermometer. (*Actual cooking time will depend on the thickness and size of the chicken breast.*)

Remove from oven, cover lightly with tented aluminum foil, and allow to rest 10 minutes.

To serve, remove twine and slice diagonally across the horizontal center of the roulade or into ½" (1.3cm) wide medallions. Serve with warmed **Fig & Honey Sauce**, **fresh figs** sliced in halves or quarters, and chopped **fresh parsley** for garnish.

GRILLING METHOD:
After searing and transferring the roulades to the cooler side of the grill, continue cooking for 8 to 10 minutes, or until the chicken reaches an internal temperature of 165°F (74°C) using a stem thermometer. (*Actual cooking time will depend on the thickness and size of the chicken breast.*)

Remove from heat, cover lightly with tented aluminum foil, and allow to rest for 10 minutes.

To serve, remove twine and slice diagonally across the horizontal center of the roulade or into ½" (1.3cm) wide medallions. Serve with warmed **Fig & Honey Sauce**, **fresh figs** sliced in halves or quarters, and chopped **fresh parsley** for garnish.

MAKE IT A FREEZER MEAL:

Package Chicken Roulades.

- Place seared roulades in the refrigerator to cool completely. They will be raw in the middle.
- Once the chicken is completely cooled, place roulades (as many as are needed at each meal service) into a resealable zippered or vacuum-sealable bag, removing as much air as possible before sealing.
- Apply label titled *"Prosciutto-Stuffed Chicken Breasts with Fig & Honey Sauce."*

Package Fig & Honey Sauce.

- Pour sauce into shallow dish and place in refrigerator to cool.
- Once cooled, pour the sauce into freezable containers or resealable zippered or vacuum-sealable bags, according to the number of servings needed for meal service. The standard serving is 2 to 4 TBSPs (29mL to 58mL) of sauce per serving of chicken.
- Apply label titled *"Fig & Honey Sauce for Prosciutto-Stuffed Chicken Breasts"* and place in freezer.

FREEZER LABELS

Find and print freezer meal labels for this dish at www.frozenandfabulous.com. (See also *Chapter 13: Quick Guide to Online Tools.*")

SUGGESTED PAIRINGS

SIDE DISH PAIRINGS

- Leek or Wild Mushroom Risotto
- Balsamic-Glazed Carrots
- Roasted Brussel Sprouts with Garlic
- Celery Root Puree
- Braised Leeks
- Rice Pilaf
- New Potatoes

WINE AND/OR ALCOHOL PAIRINGS

- Spätlese Riesling
- Shiraz
- Pinot Noir
- Fino Sherry

ONLINE RESOURCES

Scan this QR code for a direct link to an instructional cooking video for this recipe on www.frozenandfabulous.com, along with these helpful "How It's Done" videos.

- How to Butterfly-Cut a Chicken Breast
- How to Sear Meat

VARIATIONS

MAKE IT GLUTEN-FREE	MAKE IT VEGETARIAN	MAKE IT "FIT-FRIENDLY"	MAKE IT BUDGET-FRIENDLY
Use white rice flour in the Fig & Honey Sauce. No other changes are required, as this dish is otherwise naturally gluten-free.	Stuff portobello mushrooms with the stuffing mixture, sans prosciutto, then drizzle with the Fig & Honey Sauce.	To save calories, reduce or eliminate the fig jam and prosciutto, or choose a smaller portion.	To save money when preparing this dish, exchange prosciutto for thinly sliced bacon and reduce the amount of walnuts.

CHICKEN

Butter Chicken
(a/k/a Indian Chicken Makhani)

Butter Chicken, also known as Chicken Makhani, is my personal favorite Indian-style dish. I love the warm curry spices, the creaminess of the sauce, and how the tender, roasted chicken brings a heartiness that is oh-so-comforting!

The first time I was introduced to Butter Chicken was when I walked into a frozen prepared-meals store in Redmond, Washington, which at the time was known as Savory Moment. Based on the recommendation of the then-owner, Kay, I tried this dish and immediately fell in love. I could not believe any food could retain such an intensity of flavor after being frozen. It completely changed my mind about frozen meals!

As it turned out, I purchased Savory Moment and began my education into the secrets behind creating fabulous meals for the freezer that retain flavor, texture and freshness.

This Butter Chicken recipe was inspired by a Savory Moment guest chef, Paramjit, who would come into the kitchen to make this dish for our customers. I made some changes to her recipe but have stayed true to its authentic Indian heritage by using imported, premium spices and her unique flavor profile.

The main change that I made – which is NOT authentic to traditional Indian cuisine – was to swap half-and-half cream for half of the coconut milk. Traditional Indian cooking does not feature cow's milk-based ingredients; however, I find that real cream brings a richer texture, silkier mouthfeel and enhanced flavor to the dish so I prefer to use it. If you want to stay absolutely true to this dish's authentic heritage, simply replace half-and-half with coconut milk.

Enjoy!

INGREDIENTS:

No of Servings				
4		**6**	**10**	**14**
qty | msmt (weight)		qty | msmt (weight)	qty | msmt (weight)	qty | msmt (weight)
ROASTED CHICKEN BREAST				
2 LB (912g)	Boneless Chicken Breasts or Thighs	3 LB (1368g)	5 LB (2280g)	7 LB (3192g)
	* If using Chicken Breasts, pre-brine with **Quick Brine for Chicken Breasts** (see *Chapter 11: Meat Brines*)			
½ tsp (4g)	Salt	¾ tsp (5g)	1 ¼ tsp (9g)	1 ¾ tsp (12g)
¼ tsp (1g)	Black Pepper	½ tsp (1g)	¾ tsp (1g)	1 tsp (2g)
2 TBSP (1mL)	Olive Oil	3 TBSP (2mL)	⅓ cup (3mL)	½ cup (4mL)
MAKHANI SAUCE				
2 TBSP (14mL)	Olive Oil	3 TBSP (21mL)	⅓ cup (35mL)	½ cup (49mL)
2 each (452g)	Medium Yellow Onion, chopped into small dice	3 each (678g)	5 each (1130g)	7 each (1582g)
4 each (11g)	Garlic Cloves, minced	6 each (17g)	10 each (28g)	14 each (39g)
1 TBSP (9g)	Fresh Ginger Root, peeled and grated or minced	1 ½ TBSP (14g)	2 ½ TBSP (23g)	3 ½ TBSP (32g)
½ TBSP (14g)	Butter (Salted)	¾ TBSP (21g)	1 ¼ TBSP (35g)	1 ¾ TBSP (49g)
2 TBSP (17g)	**Chef Gail's Indian Butter Chicken Spice Blend** (see Recipe in *Chapter 10: Spice Blends*)	3 TBSP (26g)	5 TBSP (43g)	7 TBSP (60g)
11 fl oz (325mL)	Half & Half Cream	17 fl oz (488mL)	28 fl oz (813mL)	39 fl oz (1139mL)
11 fl oz (325mL)	Coconut Milk	17 fl oz (488mL)	28 fl oz (813mL)	39 fl oz (1139mL)
1 ½ TBSP (24g)	Tomato Paste	2 ½ TBSP (36g)	4 TBSP (60g)	5 ½ TBSP (85g)
¾ TBSP (2g)	Kasoori Methi (dried fenugreek leaves)	1 TBSP (3g)	2 TBSP (6g)	2 ½ TBSP (8g)
1 TBSP (5g)	Fresh Cilantro Leaves, finely chopped *(1 avg bunch =1 cup chopped)	1 ½ TBSP (7g)	2 ½ TBSP (12g)	3 ½ TBSP (17g)
1 tsp (7g)	Salt	1 ½ tsp (11g)	2 ½ tsp (18g)	3 ½ tsp (25g)
1 drop (<1g)	Red Food Coloring (liquid)	2 drops (<1g)	3 drops (<1g)	4 drops (1g)

NUTRITION FACTS:

Serving Size 8 oz   **Calories** 210   **Total Fat** 7g   **Total Carbohydrates** 8g   **Protein** 27g

The portion size shown is based on industry dietary standards and may be smaller than the portion size allowed for in recipe.

MAIN DISH DINNER RECIPES | CHICKEN

INSTRUCTIONS:

Prepare Roasted Chicken.
If using **chicken breasts**, place in **Quick Brine for Chicken Breasts** for 15 minutes. Remove from brine and place on a rack to dry.

Preheat oven to 375°F (190°C). Spray a baking sheet with non-stick spray.

If using **chicken breasts**, split each breast in half. Place on a cutting board, place palm firmly on top to hold in place, then cut horizontally through the middle. (*See our online video, "How to Split a Chicken Breast."*) Top with plastic wrap and pound with a mallet until the pieces are tenderized and of even thickness, being careful not to tear the meat. Lay the pieces out flat on a baking sheet.

If using **chicken thighs**, open up each thigh piece and lay flat on a baking sheet.

Sprinkle the top and bottom of each **chicken** piece with **salt** and **black pepper**. Brush or drizzle **olive oil** on the top of each piece, then place in the oven for roasting.

Bake at 375°F (190°C) for 12-15 minutes, or until internal temperature reaches 165°F (74°C) using a stem thermometer into the thickest area of the chicken breast or thigh (thighs will cook more quickly). Remove from oven and allow to cool completely. Once cooled, cut chicken into 1" (2.5cm) square pieces. Set aside.

Prepare Makhani Sauce.
In a saucepan, heat **olive oil** over MEDIUM-HIGH heat and sweat **onions** until translucent. Add minced **ginger**, **garlic** and **butter**. Once butter is nearly melted, add **Chef Gail's Indian Butter Chicken Spice Blend** and allow spices to bloom until very fragrant (about 1 to 2 minutes).

Whisk in **half & half**, **milk** and **tomato paste**. Bring to a simmer (do not boil) and allow the sauce to reduce by 10-15% (about 15 minutes). Add **kasoori methi**, fresh **cilantro, salt, black pepper** and **food coloring** (optional). Whisk well, then add in cooked chicken pieces. Allow to cook for an additional 1 to 2 minutes, then remove from heat.

MAKE IT NOW!

If the above instructions have been followed, all items are ready to serve. Chef Gail recommends serving over Basmati or Jasmine Rice, as the rice will soak up some of the sauce and provide a delicious meal.

MIS EN PLACE

1. Assemble Chef Gail's Indian Butter Chicken Spice Blend, if it is not already on hand. Place in sealed container for use in this and other recipes.
2. Prep chicken for roasting.
3. Dice onions and mince fresh garlic and ginger root.
4. Chop fresh cilantro.

CHEF NOTES

What does it mean to "bloom" the spices? When you cook dry spice in butter or fat, it causes the spice to "bloom" its flavor. It "wakes up" the spice to its fullest potential, and will bring tremendous flavor volume to your dish.

In Indian cooking, it is a sign of authenticity when you bloom the spices in butter until they become very aromatic. However, Chef Gail uses this technique across all genres of cooking because of the brilliance of flavor tones that can be achieved. See our how-to video on *"How to Bloom Spices"* in our Resources section of the website.

QUICK TIPS: CILANTRO: If you don't have fresh cilantro on hand, substitute 1 tsp (3g) dried cilantro for every 1 TBSP (<1g) fresh cilantro called for in this recipe.

MAKE IT A FREEZER MEAL:

Pour chicken and sauce mixture into a shallow pan and allow to cool completely. Transfer to a freezer-safe container. It is preferable to use a container that is oven-safe and/or microwave-safe for easy reheating. Apply label titled *"Butter Chicken."* When ready to serve, follow reheating instructions on the label.

CHEF NOTES

What is Kasoori Methi (or Kasuri Methi)? Kasoori methi are dried fenugreek leaves. It brings bold, savory flavor to the dish, with a slight bitterness. Its flavor profile is similar to an edgier version of celery and fennel. It is a common ingredient for Indian dishes and curries, and is sprinkled on near the end of cooking time. It is typically found in specialty grocery stores.

If using fresh fenugreek leaves, use 1 TBSP (<1g) of fresh for each 1 tsp (2g) of dried called for in this recipe.

Can't find fenugreek or Kasoori Methi? An acceptable alternative for this dish is fresh, chopped celery leaves. Substitute 1 TBSP (3g) chopped, fresh celery leaves for each 1 tsp of (2g) dried Kasoori Methi called for in the recipe.

FREEZER LABELS

Find and print freezer meal labels for this dish at www.frozenandfabulous.com. (See also *"Chapter 13: Quick Guide to Online Tools."*)

SUGGESTED PAIRINGS

SIDE DISH PAIRINGS

- Jasmine Rice
- Basmati Rice
- Warm Naan
- Roasted Cauliflower
- Gobi (Spicy Roasted Cauliflower)

WINE AND/OR ALCOHOL PAIRINGS

- Lager Beer
- Pilsner Beer
- Munich-style Helles Beer
- Red wine, such as Syrah or Blaufrankisch

ONLINE RESOURCES

Scan this QR code for a direct link to an instructional cooking video for this recipe on www.frozenandfabulous.com, along with this helpful "How It's Done" video.

- How to Split a Chicken Breast

VARIATIONS

MAKE IT GLUTEN-FREE

This dish is naturally gluten-free.

MAKE IT VEGETARIAN

The roasted chicken in this dish could be replaced with roasted potatoes or turnips for a delicious vegetarian dish.

MAKE IT "FIT-FRIENDLY"

Replace Half & Half with Skim, 2% or Coconut milk for a lower-calorie version of this flavorful dish.

MAKE IT BUDGET-FRIENDLY

If you don't frequently use some of these specialty ingredients and spices, it may be more affordable to purchase a pre-mixed blend from our website at www.frozenandfabulous.com.

MAIN DISH DINNER RECIPES | CHICKEN

CHICKEN

Chicken Ballotine
with Rosemary Beurre Blanc Sauce

Chicken stuffed with chicken? Yes - and it's amazing!

Ballotine is French for "a package" and refers to a de-boned chicken breast or thigh stuffed with meat – usually a forcemeat made with chicken or sausage - and formed into a tight little package.

In this version, I stuff chicken breast with a flavorful medley of chicken thigh pureed with fresh herbs, cream cheese, sour cream and crunchy bacon, and roll into a cylindrical shape. I then wrap it all up with prosciutto, sear to perfection, and serve with a rich, creamy beurre blanc-style sauce garnished with gorgeous microgreens and crispy bacon.

Seriously... it's to die for!

For optimal moisture, I recommend using the sous vide cooking technique outlined in this recipe. If you don't have an immersion circulator or sous vide cooking vessel, then the "sear and finish in the oven" technique will work beautifully. Just keep a close eye to avoid overcooking.

The Beurre Blanc Sauce is also a great stand-alone sauce and can be used for a variety of dishes. It will pair beautifully with chicken or pork as is, or adjust the flavor profile by incorporating a variety of fresh herbs to suit your taste. It is one of my favorite sauces - just silky and velvety on the palate, and brings gorgeous flavor to any plate.

Bon appetit, and I hope you enjoy this little "package" of deliciousness!

INGREDIENTS:

No of Servings				
4 qty | msmt (weight)		**6** qty | msmt (weight)	**10** qty | msmt (weight)	**14** qty | msmt (weight)
CHICKEN BREAST				
4 each (680g)	Boneless Whole Chicken Breasts, approx 6 oz (170g) each	6 each (1021g)	10 each (1701g)	14 each (2381g)
	* Pre-brine with **Quick Brine for Chicken Breasts** (see *Chapter 11: Meat Brines*)			
4 TBSP (60mL)	Olive Oil, divided	6 TBSP (90mL)	⅓ cup (150mL)	½ cup (210mL)
⅛ tsp (1g)	Salt	¼ tsp (1g)	⅓ tsp (2g)	½ tsp (3g)
⅛ tsp (<1g)	Black Pepper	¼ tsp (<1g)	⅓ tsp (1g)	½ tsp (1g)
2 tsp (11g)	Dijon Mustard	1 TBSP (17g)	1 2/3 TBSP (28g)	2 ⅓ TBSP (40g)
4 strips (113g)	Hickory-Smoked Bacon, thick cut, chopped into ¼" (.6cm) pieces, divided	6 strips (170g)	10 strips (284g)	14 strips (397g)
8 slices (112g)	Prosciutto, thinly sliced, reserved *(there are approximately 30 slices of prosciutto per pound)	12 slices (168g)	20 slices (280g)	28 slices (392g)
STUFFING FOR CHICKEN BREAST				
4 tsp (23g)	Dijon Mustard	2 TBSP (34g)	4 TBSP (57g)	5 TBSP (79g)
1 TBSP (4g)	Fresh Rosemary Leaves, finely chopped	1 ½ TBSP (6g)	2 ½ TBSP (10g)	3 ½ TBSP (13g)
2 each (6g)	Garlic Cloves, peeled & smashed	3 each (8g)	5 each (14g)	7 each (20g)
½ each (4g)	Medium Shallot, whole, peeled and rough-chopped	¾ each (5g)	1 ¼ each (9g)	1 ¾ each (12g)
¼ cup (8g)	Cream Cheese	½ cup (11g)	¾ cup (19g)	1 cup (26g)
¼ TBSP (4g)	Sour Cream	1 ½ TBSP (6g)	1 ¾ TBSP (9g)	2 TBSP (13g)
2 each (170g)	Boneless Chicken Thighs, approx 3 oz (85g) each	3 each (255g)	5 each (425g)	7 each (595g)
1 TBSP (14g)	Butter (Salted)	2 TBSP (21g)	3 TBSP (35g)	4 TBSP (49g)
1 tsp (5mL)	Olive Oil	1 ½ tsp (8mL)	2 ½ tsp (13mL)	3 ½ tsp (18mL)
⅛ tsp (1g)	Salt	¼ tsp (1g)	⅓ tsp (2g)	½ tsp (3g)
⅛ tsp (<1g)	Black Pepper	¼ tsp (<1g)	⅓ tsp (1g)	½ tsp (1g)
ROSEMARY BEURRE BLANC SAUCE				
1 TBSP (14g)	Butter (Salted)	1 ½ TBSP (21g)	2 ½ TBSP (35g)	3 ½ TBSP (49g)
2 TBSP (14g)	Medium Shallot, finely chopped	3 TBSP (21g)	⅓ cup (35g)	½ cup (50g)
1 TBSP (4g)	Fresh Rosemary Leaves, finely chopped	1 ½ TBSP (6g)	2 ½ TBSP (10g)	3 ½ TBSP (13g)
1 each (6g)	Garlic Cloves, minced	1 ½ each (8g)	2 ½ each (14g)	3 ½ each (19g)
3 TBSP (44mL)	White Wine Vinegar	⅓ cup (67mL)	½ cup (111mL)	2/3 cup (155mL)
2 TBSP (30mL)	Dry White Wine	3 TBSP (44mL)	⅓ cup (74mL)	½ cup (104mL)
½ tsp (3g)	Dijon Mustard	¾ tsp (4g)	1 ¼ tsp (7g)	1 ¾ tsp (10g)
⅓ cup (79mL)	Heavy Whipping Cream	½ cup (118mL)	1 cup (197mL)	1 ¼ cup (276mL)
⅛ tsp (1g)	Salt	¼ tsp (1g)	⅓ tsp (2g)	½ tsp (3g)
⅛ tsp (<1g)	Black Pepper	¼ tsp (<1g)	⅓ tsp (1g)	½ tsp (1g)
½ cup (7g)	Butter (Salted), cut into ½" (1.3cm) square pieces	¾ cup (11g)	1 ¼ cup (18g)	1 ¾ cup (25g)

MAIN DISH DINNER RECIPES | CHICKEN

NUTRITION FACTS:

Serving Size 8 oz   **Calories** 490   **Total Fat** 34g   **Total Carbohydrates** 3g   **Protein** 40g

The portion size shown is based on industry dietary standards and may be smaller than the portion size allowed for in recipe.

INSTRUCTIONS:

Prepare Chicken.
Place **chicken breasts** in **Quick Brine for Chicken Breasts** for 15 minutes. Remove from brine and place on a rack to dry.

Split chicken breasts in half. Place chicken breast on cutting board, place palm firmly on top to hold in place, then cut horizontally through the middle. (*See our online video, "How to Split a Chicken Breast."*)

Lay the breast pieces on the cutting board, cut side up, and cover lightly with plastic wrap. Pound with a mallet until the pieces are tenderized and approximately ½" (1.27cm) thick, being careful not to tear the meat. Remove plastic wrap.

Brush both sides of each chicken breast with **olive oil** and sprinkle generously with **salt** and **black pepper**, then lay out flat on a clean work surface. The outside of the chicken breast should be facing down so the inside is facing up. Brush **Dijon mustard** on the inside of each chicken breast piece and set aside.

Prepare Bacon.
Place HALF of the chopped **bacon** portion into a cold skillet. Turn heat to MEDIUM-LOW and cook until fat is rendered and bacon pieces are crispy. Remove from heat and set aside.

Prepare Stuffing.
Place **Dijon mustard, rosemary leaves,** uncooked **bacon, garlic** cloves and **shallot** into a food processor. Pulse or puree until items are finely chopped. Add **remaining ingredients,** then continue to run the processor until all **chicken thighs** are pureed and the mixture is well blended.

Remove processor bowl from the machine, then BY HAND stir in ¾ of the cooked **bacon**. Reserve the remaining ¼ for garnish.

Stuff, Roll and Wrap Chicken Breasts to Create "Packages"
Divide the **Stuffing** across the number of chicken breasts, then press the **Stuffing** on the inside of each chicken piece evenly. Try to cover the entire breast area while leaving ¼" (.6cm) open around the edges.

Starting on the short end of the breast, begin to roll up (or roulade) the chicken, being careful to keep the filling evenly distributed. Tuck in any loose end pieces to create a cylindrical shape.

MIS EN PLACE

1. Place chicken breasts in Quick Brine for 15 minutes, then cut in half.
2. Chop rosemary leaves, then separate out the portions for stuffing and sauce.
3. Chop up the bacon, then separate HALF to cook separately, HALF to go into the food processor for the stuffing.
4. Chop shallot and garlic for the sauce (the shallot and garlic for the stuffing will go straight into the food processor without pre-cutting).
5. Measure remaining ingredients.

Wrap each cylinder in a piece of the thinly sliced **prosciutto**, tucking around carefully to help seal the package together.

Spread out a piece of plastic wrap, then place the cylinder-shaped "package" approximately 2" (5cm) from the edge of the plastic wrap. Then take the edge of the plastic, pull it over the cylinder, tuck it in firmly, then roll the cylinder across the plastic wrap until it is completely wrapped. Swirl the plastic on each end of the cylinder to tighten and seal, then tuck the ends back over the cylinder and place on baking sheet with the tucked ends facing downward to hold in place.

Place wrapped chicken "packages" in the refrigerator for one hour to chill and set the shape.

STOVETOP/OVEN METHOD:

Fifteen minutes before cooking time, remove "packages" from the refrigerator and set on counter. When ready to cook, remove plastic wrap.

Heat skillet (preferably cast-iron) over MEDIUM-HIGH heat. Add a portion of the remaining **olive oil** to the pan, reserving enough to sear all of the "packages."

Place "package" into the pan, then sear on all sides until golden brown (approximately 1 to 2 minutes per side). Do not overfill the pan. Transfer seared "packages" to baking sheet. Leave any leftover bits and oils in the skillet, as they will add flavor when making the sauce.

CHEF NOTES

Important note about TEMPERATURE when cooking with the sous vide method.

In traditional methods of cooking chicken, we cook to an internal temperature of 165°F (74°C) to hit the kill step for bacteria. This is because bacteria is killed instantly at this temperature.

However, you can also kill bacteria by using time and temperature – this eliminates the need to hit such a high temperature which will yield a more juicy, softer, tender and flavorful meat.

For chicken cooked properly with the sous vide method, submerging in water at a steady 140°F (60°C) for at least 1 hour will hit the kill stage and the chicken will be safe (and very delicious) to eat. You can leave the chicken in the water bath (at the same consistent temperature) up to 4 hours with this method.

When cooking frozen chicken, simply add 1 hour to the cooking time.

MAKE IT NOW

Preheat oven to 375°F (190°C).

Place baking sheet of seared "packages" in preheated oven. Bake 8 to 12 minutes, or until the center of the "package" reaches an internal temperature of 165°F (74°C) using a stem thermometer.

While meat is in the oven, make the **Rosemary Beurre Blanc** sauce (instructions below).

Remove "packages" from the oven, cover lightly with tented aluminum foil, and allow to rest 10 minutes before cutting or serving.

To serve, remove twine (if used), then serve with warmed **Rosemary Beurre Blanc** Sauce. Garnish with remaining **cooked** bacon, and chopped **fresh parsley** or **microgreens**.

MAKE IT A FREEZER MEAL

Place seared "packages" in the refrigerator to cool completely. They will be raw in the middle.

Once the "packages" are cooled, remove from the refrigerator and place "packages" (as many as are needed at each meal service) into a resealable, zippered or vacuum-sealed bag.

Remove as much air as possible before sealing.

Apply label titled *"Chicken Ballotine w/ Rosemary Beurre Blanc Sauce (Oven/Stovetop Method)."*

Package the remaining bacon in a separate resealable, zippered bag. Apply label, *"Bacon for: Chicken Ballotine w/ Rosemary Beurre Blanc Sauce."*

Package the **Rosemary Beurre Blanc Sauce** separately – see instructions below.

Place all packaged components into a single resealable, zippered bag before placing in freezer.

When ready to serve, follow the cooking instructions on the label.

SOUS VIDE COOKING METHOD:

MAKE IT NOW (SOUS VIDE)

Set immersion circulator temperature to 140°F (60°C).

- When the water reaches the appropriate temperature, place tightly wrapped and vacuum-sealed "packages" into the water. Allow to stay submerged in the water at an even 140°F (60°C) temperature for 90 minutes (up to 4 hours).

MAIN DISH DINNER RECIPES | CHICKEN

- Remove "packages" from water and allow to rest 5 minutes before removing from vacuum-sealed bag and individual plastic wrap. Once removed, place each "package" on a rack to air-dry before searing.
- To sear the outside: Heat skillet (preferably cast-iron) over HIGH heat. Spray with non-stick pan spray and add **olive oil** to the pan.
- Place "package" into the pan, then sear on all sides until golden brown (approximately 1 to 2 minutes per side – do not overcook). The chicken will move easily in the pan once the sear is done.

> **Note:** The chicken will be fully cooked from the *sous vide* process. You sear the outside only to create the golden caramelization that will provide texture and flavor. Do not overcook during the searing process.

- Once seared, transfer "package" to cutting board. Allow to rest 5 minutes before serving.

Serve with warmed **Rosemary Beurre Blanc Sauce**. Garnish with **cooked bacon**, and chopped **fresh parsley or microgreens**.

MAKE IT A FREEZER MEAL (SOUS VIDE)

- Remove plastic-wrapped raw chicken "packages" from the refrigerator.
- Place "packages" (as many as are needed at each meal service) into a resealable, zippered or vacuum-sealed bag.
- Remove as much air as possible before sealing.
- Apply label titled *"Chicken Ballotine w/ Rosemary Beurre Blanc Sauce (Sous Vide Method)."*
- Package the remaining bacon in a separate resealable, zippered bag. Apply label, *"Bacon for: Chicken Ballotine w/ Rosemary Beurre Blanc Sauce"*
- Package the **Rosemary Beurre Blanc Sauce** separately – see instructions below.
- Place all packaged components into a single resealable, zippered bag before placing in freezer.
- When ready to serve, follow the cooking instructions on the label.

Prepare Rosemary Beurre Blanc Sauce
Using a skillet, melt **butter** over MEDIUM heat, then add in chopped **shallots** and **rosemary** leaves. Stir together until shallots are softened and half the butter is absorbed, then add minced **garlic**. Toss for 1 minute (be careful not to burn the garlic), then add in **white wine vinegar**, **dry white wine**, and **Dijon mustard**. Whisk together and allow to reduce by $1/3$. Add **heavy whipping cream**, **salt** and **black pepper** and bring to a simmer. Taste and adjust salt and black pepper as needed.

If serving now:
Reduce heat, then add chunks of **butter** to the simmering sauce. Do not stir! Swirl the pan around gently to allow the butter to melt into the sauce – this will create a satiny feel and prevent the sauce from breaking or separating.

If freezing the sauce:
IMPORTANT - the pieces of **butter** will be incorporated into the sauce when you reheat, so do not add them at this stage.

Remove sauce from heat, transfer to a shallow container, and cool completely in the refrigerator. Divide the cooled sauce into freezable containers, resealable zippered bags, or vacuum-sealed packaging according to the number of servings you will want to serve at each meal.

Divide the butter pieces according to the number of servings you will want to serve at each meal, then place those pieces into each container of the cold sauce. These butter pieces will melt and "swirl" into the sauce when you reheat at the time of service.

Apply label titled *"Rosemary Beurre Blanc Sauce for Chicken Ballotine."* When ready to serve, follow the cooking instructions on the label.

FREEZER LABELS

Find and print freezer meal labels for this dish at www.frozenandfabulous.com. (See also *"Chapter 13: Quick Guide to Online Tools."*)

SUGGESTED PAIRINGS:

SIDE DISH PAIRINGS

- Fresh green salad using mixed greens, spinach and romaine. The richness of the sauce is beautifully balanced with fresh, seasonable vegetables.
- Rice Pilaf, or any other light rice dish
- Roasted root vegetables
- Rice Pilaf with Porcini, Spinach & Walnuts
- Pureed Cauliflower & Celery Root with Parmigiano-Reggiano
- Roasted Cauliflower with Lemon, Capers & Toasted Almonds

WINE AND/OR ALCOHOL PAIRINGS

- Sauvignon Blanc
- Dry Riesling
- Chardonnay

ONLINE RESOURCES

Scan this QR code for a direct link to an instructional cooking video for this recipe on www.frozenandfabulous.com, along with these helpful "How It's Done" videos.

- How to Split a Chicken Breast
- How to Sear Meat
- Sous Vide Cooking Basics

VARIATIONS

MAKE IT GLUTEN-FREE

This dish is naturally gluten-free when prepared as instructed.

MAKE IT VEGETARIAN

Replace the chicken breast with long strips of squash laid flat and weaved together using an "under and over" technique. For the stuffing, replace the chicken with pureed root vegetables, then place the stuffing inside your weaved squash strips. Wrap the squash strips around, secure with toothpicks, and bake until the stuffing is heated to 145°F (63°C) and outside squash wrap is golden brown.

MAKE IT "FIT-FRIENDLY"

The cream cheese, sour cream and butter add calories to this dish, but they are also essential components of its amazing flavor and creamy texture. To reduce calories, swap cream cheese for Neufchatel, cottage cheese or pureed cauliflower, and use a reduced-fat sour cream. The heavy whipping cream could be replaced with half and half or milk but know that the texture and richness of the dish will be compromised when you make these changes. You could also reduce or omit the bacon.

MAKE IT BUDGET-FRIENDLY

This dish is a great way to use up extra pieces of chicken (in the stuffing). To save money, buy chicken in bulk so it can be used across several recipes.

CHICKEN

Spinach & Feta Stuffed Chicken
with Pesto & Mediterranean Salsa

This is a wonderful spring and summer chicken dish with its bold, piquant Mediterranean flavors. The pesto-brushed chicken is fabulous on its own, but "next level" when paired with lively Mediterranean Salsa, a recipe inspired by my very talented chef friend, Kay Conley.

To bring the "Wow!" factor to this dish for catering events, I like to garnish with caper berries with the stems attached. They are so beautiful and bring a vibrant zing to the palate. For this recipe, I have indicated regular non-pareil capers for use in the salsa because they are easy to find and are small enough not to overpower the bite. But for garnishment, it's caper berries with stems attached for the win!

I like to make my own pesto sauce so I have included the recipe here, but if you want to save time there are some yummy brands of pre-made pesto on the market that will work just as well.

When making pesto from scratch, I recommend using a food processor rather than a blender. It's important to get a suitable emulsion without over-blending the oil. Over-blended oil will become bitter and unpleasant tasting.

It's also essential to follow the instructions for making pesto carefully to ensure the fresh basil keeps its bright green color. Avoid adding the basil too soon, as it will become brown in color and less appetizing in appearance.

So I hope you enjoy making this little Mediterranean delight. If you're anything like me, you may need to buy extra olives for snacking. Once the jar is opened, I can't seem to stay out of it!

INGREDIENTS:

No of Servings 4 qty | msmt (weight)		6 qty | msmt (weight)	10 qty | msmt (weight)	14 qty | msmt (weight)
CHICKEN BREASTS				
4 each (85g)	Boneless Whole Chicken Breasts, approx 6 oz (170g) each	6 each (128g)	10 each (213g)	14 each (298g)
	*Pre-brine with **Quick Brine for Chicken Breasts** (see Chapter 11: Meat Brines)			
2 TBSP (30mL)	Olive Oil	3 TBSP (45mL)	⅓ cup (75mL)	½ cup (105mL)
1 pinch (<1g)	Black Pepper	2 pinches (<1g)	⅛ tsp (1g)	¼ tsp (1g)
1 pinch (<1g)	Salt	2 pinches (<1g)	⅛ tsp (1g)	¼ tsp (1g)
STUFFING FOR CHICKEN BREASTS				
2 cups (60g)	Fresh Spinach Leaves, chopped	3 cups (90g)	5 cups (150g)	7 cups (210g)
2 each (6g)	Garlic Cloves, minced	3 each (9g)	5 each (15g)	7 each (21g)
1 cup (150g)	Feta Cheese, crumbled	1 ½ cups (225g)	2 ½ cups (375g)	3 ½ cups (525g)
⅛ tsp (<1g)	Black Pepper	¼ tsp (<1g)	⅓ tsp (1g)	½ tsp (1g)
¼ tsp (2g)	Salt	½ tsp (3g)	¾ tsp (4g)	1 tsp (6g)
PESTO SAUCE				
¼ cup (64g)	Pine Nuts, lightly toasted	½ cup (96g)	¾ cup (160g)	1 cup (224g)
1 each (8g)	Garlic Cloves, whole, peeled	2 each (12g)	3 each (20g)	4 each (28g)
3 cups (106g)	Fresh Basil Leaves (packed), rough chopped	4 ½ cups (159g)	7 ½ cups (265g)	10 ½ cups (371g)
⅓ cup (33g)	Grated Parmesan Cheese	½ cup (50g)	¾ cup (83g)	1 cup (116g)
½ tsp (2g)	Kosher Salt	¾ tsp (3g)	1 ¼ tsp (5g)	1 ¾ tsp (7g)
¼ tsp (1g)	Black Pepper	½ tsp (2g)	¾ tsp (3g)	1 tsp (4g)
3 fl oz (113mL)	Olive Oil (drizzled in while mixing in food processor) *choose a high-quality Extra Virgin Olive Oil	5 fl oz (170mL)	8 fl oz (283mL)	11 fl oz (396mL)
MEDITERRANEAN SALSA				
1 (14.5 oz can) (411g)	Fire-Roasted Small-Diced Tomatoes, drained	2 (14.5 oz cans) (617g)	3 (14.5 oz cans) (1028g)	4 (14.5 oz cans) (1439g)
⅓ each (75g)	Red Onion, cut into small squares (small dice cut)	½ each (113g)	¾ each (188g)	1 each (264g)
9 each (45g)	Italian Castelvetrano Green Olives, pitted, cut into slivers	13 each (68g)	22 each (113g)	32 each (158g)
2 each (6g)	Garlic Cloves, minced	3 each (9g)	5 each (15g)	7 each (21g)
8 each (<1g)	Fresh Basil Leaves, cut into ribbons (chiffonade style)	12 each (1g)	20 each (1g)	28 each (2g)
2 tsp (<1g)	Fresh Flat-Leaf Italian Parsley, finely chopped	3 tsp (<1g)	5 tsp (<1g)	7 tsp (1g)
1 TBSP (11g)	Capers, non-pareil, drained	1 ½ TBSP (17g)	2 ½ TBSP (28g)	3 ½ TBSP (39g)
½ tsp (1g)	Smoked Paprika (Spanish)	¾ tsp (2g)	1 ¼ tsp (3g)	1 ¾ tsp (4g)
¼ tsp (<1g)	Oregano Leaves, Dried	½ tsp (<1g)	¾ tsp (1g)	1 tsp (1g)
1 TBSP (15mL)	Red Wine Vinegar	1 ½ TBSP (23mL)	2 ½ TBSP (38mL)	3 ½ TBSP (53mL)
2 tsp (10mL)	Lemon Juice	3 tsp (15mL)	1 2/3 TBSP (25mL)	2 ⅓ TBSP (35mL)
1 TBSP (15mL)	Olive Oil (drizzled in while while whisking) *choose a high-quality Extra Virgin Olive Oil	1 ½ TBSP (23mL)	2 ½ TBSP (38mL)	3 ½ TBSP (53mL)
1 pinch (<1g)	Black Pepper	2 pinches (<1g)	⅛ tsp (1g)	¼ tsp (1g)
1 pinch (<1g)	Kosher Salt	2 pinches (<1g)	⅛ tsp (1g)	¼ tsp (1g)

NUTRITION FACTS:

Serving Size 8 oz **Calories** 470 **Total Fat** 42g **Total Carbohydrates** 11g **Protein** 14g

The portion size shown is based on industry dietary standards and may be smaller than the portion size allowed for in recipe.

INSTRUCTIONS:

Prepare Chicken.
Place **chicken breasts** in **Quick Brine for Chicken Breasts** for 15 minutes. Remove, place on a rack to dry.

To create a "pocket" inside the chicken breast (to hold the stuffing), place the chicken breast on a cutting board and hold in place firmly with the palm of your hand. Then insert a chef knife into the side of the breast (at the thickest part) to create an opening about 2" to 3" (5cm to 7cm) wide. Insert the knife deeply enough to reach past the center but not all the way through to the other side. Inside the breast, wiggle the tip of the knife from side to side to create separation inside the breast and create a hollow area without cutting through to the other side.

Once the pocket is created, lay the chicken pieces on the cutting board. Cover lightly with plastic wrap and pound with a mallet just until the thickest parts of the breasts are tenderized, being careful not to tear the meat or let the breasts get too thin. Remove plastic wrap and pat each breast dry with a paper towel.

Sear the Chicken Breast.
Once dry, brush both sides of each breast with a portion of the **olive oil** and sprinkle with **black pepper** and **salt**.

Heat grill or cast-iron skillet to HIGH heat. Add remaining **olive oil**. When hot (but not smoking), place chicken breasts into pan. Do not overcrowd the pan. Allow breasts to sear (1 to 2 minutes per side), then remove from pan and place on baking sheet. (**The breasts will not be fully cooked** – just grill-marked or seared on the outside.)

Set aside to cool.

Prepare Stuffing for Chicken Breast.
In a small bowl, mix chopped **spinach**, **garlic**, **feta cheese**, **black pepper** and **salt**.

Make Pesto.
Toast **pine nuts** over MEDIUM heat in a dry skillet.

In a food processor, pulse toasted pine nuts several times, then add **garlic cloves**. Blend well, scraping down sides as needed. Add in fresh **basil** – pulse a few times to start to break down – then add **parmesan cheese**, **kosher salt** and **black pepper**.

Turn processor on, then while the processor is running, drizzle in the **olive oil** until the mixture is blended and of the desired consistency. Do not overmix.

MIS EN PLACE

1. Place chicken breasts in quick-brine for 15 minutes.
2. Drain fire-roasted tomatoes and capers through a mesh strainer until ready to use.
3. Toast pine nuts for Pesto Sauce.
4. Prep garlic - enough for all recipe components, then separate out for Stuffing for Chicken (minced), Pesto Sauce (no chopping needed) and Mediterranean Salsa (minced).
5. Prepare fresh basil by removing leaves from stems, then measure out for Pesto Sauce (no chopping needed) and Mediterranean Salsa (cut chiffonade style).
6. Prepare fresh spinach by removing leaves from stems, then measure out for Stuffing for Chicken (chopped small) and Pesto Sauce (rough chopped).
7. Prepare fresh flat-leaf Italian parsley by removing leaves from stems, then chopping finely for Mediterranean Salsa.
8. Chop red onion for Mediterranean Salsa
9. Cut green olives into slivers.
10. Assemble remaining ingredients.

To store extra pesto (not used in this recipe), run a light drizzle of olive oil on top, cover tightly, then place in the refrigerator. It will last up to 6 weeks in the fridge or one year in the freezer if packaged properly.

Stuff the Chicken Breasts.
Divide the stuffing into equal parts for each chicken breast and form each portion into a ball. Then stuff the "ball" into the pocket you created on the side of the chicken breast. Push to the center of the breast and into the back of the pocket, then secure the open edge with a toothpick.

Brush the top of the breast generously with **Pesto Sauce**. Set aside.

(*If you want to see this process demonstrated, please visit www.frozenandfabulous.com to watch the video that goes with this recipe.*)

Make Mediterranean Salsa.
Place the drained **tomatoes**, **red onion**, **olives**, **garlic**, fresh **basil**, fresh **parsley**, **capers**, **smoked paprika** and dried **oregano** leaves into a bowl.

In a separate bowl or pitcher, whisk together the **red wine vinegar** and **lemon juice**, then drizzle in the **olive oil** while whisking to create an emulsion. (To see this technique demonstrated, see *Chapter 13: Quick Guide to Online Tools.*)

Pour the liquid mixture over the tomato mixture and mix well. Add **black pepper** and **kosher salt** to taste, then refrigerate.

MAKE IT NOW!

Preheat oven to 375°F (190°C). If refrigerated, set **Spinach & Feta Stuffed Chicken** breasts out on the counter for 30 minutes to come to room temperature. If they are already at room temperature, skip this step.

Bake chicken breasts for 20 to 25 minutes or until the internal temperature reaches 165°F (73°C) using a stem thermometer. Allow to rest 5 minutes before serving.

> **NOTE:** When taking the temperature, make sure the thermometer is inserted into the meat (not the stuffing) to ensure the chicken is fully cooked. Also, confirm that the stuffing has reached the proper temperature as well.

Remove toothpicks, then serve with **Mediterranean Salsa**.

CHEF NOTES

To grill-mark or sear meat properly, it should be dry before placing onto the oiled grill or hot pan.

Then do not disturb. If the meat is sticking to the pan, it means it isn't done yet. When it is properly seared, it will release from the pan and you can remove without tear the meat or losing the golden crisp sear or dark grill marks.

If you have too much liquid in your pan or if the temperature is too low, it will not sear properly.

For more tips on how to create a beautiful grill-mark or sear on your meats, see our "how it's done" video - *Chapter 18: Quick Guide to Online Tools.*

MAKE IT A FREEZER MEAL:

This dish will be packaged partially cooked (grill-marked or seared only). You will finish cooking the chicken at the time of service.

Place the **Spinach & Feta Stuffed Chicken** on a flat surface (with space between) in the freezer for about 15 to 30 minutes, or long enough for the pesto sauce on top to freeze and adhere to the chicken. This will prevent the pesto sauce from coming off when it's time to remove chicken from its' packaging.

Remove the toothpicks from each breast. Place the frozen **Spinach & Feta Stuffed Chicken** in a vacuum-sealed bag, or a resealable bag with all air removed, that has been sprayed inside with non-stick pan spray. Apply label for "*Chicken for: Spinach & Feta Stuffed Chicken with Pesto.*"

Package **Mediterranean Salsa** in a separate vacuum-sealed bag, resealable zippered bag, or a freezable container. Apply label for "*Mediterranean Salsa for: Spinach & Feta Stuffed Chicken with Pesto.*"

Place both the packaged **Spinach & Feta Stuffed Chicken** and packaged **Mediterranean Salsa** into a single resealable zippered bag and place in the freezer.

MAIN DISH DINNER RECIPES | CHICKEN

A FEW NOTES ABOUT MEDITERRANEAN SALSA

If you are making this dish to enjoy now, swap the canned tomatoes for fresh grape tomatoes cut in half lengthwise. However, when making as a freezer meal, the canned tomatoes will hold up better.

It is also tasty to add crumbled feta to the salsa at the time of service; however, it won't hold up to storing in the fridge or freezer so treat it more like a garnish at time of service.

Kalamata olives are a wonderful alternative to the Italian Castelvetrano Green Olives, or even mix them together. It's also tasty to add a splash of Balsamic Vinegar to the mix.

Fresh mint is also a nice addition, if you have some on hand.

This salsa freezes well so make a large batch to keep extra on hand. It is wonderful served with fresh cucumber for an easy summer appetizer!

FREEZER LABELS

Find and print freezer meal labels for this dish at www.frozenandfabulous.com. (See also *Chapter 13: Quick Guide to Online Tools.*)

SUGGESTED PAIRINGS

SIDE DISH PAIRINGS

- Garlic Toast
- Chopped Greek Salad
- Couscous
- Roasted Sweet Potatoes and Red Onion
- Artichokes Stuffed w/ Lemon, Red Onion and Capers
- Feta & Cucumber Salad
- Roasted Carrots
- Grills Zucchini w/ Feta

WINE AND/OR ALCOHOL PAIRINGS

- Moscatos
- Sangiovese
- Gamay
- Blush wines (Reisling or Zinfandel)

ONLINE RESOURCES

How to Create an Emulsion for Oil-based Marinades and Dressings
How to Grill-Mark Meat
How to Sear Meat
The "Breast Pocket" Stuffed Chicken Technique

- How to Create an Emulsion for Oil-based Marinades and Dressings
- How to Grill-Mark Meat
- How to Sear Meat
- The "Breast Pocket" Stuffed Chicken Technique

VARIATIONS

MAKE IT GLUTEN-FREE	MAKE IT VEGETARIAN	MAKE IT "FIT-FRIENDLY"	MAKE IT BUDGET-FRIENDLY
This dish is naturally gluten-free when prepared as written.	Swap chicken for sliced cauliflower. Place stuffing mixture directly on the cauliflower "steak," then top with the Mediterranean Salsa. This dish would also be delicious as a stuffed portobello mushroom.	This dish is already very light on calories, but to reduce calories use less feta cheese and pine nuts.	Eliminate or reduce the amount of pesto sauce used in the dish, or purchase an affordable ready-made version in small quantities.

CHEF GAIL KURPGEWEIT @ASKCHEFGAIL

CHICKEN

Southern-Fried Bacon-Wrapped
Chicken & Waffles

Read that again: Fried chicken..... bacon..... waffles..... it's like the best food on the planet all got together for a party and you're invited!

My catering company, Taste of Amazing, is famous for its' Southern-Fried Bacon-Wrapped Chicken and Waffle appetizers – it is one of our most requested dishes.

But at home – where it really matters - this is the dish that brings my daughter, Kaitlyn, to the table! It is easily her all-time favorite dish and I love making it for her, knowing how much she enjoys it. Between college and working, her days are full so if there's any force on earth that can make her stop, sit at the table and enjoy a meal (and conversation) with her momma, this one is it! For that reason alone, I love to keep this one on hand. For caterings, we frequently serve this dish as an appetizer on skewers with ¼ waffle and ¼-size bacon-wrapped chicken drizzled with our decadent **Bourbon-Maple Sauce**. It is too-die-for delicious!

I did not include the **Bourbon-Maple Sauce** recipe that we use for Caterings here because it doesn't freeze well – any dish with too high of a sugar content tends to be difficult to freeze. However, you can find this recipe in the Members-Only section of our website at www.frozenandfabulous.com.

You will also find the recipe for our **Southern Waffles** on the Members-Only site. I didn't include the recipe here because it is far easier to meal prep with premium, high-quality Belgian waffles found in the freezer section of your local grocery store. If you're preparing this as a "Make it Now!" dish and have the time to put into it, I highly recommend grabbing the recipe for our incredible sauce and waffles to serve with this spicy fried chicken dish. It makes for a decadent meal you will really enjoy!

For now, here's the simplified, freezer-friendly version of the recipe.

MAIN DISH DINNER RECIPES | CHICKEN

INGREDIENTS:

No of Servings 4		6	10	14
qty | msmt (weight)		qty | msmt (weight)	qty | msmt (weight)	qty | msmt (weight)
CHICKEN & BRINE				
2 ½ LB (1140g)	Boneless Chicken Thighs, cut in half	3 ¾ LB (1710g)	6 ¼ LB (2850g)	8 ¾ LB (3990g)
1 ea (43g)	Eggs, whisked well	2 ea (65g)	3 ea (108g)	4 ea (151g)
10 fl oz (303mL)	Buttermilk	15 fl oz (455mL)	25 fl oz (758mL)	35 fl oz (1061mL)
10 fl oz (303mL)	Frank's Red Hot Sauce (Original)	15 fl oz (455mL)	25 fl oz (758mL)	35 fl oz (1061mL)
1 TBSP (13g)	Kosher Salt	1 ½ TBSP (20g)	2 ½ TBSP (33g)	3 ½ TBSP (46g)
DREDGE MIXTURE				
2 cups (280g)	Self-Rising Flour	3 cups (420g)	5 cups (700g)	7 cups (980g)
1 ½ cups (282g)	Yellow Cornmeal	2 ¼ cups (423g)	3 ¾ cups (705g)	5 ¼ cups (987g)
1 tsp (7g)	Salt	1 ½ tsp (11g)	2 ½ tsp (18g)	1 TBSP (25g)
2 TBSP (27g)	**Chef Gail's Southern Spice Blend** (see Recipe in *Chapter 10: Spice Blends*)	3 TBSP (41g)	⅓ cup (68g)	½ cup (95g)
BACON				
4 strips (113g)	Hickory-Smoked Bacon, thick-cut (cut in half)	6 strips (170g)	10 strips (284g)	14 strips (397g)
OIL FOR FRYING				
1 quart (946mL)	Peanut Oil (*use more or less as required to to fill cooking pan 3-4" (7.5cm to 12.5cm) deep*)	1 quart (946mLmL)	1 ½ quart (1419mL)	1 ½ quart (1419mL)
1 TBSP (14g)	Popcorn Kernals (unpopped) (*optional*)	1 ½ TBSP (21g)	2 ½ TBSP (35g)	3 ½ TBSP (50g)
WAFFLES & SYRUP				
4 each (454g)	Belgium Waffles (frozen)	6 each (680g)	10 each (1134g)	14 each (1588g)
8 TBSP (118mL)	Maple Syrup	¾ cup (177mL)	1 ¼ cups (296mL)	1 ¾ cups (414mL)

NUTRITION FACTS:

Serving Size 10 oz   **Calories** 560   **Total Fat** 24g   **Total Carbohydrates** 45g   **Protein** 40g

The portion size shown is based on industry dietary standards and may be smaller than the portion size allowed for in recipe.

INSTRUCTIONS:

Prepare Chicken.
Open **chicken thighs** flat, then cut in half down the middle so you have two equally-sized portions, and set aside.

Prepare Wet Brine.
Whisk **eggs**, then add in **buttermilk, Frank's Red Hot Sauce (Original)**, and **kosher salt**.

Note: This version is very spicy. If you want to reduce the heat, reduce the amount of hot sauce and increase the amount of buttermilk by that same amount. This recipe calls for a 1:1 hot sauce to buttermilk ratio, but the ratio can be adjusted according to your preference.

Whisk together until well blended, then add in cut chicken thigh pieces. Make sure all chicken pieces are fully submerged in the brine.

Place in refrigerator and allow chicken to sit in the brine for 4 hours (no longer than 8 hours).

> **IMPORTANT:** 45 minutes before you are ready to begin dredging and frying the chicken, remove the chicken and brine from the refrigerator and set on the counter. It is important to let the chicken come to room temperature before frying.
>
> **What could go wrong?** If you try to put cold chicken into the frying oil, the oil temperature will drop quickly. This will cause the chicken to absorb too much oil, leaving you with greasy chicken. It will also cause the chicken to cook unevenly, resulting in over- or under-cooking the center.

Prepare Dredge Mixture.

In a shallow dish, whisk together **self-rising flour, yellow cornmeal, salt** and **Chef Gail's Southern Spice Blend**.

> **NOTE:** If you are making a large batch of fried chicken, place about 1 to 2 cups of the dredge in a shallow dish, start dredging the chicken pieces, and then add more of the dredge mixture as needed to keep the dry mixture fresh. As you dredge pieces of chicken, the dry ingredients can get wet, making it hard to get the breading to stick to the chicken. Using only part of your dry mixture at a time will solve this problem.

Cut bacon slices.
Cut each slice of **bacon** in half so you have two shorter pieces. Set aside.

Prepare oven for baking and oil for frying.
If using the "Make it Now!" method, preheat the oven to 375°F (190°C). If making a freezer meal, skip this step.

If you have a deep fryer, follow the manufacturer's instructions to bring the oil temperature up to 350°F (177°C).

If frying on the stovetop, choose a heavy-bottomed pan, cast-iron skillet or Dutch oven. Add **peanut oil** until you have 3" to 4" (7.5cm to 12.5cm) of oil depth and 3" to 4" (7.5cm to 12.5cm) space at the top of the pan. Do not overfill the pan with oil.

Set heat to MEDIUM and bring the oil to 350°F (177°C) – do not go over 350°F (177°C). Try to keep this temperature steady by using an immersion thermometer or *"The Popcorn Method."*

> **MIS EN PLACE**
>
> 1. Cut chicken thighs in half. This will allow you to roll the half piece of bacon around each piece of chicken thigh without over-folding. If the chicken is folded too tightly or over-rolled, the breading inside won't get crispy.
> 2. Cut bacon strips in half to create two short strips from each single piece.
> 3. Whisk eggs in a bowl large enough to hold all wet ingredients for the brine. Once eggs are whisked, add remaining brine ingredients.
> 4. Assemble dredging ingredients (dry).
> 5. Make a batch of Chef Gail's Southern Spice Blend if you don't already have it on hand.

> **CAUTION: PEANUT ALLERGIES**
>
> If someone with a peanut allergy will be enjoying this dish, swap vegetable oil for the peanut oil called for in this recipe. No other change in process is required.

Dredge chicken and wrap in bacon.

- Remove the chicken pieces from the wet brine and set on a rack to allow excess liquid to drip away.
- Dredge chicken in dry flour/spice mixture.
- Wrap the half-piece of bacon around the dredged piece of chicken. Secure with a toothpick, wooden food pick or paddle-style bamboo pick. (Do not use plastic picks.)
- Place on rack or baking sheet.

MAIN DISH DINNER RECIPES | CHICKEN

Fry the bacon-wrapped chicken.

- When peanut oil is EXACTLY 350°F (177°C), place the bacon-wrapped chicken piece (secured by pick) into the oil.
- Fry pieces for **precisely 4 minutes**. They will be golden brown and crispy, but not fully cooked inside.
- Remove immediately from hot oil and place on a wire rack or baking sheet.
- Make sure not to over-crowd the pan, and always bring the oil temperature back to exactly 350°F (177°C) before adding more chicken to the oil.

MAKE IT NOW!

Place fried chicken pieces on a baking sheet and place in oven preheated to 375°F (190°C). Bake for 11 to 15 minutes, or until the internal temperature of the chicken (using a stem thermometer) reaches 165°F (74°C). Allow to rest 5 minutes before serving.

Follow manufacturer's instructions to heat *waffles*. Heat *maple syrup* on the stovetop until just warmed.

Remove picks from bacon-wrapped fried chicken pieces. Serve two pieces over a warmed waffle, then drizzle with warmed maple syrup.

MAKE IT A FREEZER MEAL:

Allow partially cooked fried chicken pieces to cool and partially freeze on a baking sheet or tray in the freezer. Make sure the pieces don't touch. (This process is called "IQF" (Individually Quick Frozen) – see *Chapter 2: From Planning to Plate*, section *Organizing Freezer Space for Quick Freezing*.)

Once the pieces are frozen (about 20 to 30 minutes), place them in a resealable bag and apply the label *"Bacon-Wrapped Chicken."* If you have performed the IQF process correctly, when you're ready to serve you'll be able to remove as many pieces of chicken as you want and they won't be frozen together.

To extend shelf life, remove as much air as possible from the resealable bag, then place it inside a second resealable bag, again removing as much air as possible.

Place frozen **Belgium waffles** in a resealable bag, removing all excess air (or just leave in the manufacturer's packaging). Apply label *"Waffles for: Fried Chicken & Waffles."*

THE POPCORN METHOD FOR FRYING

A kernel of popcorn will pop at 350°F (177°C), which is the PERFECT TEMPERATURE for frying chicken.

If you don't have an immersion thermometer to keep track of your oil's temperature, I recommend using this simple popcorn method instead.

Start warming the oil and when it starts to get small bubbles add 3 to 4 kernels of popcorn. They will settle to the bottom of the pan.

Wait - be patient. Once the oil reaches 350°F (177°C) the kernels will POP, letting you know it's time to fry a few pieces of the chicken (don't overfill the pan).

Remove the popped corn to avoid burning and ruining the taste of the oil.

When the chicken pieces are fried and golden (see cooking instructions) remove from the oil and transfer to a wire rack or baking sheet.

Then (VERY IMPORTANT) add a few new kernels to the pan and WAIT for the oil temperature to come back up to temperature. When the kernels pop, it's time to fry the next batch of chicken pieces.

Repeat this process until all your chicken is fried.

One more thing: I always recommend using 3 to 4 popcorn kernels at a time, just in case 1 or 2 of them don't pop. If popcorn kernals are old or dried out, they won't pop well, so it's good to have a few backups.

When ready to serve, follow cooking instructions on label. It is important to bring the internal temperature of the chicken to 165°F (74°C) before consuming it.

IMPORTANT TIPS ABOUT OIL FOR FRYING

This recipe calls for Peanut Oil for frying the chicken because it adds such wonderful flavor.

However, if there is any chance you will be serving this dish to someone who might have a peanut or nut allergy, please use pure vegetable or canola oil instead.

I have created two freezer labels for this recipe - if you use peanut oil in the recipe, please use the label that includes a nut allergen warning to be safe. You will find both labels at www.frozenandfabulous.com.

ALTERNATIVE OILS FOR FRYING

Pure vegetable oil and canola oil work really well for fried chicken.

However, DO NOT USE OLIVE OIL. It can't sustain the high heat and will create a bad taste in your food.

FREEZER LABELS

Find and print freezer meal labels for this dish at www.frozenandfabulous.com. (See also *Chapter 13: Quick Guide to Online Tools.*)

SUGGESTED PAIRINGS

SIDE DISH PAIRINGS

- Corn on the Cob
- Collard Greens w/ Bacon
- Sautéed Spinach w/ Bacon
- Dirty Rice
- Cheesy Grits
- Macaroni & Cheese

WINE AND/OR ALCOHOL PAIRINGS

- Sparkling Rosé
- Champagne or Crémant
- Extra-Dry Prosecco
- Tempranillo
- Riesling
- Lambrusco

ONLINE RESOURCES

Scan this QR code for a direct link to an instructional cooking video for this recipe on www.frozenandfabulous.com.

VARIATIONS

MAKE IT GLUTEN-FREE

Exchange the self-rising flour for a gluten-free all-purpose flour blend, then add 1 tsp (5g) baking powder per cup (120g) of gluten-free flour. Purchase frozen gluten-free waffles.

MAKE IT VEGETARIAN

Swap chicken for plant-based faux-chicken products.

MAKE IT "FIT-FRIENDLY"

Use an air fryer to fry the chicken instead of frying in oil, exchange chicken breast for chicken thighs, and omit the bacon.

Or leave it alone and serve it on a "cheat day" because it's friggin' delicious as is!

MAKE IT BUDGET-FRIENDLY

Omit the bacon and use vegetable oil instead of peanut oil for frying. Make your own buttermilk by adding 1/2 tsp (2.5) of lemon juice per cup (253g) of milk. This will accomplish the acidic response needed to tenderize the chicken.

MAIN DISH DINNER RECIPES | CHICKEN

CHICKEN

Cilantro-Grilled Chicken
with Mango Salsa

This is a fresh, simple dish perfect for weeknight meals, and kids will love the sweet mango salsa paired with tender, savory chicken.

Bright, colorful and easy-on-the-waistline – the whole family will enjoy this creation. I was first introduced to it by my talented gluten-free chef friend, Kay Conley. I just loved her version and have only made a few tweaks.

The mango salsa is delicious either warmed or chilled, so one of my favorite ways to serve this dish is to marry it with a crisp summer salad. Simply cut the fully-cooked chicken into cubes, toss it in with the mango salsa, and serve over a generous plate of locally-sourced, seasonal mixed greens. It's a refreshing take on healthy eating, perfect for summer meals by the pool.

Although the red onions give this dish a lively vibrancy, some people (especially kids) aren't fond of raw onions. If that is true for your kiddos, I recommend putting the red onions in a separate resealable bag so when it's time to serve you can add them to your portion of the salsa (for optimal taste) and keep the salsa onion-free for everyone else.

One more tip about red onions: They have a very strong smell when served raw. The easiest way to tone down the aroma is to soak cut onions in cold water for about 20 to 30 minutes, then drain and pat dry with paper towels. Then, when it's time to add fresh cut red onion to your dish, the aroma will be pleasant and not overpowering.

Cheers to summer eating – enjoy!

CHEF GAIL KURPGEWEIT @ASKCHEFGAIL

INGREDIENTS:

No of Servings				
4		**6**	**10**	**14**
qty | msmt (weight)		qty | msmt (weight)	qty | msmt (weight)	qty | msmt (weight)
	CHICKEN			
4 each (170g)	Boneless Whole Chicken Breasts, approx 6 oz (170g) each * Pre-brine with **Quick Brine for Chicken Breasts** (see *Chapter 11: Meat Brines*)	6 each (255g)	10 each (425g)	14 each (595g)
1 TBSP (14mL)	Olive Oil (reserved for grill-marking chicken)	1 ½ TBSP (21mL)	2 ½ TBSP (35mL)	3 ½ TBSP (49mL)
	CILANTRO MARINADE			
¼ cup (59mL)	Lime Juice	½ cup (89mL)	¾ cup (148mL)	1 cup (207mL)
1 TBSP (21g)	Honey	1 ½ TBSP (32g)	2 ½ TBSP (53g)	3 ½ TBSP (74g)
½ each (113g)	Red Onion, cut into long strips (julienne cut)	¾ each (170g)	1 ¼ each (283g)	1 ¾ each (396g)
½ each (8g)	Jalapeno Pepper, seeds removed and cut into thin strips (julienne cut)	¾ each (12g)	1 ¼ each (20g)	1 ¾ each (28g)
2 each (6g)	Garlic Cloves, peeled & smashed	3 each (8g)	5 each (14g)	7 each (20g)
½ cup (40g)	Fresh Cilantro Leaves, chopped	¾ cup (59g)	1 ¼ cups (99g)	1 ¾ cups (138g)
½ tsp (4g)	Salt	¾ tsp (5g)	1 ¼ tsp (9g)	1 ¾ tsp (12g)
¼ tsp (1g)	Black Pepper	½ tsp (1g)	¾ tsp (1g)	1 tsp (2g)
1 TBSP (14mL)	Olive Oil (drizzled in while whisking)	1 ½ TBSP (21mL)	2 ½ TBSP (35mL)	3 ½ TBSP (49mL)
	GLAZE FOR CHICKEN			
2 TBSP (42g)	Honey	3 TBSP (63g)	⅓ cup (105g)	½ cup (147g)
1 TBSP (17mL)	Lime Juice	1 ½ TBSP (26mL)	2 ½ TBSP (43mL)	3 ½ TBSP (60mL)
1 tsp (<1g)	Fresh Cilantro Leaves, chopped	1 ½ tsp (<1g)	1 TBSP (<1g)	1 ½ TBSP (1g)
	MANGO SALSA			
1 ¼ cups (284g)	Mango (fresh or frozen), cut into small squares (petite dice cut)	2 cups (425g)	3 ¼ cups (709g)	4 ½ cups (992g)
½ each (113g)	Red Onion, cut into small squares (petite dice cut)	¾ each (170g)	1 ¼ each (283g)	1 ¾ each (396g)
1 each (25g)	Jalapeno Peppers, de-seeded and cut into small squares (petite dice cut)	1 ½ each (38g)	2 ½ each (63g)	3 ½ each (88g)
1 each (3g)	Garlic Cloves, minced	2 each (5g)	3 each (8g)	4 each (11g)
2 TBSP (16g)	Fresh Cilantro Leaves, chopped	3 TBSP (24g)	⅓ cup (40g)	½ cup (55g)
3 TBSP (51mL)	Lime Juice	4 ½ TBSP (77mL)	½ cup (128mL)	2/3 cup (179mL)
⅛ tsp (1g)	Salt	¼ tsp (1g)	½ tsp (2g)	¾ tsp (3g)
⅛ tsp (<1g)	Black Pepper	¼ tsp (<1g)	½ tsp (1g)	¾ tsp (1g)
1 pinch (<1g)	Cayenne Pepper	1 ½ pinch (<1g)	⅛ tsp (<1g)	¼ tsp (1g)

NUTRITION FACTS:

Serving Size 9 oz **Calories** 300 **Total Fat** 7g **Total Carbohydrates** 19g **Protein** 40g

The portion size shown is based on industry dietary standards and may be smaller than the portion size allowed for in recipe.

MAIN DISH DINNER RECIPES | CHICKEN

INSTRUCTIONS

Prepare Chicken.
Place **chicken breasts** in **Quick Brine for Chicken Breasts** for 15 minutes. Remove from brine and place on a rack to dry.

Prepare Marinade.
Whisk together all the **Marinade ingredients**, saving the **olive oil** until the end. To add the olive oil, you'll want to create an emulsion to keep the marinade from separating. To accomplish this, slowly drizzle the oil into the other combined ingredients while whisking quickly. (To see this technique demonstrated, watch our online video *"How to Create an Emulsion for Oil-based Marinades and Dressings."*

Place brined chicken pieces into a resealable zippered bag or shallow container, then pour **Marinade** over the top. Make sure the **Marinade** fully covers all chicken pieces.

Allow chicken to marinate on the counter for 1 hour (room temperature) or in the refrigerator for up to 24 hours.

Prepare Glaze for Chicken.
Whisk together the **Glaze ingredients**. Set aside.

Grill-Mark or Sear & Glaze Chicken.
Remove chicken from **Marinade** and place on a rack to allow the marinade to drip away from chicken breasts. After 5 minutes, turn breasts over to make sure all excess liquids are trickled away, and the skin of the breasts is dry or nearly dry.

Heat grill or cast-iron skillet to HIGH heat. Add **olive oil** (reserved for grill-marking chicken). When hot (but not smoking), place chicken breasts into pan or on grill, top side of breast down first. Do not overcrowd the pan. Allow breasts to sear (1 to 2 minutes per side), then remove from pan and place on baking sheet. (**The breasts will not be fully cooked** – just grill-marked or seared on the outside.)

Brush both sides of the seared breast with a generous amount of **Glaze for Chicken**. (*Continue to "Make it a Freezer Meal" or "Make it Now" instructions to finish preparing chicken.*)

Prepare Mango Salsa.
Toss all **Mango Salsa ingredients** into a bowl. Taste. Add additional salt and pepper if needed according to your taste preference, then refrigerate.

MIS EN PLACE

The same ingredients are found in the Marinade as in the Salsa. It's super quick and easy to cut and prep the full amount needed for all components in the recipe – then just split out what you need between the marinade, glaze and salsa.

WARNING: Do not re-use the marinade or add it to the salsa once it has touched the raw chicken, as it will no longer be safe for raw consumption.

1. Place chicken breasts in Quick Brine.
2. Chop red onion - a portion can be rough cut into strips (for the Marinade) and the remaining portion for the Mango Salsa should be petite dice cut.
3. De-seed and slice jalapeno peppers for the Marinade, then dice-cut the remainder for the Mango Salsa.
4. Chop garlic cloves - the portion for the Marinade can be smashed or rough cut, then mince the remainder for the Mango Salsa.
5. Remove leaves from fresh cilantro, chop finely, then separate quantities for Marinade, Glaze and Mango Salsa. When measuring for fresh cilantro, 1 average-sized bunch will yield approximately 1 cup of chopped cilantro.
6. Cut the mango into small ½" (1.3cm) squares or measure out pre-cut frozen mango.
7. Measure remaining ingredients.

MAKE IT NOW!

Preheat oven to 375°F (190°C). If refrigerated, set grill-marked (or seared), glazed chicken breasts out on the counter for 30 minutes to come to room temperature. If they are already at room temperature, or warm, skip this step.

Bake chicken breasts for 15 to 20 minutes or until the internal temperature reaches 165°F (74°C) using a stem thermometer. Allow to rest 5 minutes before serving.

Serve with warm or cold **Mango Salsa**. To warm the salsa, place in microwave for 1 to 2 minutes or until heated to the desired temperature.

> ### CHEF NOTES
>
> To grill-mark or sear meat properly, the skin should be dry before placing onto the oiled grill or hot pan.
>
> Then do not disturb. If the meat is sticking to the pan, it means it isn't done yet. When it is properly seared, it will release from the pan and you can remove without tearing the meat or losing the golden crisp sear or dark grill marks.
>
> If you have too much liquid in your pan or if the temperature is too low, it will not sear properly.
>
> For more tips on how to create a beautiful grill-mark or sear on your meats, see our "how it's done" video - *Chapter 18: Quick Guide to Online Tools.*

MAKE IT A FREEZER MEAL

Cool **Cilantro Grilled Chicken** completely in refrigerator, then place into a vacuum-sealed bag or resealable zippered bag with all air removed. Apply label for *"Chicken for: Cilantro Grilled Chicken with Mango Salsa."* (The chicken will finish cooking after freezing on the day of service.)

Package **Mango Salsa** in a separate vacuum-sealed bag, resealable zippered bag, or a freezable container. Apply label for *"Mango Salsa for: Cilantro Grilled Chicken with Mango Salsa."*

Place both the packaged **Cilantro Grilled Chicken** and packaged **Mango Salsa** into a single resealable zippered bag and place in the freezer.

FREEZER LABELS

Find and print freezer meal labels for this dish at www.frozenandfabulous.com. (See also *"Chapter 13: Quick Guide to Online Tools."*)

SUGGESTED PAIRINGS

SIDE DISH PAIRINGS
- Red Cabbage Slaw
- White or Brown Rice, plain or with fresh cilantro and lemon
- Steamed Vegetables
- Roasted Root Vegetables

WINE AND/OR ALCOHOL PAIRINGS
- Chardonnay
- Sparkling Rosé
- Stella Beer
- Corona with Lime

ONLINE RESOURCES

Scan this QR code for a direct link to an instructional cooking video for this recipe on www.frozenandfabulous.com, along with these helpful "How It's Done" videos.

- How to Create an Emulsion for Oil-based Marinades and Dressings
- How to Grill-Mark Meat
- How to Sear Meat

VARIATIONS

MAKE IT GLUTEN-FREE	MAKE IT VEGETARIAN	MAKE IT "FIT-FRIENDLY"	MAKE IT BUDGET-FRIENDLY
This dish is naturally gluten-free when prepared as written.	Swap chicken for grilled portobello mushrooms or a plant-based faux-chicken product.	This dish is already very light on calories. To reduce even more, exchange agave for the honey and omit the "Glaze for Chicken."	Use frozen, pre-cut mango. The yield is 100% on frozen products, but with fresh you'll have waste from peeling and cutting.

CHICKEN

Oven-Baked Parmesan Chicken

This was my kids' favorite dish when they were little for both meals and snacks, and they particularly enjoyed helping me prepare it. There's something about the process of breading chicken that seems really fun to kids, probably because they can make quite a mess.

When I opened my first restaurant, my oldest daughter, Ashley, was only three years old. She'd sit on the counter back in the kitchen and "help" dredge the chicken for the day's orders. She was just adorable and it's one of my favorite memories from that first restaurant – her sweet little hands and face covered in flour and parmesan cheese and having her with me during those very long days.

This chicken also makes a great "picnic" chicken. My kids always love it when I pack up this dish for days at the beach or the park. When they were little, they'd grab a piece right out of the cooler, eat it with their hands along with a slice of watermelon, and run off again to play with their friends. It just wasn't a beach day without their favorite Parmesan chicken!

Traditionally, Parmesan chicken is served with Marinara sauce, which also goes beautifully with this version. However, I love this chicken as a stand-alone dish because it is so versatile and can go with pretty much anything.

This chicken can be served warm or cold, alone or over pasta or rice, or as a tasty salad topper. For a "kid-friendly" dish, make it "dippable" by pairing it with Marinara Sauce or Ranch Dressing.

So grab someone little and let them dredge their hands in the flour and grated cheese. I swear it'll make this chicken even more tasty!

INGREDIENTS

No of Servings				
4 qty | msmt (weight)		**6** qty | msmt (weight)	**10** qty | msmt (weight)	**14** qty | msmt (weight)
CHICKEN, BRINE & WET DREDGE				
1 cup (237mL)	Buttermilk	1 ½ cups (356mL)	2 ½ cups (593mL)	3 ½ cups (830mL)
1 each (43g)	Eggs, whisked well	2 each (65g)	3 each (108g)	4 each (151g)
2 fl oz (30mL)	Frank's Red Hot Sauce (Original)	3 fl oz (45mL)	5 fl oz (76mL)	7 fl oz (106mL)
¼ tsp (1g)	Kosher Salt	½ tsp (2g)	¾ tsp (3g)	1 tsp (4g)
½ tsp (2g)	Corn Starch	½ tsp (2g)	1 tsp (4g)	1 tsp (5g)
2 LB (912g)	Boneless Chicken Thighs OR Chicken Tenderloins	3 LB (1368g)	5 LB (2280g)	7 LB (3192g)
½ tsp (4g)	Salt	¾ tsp (5g)	1 ¼ tsp (9g)	1 ¾ tsp (12g)
¼ tsp (1g)	Black Pepper	½ tsp (1g)	¾ tsp (1g)	1 tsp (2g)
BREADING				
1 cup (10g)	All-Purpose Flour (divided)	1 ½ cups (15g)	2 ½ cups (25g)	3 ½ cups (35g)
1 cup (99g)	Grated Parmesan Cheese	1 ½ cups (149g)	2 ½ cups (248g)	3 ½ cups (347g)
½ cup (68g)	Panko Bread Crumbs	¾ cup (102g)	1 ¼ cups (170g)	1 ¾ cups (238g)
1 TBSP (8g)	Italian Seasoning (dried)	1 ½ TBSP (12g)	2 ½ TBSP (20g)	3 ½ TBSP (28g)
½ tsp (4g)	Salt	¾ tsp (5g)	1 ¼ tsp (9g)	1 ¾ tsp (12g)
¼ tsp (1g)	Black Pepper	½ tsp (1g)	¾ tsp (1g)	1 tsp (2g)
¼ tsp (<1g)	Cayenne Pepper (optional)	½ tsp (<1g)	¾ tsp (1g)	1 tsp (1g)

NUTRITION FACTS:

Serving Size 6 oz **Calories** 240 **Total Fat** 9g **Total Carbohydrates** 4g **Protein** 35g

The portion size shown is based on industry dietary standards and may be smaller than the portion size allowed for in recipe.

INSTRUCTIONS

Prepare Brine/Wet Dredge and Brine the Chicken. Whisk together **buttermilk, eggs, hot sauce, kosher salt** and **corn starch**. Place **chicken** pieces into the brine/wet dredge, making sure they are fully submerged. Place in refrigerator for one hour (no longer than 8 hours).

Remove chicken and place on a rack so excess brine liquid will drip off the chicken pieces. Sprinkle both sides with **salt** and **black pepper**. Reserve the **Brine/Wet Dredge mixture** for use in "Step 2" of the breading process.

Prepare Breading Dredge.
Pull out ⅓ of the **all-purpose flour** measurement and place in a shallow dish – we will use this for "Step 1" of the breading process.

Whisk together the **remaining dry ingredients** and place in a shallow dish. Set aside to use for "Step 3" of the breading process.

Preheat oven to 400°F (204°C). Prepare a baking sheet by spraying with non-stick spray.

> **MIS EN PLACE**
> 1. Assemble brine, then brine the chicken.
> 2. Assemble remaining ingredients.
> 3. Assemble dry/wet/dry breading station.

Breading Process for Chicken.
Step 1: Place chicken pieces into the all-purpose flour until lightly coated. Shake off to remove all excess flour.
Step 2: Place pieces of lightly-floured chicken into the **Wet Dredge** liquid, making sure to fully submerge. Tap off excess liquid.
Step 3: Place chicken pieces into the **Breading Dredge**, making sure all sides are covered and breading sticks to the chicken.

Step 4: Place chicken on the pre-sprayed baking sheet with at least ½" (1.3cm) spacing between pieces. Press firmly on each piece to help breading adhere.

Bake Chicken.
Bake in preheated oven for 10 minutes. Turn each piece over with a spatula to keep breading intact, then continue baking another 8-12 minutes or until chicken is golden brown, crispy and the internal temperature reaches 165°F (74°C). Check the temperature with a stem thermometer into the thickest part of the largest piece. The length of cooking time required will depend on the size and thickness of the chicken pieces being cooked. (If using chicken breast, it will take longer to cook than thighs.) Allow to rest on baking sheet 5 minutes after removing from the oven before serving.

MAKE IT NOW!

This chicken is ready to serve fresh out of the oven.

MAKE IT A FREEZER MEAL

Chill fully-cooked chicken on a baking sheet or tray in the freezer. Make sure the pieces don't touch. (This process is called "IQF" (Individual Quick Frozen) – see *Chapter 2: From Planning to Plate*, section *Organizing Freezer Space for Quick Freezing*.

Once the pieces are frozen (about 20 to 30 minutes), place in a resealable bag and apply the label "*Oven-Baked Parmesan Chicken.*" To extend shelf life, remove as much air as possible from the resealable bag, then place it inside a second resealable bag, again removing as much air as possible.

FREEZER LABELS

Find and print freezer meal labels for this dish at www.frozenandfabulous.com. (See also "*Chapter 13: Quick Guide to Online Tools.*")

SUGGESTED PAIRINGS

SIDE DISH PAIRINGS
- Buttery Noodles
- Any cream-style pasta dish with an Italian flavor profile
- Serve with dipping sauce (kids love Marinara or Ranch)

WINE AND/OR ALCOHOL PAIRINGS
- White or Red Wine
- Marsanne
- Roussane
- Pinot Grigio
- Merlot or Pinot Noir (when serving with a rich marinara pasta sauce)
- Stella Beer

ONLINE RESOURCES

Scan this QR code for a direct link to an instructional cooking video for this recipe on www.frozenandfabulous.com, along with this helpful "How It's Done" video.

- Dry/Wet/Dry Breading Method

VARIATIONS

MAKE IT GLUTEN-FREE	MAKE IT VEGETARIAN	MAKE IT "FIT-FRIENDLY"	MAKE IT BUDGET-FRIENDLY
Replace the all-purpose flour with a gluten-free flour blend.	Use this breading for root vegetables or large mushrooms, such as portobello.	Increase the ratio of parmesan cheese over all-purpose flour. The current recipe calls for 50/50 of each, but if you increase to 60% parmesan cheese and 40% flour, it will still create a crispy breading but will have a higher protein content.	You can save money on chicken by purchasing the whole chicken and cutting it into parts. One single breast can yield 3 to 4 "strips" that would be perfect for this breading process.

LAMB

Lamb Cutlets
with Mint Orange Cointreau Sauce

I originally created this Cointreau sauce when my first grandchild, Parker, was born.

I was kissing his sweet, soft little head that felt like velvet and was overwhelmed with emotion. So many thoughts and feelings racing through my head, from remembering his sweet momma (my Ashley) as a baby girl, to holding my breath in awe as his sweet little hand was holding tightly to my finger. I still tear up a little when I think about what an amazing experience it was to become a gramma – our handsome Parker-man owns my heart, for sure!

Inspired by the sweet complexity of the experience, this sauce brings a medley of flavors that elevate the forward notes of orange and mint. Bright flavors with a silky softness on the palate that are so perfectly balanced, together they bring elegance to the simplicity of the lamb shank.

Whatever you do, don't skip the Cointreau and follow the process for making the sauce exactly as written. If the Cointreau is added too soon, it becomes overly sweet with reduction; however, adding at the end elevates the beauty of this spirit and delivers a lovely balance of flavors.

Savourer l'instant!

INGREDIENTS

No of Servings				
4		**6**	**10**	**14**
qty | msmt (weight)		qty | msmt (weight)	qty | msmt (weight)	qty | msmt (weight)
GRILLED MANDARIN ORANGES				
20 supremes (160g)	Supremes from Mandarin Oranges (Avg 8-10 supremes per orange)	30 supremes (240g)	50 supremes (400g)	70 supremes (560g)
1 TBSP (15mL)	Olive Oil	1 ½ TBSP (23mL)	2 ½ TBSP (38mL)	3 ½ TBSP (53mL)
MINT ORANGE COINTREAU SAUCE				
4 fl oz (118mL)	Cointreau (French Orange Liqueur)	6 fl oz (177mL)	10 fl oz (296mL)	14 fl oz (414mL)
4 sprigs (4g)	Fresh Rosemary, whole sprigs, divided	6 sprigs (6g)	10 sprigs (10g)	14 sprigs (13g)
4 sprigs (4g)	Fresh Thyme, whole sprigs, divided	6 sprigs (6g)	10 sprigs (10g)	14 sprigs (13g)
4 sprigs (<1g)	Fresh Mint, whole sprigs, divided	6 sprigs (<1g)	10 sprigs (1g)	14 sprigs (1g)
2 TBSP (30mL)	Olive Oil	3 TBSP (45mL)	⅓ cup (75mL)	½ cup (105mL)
1 each (28g)	Medium Shallot, whole, peeled and rough chopped	1 ½ each (43g)	2 ½ each (71g)	3 ½ each (99g)
2 each (6g)	Garlic cloves, peeled & smashed	3 each (8g)	5 each (14g)	7 each (20g)
2 fl oz (59mL)	White Wine	3 fl oz (89mL)	5 fl oz (148mL)	7 fl oz (207mL)
¾ cup (177mL)	Juice from Valencia or Naval Oranges *(Avg ¼ cup (59mL) juice per orange)	1 ⅛ cups (266mL)	2 cups (444mL)	2 2/3 cups (621mL)
2 TBSP (8g)	Zest from Valencia or Naval Oranges (Avg 2 TBSP (8g) zest per orange)	3 TBSP (12g)	⅓ cup (20g)	½ cup (28g)
½ cup (118mL)	Juice from Mandarin Oranges (Avg ⅓ cup (78g) juice per orange)	¾ cup (177mL)	1 ¼ cup (296mL)	1 ¾ cup (414mL)
1 TBSP (4g)	Zest from Mandarin Oranges (Avg 1 TBSP (4g) zest per orange)	1 ½ TBSP (6g)	2 ½ TBSP (10g)	3 ½ TBSP (14g)
4 fl oz (118mL)	Chicken Stock or Broth	6 fl oz (177mL)	10 fl oz (296mL)	14 fl oz (414mL)
10 supremes (100g)	Supremes from Valencia or Naval Orange (Avg 8-10 supremes per orange)	15 supremes (150g)	25 supremes (250g)	35 supremes (350g)
1 tsp (6g)	Chicken Base (Chef Gail recommends "Better Than Bouillon Chicken Base")	1 ½ tsp (9g)	2 ½ tsp (15g)	3 ½ tsp (21g)
1 tsp (5g)	Sugar	1 ½ tsp (8g)	2 ½ tsp (13g)	3 ½ tsp (18g)
3 TBSP (44mL)	White Balsamic Vinegar	4 ½ TBSP (67mL)	3 ¾ fl oz (111mL)	5 ¼ fl oz (155mL)
1 pinch (<1g)	Cayenne Pepper	2 pinches (<1g)	⅛ tsp (<1g)	¼ tsp (1g)
1 pinch (<1g)	Salt	2 pinches (<1g)	⅛ tsp (1g)	¼ tsp (1g)
1 pinch (<1g)	Black Pepper	2 pinches (<1g)	⅛ tsp (1g)	¼ tsp (1g)
1 TBSP (14g)	Butter (Salted), cut into ½" (1.3cm) square pieces	1 ½ TBSP (21g)	2 ½ TBSP (35g)	3 ½ TBSP (49g)
2 tsp (<1g)	Fresh Flat-Leaf Italian Parsley, finely chopped (for garnish)	3 tsp (1g)	1 2/3 TBSP (1g)	2 ⅓ TBSP (1g)
2 TBSP (13g)	Pistachio Nuts, chopped (for garnish)	3 TBSP (19g)	⅓ cup (31g)	½ cup (44g)
LAMB CUTLETS				
8 each (1120g)	Lamb Cutlets	12 each (1680g)	20 each (2800g)	28 each (3920g)
2 TBSP (30g)	Olive Oil	3 TBSP (45g)	⅓ cup (75g)	½ cup (105g)
⅛ tsp (1g)	Salt	¼ tsp (1g)	⅓ tsp (2g)	½ tsp (3g)
⅛ tsp (<1g)	Black Pepper	¼ tsp (<1g)	⅓ tsp (1g)	½ tsp (1g)
2 sprigs (2g)	Fresh Rosemary, whole sprigs	3 sprigs (3g)	5 sprigs (5g)	7 sprigs (7g)
2 sprigs (2g)	Fresh Mint, whole sprigs	3 sprigs (3g)	5 sprigs (5g)	7 sprigs (7g)
2 sprigs (2g)	Fresh Thyme, whole sprigs	3 sprigs (3g)	5 sprigs (5g)	7 sprigs (7g)

MAIN DISH DINNER RECIPES | LAMB

NUTRITION FACTS:

Serving Size 8 oz　　**Calories** 480　　**Total Fat** 39g　　**Total Carbohydrates** 13g　　**Protein** 19g

The portion size shown is based on industry dietary standards and may be smaller than the portion size allowed for in recipe.

INSTRUCTIONS

Grill Mandarin Oranges.
Heat grill to MEDIUM-HIGH heat.

Peel and separate **Mandarin orange** segments into supremes. (If you are unfamiliar with this technique, see our tutorial video at www.frozenandfabulous.com.)

Brush both sides of each supreme with *olive oil (or toss lightly in a bowl so both sides are oiled)*, then place on grill, turning once, approximately 1 minute per side. Remove from heat and set aside.

Prepare Sauce.
Pour **Cointreau** into a glass or container and add HALF the sprigs of **rosemary, thyme** and **mint** so they are fully submerged. Set aside.

In a skillet over MEDIUM heat, warm **olive oil**, then add in rough-chopped **shallots** and smashed **garlic cloves**. Toss until shallots are softened and garlic is starting to caramelize. Whisk in **white wine** to deglaze the pan and allow to reduce until pan is nearly dry.

Add in the remaining HALF of the sprigs of **rosemary, thyme** and **mint**, the **juice and zest from Valencia and Mandarin oranges, chicken stock,** sections from **Valencia oranges, chicken base, sugar, white balsamic vinegar, cayenne pepper, salt** and **black pepper**.

Allow to simmer over MEDIUM-LOW heat until the sauce has reduced by half and begins to coat the back of a spoon.

Add in the infused Cointreau.
Strain sauce through a fine-mesh strainer into a separate container, clean out the skillet with a paper towel, then strain the sauce again back into the skillet. Return heat to MEDIUM.

Continue cooking for 1 minute, then taste. If the sauce is bitter, add sugar. If the sauce is too sweet, add white balsamic vinegar. Add more salt, black pepper and cayenne pepper to taste. Do not cook too long at this stage or the Cointreau will over-reduce.

Add in **grilled mandarin orange supremes**, then place **butter pieces** into the sauce. Swirl until butter melts and is incorporated. (Do not stir.)

Remove from heat and set aside.

MAKE IT NOW!

Prepare Lamb Cutlets and Serve.
Brush both sides of **lamb cutlets** with **olive oil**, then sprinkle both sides with **salt** and **black pepper**.

Heat grill or cast-iron skillet over HIGH heat until very hot. Grill for 2 to 3 minutes on each side (depending on how thick the cuts are), then remove from skillet or grill and allow to rest for 5 minutes.

The lamb should be seared on the outside and VERY PINK inside. The internal temperature for rare will be 120°F (49°C) or medium-rare 130°F (54°C). Overcooked lamb cutlets will be tough and taste "gamey" so cooking to the rare or medium-rare stage will yield the best taste and texture.

> **Note:** To avoid over-cooking, I typically pull lamb from the oven at 115°F (46°C) for rare or 125°F (52°C) for medium-rare and let it come up to temp while resting.

Drizzle lamb cutlets with **Mint Orange Cointreau Sauce**, garnish with chopped **pistachios**, chopped **parsley** and a sprig of **fresh mint**. Enjoy!

MIS EN PLACE

1. Extract juice and zest from Mandarin and Valencia oranges.
2. Remove supremes from Mandarin and Valencia oranges (not the same ones used for juicing). The pieces of the Valencia oranges can be roughly separated, but the Mandarine pieces should be clean with all pith removed and without tears in the skin.
3. Rough chop shallots and garlic.
4. Chop parsley.
5. Chop pistachio nuts.
6. Assemble all remaining ingredients.

CHEF NOTES

I do not recommend using canned mandarin oranges. They are typically canned in a sugary syrup and the extra sugar will over-sweeten the sauce.

However, if you really need to use canned, then rinse away the syrup or use a no-sugar-added, packed in water version.

MAKE IT A FREEZER MEAL

Place sauce in a shallow container in the refrigerator and allow it to cool completely.

Brush both sides of **lamb cutlets** with **olive oil**, then sprinkle both sides with **salt** and **black pepper**.

HEAT grill or cast-iron skillet over HIGH heat until very hot. Grill for 2 to 3 minutes on each side just to get a good grill mark, then remove from skillet or grill and allow to cool completely. They will only be partially cooked and raw on the inside.

Once cooled, placed seared chops in a vacuum-seal or zippered bag and seal tightly, removing all excess air. Apply label *"Lamb Cutlets for: Lamb Cutlets with Mint Orange Cointreau Sauce"* and place in freezer. Follow cooking instructions when ready to serve.

Place cooled Mint Orange Cointreau Sauce into a freezable container and seal tightly. Apply label *"Sauce for Lamb Cutlets with Mint Orange Cointreau Sauce."* Follow reheating instructions when ready to serve.

FREEZER LABELS

Find and print freezer meal labels for this dish at www.frozenandfabulous.com. (See also *"Chapter 13: Quick Guide to Online Tools."*)

SUGGESTED PAIRINGS

SIDE DISH PAIRINGS

- Grilled Asparagus
- Haricot Vert with Rosemary and Mint Butter
- Rice Pilaf
- Baked Brie and Pasta
- Fennel, Mandarin Orange and Mixed Greens Salad

WINE AND/OR ALCOHOL PAIRINGS

- Barbera
- Syrah
- Mourvèdre
- Tempranillo

ONLINE RESOURCES

Scan this QR code for a direct link to an instructional cooking video for this recipe on www.frozenandfabulous.com, along with this helpful "How It's Done" video.

- How to Supreme an Orange
- How to Grill-Mark Meat

VARIATIONS

MAKE IT GLUTEN-FREE

All the ingredients in this dish are naturally gluten-free; however, check the label on the chicken base and chicken stock you choose, as some brands contain gluten.

MAKE IT VEGETARIAN

This sauce is delicious served over cauliflower or eggplant steaks in place of the lamb cutlets. For the sauce, exchange the chicken stock and base for vegetarian versions.

MAKE IT "FIT-FRIENDLY"

Exchange sugar for honey and reduce the amount of sauce served with the lamb.

MAKE IT BUDGET-FRIENDLY

Chicken breasts or thighs are a delicious pairing for this sauce and are generally less expensive than lamb.

LAMB

Chipotle Roasted Leg of Lamb

Lamb is one of my favorite meats to work with for its' rich, earthy flavor and (when prepared properly) its' tender bite, which is easily as luxurious as a perfectly-rare prime rib.

For this recipe, the spicy chipotle rub brings a lively kick to the richness of the lamb while the sauce finishes with a silky mouthfeel to the palate. Adjust the heat level by adding more or less chipotle peppers and chipotle spice blend, depending on your taste preferences.

Although I typically recommend choosing locally-grown meat, it is different when choosing lamb. I only use Australian- or New Zealand-grown lamb versus U.S.-grown, New Zealand being my favorite.

Australian and New Zealand lamb are grass-fed in open pastures without hormones. The lambs are younger, smaller and the meat much more rich, flavorful and tender. If you can find it, Icelandic lamb is even more petite and tender, though difficult to find in most markets.

In contrast, even grass-fed lamb in the U.S. is typically finished with grain, and the animals are allowed to grow much larger. This negatively affects the taste and texture of the meat, which is why I avoid it. If you choose a U.S.-grown lamb, look for organic, 100% grass-fed, and butchered under one year.

With lamb, cooking to rare 120°F (49°C) or medium-rare 130°F (54°C) is always going to provide the best taste and texture. Over-cooking past medium-rare will result in a tougher bite and a more gamey taste. It should be **very pink to bright red** in the center. To avoid over-cooking, I typically pull the roast from the oven at 115°F (46°C) for rare or 125°F (52°C) for medium-rare and let it come up to temp while resting.

For those of you who haven't tried lamb yet, I often tell my clients that they will usually enjoy a leg of lamb if they like prime rib. The textures and taste are similar, but the lamb has a bit more depth to its' flavor. On the other hand, if you are someone who must have their meat cooked to well-done, and get squeamish at the sight of pink, then you aren't likely to enjoy it as much.

For all of you who try this dish, I hope you love every unctuous bite!

INGREDIENTS

No of Servings				
4 qty | msmt (weight)		**6** qty | msmt (weight)	**10** qty | msmt (weight)	**14** qty | msmt (weight)
	LEG OF LAMB & RUB			
¼ cup (20g)	**Chef Gail's Chipotle Dry Rub** (see Recipe in *Chapter 10: Spice Blends*)	½ cup (30g)	¾ cup (50g)	1 cup (70g)
1 TBSP (14g)	Chipotle Chiles in Adobo Sauce (canned), cut into small pieces	1 ½ TBSP (21g)	2 ½ TBSP (35g)	3 ½ TBSP (49g)
4 TBSP (56mL)	Olive Oil, divided	6 TBSP (84mL)	10 TBSP (140mL)	14 TBSP (196mL)
2 fl oz (59mL)	Bourbon Whiskey	3 fl oz (89mL)	5 fl oz (148mL)	7 fl oz (207mL)
3 LB (1368g)	Leg of Lamb Roast, bone-in or boneless, trimmed	4 ½ LB (2052g)	7 ½ LB (3420g)	10 ½ LB (4788g)
4 each (11g)	Garlic Cloves, whole, peeled	6 each (17g)	10 each (28g)	14 each (39g)
1 TBSP (13g)	Kosher Salt	1 ½ TBSP (20g)	2 ½ TBSP (33g)	3 ½ TBSP (46g)
1 tsp (2g)	Black Pepper	1 ½ tsp (3g)	2 ½ tsp (5g)	3 ½ tsp (7g)
	CHIPOTLE PAN SAUCE			
½ TBSP (7mL)	Olive Oil	¾ TBSP (11mL)	1 ¼ TBSP (18mL)	1 ¾ TBSP (25mL)
1 each (28g)	Medium Shallot, whole, peeled and rough-chopped	1 ½ each (43g)	2 ½ each (71g)	3 ½ each (99g)
2 each (6g)	Garlic Cloves, peeled & smashed	3 each (8g)	5 each (14g)	7 each (20g)
½ tsp (1g)	**Chef Gail's Chipotle Dry Rub** (see Recipe in *Chapter 10: Spice Blends*)	½ tsp (2g)	¾ tsp (3g)	1 tsp (4g)
3 fl oz (89mL)	Bourbon Whiskey	4 ½ fl oz (133mL)	7 ½ fl oz (222mL)	10 ½ fl oz (311mL)
as available	Reserved Pan Drippings, strained	as available	as available	as available
8 fl oz (237mL)	Lamb or Beef Stock	12 fl oz (355mL)	20 fl oz (591mL)	28 fl oz (828mL)
1 tsp (6g)	Beef Base (*Chef Gail recommends "Better Than Bouillon Beef Base"*)	1 ½ tsp (9g)	2 ½ tsp (15g)	1 TBSP (21g)
½ TBSP (7mL)	Chipotle Chiles in Adobo Sauce (canned), cut into small pieces	¾ TBSP (11g)	1 ¼ TBSP (18g)	1 ¾ TBSP (25g)
3 TBSP (51mL)	Lime Juice	4 ½ TBSP (77mL)	½ cup (128mL)	2/3 cup (179mL)
4 sprigs (4g)	Fresh Mint, whole sprigs, divided	6 sprigs (6g)	10 sprigs (10g)	14 sprigs (13g)
1 pinch (<1g)	Cayenne Pepper	2 pinches (<1g)	⅛ tsp (<1g)	¼ tsp (1g)
1 pinch (<1g)	Salt	2 pinches (<1g)	⅛ tsp (1g)	¼ tsp (1g)
1 pinch (<1g)	Black Pepper	2 pinches (<1g)	⅛ tsp (1g)	¼ tsp (1g)
1 TBSP (14g)	Butter (Salted), cut into ½" (1.3cm) square pieces	2 TBSP (21g)	3 TBSP (35g)	4 TBSP (49g)

NUTRITION FACTS:

Serving Size 7 oz   **Calories** 240   **Total Fat** 13g   **Total Carbohydrates** 2g   **Protein** 29g

The portion size shown is based on industry dietary standards and may be smaller than the portion size allowed for in recipe.

INSTRUCTIONS

Prepare Rub.
Place **Chef Gail's Chipotle Dry Rub**, **chipotle chiles** (**in sauce**), HALF of the **olive oil**, and **Bourbon whiskey** in a small container. Stir well to combine into a paste.

Prepare the Lamb Roast.
If using a bone-in leg of lamb, see "**chef notes** - Trimming the Bone-in Leg of Lamb."

Pat the *lamb roast* dry with paper towels, then place on a cutting board with the fat side up. With a sharp knife, make several cuts into the fat layer in a hashtag pattern. Each cut should be deep enough to penetrate the fat layer without cutting into the meat underneath.

Smash the whole **garlic cloves**, then push into a few of the crevices of the fat cap and roast on all sides.

Again, pat the roast dry with paper towels, then sprinkle generously on all sides with **kosher salt** and **black pepper**.

Apply Rub and Insert Garlic.
Prepare roasting pan by spraying the bottom with non-stick spray and placing a roasting rack inside.

Place lamb, fat side facing up, on the roasting rack. Spread the wet rub evenly over the lamb, using your hands to push the mixture into areas between the scored cuts.

Cover lightly with plastic wrap (sprayed with non-stick spray to prevent rub from adhering to plastic) and place in the refrigerator for 4 hours to allow the seasonings to penetrate the meat.

MAKE IT NOW

Finish the Roast.
Sixty to 90 minutes before cooking, remove from the refrigerator and place on the counter. The roast must come to room temperature before cooking to prevent uneven doneness.

Preheat oven to 400°F (204°C). If you have an oven-safe stem thermometer to place in the meat while cooking, insert it to reach the center of the thickest part of the roast.

Remove plastic wrap and replace with aluminum foil, sprayed with non-stick spray and tented over the roast. (It shouldn't touch the lamb but allow air to circulate underneath).

MIS EN PLACE

1. Trim the lamb roast, if necessary.
2. If you don't already have some on hand, prepare a batch of Chef Gail's Chipotle Dry Rub.
3. Peel and prep garlic for both the roast and sauce.
4. Rough-chop shallots for sauce.
5. Assemble remaining ingredients.

Place in preheated 400°F (204°C) oven and roast for 8 minutes, then reduce oven temperature to 325°F (163°C) without opening the oven door.

Continue cooking for one more hour, then check the internal temperature and remove aluminum foil.

About 30 minutes of additional cooking time (uncovered) may be required. The total cooking time needed will depend on whether your roast is bone-in or boneless and the thickness of the roast, but a good rule of thumb is about 15 minutes total cooking time per pound. Always use a stem thermometer to prevent over-cooking, and make sure the stem isn't touching the bone (if using a bone-in roast).

For medium-rare (*which is perfect*), pull the roast from the oven when the internal temperature reaches 130°F (54°C). Then allow the meat to rest for 15 minutes, covered lightly with tented aluminum foil. During the rest time, it will reach an internal temperature of 135°F (57°C). If you prefer a different level of doneness, here is a helpful temperature guide:

LAMB ROASTS & STEAKS

120°F (49°C)	130°F (54°C)	140°F (60°C)	150°F (65°C)	160°F (71°C)
Rare	Medium-Rare	Medium	Medium-Well	Well Done

Prepare the Sauce.
In a skillet, heat **olive oil** over MEDIUM-HIGH heat. Sauté **shallots** and **garlic** until softened, then add **Chef Gail's Chipotle Dry Rub** and allow to "bloom" in the oil until aromatic. (If pan is dry, add a bit of oil or butter before adding in the spices.)

> **CHEF NOTES: TRIMMING THE BONE-IN LEG OF LAMB**
>
> Most butchers will trim the leg of lamb for you; however, if your roast has not been trimmed it is easy to do.
>
> Remove 1-½ inches (3.75cm) of flesh from the shank bone with a sharp knife so the bone is clean.
>
> For both bone-in and boneless, remove the fell. Fell is a very thin outer layer of fat that sits on top of the regular fat.
>
> After removing the fell, remove excess fat, if any. Be careful at this point, as the fat brings a lot of flavor and moisture to the meat so you don't want to remove too much. If you're not sure, just cut hashtags about ½" (1.25cm) deep through the fat layer to break it up and allow the seasonings to reach the meat.
>
> Use kitchen shears to remove the fat pads around the larger end of the roast.

Cook for 1 to 2 minutes longer or until pan is almost dry and ingredients are sticking, then add **Bourbon whiskey**. Cook until Bourbon is reduced and the pan is almost dry (au sec), then whisk in the **pan drippings**, **lamb or beef stock**, and **beef base**. Add **chipotle chiles in sauce**, **lime juice**, and ¾ of the **fresh mint** sprigs (*the remaining ¼ will be used for garnish*), then stir together and bring to a boil.

Reduce heat and continue cooking over MEDIUM-LOW heat until sauce is reduced by half. Strain the sauce through a mesh strainer, clean out the pan with a paper towel, then return the strained sauce to the pan. Add **cayenne pepper**, **salt** and **black pepper** (to taste).

Place **butter pieces** into the sauce and swirl to incorporate (do not stir), then remove from heat.

To serve, spoon the sauce over sliced lamb and garnish with freshly chopped **mint**.

MAKE IT A FREEZER MEAL

Package the Meat.
For best taste at time of service, package the meat raw, with its' rub intact, then cook at the time of service.

Wrap rubbed roast in a tight layer of plastic wrap to make sure the rub mixture stays adhered to all sides of the meat. Then place the wrapped roast into a resealable zippered or vacuum-sealable bag with all air removed. Apply label *"Chipotle Roasted Leg of Lamb"* and follow cooking instructions at time of service.

However, it is also okay to PARTIALLY cook the meat, then finish cooking at the time of service if you need to save time later. Follow the cooking instructions under the "Make it Now" section above but stop cooking half-way through the suggested cooking time. If you use this method, it is IMPORTANT to mark on your freezer label that the meat is partially cooked and notate the required cooking temperature for finishing in the oven. It is also important to make sure the partially-cooked roast is cooled completely before packaging.

Prepare the Sauce.
Follow the **Prepare the Sauce** instructions in the "Make it Now" section above; however, do not incorporate the butter into the sauce if you plan to freeze it.

Transfer the finished sauce to a shallow container and place in refrigerator until cooled completely. Add in the pieces of butter. (As long as the sauce is cold when butter is added, the butter will melt properly when reheated at time of service.)

Once cooled, place the sauce (with pieces of butter) in a freezable container, resealable zippered or vacuum-sealable bag with all air removed. Apply label *"Chipotle Pan Sauce for: Chipotle Roasted Leg of Lamb"* and follow instructions for heating at time of service.

Place packaged roast and sauce into a single resealable zippered bag for convenient storage in the freezer.

FREEZER LABELS

Find and print freezer meal labels for this dish at www.frozenandfabulous.com. (See also *"Chapter 13: Quick Guide to Online Tools."*)

MAIN DISH DINNER RECIPES | LAMB

CHEF NOTES: BONELESS OR BONE-IN?

If you are serving seven or more, I recommend using a bone-in leg of lamb that has been trimmed by your butcher. The bone brings tremendous flavor and adds a rich silkiness to the pan sauce.

However, if you are serving fewer than seven then you'll want to choose a boneless roast because you can more easily adjust for servings. (Bone-in roasts are usually 5 to 6 pounds.)

IMPORTANT: If you choose a boneless roast, you'll need kitchen twine on hand so you can tie the roast together for cooking.

SUGGESTED PAIRINGS

SIDE DISH PAIRINGS

- Potatoes au Gratin
- Buttery Herbed Hasselback Potatoes
- Roasted Root Vegetables
- Rice Pilaf
- Mushroom Risotto

WINE AND/OR ALCOHOL PAIRINGS

- Cabernet Sauvignon
- Ribera del Duero
- Malbec
- Riesling
- Côtes du Rhône

ONLINE RESOURCES

Scan this QR code for a direct link to an instructional cooking video for this recipe on www.frozenandfabulous.com.

VARIATIONS

MAKE IT GLUTEN-FREE

This dish is naturally gluten-free when prepared as written.

MAKE IT VEGETARIAN

The rub mixture would be delicious paired with jackfruit, eggplant or potatoes.

MAKE IT "FIT-FRIENDLY"

Serve a smaller portion of the lamb and omit the butter from the sauce.

MAKE IT BUDGET-FRIENDLY

Unfortunately, good quality lamb is expensive. The best way to save costs on this dish is to exchange the bourbon whiskey for a cheaper white wine and swap the lamb for a pork or beef roast, or whole chicken.

CHEF GAIL KURPGEWEIT @ASKCHEFGAIL

PORK

The "Little Black Dress" of White Meat

Pork Tenderloin is an incredibly versatile, flavorful and tender cut of meat. I highly recommend keeping several partially-prepared, flavor-neutral pork tenderloins in the freezer for quick and easy meals.

To prepare, clean the pork by removing the silver skin. For detailed instructions on this process, see our online "how-to" video called "How to Prep Pork Tenderloin for Cooking."

Then simply brush with olive oil, rub with a mixture of salt, black pepper and freshly chopped rosemary, and sear in a cast-iron skillet (leave it raw on the inside). Allow to cool completely, then store in a resealable zippered bag with all air removed or a vacuum-sealed bag.

When it's time to serve just thaw, finish in the oven, and pair with your favorite sauce. Easy peasy and so delicious!

PORK

Cherry-Stuffed Pork Loin with Black Cherry Chutney

Because of its intense, vibrant color, this is easily my favorite dish to make around the holidays. Still, it is delicious any time of year with its bold flavor of cherry and balsamic vinegar paired with tender pork and the crunch of walnuts.

This version calls for pork loin stuffed with a flavorful black cherry mixture and served with a decadent black cherry chutney; however, it can just as easily be paired with pork tenderloin. Just prepare pork tenderloin with salt, black pepper and fresh rosemary, skip the stuffing and pair with the black cherry chutney for a decadent meal.

When choosing a pork loin roast, select one with a generous fat cap to get the best flavor. If your pork loin roast doesn't have a significant fat cap, then I recommend placing strips of bacon across the top of the roast to provide the fat necessary to build flavor in this lean cut of pork.

There are two ways to stuff a pork loin roast. For this recipe, I recommend an "open-book style" because it provides a higher ratio of meat to stuffing. This allows the taste of the pork to shine through, and the filling complements the hearty chutney. The pork is slow-roasted to enhance its flavor, while the overall dish remains balanced.

You could also butterfly-cut the loin to about ½" (1.3cm) thickness, pound, then add the stuffing and roll up like a roulade. I find this technique to deliver the most tender meat, and it cooks faster than the "open-book" method; however, the stuffing will take on a more forward role which may not be as pleasant when paired with the chutney. One way to make the butterfly-cut technique work would be to run the chutney through a mesh strainer and serve the remaining sauce with the roulade-style stuffed tenderloin.

The sauce will take awhile to freeze, and will thaw quickly because of its high sugar content. The sugar is needed to balance out the sourness of the cherries so if you are looking for a low-calorie sauce this isn't it. It is extraordinary, though, with its gorgeous flavor and presentation, and a real crowd-pleaser when entertaining.

INGREDIENTS

No of Servings				
4		**6**	**10**	**14**
qty | msmt (weight)		qty | msmt (weight)	qty | msmt (weight)	qty | msmt (weight)
BRINE PORK LOIN				
2 LB (912g)	Boneless Pork Loin Roast	3 LB (1368g)	5 LB (2280g)	7 LB (3192g)
	* Pre-brine with **Overnight Brine for Pork** (see *Chapter 11: Meat Brines*)			
CHERRY & WALNUT STUFFING				
1 TBSP (8g)	Dried Tart Cherries	1 ½ TBSP (11g)	2 ½ TBSP (19g)	3 ½ TBSP (26g)
¼ cup (59mL)	Red Wine	½ cup (89mL)	¾ cup (148mL)	1 cup (207mL)
2/3 cup (93g)	Black Cherries, (fresh or frozen) pitted and cut into quarters	1 cup (140g)	1 2/3 cups (233g)	2 1/3 cups (327g)
¼ each (57g)	Medium White Onion, chopped into small squares (small dice cut)	½ each (85g)	¾ each (141g)	1 each (198g)
1 each (6g)	Garlic Cloves, minced	2 each (8g)	3 each (14g)	4 each (19g)
2 tsp (5g)	Walnuts, roughly chopped	3 tsp (7g)	5 tsp (12g)	2 1/3 TBSP (16g)
1 tsp (1g)	Fresh Rosemary Leaves, finely chopped	1 ½ tsp (2g)	2 ½ tsp (3g)	3 ½ tsp (4g)
1 tsp (2g)	Lemon Zest, fresh (Zest of 1 lemon = 3 tsp or 1 TBSP)	1 ½ tsp (3g)	2 ½ tsp (5g)	3 ½ tsp (7g)
1 pinch (<1g)	Salt	2 pinches (<1g)	1/8 tsp (1g)	¼ tsp (1g)
1 pinch (<1g)	Black Pepper	2 pinches (<1g)	1/8 tsp (1g)	¼ tsp (1g)
PREPARE PORK LOIN				
1 TBSP (14g)	Butter (Salted), room temperature	1 ½ TBSP (21g)	2 ½ TBSP (35g)	3 ½ TBSP (49g)
½ tsp (4g)	Salt	¾ tsp (5g)	1 ¼ tsp (9g)	1 ¾ tsp (12g)
½ tsp (1g)	Black Pepper, divided	¾ tsp (2g)	1 ¼ tsp (3g)	1 ¾ tsp (4g)
½ tsp (2g)	Kosher Salt	¾ tsp (3g)	1 ¼ tsp (5g)	1 ¾ tsp (8g)
1 tsp (1g)	Fresh Rosemary Leaves, finely chopped	1 ½ tsp (2g)	2 ½ tsp (3g)	3 ½ tsp (4g)
8 each (22g)	Garlic Cloves, whole, peeled	12 each (34g)	20 each (56g)	28 each (78g)
BLACK CHERRY CHUTNEY				
½ TBSP (8mL)	Olive Oil	¾ TBSP (11g)	1 ¼ TBSP (19g)	1 ¾ TBSP (26g)
¾ each (170g)	Medium White Onion, chopped into small squares (small dice cut)	1 each (254g)	1 ¾ each (424g)	2 ½ each (593g)
½ TBSP (7g)	Butter (Salted)	¾ TBSP (11g)	1 ¼ TBSP (18g)	1 ¾ TBSP (25g)
¼ tsp (1g)	Ground Coriander	½ tsp (1g)	¾ tsp (2g)	1 tsp (2g)
¼ tsp (1g)	Ground Cinnamon	½ tsp (1g)	¾ tsp (2g)	1 tsp (3g)
2 each (11g)	Garlic Cloves, minced	3 each (17g)	5 each (28g)	7 each (39g)
1 tsp (1g)	Fresh Rosemary Leaves, finely chopped	1 ½ tsp (2g)	2 ½ tsp (3g)	3 ½ tsp (4g)
¼ cup (59mL)	Red Wine	½ cup (89mL)	¾ cup (148mL)	1 cup (207mL)

⅓ cup (79mL)	Balsamic Vinegar	⅔ cup (118mL)	1 cup (197mL)	1 ⅓ cups (276mL)
½ (14.5-oz can) (210g)	Red Tart Cherries, canned in water or juice * if canned in heavy syrup, reduce the sugar called for in the recipe by half	¾ (14.5-oz can) (315g)	1 ¼ (14.5-oz cans) (525g)	1 ¾ (14.5-oz cans) (735g)
½ cup (114g)	Sugar	¾ cup (171g)	1 ¼ cup (285g)	1 ¾ cup (399g)
2 TBSP (11g)	Dried Pomegranate Arils, divided	3 TBSP (16g)	⅓ cup (26g)	½ cup (37g)
⅓ cup (50g)	Black or Golden Raisins, divided	½ cup (75g)	¾ cup (125g)	1 cup (175g)
1 cup (140g)	Black Cherries, (fresh or frozen) pitted and cut into ¼'s, divided	1 ½ cups (210g)	2 ½ cups (350g)	3 ½ cups (490g)
½ tsp (4g)	Salt	¾ tsp (5g)	1 ¼ tsp (9g)	1 ¾ tsp (12g)
¼ tsp (1g)	Black Pepper	½ tsp (1g)	¾ tsp (1g)	1 tsp (2g)
⅛ tsp (<1g)	Cayenne pepper	⅛ tsp (<1g)	⅓ tsp (1g)	½ tsp (1g)
2 tsp (6g)	Lemon Zest, fresh (Zest of 1 lemon = 1 TBSP)	1 TBSP (9g)	1 ⅔ TBSP (15g)	2 ⅓ TBSP (21g)
1 TBSP (7g)	Walnuts, chopped into small pieces	1 ½ TBSP (11g)	2 ½ TBSP (18g)	3 ½ TBSP (25g)

NUTRITION FACTS:

Serving Size 8 oz　　**Calories** 410　　**Total Fat** 12g　　**Total Carbohydrates** 42g　　**Protein** 34g

The portion size shown is based on industry dietary standards and may be smaller than the portion size allowed for in recipe.

INSTRUCTIONS

Prepare Boneless Pork Loin Roast
To prevent overcooking, it is best to work with roasts between two and four pounds. If you are working with a larger roast, cut it into 2 to 3-pound pieces, cutting vertically to make sure each piece has its own fat cap.

Place **boneless pork loin** in **Overnight Brine for Pork** for 12 to 24 hours.

Remove the pork loin from the brine. Brush away the aromatics and pat dry with a paper towel.

With the fat cap of the pork loin facing up, score the top with your Chef knife to make a hashtag # pattern. The cuts should be shallow – just deep enough to open the fat so the seasonings will adhere, but not so deep that it breaks through to the meat underneath.

Set aside.

Prepare Cherry & Walnut Stuffing.
Place **dried tart cherries** in the bottom of a bowl, then add **red wine**. Mix, then allow to sit for 10 minutes.

Add in the **black cherries**, diced **onion**, minced **garlic**, chopped **walnuts**, chopped fresh **rosemary**, **lemon zest**, **salt** and **black pepper**. Mix well, then cover the bowl with plastic wrap and place in the refrigerator while preparing the loin roast.

MIS EN PLACE

One day ahead:
Prepare the Overnight Brine for Pork, place pork loin in brine, then refrigerate.

On prep day:
1. Pull butter out of fridge and set on counter.
2. Pit and slice black cherries into quarters for Stuffing and Chutney.
3. Chop onion, garlic, walnuts and fresh rosemary for Stuffing and Chutney.
4. Zest lemons for Stuffing and Chutney.
5. Prepare pork loin roast by scoring and rubbing with kosher salt and black pepper.
6. Assemble remaining ingredients

Butterly-Cut Boneless Pork Loin Roast (a/k/a Open Book Cut).

To butterfly cut the pork roast, place the roast with fat-cap side up on a cutting board. Place the palm of your hand on the top of the fat cap, then using a sharp Chef's knife cut horizontally through the center until you reach approximately 1" (2.5cm) from the other side. Do not cut all the way through.

> **Note:** *To see this technique demonstrated, visit www.frozenandfabulous.com for a full demo of this recipe, or visit the Resources section for a video called "How to Butterfly-Cut a Pork Loin Roast."*

Open the pork roast like a "book" or butterfly shape (the fat cap side will be face down on the table opposite the bottom-side of the roast). Continue to make light cuts through the center until the "book" is of even thickness on both sides.

Cover the opened pork loin with plastic wrap. Using a meat mallet, pound both sides until they are evenly sized and tenderized.

Brush softened **butter** evenly on both sides of the pork loin "book," then sprinkle with **salt** and a portion of the **black pepper**.

Drain the **Cherry & Walnut Stuffing** through a mesh strainer to remove excess liquid, then spoon into the center of the open pork loin and spread to evenly disbursed on both sides. Bring both sides of the "book" back together, then tie the pork loin about every 2" to 3" (5cm to 7.5cm) using kitchen twine to keep the stuffing in place.

Once the pork loin is tied off, roll so the fat cap is facing up. Place the **kosher salt**, remaining **black pepper**, and chopped fresh **rosemary** into a small bowl, mix together, and then generously rub the mixture all over the fat cap and all sides of the roast. Stuff whole **garlic cloves** evenly throughout the cuts of the fat cap.

Prepare Black Cherry Chutney.

While the roast is cooking, heat **olive oil** over MEDIUM heat in a cast-iron skillet or saucepan. Add in rough-chopped **onions** and cook until softened and transparent. Move the onions to one side of the pan, then place the **butter** on the other so it melts. Stir the **ground coriander** and **cinnamon** into the melted butter and continue stirring until they "bloom" and become very fragrant. Then mix together with the cooked onions and add the minced **garlic** and chopped fresh **rosemary**.

Continue cooking until the garlic becomes softened and the pan is nearly dry, then add the **red wine** to deglaze the pan. Reduce until the red wine is nearly gone, then add **balsamic vinegar, tart cherries (with juice), sugar** and HALF each of the **dried pomegranates, raisins** and **black cherries**.

Bring to a boil, then immediately reduce to simmer. Allow sauce to cook for 20-30 minutes or until liquids are reduced by one-third.

Strain the sauce into another container, wipe out any large "bits" remaining in the pan, then place the liquid back into the saucepan. Add the reserved HALF of the **dried pomegranates, raisins** and **black cherries**. Bring back to a simmer and continue cooking for 4 to 5 minutes or until the liquid is reduced by half.

Add **salt, black pepper, cayenne pepper** and fresh **lemon zest**. Taste and add more if needed.

Add in the **chopped walnuts**. Stir and remove from the heat.

MAKE IT NOW!

Preheat oven to 375°F (190°C).

Place stuffed, tied pork loin on a rimmed baking sheet or in a roasting pan with the fat cap side up. Roast uncovered for 55 to 70 minutes, or until the internal temperature reaches 145°F (63°C). (*Make sure the stem thermometer is inserted into the center of the meat and not the stuffing to avoid under- or overcooking.*) Remove from oven and place on counter to rest for 10 minutes.

After resting, remove the twine and cut the roast into ¾" (2cm) wide slices so each piece gets some of the stuffing and the flavor-rich fat cap. Serve the warm **Black Cherry Chutney** on top or slightly off to the side of the sliced roast.

(Optional) Garnish with freshly chopped Italian flat-leaf parsley.

MAKE IT A FREEZER MEAL

Place uncooked, stuffed, tied pork loin into a resealable zippered or vacuum-sealable bag, then seal, making sure all air is removed.

Note: *If using a resealable zippered bag, wrap the loin in plastic wrap before placing it in the bag to keep all the seasonings and stuffing intact. It will also extend the shelf life of your roast if you double-bag for additional protection. These steps are not necessary if using a quality vacuum-sealed bag.*

Apply label "*Cherry-Stuffed Pork Loin*" and place in freezer. Follow cooking instructions when ready to serve.

Pour finished **Black Cherry Chutney** into a shallow container and place in refrigerator to cool completely.

Once cooled completely, package Chutney in a resealable zippered or vacuum-sealable bag with all air removed, or a freezer-safe, air-tight microwaveable container. Apply label, "*Black Cherry Chutney for Cherry-Stuffed Pork Loin.*" Follow reheating instructions when ready to serve.

FREEZER LABELS

Find and print freezer meal labels for this dish at www.frozenandfabulous.com. (See also "*Chapter 13: Quick Guide to Online Tools.*")

SUGGESTED PAIRINGS

SIDE DISH PAIRINGS

- Cranberry Rice Pilaf
- Buttery French Bread
- Mushroom Risotto
- Seasonal Fresh Mixed Greens

WINE AND/OR ALCOHOL PAIRINGS

- Pinot Noir
- Zinfandel
- Beaujolais
- Merlot

ONLINE RESOURCES

Scan this QR code for a direct link to an instructional cooking video for this recipe on www.frozenandfabulous.com, along with these helpful "How It's Done" videos.

- How to Butterfly-Cut a Pork Loin Roast
- How to Roulade-Cut a Pork Loin Roast

VARIATIONS

MAKE IT GLUTEN-FREE

This dish is naturally gluten-free when prepared as written.

MAKE IT VEGETARIAN

This Black Cherry Chutney is delicious when paired with sliced fresh mozzarella and fresh spinach. It also makes a lovely pairing with baked brie.

MAKE IT "FIT-FRIENDLY"

Reduce the sugar and use tart cherries canned in water instead of juice or syrup.

MAKE IT BUDGET-FRIENDLY

Pork loin roast and the ingredients used in this recipe are already relatively budget-friendly, so to reduce cost try to find items on sale or purchase in bulk for use in other recipes.

PORK

Pork Tenderloin
with Bourbon Pear Sauce

Imagine a slow dance with someone you really love, the sway, an ease so warm and comfortable time slows and you could stay in the moment forever.

That is this dish. Sweet, easy comfort with flavors that move across your palate in the most luscious, rich and intimate way.

Yes, I had someone on my mind when I created this dish – and it was his favorite. He would follow this meal with a snifter of whiskey and a cigar, and time would take on a decadently slower pace whenever he was nearby. Those were good days.

Bourbon brings deep caramel flavor to the pears, while shallots, white wine vinegar and just a pinch of cayenne provide savory notes for a rich, silky finish. This dish works best with firm pears that haven't over-ripened or become too soft.

When serving this dish over the holidays, add a few dried cranberries – it will pair perfectly and add festive color and flavor.

This dish is extraordinary, so put on your pretty clothes, pour a glass of wine, and enjoy every romantic bite!

INGREDIENTS

No of Servings				
4 qty | msmt (weight)		**6** qty | msmt (weight)	**10** qty | msmt (weight)	**14** qty | msmt (weight)
PORK TENDERLOIN				
2 each (912g)	Pork Tenderloins (approx 1 LB (456g) each)	3 each (1368g)	5 each (2280g)	7 each (3192g)
2 TBSP (30mL)	Olive Oil, divided	3 TBSP (45mL)	5 TBSP (75mL)	7 TBSP (105mL)
1 TBSP (4g)	Fresh Rosemary Leaves, finely chopped	3 TBSP (5g)	3 TBSP (9g)	4 TBSP (13g)
1 tsp (7g)	Salt	1 ½ tsp (11g)	2 ½ tsp (18g)	3 ½ tsp (25g)
1 tsp (2g)	Black Pepper	1 ½ tsp (3g)	2 ½ tsp (5g)	3 ½ tsp (7g)
BOURBON PEAR SAUCE (PART 1)				
2 TBSP (30mL)	Olive Oil	3 TBSP (45mL)	5 TBSP (75mL)	7 TBSP (105mL)
1 each (28g)	Medium Shallot, whole, peeled and rough-chopped	1 ½ each (43g)	2 ½ each (71g)	3 ½ each (99g)
1 each (3g)	Garlic Cloves, peeled & smashed	1 ½ each (4g)	2 ½ each (7g)	3 ½ each (10g)
1 TBSP (4g)	Fresh Rosemary Leaves, finely chopped	1 ½ TBSP (5g)	2 ½ TBSP (9g)	3 ½ TBSP (13g)
2 fl oz (59mL)	Bourbon Whiskey	3 fl oz (89mL)	5 fl oz (148mL)	7 fl oz (207mL)
10 fl oz (296mL)	Chicken Broth or Stock	15 fl oz (444mL)	25 fl oz (739mL)	35 fl oz (1035mL)
1 tsp (6g)	Chicken Base (Chef Gail recommends "Better Than Bouillon Chicken Base")	1 ½ tsp (9g)	2 ½ tsp (15g)	3 ½ tsp (21g)
1 (14.5 oz can) (411g)	Canned Sliced Pears with Juice or Syrup	1 ½ (14.5 oz cans) (617g)	2 ½ (14.5 oz cans) (1028g)	3 ½ (14.5 oz cans) (1439g)
1 TBSP (6g)	Lemon Zest *Average 1 TBSP (6g) of zest per lemon	1 ½ TBSP (10g)	2 ½ TBSP (16g)	3 ½ TBSP (22g)
BOURBON PEAR SAUCE (PART 2)				
2 TBSP (30mL)	Olive Oil	3 TBSP (45mL)	⅓ cup (75mL)	½ cup (105mL)
1 each (142g)	Fresh Anjou Pear, peeled and sliced, seeds removed	1 ½ each (213g)	2 ½ each (355g)	3 ½ each (497g)
1 each (142g)	Fresh Bartlett or Bosc Pear, peeled and sliced, seeds removed	1 ½ each (213g)	2 ½ each (355g)	3 ½ each (497g)
4 fl oz (118mL)	Bourbon Whiskey, divided	6 fl oz (177mL)	10 fl oz (296mL)	14 fl oz (414mL)
1 TBSP (15mL)	White Wine Vinegar	1 ½ TBSP (22mL)	2 ½ TBSP (37mL)	3 ½ TBSP (52mL)
1 TBSP (1g)	Sugar	1 ½ TBSP (1g)	2 ½ TBSP (2g)	3 ½ TBSP (2g)
1 pinch (<1g)	Cayenne Pepper	2 pinches (<1g)	⅛ tsp (<1g)	¼ tsp (1g)
1 tsp (7g)	Salt	1 ½ tsp (11g)	2 ½ tsp (18g)	3 ½ tsp (25g)
1 tsp (2g)	Black Pepper	1 ½ tsp (3g)	2 ½ tsp (5g)	3 ½ tsp (7g)
2 TBSP (28g)	Butter (Salted), cut into ½" (1.3cm) square pieces	3 TBSP (42g)	5 TBSP (70g)	7 TBSP (98g)

NUTRITION FACTS:

Serving Size 6.5 oz **Calories** 280 **Total Fat** 14g **Total Carbohydrates** 19g **Protein** 20g

The portion size shown is based on industry dietary standards and may be smaller than the portion size allowed for in recipe.

INSTRUCTIONS

Prepare Pork.
Clean the **pork tenderloins** by removing silver skin. For detailed instructions on this process, see our online "how-to" video called *"How to Prep Pork Tenderloin for Cooking"* (see *Chapter 13: Quick Guide to Online Tools*).

Dry all sides of the pork tenderloins by patting with a paper towel, then brush lightly with a portion of the **olive oil**. Sprinkle all sides generously with chopped fresh **rosemary leaves**, **salt**, and **black pepper**.

Heat remaining **olive oil** over HIGH heat in a cast-iron skillet. When the pan is hot, sear tenderloins on all sides (about 1 to 2 minutes per side) until each side is golden brown. Remove tenderloins from the pan and set aside (they will be uncooked in the center).

Prepare Bourbon Pear Sauce (Part 1 Process).
In the same skillet used to sear Pork Tenderloins, heat **olive oil** over MEDIUM heat. Sauté **shallot**, **garlic** and **rosemary leaves** until softened and beginning to brown and stick to the pan.

Deglaze pan with **Bourbon whiskey**, then whisk in **chicken broth or stock** and **chicken base**. Stir in **canned pears** and **lemon zest**. (If desired, add the juice of the lemon used for zest to the sauce.)

Bring to a boil, then reduce heat to MEDIUM-LOW. Continue to simmer until sauce is reduced by half and pears are beginning to break apart.

Strain through a wire mesh and set aside the strained liquid. (*It's a good idea to place the strainer over a container so it can strain for several minutes.*)

Prepare Bourbon Pear Sauce (Part 2 Process).
In the same skillet used for the pork and part 1 of the sauce, remove the leftover bits with a paper towel, then add **olive oil** and heat the skillet to MEDIUM-HIGH. Toss in the **fresh cut pears**. Allow to brown lightly on both sides, being careful not to break the pieces.

Pour in HALF of the **Bourbon whiskey**, reduce heat to MEDIUM-LOW, and allow to simmer for 1 to 2 minutes or until reduced by one-third. Add in the **white wine vinegar**, **sugar**, **cayenne pepper** and remaining HALF of the **Bourbon whiskey**. Cook for 2 to 3 minutes or until pears are easily pierced with a fork. Pears should be softened but slightly tender (not mushy).

Add **salt** and **black pepper**. Taste and add more salt and black pepper if desired.

Place **butter pieces** on top of the sauce and allow butter to melt by gently SWIRLING the pan (do not stir). Remove pan from heat and set aside.

MIS EN PLACE

1. Clean pork tenderloins and remove silverskin.
2. Chop fresh rosemary leaves.
3. Rough chop shallot and garlic cloves.
4. Carefully peel pears, remove seeds, and cut into evenly sized pieces.
5. Cut butter into pieces and keep chilled.
6. Assemble remaining ingredients.

Note: *If making a freezer meal, reserve the butter pieces and package them separately. Then swirl into the sauce at the time of re-heating. This is an optional step, but will give your sauce a more satiny mouth-feel at time of service.*

MAKE IT NOW!

Preheat oven to 375°F (190°C). Spray a baking sheet with non-stick pan spray, then place seared pork tenderloins on the sheet.

Bake for 12 to 14 minutes or until the tenderloins reach an internal temperature of 145°F (63°C). DO NOT OVERCOOK. The meat should be quite pink inside. Allow meat to rest for 10 minutes, then slice into ¾" (2cm) medallions. Drizzle with warm **Bourbon Pear Sauce** and serve with extra sauce.

MAKE IT A FREEZER MEAL

Allow seared pork tenderloins to cool completely on a rack, then package in a resealable zippered bag with all air removed, or a vacuum-sealed bag. Apply label *"Pork for: Pork Tenderloin with Bourbon Pear Sauce."* Place in the freezer and follow cooking instructions when ready to serve.

Place cooled **Bourbon Pear Sauce** into a freezable container and seal tightly. Apply label *"Sauce for: Pork Tenderloin with Bourbon Pear Sauce."* Follow reheating instructions when ready to serve.

FREEZER LABELS

Find and print freezer meal labels for this dish at www.frozenandfabulous.com. (See also *"Chapter 13: Quick Guide to Online Tools."*)

SUGGESTED PAIRINGS

SIDE DISH PAIRINGS

- Rice Pilaf
- Roasted Garlic Fingerling Potatoes
- Roasted Brussel Sprouts

WINE AND/OR ALCOHOL PAIRINGS

- Sauvignon Blanc
- Champagne
- Cabernet Sauvignon

ONLINE RESOURCES

Scan this QR code for a direct link to an instructional cooking video for this recipe on www.frozenandfabulous.com, along with this helpful "How It's Done" video.

- How to Prep Pork Tenderloin for Cooking

VARIATIONS

MAKE IT GLUTEN-FREE

This dish is naturally gluten-free as written but check labels to make sure the chicken stock and base are gluten-free versions.

MAKE IT VEGETARIAN

This sauce will pair beautifully with a salad of fennel, endive and steamed parsnips.

MAKE IT "FIT-FRIENDLY"

Exchange the canned pears (which are packed in syrup) with fresh pears. They will require a longer cooking time, and for the first part of the sauce-making process it would be beneficial to smash the pears to extract as much juice and flavor as possible. The process for the second part of the sauce will be the same.

MAKE IT BUDGET-FRIENDLY

Find pork tenderloins on sale and purchase pears in season for the most cost-effective way to build this dish. The pork tenderloins could also be exchanged for pork chops or a white fish.

MAIN DISH DINNER RECIPES | PORK

PORK

Bourbon BBQ Babyback Ribs

Fall off the bone tender! Infuse meaty babyback ribs with a smoky spice blend before slowly cooking to create grab-it-with-both-hands, hope-you're-wearing-a-bib, unforgettable flavor! Baste and serve with Carolina-style BBQ sauce to add sweet, tangy vibrancy to the dish.

The BBQ sauce was originally created by my chef friend, Kay Conley. Her freezer-friendly sauce had so much flavor, even after being frozen, it became my go-to sauce (with just a few tweaks to make it my own).

One of the most essential "chef secrets" to creating tender, flavorful ribs is preparing the meat in advance by removing the thick skin from inside the ribs. This process allows the spicy rub flavors to infuse with the meat and break down tough fibers. As part of this recipe, you'll find step-by-step instructions on preparing the ribs for a memorable taste experience. I have also created a tutorial video available online – just search for the "Preparing Ribs" video in our Members-Only section of the frozenandfabulous.com website. See also Chapter 13: Quick Guide to Online Tools.

The BBQ Sauce included with this recipe marries together the sweetness of brown sugar, tartness of vinegar, and depth of flavor with spicy mustard and Worcestershire sauce. It pairs beautifully with chicken, so it's a great idea to make a large batch and store extra in the freezer for a quick, easy and popular weeknight dinner. Even the kids love this sauce, probably because their little taste buds recognize the ketchup flavor used to amp up the tomato profile.

So fire up the grill, grab some friends, and enjoy these amazing ribs all summer long!

CHEF GAIL KURPGEWEIT @ASKCHEFGAIL

INGREDIENTS

No of Servings				
4		**6**	**10**	**14**
qty | msmt (weight)		qty | msmt (weight)	qty | msmt (weight)	qty | msmt (weight)
BOURBON BBQ BABYBACK RIBS				
¼ cups (36g)	**Chef Gail's BBQ Dry Rub** (see Recipe in *Chapter 10: Spice Blends*)	½ cup (54g)	¾ cup (91g)	1 cup (127g)
2 racks (3192g)	Babyback Ribs, bone-in, cleaned (skin removed)	3 racks (4788g)	5 racks (7980g)	7 racks (11172g)
BOURBON BBQ SAUCE				
½ each (43g)	Medium Sweet White Onion, chopped into small squares (small dice cut)	1 each (64g)	1 ¼ each (106g)	2 each (149g)
2 each (11g)	Garlic Cloves, minced	3 each (17g)	5 each (28g)	7 each (39g)
⅓ each (7g)	Jalapeno Peppers, de-seeded and cut into small squares (small dice cut)	½ each (10g)	1 each (17g)	1 ¼ each (23g)
1 TBSP (15mL)	Olive Oil	1 ½ TBSP (23mL)	2 ½ TBSP (38mL)	3 ½ TBSP (53mL)
½ tsp (3g)	Spicy Brown Mustard	¾ tsp (4g)	1 ¼ tsp (6g)	1 ¾ tsp (9g)
1 tsp (3g)	**Chef Gail's BBQ Dry Rub** (see Recipe in *Chapter 10: Spice Blends*)	1 ½ tsp (5g)	2 ½ tsp (8g)	3 ½ tsp (11g)
½ cup (8g)	Dark Brown Sugar, firmly packed	¾ cup (12g)	1 ¼ cups (20g)	1 ¾ cups (28g)
3 TBSP (48g)	Ketchup	4 ½ TBSP (72g)	½ cup (120g)	2/3 cup (168g)
½ cup (8g)	Tomato Paste	¾ cup (12g)	1 ¼ cups (20g)	1 ¾ cups (28g)
5 fl oz (148mL)	Beef Stock or Broth	8 fl oz (222mL)	13 fl oz (370mL)	18 fl oz (518mL)
3 TBSP (45mL)	Worcestershire Sauce	4 ½ TBSP (68mL)	½ cup (113mL)	2/3 cup (158mL)
¼ cup (4mL)	Apple Cider Vinegar	½ cup (6mL)	¾ cup (9mL)	1 cup (13mL)
4 fl oz (118mL)	Apple Juice	6 fl oz (177mL)	10 fl oz (296mL)	14 fl oz (414mL)
2 TBSP (30mL)	Bourbon Whiskey, divided	3 TBSP (45mL)	5 TBSP (75mL)	7 TBSP (105mL)
½ tsp (4g)	Salt	¾ tsp (5g)	1 ¼ tsp (9g)	1 ¾ tsp (12g)
¼ tsp (1g)	Black Pepper	½ tsp (1g)	¾ tsp (1g)	1 tsp (2g)

NUTRITION FACTS:

Serving Size 8 oz   **Calories** 830   **Total Fat** 38g   **Total Carbohydrates** 35g   **Protein** 45g

The portion size shown is based on industry dietary standards and may be smaller than the portion size allowed for in recipe.

INSTRUCTIONS

If you don't already have it on hand, mix together a batch of **Chef Gail's BBQ Dry Rub**, enough for both the ribs and sauce – or even more to keep on hand for use in other recipes.

Prepare Ribs
Clean **ribs** by removing the thin layer of skin on the backside of the rack. This is an essential step because it allows the seasoning to permeate and tenderize the meat. Also, the skin, if left intact, becomes a tough barrier when eating the cooked ribs.

Method 1: Loosen the skin with a knife, then grab a large piece of the skin with a paper towel gripped between thumb and fingers. Pull to one side, trying to keep the entire piece of skin in one piece as you pull across.

> **Note:** To see this method demonstrated, please see the "Preparing Ribs" video tutorial on our website at www.frozenandfabulous.com.

Method 2: If you cannot remove the skin, it is okay to "score" it. Make cuts across the rib bones in a cross-hatch pattern (###) with a sharp knife. This will break up the skin enough to allow the seasoning to reach the meat, and more of it will dissolve during cooking.

Separate **Chef Gail's BBQ Dry Rub** seasoning into quantities for the ribs and **Bourbon BBQ Sauce**.

Liberally coat all sides of the ribs with **BBQ Dry Rub** seasoning (approximately 2 TBSP per side) and rub the seasoning into the meat, making sure sides and ends are covered.

> **Note:** Extra rub may be stored in the freezer or spice cupboard, and is delicious with chicken, pulled pork and a variety of vegetables.

Place rack of rib on top of a piece of aluminum foil, about twice the size of the rack. Then wrap foil around the rack of ribs, tucking in ends. Wrap each rack of rib individually in foil.

MIS EN PLACE

1. Prepare BBQ Dry Rub if not already on hand.
2. Clean ribs by removing silver skin.
3. Chop onion, garlic and jalapeno peppers.
4. Assemble remaining ingredients.

Place wrapped ribs on a baking sheet, refrigerate for a minimum of 4 hours or overnight, then follow instructions for "Make it a Freezer Meal" or "Make it Now!"

Prepare Bourbon BBQ Sauce
Heat **olive oil** over MEDIUM heat, then sweat **onions** until translucent. Add **garlic** and **jalapeno** and toss until softened. Add **spicy brown mustard** and **BBQ Dry Rub**, then stir to allow spices to "bloom" or begin to release aroma (1 to 2 minutes).

> **Note:** If the pan is dry when you add the rub, add a bit of oil. The fat is needed to properly "bloom" the spices.

Add **dark brown sugar, ketchup, tomato paste, beef stock, Worcestershire sauce, apple cider vinegar, apple juice** and 2/3 of the **Bourbon whiskey** measurement.

Bring to a boil, then reduce heat and continue to simmer for 20 to 30 minutes or until reduced by 25%.

> **Note:** Sauce will be thick and may splatter a lot while simmering. Create a "tent" around the sides of the pot, leaving a large space open at the top. This will allow the sauce to cook uncovered while the foil will catch splatters.

Once the sauce is reduced and thickened, add **salt, black pepper** and the remaining 1/3 of **Bourbon whiskey** measurement. Cook 1 more minute, taste, and add additional salt and pepper to taste. Remove from heat and follow instructions for "Make it a Freezer Meal" or "Make it Now!"

Note: *If the sauce is too acidic for your taste, add a bit of sugar or apple juice. If you're missing "punch" add more Chef Gail's BBQ Dry Rub and apple cider vinegar to taste. If you prefer to taste more of the Bourbon, add a little more at the end of the cooking process and remove from heat after one minute of cooking.*

MAKE IT NOW!

Remove wrapped ribs from the refrigerator, then set out on the counter for 1 hour to allow the meat to come to room temperature. Keep wrapped in foil during this un-chilling time.

OVEN METHOD

Preheat oven to 300°F (149°C). Place wrapped ribs on a baking sheet and cook for 3 hours. Check meat – if it doesn't pull easily from the bone, cook an additional 30 minutes to one hour.

OVEN & GRILL METHOD

Preheat oven to 300°F (149°C). Place wrapped ribs on a baking sheet and bake for 3 hours. Remove from oven and allow to rest 15 minutes. Prepare grill. Remove ribs from aluminum foil, then sear both sides over MEDIUM-HIGH heat for approximately 2 minutes per side. Move to the cooler side of the grill, cover with foil, and continue cooking another 15 to 20 minutes or until meat falls easily off the bone.

Brush with **Bourbon BBQ Sauce**, then serve with extra sauce on the side.

GRILL-ONLY METHOD

Place wrapped ribs in LOW heat grill (300°F (149°C) for 4 hours. Remove ribs from aluminum foil, then sear both sides over MEDIUM-HIGH heat for approximately 2 minutes per side. Move to the cooler side of the grill, cover with foil, and continue cooking another 15 to 20 minutes or until meat falls easily off the bone.

Brush with **Bourbon BBQ Sauce**, then serve with extra sauce on the side.

SMOKER METHOD

Set the smoker to a low temperature (250°F (121°C). Remove ribs from foil, place on smoker rack, and close lid. Smoke for 6 to 8 hours or until meat falls easily off the bone.

Brush with **Bourbon BBQ Sauce**, then serve with extra sauce on the side.

MAKE IT A FREEZER MEAL

Prepare ribs for freezing:

Option 1 – Freeze Raw:
- Place rack of rib in a vacuum-sealed bag or zippered freezer bag. If bags are not large enough to hold the entire rack, cut the rack in half or quarters before placing in the bag and sealing it.
- Remove as much air from the bag as possible before sealing.
- Apply label titled *"Bourbon BBQ Babyback Ribs - Uncooked"* to the outside of bag and place in freezer. Sauce for ribs will be prepared and packaged separately.
- When ready to serve, follow the cooking instructions on the label.

Option 2 – Partially Cook, Then Freeze:
- This is the method I typically recommend (versus packing the ribs raw) as it will allow you to enjoy the convenience of a quick meal with the freshness of "just cooked."
- Preheat oven to 300°F (149°C). Place wrapped ribs on a baking sheet and cook for 2-½ hours.
- Remove from oven. Open foil to allow hot air to escape. Place in refrigerator to cool.
- Once ribs are completely cooled, place rack of rib in a vacuum-sealed bag or zippered freezer bag. If bags are not large enough to hold the entire rack, cut the rack in half before placing in the bag and sealing it.
- Remove as much air from the bag as possible before sealing.
- Apply label titled *"Bourbon BBQ Babyback Ribs – Partially Cooked"* to the outside of bag and place in freezer. Sauce for ribs will be prepared and packaged separately.
- When ready to serve, follow the cooking instructions on the label.

MAIN DISH DINNER RECIPES | PORK

Prepare sauce for freezing:

- Pour sauce into a shallow baking dish so that sauce is not more than 2" (5cm) deep. Place in refrigerator to cool approximately 30 minutes, stirring after 15 minutes.
- Once the sauce is completely cooled, transfer to a freezable container for liquids (*see Chapter 3: Packaging Options & Recommendations*). Apply label titled "*Bourbon BBQ Sauce for Babyback Ribs.*"

FREEZER LABELS

Find and print freezer meal labels for this dish at www.frozenandfabulous.com. (See also "*Chapter 13: Quick Guide to Online Tools.*")

SUGGESTED PAIRINGS

SIDE DISH PAIRINGS

- Red Beans & Rice
- Southern-Style Grits
- Grilled Vegetables
- Potato Salad
- Cole Slaw

WINE AND/OR ALCOHOL PAIRINGS

- Beer
- Craft Beers, particularly Stout styles
- Belgian Saison
- American IPA
- Guinness Extra Stout
- Sparkling Wines (Prosecco or Cava)
- Red Wines (Bordeaux, California Cabernet or Barolo)

ONLINE RESOURCES

Scan this QR code for a direct link to an instructional cooking video for this recipe on www.frozenandfabulous.com, along with these helpful "How It's Done" videos.

- Preparing Ribs
- How to Speed Up Production with a Kitchen Scale

VARIATIONS

MAKE IT GLUTEN-FREE

This dish is naturally gluten-free. No changes are required.

MAKE IT VEGETARIAN

This BBQ Dry Rub pairs well with grilled eggplant, tofu or cauliflower.

You can also make "pulled jackfruit" and marry it with the Bourbon BBQ Sauce for lovely faux-pulled pork for sandwiches.

MAKE IT "FIT-FRIENDLY"

To save calories with this dish, exchange the babyback ribs for chicken breast. Also, to reduce calories in the sauce, reduce the amount of sugar and ketchup used.

MAKE IT BUDGET-FRIENDLY

To save money, choose pork loin roast cut into strips or chicken.

FISH & SEAFOOD

Seafood-Stuffed Portobello Mushrooms

Oooooh how I love this decadent surf and turf-inspired dish! The shrimp and bay scallops married with the earthiness of portobello mushrooms deliver beautiful texture and bold flavor for a hearty, enjoyable meal.

And damn... it's just so pretty!

I always make a little extra of this seafood-rich filling, then freeze individual portions for an extravagant pairing to a juicy, grilled steak. It's the perfect marriage of "special occasion" style dining with the ease of heat and serve.

You may be surprised to see goat and parmesan cheese in this recipe since cheese is not typically paired with seafood. However, they harmonize perfectly in this case, and the combination provides a lovely creaminess to the stuffing.

These stuffed portobellos will freeze beautifully if packaged correctly, so I have included detailed instructions with the recipe. However, it is important to know that raw portobellos don't freeze well, so cooking them prior to stuffing is an important step. If you don't have access to fresh, quality portobellos, you can make the stuffing, freeze it into individual portions, then finish the dish when portobellos come into season.

Whether you're making this dish to impress guests, or enjoying an indulgent, romantic meal for two, this dish is a show stopper!

Cheers to making every day a special occasion, and treating yourself like the guest of honor.

INGREDIENTS

No of Servings				
4		**6**	**10**	**14**
qty | msmt (weight)		qty | msmt (weight)	qty | msmt (weight)	qty | msmt (weight)
	PORTOBELLO MUSHROOMS			
4 ea (636g)	Portobello Mushrooms, avg 4.5" (11.25cm) wide, de-stemmed and cleaned	6 ea (954g)	10 ea (1590g)	14 ea (2226g)
2 TBSP (30mL)	Olive Oil	3 TBSP (45mL)	5 TBSP (75mL)	7 TBSP (105mL)
1 tsp (5g)	Sea Salt (fine)	1 ½ tsp (7g)	1 2/3 TBSP (12g)	2 ⅓ TBSP (17g)
1 tsp (2g)	Black Pepper	1 ½ tsp (3g)	1 2/3 TBSP (5g)	2 ⅓ TBSP (7g)
	SEAFOOD STUFFING			
4 TBSP (56g)	Butter (Salted)	6 TBSP (84g)	10 TBSP (140g)	14 TBSP (196g)
1 TBSP (15mL)	Olive Oil	1 ½ TBSP (23mL)	2 ½ TBSP (38mL)	3 ½ TBSP (53mL)
½ LB (228g)	Raw Shrimp, peeled and deveined, tail-off	¾ LB (342g)	1 ¼ LB (570g)	1 ¾ LB (798g)
½ LB (228g)	Small Whole Bay Scallops (80-120 scallops per pound (456g))	¾ LB (342g)	1 ¼ LB (570g)	1 ¾ LB (798g)
2 tsp (14g)	Salt, divided	3 tsp (21g)	5 tsp (35g)	2 ⅓ TBSP (49g)
1 tsp (2g)	Black Pepper, divided	1 ½ tsp (3g)	2 ½ tsp (5g)	3 ½ tsp (7g)
2 each (136g)	Carrots, medium-sized (sliced and cut into small-sized squares (small dice cut)	3 each (204g)	5 each (340g)	7 each (476g)
1 each (226g)	Medium Sweet White Onion, chopped into small squares (small dice cut)	1 ½ each (339g)	2 ½ each (565g)	3 ½ each (791g)
1 each (106g)	Red Bell Peppers, de-seeded and cut into small-sized squares (small dice cut)	1 ½ each (159g)	2 ½ each (266g)	3 ½ each (372g)
2 TBSP (30g)	Garlic Cloves, minced	3 TBSP (45g)	⅓ cup (75g)	½ cup (105g)
2 TBSP (1g)	Fresh Flat-Leaf Italian Parsley, finely chopped	3 TBSP (2g)	⅓ cup (3g)	½ cup (4g)
½ tsp (12g)	Crushed Red Pepper Flakes	¾ tsp (17g)	1 ¼ tsp (29g)	1 ¾ tsp (40g)
½ cup (50g)	Grated Parmesan Cheese, **divided**	¾ cup (74g)	1 ¼ cup (124g)	1 ¾ cup (174g)
½ cup (119g)	Chevre Goat Cheese	¾ cup (178g)	1 ¼ cup (296g)	1 ¾ cup (415g)
4 fl oz (63mL)	Milk (Whole or 2%)	6 fl oz (95mL)	10 fl oz (158mL)	14 fl oz (221mL)

NUTRITION FACTS:

Serving Size 11 oz **Calories** 210 **Total Fat** 8g **Total Carbohydrates** 15g **Protein** 19g

The portion size shown is based on industry dietary standards and may be smaller than the portion size allowed for in recipe.

INSTRUCTIONS

Prepare Portobello Mushrooms.
Preheat oven to 350°F (177°C).

Remove stems from the **portobello mushrooms**, then use a spoon to lightly scrape away the black gills on the bottom of the mushrooms without tearing or damaging the rounded caps. Use a paper towel to wipe away any dirt or leftover debris. (Never use water to clean mushrooms.)

MAIN DISH DINNER RECIPES | FISH & SEAFOOD

Brush the top and bottom of the cleaned portobello with **olive oil**, then sprinkle lightly on both sides with **sea salt** and **black pepper**.

Spray a baking sheet with non-stick spray, then place portobellos on the baking sheet cap-side facing up. Bake for 7 minutes in a preheated oven, remove from oven and allow to cool.

Prepare Shrimp and Scallops.

Heat **butter** and **olive oil** in a skillet over MEDIUM heat. Toss **shrimp** and **scallops** in the melted butter and oil and cook until opaque (*do not overcook – they will fully cook in 2 to 3 minutes*). Sprinke with a portion of the **salt** and **black pepper**. Remove shrimp and scallops, leave the juice and oils in the pan, and set aside.

Prepare Stuffing Mixture.

Increase oven temperature to 400°F (204°C).

In the reserved juice and oils in the pan over MEDIUM heat, cook the chopped **carrots** for about 2 minutes, then add in **onions**, and **red bell peppers** until onions are opaque. Add **garlic** until softened. The bell peppers and carrots should still be firm but tender. Add in 90% of the freshly chopped **parsley**, the remaining **salt** and **black pepper**, **red pepper flakes**, **goat cheese**, and **milk**. Gradually add in **¾ only of the parmesan cheese**, making sure to stir briskly while sprinkling in the parmesan to avoid it becoming clumped up and gummy.

> **Note:** It is SUPER IMPORTANT only to add ¾ of the parmesan cheese at this stage, and to sprinkle it in lightly while stirring. If not, it can become very gummy and won't melt properly.

Cook until the mixture is creamy and cheese is melted. Taste and adjust salt if needed. Add the cooked shrimp and scallops and stir together to distribute evenly. Remove from heat.

Place the cooked portobellos on a baking sheet, cap-side down. Divide the mixture evenly across the number of portobello mushrooms. Stuff the allocated portion of the mixture into the "bowl" of the underside of the portobello. Sprinkle the remaining ¼ of the **parmesan cheese** evenly over each of the filled mushrooms. Once it bakes, the parmesan will create a crust.

MAKE IT NOW!

Preheat oven to 400°F (204°C). Roast for 7 minutes or until parmesan cheese is lightly browned (like a crust). Remove from the oven and garnish with the remaining freshly chopped parsley. Allow to rest 5 minutes before serving.

> ### MIS EN PLACE
> 1. De-stem and clean portobello mushrooms.
> 2. Clean, devein and remove tails from shrimp.
> 3. Chop onion, red bell peppers, carrots, garlic and parsley.
> 4. Assemble remaining ingredients.

MAKE IT A FREEZER MEAL

Option 1: FOR MICROWAVE REHEATING

Preheat oven to 400°F (204°C). Roast for 7 minutes or until parmesan cheese is lightly browned (like a crust). Remove from the oven and garnish with the remaining freshly chopped parsley.

Place baked, stuffed portobellos in the refrigerator to cool completely. Once cooled, place in a freezer-safe, microwave-safe and/or oven-safe container with a tight sealing lid. The container should be large enough to allow the portobellos to stay upright without toppling over, and not stacked on top of each other inside the container.

> **Note:** *For single-serving meals, the Frozen & Fabulous single-serve microwaveable bowls with a vented lid are perfect for storing these stuffed portobellos. The lid is tall enough to accommodate the stuffing, the vented lid allows the excess steam to release so the mushroom doesn't become spongy, and they will reheat perfectly in the microwave. To extend shelf life, wrap the sealed bowl in a layer of plastic wrap before freezing.*

Place sealed container in the freezer.

Option 2: FOR OVEN REHEATING

Place stuffed portobellos in the refrigerator to cool completely. Once cooled, place in an oven-safe container with a tight sealing lid. The container should be large enough to allow the portobellos to stay upright without toppling over, and not stacked on top of each other inside the container.

Place sealed container in the freezer. Follow baking instructions on the label when ready to serve.

Option 3: IQF METHOD

Preheat oven to 400°F (204°C). Roast for 7 minutes or until parmesan cheese is lightly browned (like a crust). Remove from the oven and garnish with the remaining freshly chopped parsley.

Place baked, stuffed portobellos in the refrigerator to cool completely.

Once cooled, place portobellos on a baking sheet lined with parchment about ½" (1.3cm) apart, cover lightly with plastic wrap, then place in the freezer for 1 hour. This will allow each individual stuffed portobello to freeze (this is the IQF method discussed in *Chapter 2: From Planning to Plate*).

> **Note:** *Laying the piece of plastic wrap lightly across the top of the stuffed portobellos before freezing will reduce or eliminate frost accumulating on top of the mushrooms. This is important because too much moisture will cause mushrooms to have a rubbery consistency. If you see any frost on the mushrooms, simply brush it off with a paper towel or pastry brush before packaging.*

Once frozen, place the stuffed portobellos in a resealable zippered bag or vacuum-sealable bag and seal, making sure all air is removed. Apply label "*Seafood-Stuffed Portobello Mushrooms*" and follow reheating instructions when ready to serve.

FREEZER LABELS

Find and print freezer meal labels for this dish at www.frozenandfabulous.com. (See also "*Chapter 13: Quick Guide to Online Tools.*")

SUGGESTED PAIRINGS

SIDE DISH PAIRINGS

- Fresh seasonal green salad
- Roasted root vegetables
- Rice Pilaf
- Mushroom and Leek Risotto
- Grilled Steak (*the combination of steak and these stuffed portobellos create a decadent surf-and-turf meal*)

WINE AND/OR ALCOHOL PAIRINGS

- Vodka with citrus or simple soda
- Chardonnay
- Pinot Grigio
- Pinot Gris
- Riesling
- Pinot Noir

ONLINE RESOURCES

Scan this QR code for a direct link to an instructional cooking video for this recipe on www.frozenandfabulous.com, along with these helpful "How It's Done" videos."

- How to De-Shell, Clean and De-Vein Shrimp or Prawns
- How to Clean Mushrooms

VARIATIONS

MAKE IT GLUTEN-FREE	MAKE IT VEGETARIAN	MAKE IT "FIT-FRIENDLY"	MAKE IT BUDGET-FRIENDLY
This dish is naturally gluten-free when prepared as written.	Swap the shrimp and scallops for root vegetables, tofu or diced eggplant.	This dish is already high in protein and relatively low in calories. To make it more "fit friendly," simply reduce the portion size.	Buy frozen scallops and shrimp in resealable bags so you can use what you need and keep the rest for another dish.

FISH & SEAFOOD

Macadamia Nut-Crusted Halibut
with Raspberry Sauce

This is not your typical freezer meal, for sure! It's a fine dining experience from the comfort of home, offering an incredible taste and texture appropriate for even the most special of occasions, or making a casual night at home feel like one.

That's the beauty of a well-made freezer meal – it allows us to stop time for just a moment to engage and experience incredible food with people we love and enjoy. We frequently miss these moments when time is running at full speed, everyone heading in different directions, and take-out seems like the only option.

But that narrative changes when you can put a dish on the table that is this delicious, this decadent, and do it in 10 minutes or less. Do that, and you've created something far beyond just putting food on a plate.

So I hope you will truly savor every extraordinary bite of this dish and enjoy sharing it even more! This is the perfect dish to bring everyone to the table.

INGREDIENTS

No of Servings		4	6	10	14
		qty | msmt (weight)	qty | msmt (weight)	qty | msmt (weight)	qty | msmt (weight)
HALIBUT					
	Wild Caught Halibut, skin off, cut into 6 oz (170g) or 8 oz (226g) portions	4 each (680g)	6 each (1021g)	10 each (1701g)	14 each (2381g)
	Himalayan Sea Salt, finer grind	½ tsp (3g)	¾ tsp (4g)	1 ¼ tsp (7g)	1 ¾ tsp (10g)
FLOUR AND NUT BREADING MIXTURE					
	All-Purpose Flour	¼ cup (10g)	½ cup (15g)	¾ cup (25g)	1 cup (35g)
	Salt, divided	½ tsp (4g)	½ tsp (5g)	¾ tsp (9g)	1 tsp (12g)
	Black Pepper, divided	½ tsp (1g)	½ tsp (2g)	¾ tsp (3g)	1 tsp (4g)
	Macadamia Nuts, shelled	¾ cup (94g)	1 ½ cups (141g)	2 ¼ cups (234g)	3 cups (328g)
	Panko Bread Crumbs	¼ cup (34g)	½ cup (51g)	¾ cup (85g)	1 cup (119g)
	Fresh Flat-Leaf Italian Parsley Leaves, divided	2 tsp (<1g)	1 TBSP (<1g)	1 ½ TBSP (1g)	2 TBSP (1g)
DREDGING LIQUID					
	Eggs	2 each (86g)	3 each (129g)	5 each (215g)	7 each (301g)
	Coconut Milk or Water	1 TBSP (15mL)	2 TBSP (22mL)	3 TBSP (37mL)	4 TBSP (52mL)
FOR SEARING HALIBUT (OPTIONAL)					
	Butter (Salted)	1 TBSP (14g)	2 TBSP (21g)	3 TBSP (35g)	4 TBSP (49g)
	Olive Oil	1 ½ TBSP (21mL)	2 ¼ TBSP (32mL)	3 ¾ TBSP (53mL)	5 ¼ TBSP (74mL)
RASPBERRY SAUCE					
	Fresh Raspberries	1 cup (125g)	1 ½ cups (188g)	2 ½ cups (313g)	3 ½ cups (438g)
	Raw Sugar (Turbinado Sugar)	¼ cup (51g)	½ cup (76g)	¾ cup (127g)	1 cup (178g)
	Salt	1 pinch (<1g)	2 pinches (<1g)	⅛ tsp (1g)	¼ tsp (1g)

NUTRITION FACTS:

Serving Size 7 oz **Calories** 790 **Total Fat** 66g **Total Carbohydrates** 18g **Protein** 34g

The portion size shown is based on industry dietary standards and may be smaller than the portion size allowed for in recipe.

INSTRUCTIONS

Prepare Halibut.
Remove skin from the *halibut*, then cut into 6 to 8 oz (170g to 227g) portions.

> **Note:** *It's important to cut portions similar in size and thickness so they will cook evenly. If you have thinner pieces, it's a good idea to cook them separately from the thicker ones to avoid over-cooking.*

Sprinkle both sides of each piece with **Himalayan sea salt** and set aside on a rack to dry.

Prepare Nut Breading.
Place the **all-purpose flour** and HALF of the **salt** and **black pepper** in a shallow container, whisk together and set aside.

Place **all remaining ingredients for the nut breading**, including the second HALF of the **salt** and **black pepper**, into a food processor. Pulse lightly until incorporated and the nuts are chopped small. Do not over-process – you're looking for a chunky mixture, not a powder. Transfer mixture into a shallow container and set aside.

Prepare Dredging Liquid.
Place **eggs** and **coconut milk** (**or water**) in a shallow container, then whisk until egg is broken up and liquid is incorporated and set aside.

Perform the Breading Process.
If using the "Make it Now" process: Prepare a baking sheet and rack by placing a baking rack inside the baking sheet, then spraying both with non-stick pan spray. (Cooking the halibut on a rack will allow both sides of the fish to brown without having to turn over in the middle of cooking time.)

If making a Freezer Meal: Prepare a baking sheet covered with parchment paper, then spray with non-stick pan spray.

Pat halibut pieces dry on all sides with a paper towel. Each halibut piece must be dry before starting the breading process or the breading will not stick.

Step 1: Place halibut in the all-purpose flour and shake off any excess.

Step 2: Dip halibut in the **dredging liquid** and shake off any excess.

Step 3: Firmly press the halibut into the **nut breading mixture**, coating all sides of the fish with the nut breading.

Step 4: Place coated halibut on the prepared baking rack (or parchment-covered baking sheet).

Continue this process to coat all pieces in the nut mixture.

Make the Raspberry Sauce.
Place fresh **raspberries** into a dry skillet over MEDIUM-LOW heat. Add in the **raw/turbinado sugar**, stir well, and cook until the raspberries break down and the sauce is thickened and coats the back of a spoon. The process should take about 5 to 15 minutes, depending on the size of the batch.

If the sauce tastes too tart for your preference, add a bit more raw/turbinado sugar. When done, sprinkle with **salt**, stir, and remove from heat.

> **MIS EN PLACE**
> 1. Remove skin from Halibut and cut into 6 oz (170g) or 8 oz (227g) portions. As much as possible, create filets that are similar in size and thickness so they will cook evenly.
> 2. De-shell macadamia nuts.
> 3. Chop fresh parsley leaves.
> 4. Assemble remaining ingredients.

> **Note:** *It is not a good idea to substitute regular granulated sugar for the raw/turbinado sugar. It will not reduce in the same way, and the granulated sugar will create a runny, less robust sauce. If you do not have access to raw/turbinado sugar, brown sugar would be an okay substitute, although this sauce is best when prepared as written.*

MAKE IT NOW!

Preheat oven to 400°F (204°C).

> **Note:** *It is an option to sear the fish before finishing in the oven. Macadamia nuts will burn quickly, so if you choose this option use a MEDIUM level of heat and watch the nuts carefully. Once you reach the desired color, transfer to the oven to finish cooking. The cooking time required will be 3-5 minutes less than the oven-only method.*
>
> *You can freeze pre-seared pieces and finish cooking at time of service.*

Once the oven comes to temp, place the baking sheet and rack of halibut in the oven.

Bake for 10-12 minutes or until the fish is opaque and flakes easily with a fork (thicker pieces of Halibut could take longer) and crust is golden. The internal temperature of the fish needs to be 145°F (65°C). Do not overcook.

Allow fish to rest for 5 minutes, then serve with warmed raspberry sauce.

MAKE IT A FREEZER MEAL

The fish will be packaged raw.

Place breaded fish pieces on a parchment-lined tray in the freezer about ½" (1.3cm) apart so each piece will freeze individually. (This is the IQF method - *see Chapter 2: From Planning to Plate*.)

Once frozen, package in an air-tight oven-safe container or a resealable zippered or vacuum-sealable bag with all air removed. (If using a zippered or vacuum-sealable bag, wrap each individual piece in parchment paper before packaging.)

> **Note:** Since this dish is expensive to make, I highly recommend that you choose packaging that will extend shelf life and preserve its freshness. For example, if using an oven-safe container, wrap the outside in plastic wrap for additional protection. If using a zippered freezer bag, double-bag it. My preferred method for packaging this dish is a vacuum-sealable bag stored inside a zippered freezer bag.

Place the label *"Macadamia Nut-Crusted Halibut"* on the outside of the packaging. The best way to cook this dish at the time of service is in the oven after thawing.

Once the raspberry sauce is completely cooled, place it in a freezer-safe container, resealable zippered freezer bag, or a vacuum-sealable bag. Apply the label, *"Raspberry Sauce for: Macadamia Nut-Crusted Halibut,"* and follow the instructions at time of service.

Place both the packaged fish and sauce in a single, large resealable bag.

FREEZER LABELS

Find and print freezer meal labels for this dish at www.frozenandfabulous.com. (See also *"Chapter 13: Quick Guide to Online Tools."*)

SUGGESTED PAIRINGS

SIDE DISH PAIRINGS

- Haricot Vert or Green Beans
- Roasted Fingerling or New Potatoes
- Shaved Asparagus with Mixed Greens and Raspberry Vinaigrette
- Summer Squash
- Grilled Asparagus

WINE AND/OR ALCOHOL PAIRINGS

- Pinot Grigio
- Verdicchio
- Alsace Riesling
- Zinfandel

ONLINE RESOURCES

Scan this QR code for a direct link to an instructional cooking video for this recipe on www.frozenandfabulous.com, along with these helpful "How It's Done" videos.

- Dry/Wet/Dry Breading Method
- How to Sear Meat

VARIATIONS

MAKE IT GLUTEN-FREE	MAKE IT VEGETARIAN	MAKE IT "FIT-FRIENDLY"	MAKE IT BUDGET-FRIENDLY
Use gluten-free breadcrumbs.	Replace the halibut with eggplant sliced into ½" (1.3cm) thick "steaks."	Reduce the amount of, or eliminate, raspberry sauce.	Choose a less expensive fish, such as cod, and use less costly nuts.

MAIN DISH DINNER RECIPES | FISH & SEAFOOD

FISH & SEAFOOD

Glazed Salmon
(multiple varieties)

This isn't really a "recipe" – it's more of an instruction tool to help you make any kind of glazed salmon you could possibly want. The options are endless, and it is one of the easiest and healthiest dishes to keep on hand in your freezer.

INSTRUCTIONS & INFORMATION

Fresh or Wild-Caught?
I almost exclusively choose wild-caught salmon for freshness, flavor and quality. However, there is one exception to this rule: Norwegian farmed salmon. Norwegian salmon farms are organic and well-managed, resulting in salmon that, in many cases, are even superior to wild-caught since the fish are never exposed to unrestricted ocean space where there is a potential for contact with environmental contaminants.

However, the majority of farmed salmon is of terrible quality. The salmon are restricted from their natural behavior, which causes an unnatural color to their meat (hence the need for salmon farmers to add color additives). It's nasty. And the absolute worst farmed salmon comes from Chile, where bad farming practices are employed that are hurtful to the fish, the environment and the end product that lands on your plate. Please avoid farmed salmon (unless it's the organic kind that comes from Norway) and choose wild-caught whenever possible. The taste, texture and quality will make it well worth the additional expense.

Prepare Salmon.
When preparing salmon for freezer meals, you can choose skin on or off, according to your preference.

I recommend skin off for most freezer meal applications since the skin needs a good hard sear to taste good. If you sear before freezing, it won't hold through freezing and the skin will get over-moistened. When it comes time to heat and/or cook salmon after being frozen, it will be easier if you don't have to deal with a searing step. For those reasons, I do not recommend keeping the skin on *unless* you are prepared to sear it at the time of service.

To prepare salmon for freezer meals, remove the skin, then cut into 6- to 8-oz (170g to 227g) portions. When cutting into portions, keep an eye on thickness so the pieces are as evenly sized as possible to ensure an even cooking or reheating process.

Once the pieces are cut, I like to sprinkle both sides with Himalayan sea salt, or any sea salt that I may have on hand. It will bring out the flavor of the salmon, no matter what type of glaze you choose to use.

Save a step: Just purchase frozen pre-portioned salmon and keep it in the freezer. You can apply the glaze or sauce when you're ready to serve.

Glaze Options.
Gourmet jams and jellies work perfectly as a glaze for salmon. Some of my favorite spreads to pair with salmon are fig, raspberry, jalapeno, peach, plum, apricot, and strawberry-jalapeno.

The key is to find a high-quality jam – not the sugar-laden fake-fruit kind kids like on their PB&J's. Instead,

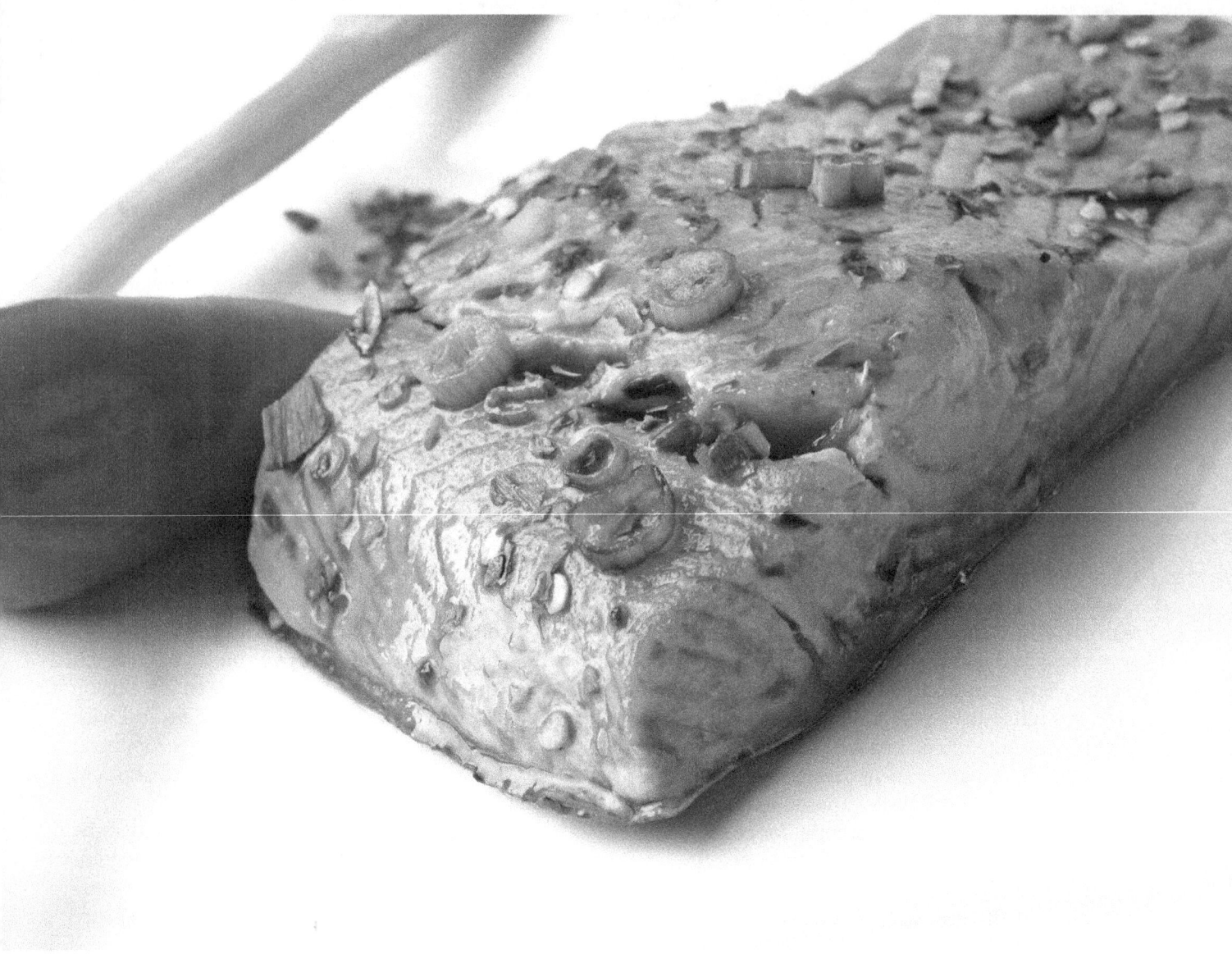

look for artisan-style jams and jellies made with real fruit and premium, natural ingredients.

For glazing sauces, choose a viscous, syrupy-style sauce that will brush on easily and adhere to the fish. Marinara sauce? No. Alfredo sauce? No. Teriyaki sauce? Yes. Maple syrup? Yes. Aren't sure? Try it on a small piece of salmon and see how you like it.

I have included some of my favorite glazing sauces to use with salmon in this cookbook.

- Teriyaki Sauce – see *Chapter 7: Grab & Go Lunch Recipes* under the recipe for **Teriyaki Chicken with Rice & Broccoli**.
- Raspberry Sauce – see *Chapter 8: Main Dish Recipes* under the recipe for **Macadamia Nut-Crusted Halibut with Raspberry Sauce**
- Fig & Honey Sauce – see *Chapter 8: Main Dish Recipes* under the recipe for **Prosciutto-Stuffed Chicken Breasts with Fig & Honey Sauce**.
- Blood Orange Glaze – see *Chapter 7: Grab & Go Lunch Recipes* under the recipe for **Blood Orange-Roasted Chicken**

Need more inspiration? Check out the **Index of Recipe Mix & Match Components** in the Resources section of this cookbook.

I also love to find new glazing sauces at the local Farmer's Market or gourmet grocery store. Creative chefs come up with new flavors every day, and a gorgeous piece of wild-caught salmon makes the perfect accompaniment.

The Glazing & Cooking Process.

MAKE IT NOW!

- Preheat oven to 425°F (220°C). Spray baking sheet with non-stick spray.
- Place **salmon** pieces that have been sprinkled with **sea salt** on a baking sheet, about 1" (2.5cm) apart.
- When oven temperature has reached 425°F (220°C), place in oven.
- Bake salmon for 5 minutes.
- Apply **glaze or sauce** generously to the top of each salmon piece. Place back in the oven.
- Bake for 5 minutes more, then test for doneness. Salmon is done when it easily flakes with a fork. (Internal temperature of the fish needs to be 145°F (65°C). **Do not overcook.**
- If not finished cooking, place back in the oven and recheck temperature in 1 to 3 minutes. Thicker pieces of salmon will take longer to cook than thinner, but even the thickest pieces of salmon will usually cook in less than 12 minutes.
- Remove from the oven and immediately apply a light layer of additional glaze or sauce, then allow salmon to rest for 5 minutes before serving.

Note: *The reason you don't glaze the salmon before it initially goes in the oven is because many glazes are high in sugar and will burn quickly. This process ensures even cooking for both the salmon and the glaze. If you use a low-sugar glaze or sauce, you can apply it at the beginning of the process.*

MAKE IT A FREEZER MEAL

Package and freeze the salmon and glaze/sauce separately.

When ready to serve, thaw the salmon and/or sauce and follow the "Make it Now!" instructions for glazing and cooking.

BUILD-YOUR-OWN SALMON BAR

I'm sure you've enjoyed or heard of the classic baked potato bar where you can choose your own toppings for a plain baked potato? Or a build-your-own pizza where you select the toppings just before your customized pizza is grilled or baked?

You can do the same with salmon. Give everyone a plain piece of salmon that has been sprinkled with sea salt and cooked for 5 minutes, then provide an assortment of glazes. Everyone can brush on their favorite glaze, bake it off in 5 to 10 minutes, and *voila*! A delicious, fun meal everyone will enjoy.

MAIN DISH DINNER RECIPES | CASSEROLES

CASSEROLES

Drunk Irishman's
Shepherd's Pie

I named this dish after the countless party-goers that have attended my Irish-themed catering events over the years. I love cooking for St. Patrick's Day parties and bringing yummy comfort food, green spirits and highly festive people together!

Irish Whiskey brings robust flavor to this hearty stew of lamb, chicken, sausage, fresh rosemary, carrots and spring peas all married together in a rich gravy. The fluffy, buttery mashed potatoes on top make this the perfect fall dish to cozy up with in front of the fire or grab friends and gather around the television for the football game. Great for groups, this dish is always a sure crowd-pleaser.

If you don't like the taste of alcohol, I recommend omitting the Whiskey from the mashed potatoes. I do this for my kids – they like the sauce with the whiskey flavor, but not the potatoes. This dish also pairs beautifully with Irish Soda Bread – so so good (although it makes the meal higher in carbs, if you're watching that sort of thing). I shared my favorite soda bread recipe on the website at www.frozenandfabulous.com so it's there if you want to try it.

And one more thing... this dish hosts three varieties of meat: Lamb, sausage and chicken. The ratios provided in the recipe provide my favorite blend of flavor, meatiness and texture; however, sometimes it can be a pain if you're only using a partial package of meat (recipe calls for ¾ lb of lamb... WTH do you do with the other ¼ lb)?

It's really okay to swap around the ratios of meat if that makes things easier. You just want a good balance of ground meats to chunky chicken for the best result. Or... just cook up the full packages of each meat, weigh out what is needed for this dish, then use the remainder in quick everyday dishes. I love to add this trio of meat to scrambled eggs, for example. Add some bell peppers, cheese and wrap in a tortilla and you have a pretty amazing breakfast burrito.

So enjoy... and "may your troubles be less and your blessings be more, and nothing but happiness come through your door."

And the luck o' the Irish cook right along with you!

INGREDIENTS

No of Servings					
4			**6**	**10**	**14**
qty | msmt (weight)			qty | msmt (weight)	qty | msmt (weight)	qty | msmt (weight)
MASHED POTATOES					
1 ¼ LB (570g)		Russet Potatoes, cleaned and peeled	2 LB (855g)	3 LB (1425g)	4 ½ LB (1995g)
1 TBSP (13g)		Kosher Salt	1 ½ TBSP (20g)	2 ½ TBSP (33g)	3 ½ TBSP (46g)
3 TBSP (42g)		Butter (Salted), softened	5 TBSP (63g)	8 TBSP (105g)	11 TBSP (147g)
5 fl oz (148mL)		Milk, Whole or 2%, warmed	7 fl oz (222mL)	12 fl oz (370mL)	17 fl oz (518mL)
½ tsp (4g)		Salt	¾ tsp (6g)	1 ¼ tsp (10g)	1 ¾ tsp (14g)
¼ tsp (1g)		Black Pepper	⅓ tsp (1g)	½ tsp (1g)	1 tsp (2g)
1 pinch (<1g)		Cayenne Pepper	2 pinches (<1g)	3 pinches (1g)	⅛ tsp (1g)
¼ cup (25g)		Parmesan Cheese, Grated	⅓ cup (37g)	½ cup (62g)	1 cup (87g)
1 TBSP (15mL)		Irish Whiskey	1 ½ TBSP (22mL)	2 ½ TBSP (37mL)	3 ½ TBSP (52mL)
SHEPHERD'S PIE FILLING					
3 fl oz (89mL)		Olive Oil, divided	6 fl oz (133mL)	9 fl oz (222mL)	12 fl oz (311mL)
¾ LB (342g)		Ground Lamb	1 LB (513g)	2 LB (855g)	2 ¾ LB (1197g)
¼ LB (114g)		Ground Italian or Chicken Sausage	½ LB (171g)	¾ LB (285g)	1 LB (399g)
1 TBSP (13g)		Salt, divided	1 ½ TBSP (20g)	2 ½ TBSP (33g)	3 ½ TBSP (46g)
1 tsp (2g)		Black Pepper, divided	1 ½ tsp (3g)	2 ½ tsp (5g)	3 ½ tsp (7g)
¼ LB (114g)		Boneless Chicken Thighs, cut into ½" (1.3cm) pieces	½ LB (171g)	¾ LB (285g)	1 LB (399g)
¼ cup (35g)		All-Purpose Flour, divided	½ cup (53g)	¾ cup (88g)	1 cup (123g)
1 rib (40g)		Celery, sliced into ¼" (.6cm) pieces	1 ½ ribs (60g)	2 ½ ribs (100g)	3 ½ ribs (140g)
1 ½ cups (129g)		Frozen Carrots, cut coin-style	2 ¼ cups (194g)	3 ¾ cups (323g)	5 ¼ cups (452g)
½ each (14g)		Medium Shallot, finely chopped	¾ each (21g)	1 ¼ each (35g)	1 ¾ each (50g)
1 each (6g)		Garlic Cloves, minced	1 ½ each (8g)	2 ½ each (14g)	3 ½ each (19g)
1 ½ tsp (2g)		Fresh Rosemary Leaves, finely chopped	2 ¼ tsp (3g)	3 ¾ tsp (5g)	5 ¼ tsp (6g)
¼ tsp (1g)		Ground Cinnamon	½ tsp (1g)	¾ tsp (2g)	1 tsp (3g)
¼ tsp (1g)		Ground Nutmeg	½ tsp (1g)	¾ tsp (2g)	1 tsp (2g)
8 fl oz (237mL)		Irish Whiskey, divided	12 fl oz (355mL)	20 fl oz (591mL)	28 fl oz (828mL)
14 fl oz (414mL)		Beef Stock or Broth (1st portion)	21 fl oz (621mL)	35 fl oz (1035mL)	49 fl oz (1449mL)
1 TBSP (18g)		Beef Base (*Chef Gail recommends "Better Than Bouillon Beef Base"*)	1 ½ TBSP (27g)	2 ½ TBSP (45g)	3 ½ TBSP (63g)
4 fl oz (118mL)		Sherry Wine	6 fl oz (177mL)	10 fl oz (296mL)	14 fl oz (414mL)
2 TBSP (32g)		Tomato Paste	3 TBSP (48g)	5 TBSP (80g)	7 TBSP (112g)
2 fl oz (59mL)		Beef Stock or Broth (2nd portion)	3 fl oz (89mL)	5 fl oz (148mL)	7 fl oz (207mL)

MAIN DISH DINNER RECIPES | CASSEROLES

½ cup (72g)	Frozen Peas	¾ cup (108g)	1 ¼ cup (180g)	1 ¾ cup (252g)
1 TBSP (14g)	Butter (Salted), cut into ½" (1.3cm) square pieces	2 TBSP (21g)	3 TBSP (35g)	4 TBSP (49g)
FINISHING SHEPHERD'S PIE				
2 TBSP (10g)	Parmesan Cheese, shredded	3 TBSP (15g)	5 TBSP (25g)	7 TBSP (35g)
½ TBSP (<1g)	Fresh Flat-Leaf Italian Parsley, finely chopped	1 TBSP (<1g)	1 ½ TBSP (<1g)	2 TBSP (1g)

NUTRITION FACTS:

Serving Size 8 oz **Calories** 370 **Total Fat** 16g **Total Carbohydrates** 25g **Protein** 20g

The portion size shown is based on industry dietary standards and may be smaller than the portion size allowed for in recipe.

INSTRUCTIONS

Boil Potatoes.
Clean and peel **potatoes**. Store peeled potatoes in a bowl of cold water until ready to boil. (This prevents the peeled potatoes from turning brown.)

Bring a large pot of water to boil over HIGH heat. Add in **kosher salt**.

> **Note:** *To reduce cooking time, cut the potatoes in half or quarters of consistent size.*

Once water is boiling, remove potatoes from cold water and add to the boiling water. Reduce heat and cook for 10-20 minutes or until potatoes are fork tender.

Strain potatoes, then place on a baking rack to dry. Make sure cooked potatoes are completely dry before proceeding to the next step (water will cause the potatoes to become gummy).

Finish Mashed Potatoes.
Push dry, peeled, boiled potatoes through a ricer and into a large bowl.

> **Note:** *If you don't have a ricer, then mash the potatoes by hand or with a mixer, being careful not to over-work them. Overworking or overmixing will create gummy potatoes.*

Warm **butter** and **milk** together in the microwave, then whisk in **salt**, **black pepper** and **cayenne pepper**. Pour this mixture over the riced potatoes, then add the shredded **parmesan cheese** and **Irish whiskey**. Gently fold all the ingredients together using a large spatula. Do not over-mix.

> ### MIS EN PLACE
> 1. Clean potatoes to prepare for roasting.
> 2. Cut chicken thighs into ½" (1.3cm) pieces.
> 3. Chop shallots, garlic and celery.
> 4. Chop fresh rosemary and parsley.
> 5. Measure remaining ingredients.

If available, load the finished potatoes into a large pastry bag and set them aside.

Cook Meats.
Heat ⅓ of the **olive oil** in a skillet over MEDIUM heat. Brown the **ground lamb** and **ground sausage** until cooked through (no longer pink). Toward the end of the cooking time, sprinkle with approximately ¼ each of the **salt** and **black pepper** quantities.

Drain meat and reserve the fat and juices in the pan. Set cooked meat aside.

In a separate container, dredge cut pieces of **chicken thighs** through HALF of the **all-purpose flour** until each piece is lightly coated.

Bring reserved fat and juices in the skillet, plus ⅓ of the **olive oil**, to MEDIUM heat, then add in the coated chicken pieces. Toss until browned and cooked through so no longer pink in the middle. Toward the end of the cooking time, sprinkle with approximately ¼ each of the **salt** and **black pepper**.

Drain cooked chicken and reserve any remaining fat or liquids. Set cooked chicken aside.

> **CHEF NOTES:**
>
> You may notice that the cooked meats don't get added into the stew until nearly the end of the stew's cooking time.
>
> This is on purpose. It prevents the meat from getting overcooked and becoming dry and tough.
>
> The flavors of the meats will still be deeply incorporated into the stew by using the pan drippings to cook the vegetables and aromatics.

Prepare Stew.
Bring reserved fat and juices in the skillet, plus ⅓ of the **olive oil**, to MEDIUM heat. Add chopped **celery** and **carrots**, cook for 1 to 2 minutes, and then add **shallot** until softened.

Add in minced **garlic**, chopped **rosemary leaves**, **cinnamon** and **nutmeg**. Toss together until rosemary and the spices have "bloomed," are very fragrant, and garlic is softened (about 1 to 2 minutes).

> **CHEF NOTES: LET'S TALK ABOUT MASHED POTATOES**
>
> When making mashed potatoes, water is the enemy! Water will make the potatoes gummy and starchy, so make sure you set them out on a rack to dry before mashing or mixing.
>
> Also, "less is more" when it comes to mixing potatoes. Over-mixing will create a tougher, gluey consistency. I prefer to use a Ricer to push the dry potatoes through, then mix in the warmed creaming ingredients using a fold-in technique.
>
> For more information on how to make delicious, fluffy and light mashed potatoes see the tutorial for this recipe on our website at www.frozenandfabulous.com.

> **Note:** *If pan is dry when ready to add the cinnamon and nutmeg, add a pinch of butter to the pan first, let it melt, then add the seasonings into the butter. This will give the spices the necessary fat to "bloom" properly.*

Add ¾ of the **Irish whiskey** and whisk to deglaze the pan, then add **beef stock (1st portion)**, **beef base**, **Sherry wine**, and **tomato paste**. Whisk together and bring to a boil, then reduce heat to MEDIUM-LOW and allow to simmer until sauce reduces, thickens and begins to coat the back of a spoon (about 30-40 minutes).

Add in cooked lamb, sausage and chicken.

To make the slurry, in a separate container whisk together the **beef stock (2nd portion)**, remaining HALF of the **all-purpose flour**, and ¼ each of the **salt** and **black pepper**.

While stew is boiling, whisk in the slurry, making sure to break up any lumps. Allow to simmer briskly for 3 minutes, then add in frozen **peas** and the remaining ¼ of the **Irish whiskey**. Allow to simmer for 1 minute more, then SWIRL in pieces of **butter** (do not stir). Continue swirling until butter is melted and incorporated into the sauce, then remove from heat.

Final Assembly of Shepherd's Pie.
Transfer filling to an **oven-safe** casserole dish. Choose a deep dish that will allow 2" to 3" (5cm to 7.5cm) of stew with ½" to 1" (1.3cm to 2.5cm) of potatoes on top. The correct ratio of stew to potatoes (in height) should be about 3 parts stew to 1 part potatoes.

Sprinkle evenly over the top: **Shredded parmesan cheese** and freshly chopped **Italian flat-leaf parsley**.

MAKE IT NOW!

Preheat oven to 350°F (176°C).

Bake for 30 minutes or until potatoes are golden brown.

MAIN DISH DINNER RECIPES | CASSEROLES

MAKE IT A FREEZER MEAL

Place assembled Shepherd's Pie, uncovered, in the refrigerator until it is completely cooled.

Once cooled: Spray aluminum foil with non-stick spray, then cover the Shepherd's Pie with the foil (sprayed side down).

Wrap foil-covered container in a second covering of aluminum foil, then wrap the entire container with plastic wrap. Apply label for *"Shepherd's Pie"* and place in freezer.

When ready to serve, follow reheating instructions on the label.

FREEZER LABELS

Find and print freezer meal labels for this dish at www.frozenandfabulous.com. (See also *Chapter 13: Quick Guide to Online Tools.*")

SUGGESTED PAIRINGS

SIDE DISH PAIRINGS

- Irish Soda Bread
- Corn Bread
- Crusty French Bread with Rosemary Butter

WINE AND/OR ALCOHOL PAIRINGS

- Spirits:
- Irish Whiskey
- Beer:
- Classic English Ale
- Guinness Draught Beer
- Stout or Porter Beer
- Wine:
- Red Pinot Noir
- Sangiovese
- Côtes-du-Rhône
- Red Rioja
- Red Bordeaux

ONLINE RESOURCES

Scan this QR code for a direct link to an instructional cooking video for this recipe on www.frozenandfabulous.com.

VARIATIONS

MAKE IT GLUTEN-FREE

Replace all-purpose flour with tapioca or rice flour, and use gluten-free versions of beef base and beef stock.

MAKE IT VEGETARIAN

Swap meats for mushrooms, eggplant and/or tofu. Replace beef stock and base for vegetarian versions.

MAKE IT "FIT-FRIENDLY"

Eliminate the all-purpose flour coating on the chicken pieces, and swap the all-purpose flour used in the slurry for cornstarch. To reduce calories, eliminate or reduce the butter used in both the stew and potatoes. Replace the mashed potatoes with pureed cauliflower and replace the chicken thighs with chicken breast.

MAKE IT BUDGET-FRIENDLY

Exchange ground beef for the lamb and sausage.

CHEF GAIL KURPGEWEIT @ASKCHEFGAIL

CASSEROLES

Roasted Vegetable
Lasagna (Vegetarian)

One of my favorite memories of this dish is when my friend, DeAnna, and I would stay up late into the night preparing it for my client, Microsoft. I turned this dish into single-serve grab-and-go meals sold in Microsoft cafés and a few other places in the Seattle area.

At the time, the manufacturing side of my business was new and I needed help. DeAnna was always the first to step up to help me in the kitchen – without pay - and she would hang in with me until all the orders were done. Sometimes that took two or three days, in a row, working 24/7, because we were so short-staffed and cash-strapped.

But when you have two great friends operating on no sleep, it can get pretty crazy. One day when we were both particularly exhausted and I had gotten a little salty with her, she yells across the table, "I love you, girl, but this is your dream, not mine!" My immediate gut response was, "This isn't my dream, either!" We both looked at each other - a little startled - like, "So what the hell are we doing here?!!" And then both burst out laughing – the kind of laughing that turns to crying from sheer exhaustion. If I had known how much work would be required to launch our frozen meals manufacturing division, I might have thought twice.

But as it turned out, I will forever cherish those days we spent in the kitchen making massive quantities of food, sometimes joined by my guardian angel and dear friend, Ellie Deets. We put out some fantastic products that were pivotal in taking my business to the next level. Other friends, too, came in and helped during those first days, and I will forever be grateful for their contributions because my business wouldn't have survived those days without them.

For freezer meal prep, using pre-cooked lasagna sheets makes this dish super quick to prepare, but you can also use traditional lasagna noodles. Just cook to al dente, rinse under cold water, and layer in the pan as instructed.

Have a meat-loving Italian in the family? Just add a layer or two of cooked Spicy Italian Sausage (add it along with the sauce). And don't be surprised if your Italian grabs your face in both hands, kisses you directly on the lips, and exclaims, "baciami sulle labbra è così delizioso!!"

MAIN DISH DINNER RECIPES | CASSEROLES

INGREDIENTS

No of Servings				
4 3 qt (88mL) casserole dish		**6** 4 qt (118mL) casserole dish	**10** split into 2 casserole dishes: 1 - 3 qt (88mL) and 1 - 4 qt (118mL)	**14** split into 3 casserole dishes: 1 - 3 qt (88mL) and 2 - 4 qt (118mL)
ROASTED VEGETABLES				
1 each (142g)	Zucchini, peeled and cut into half-moon-shaped pieces	1 ½ each (213g)	2 ½ each (354g)	3 ½ each (496g)
1 each (142g)	Yellow Squash, peeled and cut into half-moon-shaped pieces	1 ½ each (213g)	2 ½ each (354g)	3 ½ each (496g)
⅓ each (142g)	Eggplant, peeled and cut into medium-sized cubes	½ each (213g)	1 each (355g)	1 ¼ each (497g)
1 each (135g)	Bell Peppers, de-seeded and cut into medium-sized squares (diced)	1 ½ each (203g)	2 ½ each (338g)	3 ½ each (473g)
2 TBSP (30mL)	Olive Oil	3 TBSP (45mL)	5 TBSP (75mL)	½ cup (105mL)
¼ tsp (2g)	Salt	½ tsp (3g)	¾ tsp (4g)	1 tsp (6g)
⅛ tsp (<1g)	Black Pepper	¼ tsp (<1g)	⅓ tsp (1g)	½ tsp (1g)
TOMATO SAUCE MIXTURE				
2 (14.5 oz cans) (822g)	Fire-Roasted Diced Tomatoes, drained	3 (14.5 oz cans) (1233g)	5 (14.5 oz cans) (2055g)	7 (14.5 oz cans) (2877g)
2 each (6g)	Garlic Cloves, minced	3 each (8g)	5 each (14g)	7 each (20g)
¾ cup (23g)	Fresh Basil Leaves, cut into ribbons (chiffonade style)	1 ¼ cups (34g)	2 cups (56g)	2 ½ cups (79g)
¼ cup (27g)	Fresh Oregano leaves, finely chopped	½ cup (41g)	¾ cup (68g)	1 cup (95g)
½ tsp (4g)	Salt	¾ tsp (5g)	1 ¼ tsp (9g)	1 ¾ tsp (12g)
¼ tsp (1g)	Black Pepper	½ tsp (1g)	¾ tsp (1g)	1 tsp (2g)
RICOTTA CHEESE MIXTURE				
16 oz (454g)	Ricotta Cheese	24 oz (680g)	2 ½ oz (1134g)	3 ½ oz (1588g)
1 each (43g)	Eggs	2 each (64g)	3 each (106g)	4 each (149g)
¼ tsp (2g)	Salt	½ tsp (3g)	¾ tsp (4g)	1 tsp (6g)
CHEESE BLEND				
1 ¾ cups (174g)	Grated Parmesan Cheese	2 ⅔ cups (260g)	4 ½ cups (434g)	6 cups (608g)
1 ½ cups (170g)	Shredded Mozzarella Cheese	2 ¼ cups (255g)	3 ¾ cups (425g)	5 ¼ cups (595g)
NOODLES				
6 pieces (102g)	Lasagna Pasta Sheets (pre-cooked)	9 pieces (153g)	15 pieces (255g)	21 pieces (357g)

NUTRITION FACTS:

Serving Size 8.5 oz   **Calories** 280   **Total Fat** 12g   **Total Carbohydrates** 26g   **Protein** 17g

The portion size shown is based on industry dietary standards and may be smaller than the portion size allowed for in recipe.

CHEF GAIL KURPGEWEIT @ASKCHEFGAIL

INSTRUCTIONS

Prepare Roasted Vegetables.
Preheat oven to 375ºF (190ºC).

Clean and cut **zucchini, yellow squash, eggplant** and **bell peppers**. Brush or toss together with **olive oil, salt** & **black pepper**, then place on a baking sheet in a single level. Avoid piling the pieces on top of one another so you'll get a nice caramelization on each piece while roasting.

Roast vegetables in the oven for 3-5 minutes or until just fork-tender but not too soft. Remove from oven and set aside to cool.

Optional Roasting Method:
Cut vegetables in half lengthwise, roast until fork-tender, then cut into smaller pieces for layering.

For layering, slice roasted vegetables as follows:
- Zucchini and yellow squash, cut into half circles about ¼" (.6cm) thick
- Eggplant, cut into small squares (large dice cut)
- Bell Peppers, cut into small squares (large dice cut)

Prepare Tomato Sauce Mixture

In a bowl, mix together **fire-roasted diced tomatoes, garlic, fresh basil, fresh oregano, salt** and **black pepper**. Set aside and keep chilled.

> **Note:** *It's best to set the sauce mixture in a colander while assembling other ingredients. This allows the tomatoes to continue draining and you'll have a better result. Too much liquid in the tomatoes can result in soggy or watery lasagna.*

Prepare Ricotta Cheese Mixture
In a separate bowl, mix **ricotta cheese**, **eggs** and **salt**. Set aside and keep chilled.

Prepare Cheese Blend:
In a separate bowl, mix **parmesan cheese** and **mozzarella cheese**. Set aside and keep chilled.

Assemble Lasagna:
In the bottom of an **oven-safe** lasagna pan, spray with non-stick pan spray, then sprinkle a small amount of parmesan cheese on the bottom of the pan (this keeps the noodles from sticking).

> ### MIS EN PLACE
> 1. Clean, cut and prep zucchini, squash, eggplant and bell peppers for roasting.
> 2. Mince garlic, chop oregano and chiffonade fresh basil.
> 3. Assemble remaining ingredients.
> 4. Assemble all components of dish and set at workstation for organized assembly of lasagna layers.

Create layers:
BOTTOM: Place **pasta sheets** down to cover the bottom of the pan.

NEXT LAYER: Spoon a generous amount of **Tomato Sauce Mixture** over noodles.

NEXT LAYER: Spoon a generous amount of **Ricotta Cheese Mixture** on top of Tomato Sauce Mixture (it's okay if it swirls into the sauce a little).

NEXT LAYER: Sprinkle **Cheese Blend** to cover.

REPEAT: Add a layer of noodles, then continue with the layers of **Tomato Sauce Mixture**, **Ricotta Cheese Mixture** and **Cheese Blend**.

Continue repeating the layers (two to three times, depending on the height of the pan), ending with the **Cheese Blend** mixture on top. (This will create a nice crust on the top of your finished baked lasagna.)

MAKE IT NOW!

Preheat oven to 350ºF (176ºC).

Cover pan tightly with aluminum foil. If the cheese layer touches the foil, spray foil with a non-stick pan spray before placing it over the top.

Bake covered for 20 minutes, remove foil, and continue baking uncovered for another 20 minutes or until cheese is golden brown.

Remove from oven and allow to rest for 10 minutes before cutting and serving.

MAIN DISH DINNER RECIPES | CASSEROLES

MAKE IT A FREEZER MEAL (FAMILY STYLE):

DO NOT BAKE. Cover pan tightly with aluminum foil, then wrap the entire pan in plastic wrap.

Apply label titled *"Roasted Vegetable Lasagna."*

When ready to serve, follow cooking instructions on the label.

MAKE IT A FREEZER MEAL (SINGLE SERVINGS):

Preheat oven to 350°F (176°C).

Cover pan tightly with aluminum foil. If the cheese layer touches the foil, spray foil with a non-stick pan spray before placing it over the top.

Bake covered for 20 minutes, remove foil, and continue baking uncovered for another 20 minutes or until cheese is golden brown.

Remove from oven and allow to cool on the counter for 30 minutes.

Once the pan is cooled, transfer to the freezer for **1 hour**. This will allow the lasagna to partially freeze so it can be cut easily into individual pieces.

Remove pan from freezer and begin cutting single-portion pieces (about 12 oz (340g) each).

Place individual portions in a microwaveable, freezable container. Cover each individual portion tightly and apply the label titled *"Roasted Vegetable Lasagna"* to each one.

FREEZER LABELS

Find and print freezer meal labels for this dish at www.frozenandfabulous.com. (See also *"Chapter 13: Quick Guide to Online Tools."*)

SUGGESTED PAIRINGS

SIDE DISH PAIRINGS

- Garlic Bread
- Caesar Salad
- Grilled Asparagus

WINE AND/OR ALCOHOL PAIRINGS

- Languedoc Wine
- Roussillon Red Wine
- Medium Red Wines such as Merlot, Carmenere or Carignan

ONLINE RESOURCES

Scan this QR code for a direct link to an instructional cooking video for this recipe on www.frozenandfabulous.com.

VARIATIONS

MAKE IT GLUTEN-FREE

Use gluten-free lasagna noodles. If none are available, thinly slice squash or zucchini to create faux noodles.

MAKE IT "FIT-FRIENDLY"

This dish is already a very healthy choice, but the following options reduce calories even further:

- Replace noodles with high protein/low carb noodles or thinly sliced squash or zucchini "faux" noodles.
- Reduce the amount of cheese and exchange half of the ricotta cheese for low-fat cottage cheese.
- Use egg whites instead of the whole egg in the ricotta mixture.

MAKE IT BUDGET-FRIENDLY

The cheese blends used in this recipe are the most expensive items. To reduce cost, use fewer of these items or replace them with less expensive versions. For example, cottage cheese is an excellent exchange for ricotta cheese. You can also use more parmesan cheese to replace some of the mozzarella to reduce cost.

CASSEROLES

Chicken Enchiladas

Pull out the big batch pans because this is the kind of meal you'll want over and over again. Anyone you serve it to will oooh and aaaaah and beg for more.

This dish brings together a scrumptious marriage of chicken breast in rich chile pepper and cream sauce, wrapped in a flour or corn tortilla, and topped with a spicy red enchilada sauce and blend of Mexican cheeses. Pair with a salt-on-the-rim margarita on the rocks and you have yourself a fiesta!

I love to make a little extra of this dish and create a few "grab and go" single-serve meals for the freezer. These make a satisfying lunch-on-the-run, especially when paired with Spanish rice.

Fair warning, avoid the "super soft" or "extra soft" tortillas you'll find at the grocery store. These tortillas become very gummy during the cooking process. I highly recommend going with traditional flour tortillas for the best result (my favorite brand is Guerrero). Also, you can use corn tortillas if you prefer the flavor or if you're making the dish gluten-free; however, they frequently crumble during the rolling process. If you warm them gently in a dry skillet just before rolling, they will come together more easily for you.

There are many ingredients and steps to this recipe, but it really is simple to bring it all together. Just roast off the chicken and while it's cooking, start the sauce. Part of the sauce will be used for the chicken filling, so once the sauce and chicken are done, the filling will come together quickly. Then just roll, sear, garnish (and bake, if you're planning to eat it now).

And don't be surprised when you find yourself licking the plate... this one is just that good!

MAIN DISH DINNER RECIPES | CASSEROLES

INGREDIENTS

No of Servings				
4		**6**	**10**	**14**
3 qt (88mL) casserole dish		3 qt (88mL) casserole dish	6 qt (178mL) casserole dish	split into 2 casserole dishes: 2 - 4 qt (118mL)
	CHICKEN FOR FILLING			
1 ⅓ each (227g)	Boneless Whole Chicken Breasts, approx 6 oz (170g) each	2 each (340g)	3 ⅓ each (567g)	4 ⅔ each (793g)
	*Pre-brine with **Quick Brine for Chicken Breasts** (see Chapter 11: Meat Brines)			
1 TBSP (15mL)	Olive Oil	1 ½ TBSP (23mL)	2 ½ TBSP (38mL)	3 ½ TBSP (53mL)
⅛ tsp (1g)	Salt	¼ tsp (1g)	⅓ tsp (2g)	½ tsp (3g)
⅛ tsp (<1g)	Black Pepper	¼ tsp (<1g)	⅓ tsp (1g)	½ tsp (1g)
	ENCHILADA SAUCE			
1 tsp (14mL)	Olive Oil	1 ½ tsp (21mL)	2 ½ tsp (35mL)	3 ½ tsp (49mL)
⅓ each (75g)	Medium White Onion, chopped into small squares (small dice cut)	½ each (113g)	¾ each (188g)	1 each (264g)
1 each (6g)	Garlic Cloves, minced	1 ½ each (8g)	2 ½ each (14g)	3 ½ each (19g)
1 TBSP (5g)	**Chef Gail's Mexican Spice Blend** (see Recipe in Chapter 10: Spice Blends)	1 ½ TBSP (8g)	2 ½ TBSP (13g)	3 ½ TBSP (18g)
3 fl oz (710mL)	Water	4 ½ fl oz (1065mL)	7 ½ fl oz (1774mL)	10 ½ fl oz (2484mL)
2 fl oz (59mL)	Chicken Stock or Broth	3 fl oz (89mL)	5 fl oz (148mL)	7 fl oz (207mL)
1 TBSP (15mL)	Apple Cider Vinegar	1 ½ TBSP (22mL)	2 ½ TBSP (37mL)	3 ½ TBSP (52mL)
¼ tsp (1mL)	Worcestershire Sauce	½ tsp (2mL)	¾ tsp (3mL)	1 tsp (4mL)
2 tsp (10g)	Sugar	1 TBSP (15g)	1 ⅔ TBSP (25g)	2 ⅓ TBSP (35g)
2 tsp (11g)	Tomato Paste	1 TBSP (16g)	1 ⅔ TBSP (27g)	2 ⅓ TBSP (37g)
½ cup (133g)	Tomato Puree	¾ cup (200g)	1 ¼ cups (333g)	1 ¾ cups (466g)
¼ (4.5 oz can) (32g)	Diced Green Chiles (canned)	½ (4.5 oz can) (48g)	¾ (4.5 oz can) (79g)	1 (4.5 oz can) (111g)
½ tsp (3g)	Chicken Base (Chef Gail recommends "Better Than Bouillon Chicken Base")	¾ tsp (5g)	1 ¼ tsp (8g)	1 ¾ tsp (11g)
⅛ tsp (1g)	Salt	¼ tsp (<1g)	⅓ tsp (1g)	½ tsp (1g)
⅛ tsp (<1g)	Black Pepper	¼ tsp (<1g)	⅓ tsp (1g)	½ tsp (1g)
	FILLING (ADD TO CHICKEN)			
½ cup (63g)	Cauliflower Florets (fresh or frozen), cut into small pieces	¾ cup (94g)	1 ¼ cups (157g)	1 ¾ cups (219g)
1 TBSP (14g)	Cream Cheese	1 ½ TBSP (21g)	2 ½ TBSP (35g)	3 ½ TBSP (49g)
1 TBSP (15g)	Sour Cream	1 ½ TBSP (22g)	2 ½ TBSP (37g)	3 ½ TBSP (52g)

⅓ cup (84mL)	Milk (Whole or 2%), divided	½ cup (127mL)	⅔ cup (211mL)	1 cup (295mL)
4 fl oz (118mL)	**Red Enchilada Sauce** (see Recipe above)	6 fl oz (177mL)	10 fl oz (296mL)	14 fl oz (414mL)
1 TBSP (113g)	Mexican Cheese Blend (Monterey Jack, Cheddar, Asadero and Queso Quesadilla), shredded, divided	1 ½ TBSP (170g)	2 ½ TBSP (283g)	3 ½ TBSP (396g)
1 TBSP (113g)	Cheddar Cheese	1 ½ TBSP (170g)	2 ½ TBSP (283g)	3 ½ TBSP (396g)
¼ tsp (2g)	Salt	½ tsp (3g)	¾ tsp (4g)	1 tsp (6g)
½ tsp (1g)	Black Pepper	¾ tsp (2g)	1 ¼ tsp (3g)	1 ¾ tsp (4g)
4 each (164g)	7" (17.5cm) Flour or Corn Tortillas	6 each (246g)	10 each (410g)	14 each (574g)
GARNISH				
¾ cup (85g)	Mexican Cheese Blend (Monterey Jack, Cheddar, Asadero and Queso Quesadilla), shredded	1 cup (128g)	2 cups (213g)	2 ¾ cups (298g)
1 TBSP (5g)	Fresh Cilantro, finely chopped (1 avg bunch =1 cup (79g) chopped)	1 ½ TBSP (7g)	2 ½ TBSP (12g)	3 ½ TBSP (17g)

NUTRITION FACTS:

Serving Size 8.5 oz   **Calories** 350   **Total Fat** 13g   **Total Carbohydrates** 25g   **Protein** 32g

The portion size shown is based on industry dietary standards and may be smaller than the portion size allowed for in recipe.

INSTRUCTIONS

Prepare Chicken.
Place **chicken breasts** in **Quick Brine for Chicken Breasts** for 15 minutes. Remove from brine and place on a rack to dry.

Split **chicken breasts** in half. Place chicken breast on cutting board, place palm firmly on top to hold in place, then cut horizontally through the middle. (*See our online video, "How to Split a Chicken Breast."*)

Lay the breast pieces on the cutting board, cut side up, and cover lightly with plastic wrap. Pound with a mallet until the pieces are tenderized and approximately ½" (1.25cm) thick, being careful not to tear the meat. Remove plastic wrap.

Preheat oven to 375°F (190°C).

Brush both sides of chicken breasts with **olive oil** and sprinkle generously with **salt** and **black pepper**. Place chicken pieces on a baking sheet.

Roast for 10-12 minutes or until internal temperature reaches 155°F (68°C) with a stem thermometer. DO NOT GO OVER. The chicken will finish cooking with the sauce.

Allow chicken to rest for 5-10 minutes, then cut into 1" (2.5cm)-sized pieces.

Prepare Enchilada Sauce
In a saucepan or deep skillet, warm **olive oil** over MEDIUM-HIGH heat. Sauté **onions** until transparent, then add in minced **garlic** cloves until softened (about 1 minute). Add **Chef Gail's Mexican Spice Blend** and heat in the remaining oil until very fragrant. (If the pan is dry, add a little butter or olive oil before adding the spice blend so it will "bloom.")

Add in the liquids: **Water, chicken stock or broth, apple cider vinegar,** and **Worcestershire sauce**. Whisk well, then add in **sugar, tomato paste, tomato puree, diced green chiles, chicken base, salt** and **black pepper**. Whisk well, bring to a boil, then reduce heat to MEDIUM-LOW and allow to simmer.

Note: If you have trouble finding Tomato Puree at your local grocery store, substitute fresh or canned whole tomatoes that have been pureed in a food processor or blender. Another option is to mix equal parts tomato paste and water to create a similar flavor and texture.

While simmering, spoon off the orange foam that rises to the top (I call these "the bitters.") Allow the sauce to reduce by 20%.

Then taste - if the sauce is still bitter, add a bit more sugar. If you want a bit more "bite" add more apple cider vinegar. Add more salt and black pepper to taste. Remove from heat.

Make Filling.
Cook **cauliflower** in the microwave for 1 to 2 minutes until fork tender. (Or boil in lightly salted water for 3 to 4 minutes.)

Place cooked cauliflower into a blender or food processor. Add **cream cheese**, **sour cream**, and enough of the **milk** to cover without over-filling the container. Blend or puree until very smooth, then pour into a saucepan. Turn heat to MEDIUM-HIGH.

Add in remaining **milk** and the portion shown of **Red Enchilada Sauce**. (IMPORTANT: Do not add all the sauce, just the amount called for in the **Filling** part of the recipe.)

Whisk well, then stir in the **Mexican cheese blend**, **cheddar cheese**, **salt** and **black pepper**.

Bring to a boil, reduce heat to MEDIUM, and continue cooking until cheese is melted and sauce is smooth.

Add in diced chicken and reserved juices, continue cooking for 1 to 2 minutes. Taste and add additional salt and black pepper if needed.

Divide filling evenly across all the tortillas. Wrap up the filled tortillas tightly.

Bring a clean skillet to MEDIUM heat, spray with non-stick pan spray, then place the tightly rolled, stuffed tortillas into the pan, one or two at a time to avoid over-filling the pan. Sear the top and bottom until golden brown (about 1 minute per side).

> **MIS EN PLACE**
> 1. Prepare chicken by brining, roasting then cutting into 1" pieces.
> 2. Chop onion and garlic.
> 3. Chop fresh parsley for garnish.
> 4. Assemble remaining ingredients.

> **CHEF NOTES: LET'S TALK ABOUT TORTILLAS**
>
> I recommend using flour tortillas for this recipe. Although the flavor of a corn tortilla is nice, they frequently crumble during the roll-up process and don't hold well during freezing.
>
> When it comes to flour tortillas, please DO NOT use the "super soft" or "extra soft" varieties. These types of tortillas will become very gummy during the baking process, and even worse after freezing.
>
> Instead, make your own or choose an authentic Mexican brand tortilla (I personally love the Guerrero brand if I don't have time to make my own).

Transfer seared stuffed tortillas to an oven-safe casserole dish. Once all tortillas are in place, cover with **Red Enchilada Sauce**.

Apply Garnish: Top with shredded **Mexican Cheese Blend** and chopped fresh **cilantro**.

MAKE IT NOW!

Preheat oven to 375°F (190°C). Bake in a casserole dish, uncovered, for 20 minutes or until cheese is melted and sauce is bubbling. Serve with a dollop of sour cream.

MAKE IT A FREEZER MEAL

Once the entire casserole dish has cooled (sauce and filling), cover tightly with aluminum foil (spray the inside of the foil with non-stick spray). Wrap the entire container in plastic wrap once or twice, then apply the label *"Chicken Enchiladas."* Place in the freezer and follow reheating instructions when ready to serve.

FREEZER LABELS

Find and print freezer meal labels for this dish at www.frozenandfabulous.com. (See also *Chapter 13: Quick Guide to Online Tools.*)

SUGGESTED PAIRINGS

SIDE DISH PAIRINGS

- Spanish Rice.
- This dish also makes a great single-serve "Grab & Go" microwaveable meal. Place Spanish Rice at the bottom of the bowl, place 1 or 2 chicken-stuffed tortillas on top of the rice, pour some of the flavorful enchilada sauce on top, and then garnish with Mexican cheese blend and fresh cilantro. This dish is ready for freezing, then a quick heat-and-serve whenever you're ready to enjoy.
- If you're using *Frozen & Fabulous* microwaveable bowls with a vented lid, a 6" flour tortilla will fit perfectly.
- Grilled Corn Salad
- Cole Slaw
- Mexican-Style Cornbread

WINE AND/OR ALCOHOL PAIRINGS

- Mexican Beer
- Pinot Grigio
- Chenin Blanc
- Sangiovese
- Zinfandel
- Barberas

ONLINE RESOURCES

Scan this QR code for a direct link to an instructional cooking video for this recipe on www.frozenandfabulous.com, along with this helpful "How It's Done" videos.

VARIATIONS

MAKE IT GLUTEN-FREE

Use corn tortillas and check labels to make sure the chicken base and stock are both gluten-free versions.

MAKE IT VEGETARIAN

Swap the chicken breast for firm tofu cut into 1" (2.5cm) squares and marinated for 2 hours with a can of roasted, diced red peppers mixed with Chef Gail's Mexican Spice Blend.

MAKE IT "FIT-FRIENDLY"

This recipe allows for two enchiladas with sauce and cheese per portion. To save calories, reduce the portion size to one enchilada with sauce per serving.

MAKE IT BUDGET-FRIENDLY

Purchase a rotisserie chicken and use the meat to replace the chicken breast in this recipe. You'll be able to use the rest of the roasted meat as a meal or in other recipes, making it a more economical choice. You can also reduce the cost of ingredients by using a pre-made enchilada sauce.

MEATBALLS

Habanero, Turkey & Sausage Meatballs

I recently moved to Arizona (from my home state of Washington) and was looking for foods for my catering business that would represent the "Arizona experience."

This was the first recipe that my son-in-law, Nick, helped me test. Because we've lived far apart the last decade, he didn't realize that when I have food, I tend to share it with anyone within reach. I just like to feed people!

I walked up his driveway, meatballs in hand, where he was standing and visiting with a man who I hadn't previously met. I'll never forget the look on Nick's face when I offered these spicy meatballs to both of them. It turned out the man was a neighbor who Nick had only met a few minutes prior, and he wasn't expecting me to walk up and feed a stranger! It was hilarious to see the surprise on Nick's face – like, "what the hell is she doing?"

As it turns out, Nick has a wonderful discerning palate and gave me valuable feedback to make these meatballs just perfect.

These fiery bites are a lively fusion of Southwest flavors. The habaneros bring the heat, while fresh rosemary, oregano and goat cheese bring nuanced flavor and moisture for a scrumptious bite.

But what I love the most about these meatballs is how many flavor variations will pair so beautifully with them – the options seem endless.

My favorite is serving with bright Mango Salsa – the same version included in "Chapter 8: Main Dish Dinner Recipes" under **Cilantro-Grilled Chicken with Mango Salsa**. Another delicious pairing is **Mediterranean Salsa** with its piquant medley of tomato, olives and red onion. Find the recipe in "Chapter 8: Main Dish Dinner Recipes" under **Spinach & Feta Stuffed Chicken with Pesto & Mediterranean Salsa**.

When making this dish for kids who don't love spicy foods, you can turn down the heat by cutting the number of habaneros by half, or replacing them with a less spicy pepper such as jalapeno. For zero heat, while retaining the texture, use bell or banana peppers.

If you are working on a high-protein dietary lifestyle, these meatballs make a great snack, too. Just freeze some using the IQF method (see Chapter 2: From Planning to Plate), place in a resealable bag, and in just a minute or so in the microwave you'll have a delicious, satisfying protein boost.

So make a big batch – they're quick, easy and go with everything!

INGREDIENTS

No of Servings		4	6	10	14
		qty | msmt (weight)	qty | msmt (weight)	qty | msmt (weight)	qty | msmt (weight)
HABANERO, TURKEY & SAUSAGE MEATBALLS					
	Ground Pork Sausage	½ LB (228g)	¾ LB (342g)	1 ¼ LB (570g)	1 ¾ LB (798g)
	Ground Turkey	½ LB (228g)	¾ LB (342g)	1 ¼ LB (570g)	1 ¾ LB (798g)
	Habanero Peppers, de-seeded and cut into ⅛" (.3cm) small squares (brunoise cut) *Add 1 more per batch size for extra heat	2 ea (30g)	3 ea (45g)	5 ea (75g)	7 ea (105g)
	Medium White or Yellow Onion, shredded, with juice, or chopped into very small squares (petite dice cut)	¾ each (170g)	1 ¼ each (254g)	2 each (424g)	2 ¾ each (593g)
	Garlic Cloves, minced	2 each (11g)	3 each (17g)	5 each (28g)	7 each (39g)
	Fresh Oregano leaves, finely chopped	½ tsp (1g)	¾ tsp (2g)	1 ¼ tsp (3g)	1 ¾ tsp (4g)
	Fresh Rosemary Leaves, finely chopped	½ tsp (1g)	¾ tsp (1g)	1 ¼ tsp (2g)	1 ¾ tsp (2g)
	Panko Bread Crumbs	¼ cup (34g)	½ cup (51g)	¾ cup (85g)	1 cup (119g)
	Grated Parmesan Cheese	½ cup (50g)	1 cup (74g)	1 ½ cup (124g)	2 cups (174g)
	Chevre Goat Cheese	¼ cup (59g)	½ cup (89g)	¾ cup (148g)	1 cup (207g)
	Egg, whisked with fork	1 ea (43g)	2 ea (65g)	3 ea (108g)	4 ea (151g)
	Olive Oil	1 tsp (5mL)	1 ½ tsp (8mL)	2 ½ tsp (13mL)	3 ½ tsp (18mL)
	Italian Seasoning (dried)	1 TBSP (8g)	1 ½ TBSP (12g)	2 ½ TBSP (20g)	3 ½ TBSP (28g)
	Dark Chile Powder	1 tsp (3g)	1 ½ tsp (5g)	2 ½ tsp (8g)	3 ½ tsp (11g)
	Salt	1 tsp (7g)	1 ½ tsp (11g)	2 ½ tsp (18g)	3 ½ tsp (25g)
	Black Pepper	½ tsp (1g)	¾ tsp (2g)	1 ¼ tsp (3g)	1 ¾ tsp (4g)

NUTRITION FACTS:

Serving Size 6 oz   **Calories** 340   **Total Fat** 23g   **Total Carbohydrates** 9g   **Protein** 25g

The portion size shown is based on industry dietary standards and may be smaller than the portion size allowed for in recipe.

INSTRUCTIONS

Preheat oven to 375°F (190°C).
Combine **all listed ingredients for Habanero, Turkey & Sausage Meatballs** in a large mixing bowl. Mix well by hand or with a stand-mixer.

Testing for Seasoning Levels.
Once all ingredients are incorporated, remove a small portion of the mixture (approximately 1 TBSP (14g)) and cook over MEDIUM heat in a small skillet. Once cooked (takes 1-2 minutes), taste and adjust salt, pepper and crushed red pepper in the mixture as needed. Mix well, then continue testing for flavor by cooking 1 TBSP (14g) pieces until you are happy with the salt, pepper and seasoning levels – then the mixture is ready to form into meatballs.

Prepare to Bake Meatballs.
Place parchment or foil on a baking sheet and spray with non-stick pan spray. Form the mixture into 1-½" (3.8cm) round meatballs (about 1 oz (29g) each), then place on the baking sheet approximately ½" (1.3cm) apart.

MAIN DISH DINNER RECIPES | MEATBALLS

MIS EN PLACE

1. De-seed and chop habanero peppers. Avoid touching eyes while or after cutting until hands are washed, as the heat from the peppers can irritate eyes.
2. Chop onions, garlic, fresh oregano and rosemary.
3. Assemble remaining ingredients.

Bake meatballs at 375°F (190°C) for 15 to 20 minutes or until internal temperature reaches 165°F (74°C) with a stem thermometer. Allow to rest 5 minutes before serving or chilling.

MAKE IT NOW!

Meatballs are ready to eat after baking.

MAKE IT A FREEZER MEAL

Place cooled baking sheet in the freezer, making sure no meatballs are touching - this is the IQF method discussed in *Chapter 2: From Planning to Plate.* Allow to freeze for 30 to 45 minutes, or until each meatball is frozen. Transfer frozen meatballs into a resealable, zippered bag with all air removed. Attach label "Habanero, Turkey & Sausage Meatballs."

FREEZER LABELS

Find and print freezer meal labels for this dish at www.frozenandfabulous.com. (See also "*Chapter 13: Quick Guide to Online Tools.*")

SUGGESTED PAIRINGS

SIDE DISH PAIRINGS

- Pasta with Marinara Sauce
- Jasmine Rice with Mango Salsa or Mediterranean Salsa
- Mexican Rice Pilaf
- Spaghetti Squash
- Roasted root vegetables with oregano and rosemary-infused butter

WINE AND/OR ALCOHOL PAIRINGS

- Mango Habanero Vodka
- Sweet Riesling Wine
- Gewurztraminer Wine
- Sauvignon Blanc Wine
- Stella Artois Beer
- Corona Beer with Lime

ONLINE RESOURCES

Scan this QR code for a direct link to an instructional cooking video for this recipe on www.frozenandfabulous.com.

VARIATIONS

MAKE IT GLUTEN-FREE	MAKE IT VEGETARIAN	MAKE IT "FIT-FRIENDLY"	MAKE IT BUDGET-FRIENDLY
Exchange Panko breadcrumbs for gluten-free breadcrumbs.	Replace ground sausage and turkey with a mixture of 1/3 ground cauliflower, 1/3 ground mushrooms and 1/3 ground garbanzo beans.	Exchange the ground pork sausage for ground chicken or turkey sausage	Buy ground turkey and sausage in bulk, then use in multiple recipes at a reduced cost.

MEATBALLS

Swedish Meatballs
with White Gravy

This dish is most definitely one of my family's favorite, with yummy meatballs in an unctuous white gravy served over al dente ribbon pasta or buttery mashed potatoes. It is one of those meals where portion control goes out the door with everyone coming back for seconds or thirds.

I was introduced to this dish by my chef friend, Kay Conley. It was unique to find a freezable cream sauce that retained its' composition and flavor. I have used and expanded on her techniques to create really amazing, flavorful cream-based sauces for a variety of recipes.

My sweet new grandson, Oliver, especially loves these meatballs and sauce. I was babysitting him (he was about 18 months old at the time), and I gave him a little taste of sauce from the cooking pot while he sat on the counter "helping" me stir.

When Ollie wants something, he makes this little grunting sound. He makes the same sound when I'm singing to him and he wants a different song (yes, I'm happy to be his own personal Alexa). He is so adorable! He kept grunting until I gave him more, and quickly devoured an entire bowl which made my whole day! Of course, this one stays stocked in my freezer now and he knows right where to find it!

For freezer family meals, I recommend making the pasta at the time of service rather than pre-cooking and freezing; however, I have also included instructions for making this into a complete make-ahead meal with pre-cooked pasta or mashed potatoes. It makes a popular "flavor bowl" with a side, sauce and meatballs packed into individual portions in Frozen & Fabulous microwaveable bowls with vented lids (see Chapter 3: Packaging Options & Recommendations).

The best kinds of pasta to pair with this dish are cavatappi, medium-sized egg noodles, fusilli, mafalda, or tagliatelle. These meatballs are flavor-neutral and delicious paired with almost any style of sauce – marinara, alfredo, vodka, pesto and more.

So make a big batch - you'll enjoy every delightful bite!

MAIN DISH DINNER RECIPES | MEATBALLS

INGREDIENTS

No of Servings				
4		**6**	**10**	**14**
qty | msmt (weight)		qty | msmt (weight)	qty | msmt (weight)	qty | msmt (weight)
MEATBALLS				
1 TBSP (15mL)	Olive Oil	1 ½ TBSP (23mL)	2 ½ TBSP (38mL)	3 ½ TBSP (53mL)
½ each (113g)	Medium White Onion, chopped into small squares (small dice cut)	¾ each (170g)	1 ¼ each (283g)	1 ¾ each (396g)
3 each (17g)	Garlic Cloves, minced	5 each (25g)	8 each (41g)	11 each (58g)
¼ tsp (1g)	Ground Nutmeg	½ tsp (1g)	¾ tsp (2g)	1 tsp (2g)
1 each (43g)	Eggs	2 each (65g)	3 each (108g)	4 each (151g)
2 fl oz (59mL)	Milk (Whole or 2%)	3 fl oz (89mL)	5 fl oz (148mL)	7 fl oz (207mL)
1 tsp (5mL)	Worcestershire Sauce	1 ½ tsp (8mL)	2 ½ tsp (13mL)	3 ½ tsp (18mL)
2 slices (100g)	Brioche Bread, sliced ¾" (2cm) thick, cut into cubes	3 slices (150g)	5 slices (250g)	7 slices (350g)
1 LB (456g)	Angus Ground Beef (90/10 lean beef/fat ratio)	1 ½ LB (684g)	2 ½ LB (1140g)	3 ½ LB (1596g)
½ LB (228g)	Ground Italian Pork Sausage	¾ LB (342g)	1 ¼ LB (570g)	1 ¾ LB (798g)
2 tsp (6g)	Montreal Steak Seasoning (McCormick brand)	3 tsp (9g)	5 tsp (15g)	7 tsp (21g)
1 tsp (9g)	Salt	1 ½ tsp (13g)	2 ½ tsp (22g)	3 ¼ tsp (31g)
¾ tsp (2g)	Black Pepper	1 tsp (2g)	2 tsp (4g)	2 ½ tsp (5g)
WHITE GRAVY				
3 TBSP (42g)	Butter (Salted)	¼ cup (63g)	½ cup (105g)	2/3 cup (147g)
3 TBSP (30g)	All-Purpose Flour	¼ cup (45g)	½ cup (75g)	2/3 cup (105g)
20 fl oz (591mL)	Beef Stock or Broth	30 fl oz (887mL)	50 fl oz (1479mL)	70 fl oz (2070mL)
2 TBSP (28g)	Cream Cheese	3 TBSP (42g)	⅓ cup (70g)	½ cup (98g)
2 TBSP (30g)	Sour Cream	3 TBSP (45g)	⅓ cup (75g)	½ cup (105g)
½ tsp (3g)	Beef Base (Chef Gail recommends "Better Than Bouillon Beef Base")	¾ tsp (5g)	1 ¼ tsp (8g)	1 ¾ tsp (11g)
½ tsp (4g)	Salt	¾ tsp (5g)	1 ¼ tsp (9g)	1 ¾ tsp (12g)
¼ tsp (1g)	Black Pepper	½ tsp (1g)	¾ tsp (1g)	1 tsp (2g)
1 tsp (<1g)	Fresh Flat-Leaf Italian Parsley, finely chopped (for garnish)	1 ½ tsp (<1g)	2 ½ tsp (1g)	3 ½ tsp (1g)

NUTRITION FACTS:

Serving Size 8 oz   **Calories** 410   **Total Fat** 31g   **Total Carbohydrates** 16g   **Protein** 17g

The portion size shown is based on industry dietary standards and may be smaller than the portion size allowed for in recipe.

INSTRUCTIONS

Prepare Meatballs
Preheat oven to 375°F (190°C).

Heat **olive oil** in skillet over MEDIUM heat. Add in diced **onions** and cook until softened and almost translucent. Then add minced **garlic** and **nutmeg**. Toss together until the nutmeg begins to "bloom" and become aromatic, and the garlic is softened but not burned. Remove from heat and set aside to cool.

> **Note:** *If the pan is dry when it's time to add the garlic and nutmeg, add a bit of oil or butter before adding. The nutmeg will need a little fat in the pan to properly "bloom" or release its' flavor.*

In a large bowl, whisk together **eggs**, **milk** and **Worcestershire sauce**, then add **Brioche bread** pieces and toss them together by hand, keeping bread pieces intact without crushing. Allow bread to sit in the mixture 5 minutes to absorb the liquid, then add cooked onion, garlic and nutmeg, **ground beef**, **ground pork sausage**, **Montreal steak seasoning**, **salt** and **black pepper**.

Testing for Seasoning Levels
Once all ingredients are incorporated, remove a small portion of the mixture (approximately 1 TBSP (14g)) and cook over medium heat in a small skillet. Once cooked (takes 1-2 minutes), taste, then adjust salt, pepper and other seasonings in the mixture as desired. Mix well, then continue testing for flavor by cooking 1 TBSP (14g) pieces until you are happy with the salt, pepper and seasoning levels – then the mixture is ready to form into meatballs.

Place parchment or foil on a baking sheet and spray with non-stick pan spray. Firmly form the mixture into 1-½" (3.8cm) round meatballs, then place on the baking sheet approximately ½" (1.3cm) apart.

Cook Meatballs
Bake meatballs in 400°F (204°C) oven for 8-10 minutes or until golden brown and firm, but not fully cooked. Remove from oven and set aside.

Prepare White Gravy
Melt **butter** over MEDIUM heat, then whisk in **flour** to form a roux. Allow to cook 3 to 5 minutes, while whisking, until roux begins to brown and smell "nutty." Quickly whisk in HALF of the **beef stock** and bring to a boil. Whisk constantly until smooth, then add remaining **beef stock**, **cream cheese**, **sour cream** and **beef base**.

Reduce heat to MEDIUM-LOW and continue whisking until all ingredients are incorporated, the sauce is smooth, and the mixture is thickened (or starting to thicken).

When the partially-cooked **meatballs** are out of the oven, place into the **White Gravy** sauce. Allow to simmer over MEDIUM-LOW heat for 20-30 minutes, or until meatballs are cooked through and internal temperature reaches 165°F (74°C) with a stem thermometer.

When done, the meatballs should be cooked through to the proper temperature and the sauce thickened sufficiently to coat the back of a spoon.

Add **salt** and **black pepper** to taste.

> **Note:** *The sauce may be thickened slightly with heavy whipping cream, or thinned with milk, added at the end.*

MAKE IT NOW!

OPTIONAL: Prepare your favorite pasta by cooking in salted water until *al dente*; or prepare mashed potatoes to serve with the meatballs and sauce.

Serve the cooked meatballs in sauce over pasta or mashed potatoes, garnish with freshly chopped **parsley**, and enjoy!

MAKE IT A FREEZER MEAL

Option 1: Package Meatballs and Sauce Together.
When finished cooking, transfer meatballs and sauce into a 2" (5cm) deep container, then place in refrigerator to cool completely. Once cooled, store in a resealable zippered bag with all air removed, a vacuum-seal-able bag, or in a microwave- and freezer- safe container.

Attach label *"Swedish Meatballs with White Gravy,"* place in freezer, and follow reheating instructions when ready to serve.

Option 2: Package as a Meal
This packaging style is perfect for single-serving grab-and-go meals, similar to those found in *Chapter 7: Grab & Go Lunch Recipes*.

MAIN DISH DINNER RECIPES | MEATBALLS

MIS EN PLACE

1. Chop onions and garlic.
2. Cut bread into squares.
3. Chop fresh parsley for garnish.
4. Assemble remaining ingredients.

CHEF NOTES

The "coats the back of a spoon" thickening test for sauce will give you a good indication if the sauce is thickened correctly without over-thickening.

Dip a spoon into the sauce, then trace your finger across the back of the spoon. If there is a clear line where your finger ran across and the sauce doesn't immediately run to fill in the space, then it is perfect.

If you have over-thickened a sauce simply add more stock or flavorful liquid.

If you have under-thickened a sauce, whisk in cooked roux or a corn-starch slurry to the boiling sauce.

Transfer meatballs and sauce into a 2" (5cm) deep container, then place in refrigerator to cool completely.

For Pasta as a Side: Prepare pasta by cooking in salted, boiling water until **almost** *al dente*. Pasta should be firm and almost fully cooked, but not all the way. Remove pasta from boiling water and reserve the water. Set aside to cool.

Choose a freezer- and microwave-able safe container that will hold the desired portion sizes for time of service. Place cooled, par-cooked pasta in the bottom of the container, then add some of the cooled pasta cooking water, and toss lightly. (Use 2 TBSP (30mL) of the starchy water for every 1 cup (227g) of par-cooked pasta.)

Push the pasta over to one side of the container, then place the Meatballs in White Sauce on the other side.

Garnish with freshly chopped parsley. Seal the container and apply the label, *"Swedish Meatballs with White Gravy & Pasta."* Follow reheating instructions when ready to serve.

For Mashed Potatoes as a Side: Prepare mashed potatoes according to your favorite recipe.

Choose a freezer- and microwave-able safe container that will hold the desired portion sizes for time of service. Place the prepared mashed potatoes in the bottom of the container pushed to one side, then place a dollop of butter on top of the potatoes. Place the Meatballs in White Sauce on the other side of the container.

Garnish with freshly chopped parsley. Seal the container and apply the label, *"Swedish Meatballs with White Gravy & Mashed Potatoes."* Follow reheating instructions when ready to serve.

Option 3: Package Meatballs and Sauce Separately. Bake meatballs at 375°F (190°C) for 20 to 25 minutes or until internal temperature reaches 165°F (74°C) with stem thermometer.

Place cooled baking sheet in the freezer, making sure no meatballs are touching - this is the IQF method discussed in *Chapter 2: From Planning to Plate.* Allow to freeze for 30 to 45 minutes, or until each individual meatball is frozen. Transfer frozen meatballs into a resealable, zippered bag with all air removed. Attach label *"Swedish Meatballs."*

Transfer sauce into a 2" (5cm) deep container, then place in refrigerator to cool completely. Once cooled, store in a resealable zippered bag with all air removed, a vacuum-seal-able bag, or in a microwave- and freezer-safe container. Attach label *"White Gravy for: Swedish Meatballs"* and follow reheating instructions when ready to serve.

FREEZER LABELS

Find and print freezer meal labels for this dish at www.frozenandfabulous.com. (See also *"Chapter 13: Quick Guide to Online Tools."*)

SUGGESTED PAIRINGS

SIDE DISH PAIRINGS

- Pasta (*The best kinds of pasta to pair with this dish are cavatappi, medium-sized egg noodles, fusilli, mafalda, or tagliatelle*)
- Mashed Potatoes
- Pureed Cauliflower, Celery Root and Potato

WINE AND/OR ALCOHOL PAIRINGS

- Zinfandel
- Riesling
- Chardonnay
- Pinot Grigio
- Shiraz
- Shirah

ONLINE RESOURCES

Scan this QR code for a direct link to an instructional cooking video for this recipe on www.frozenandfabulous.com.

VARIATIONS

MAKE IT GLUTEN-FREE

For the Swedish Meatballs, swap the brioche bread for gluten-free bread and use a gluten-free version of Worcestershire sauce. For the White Gravy, swap the all-purpose flour for white rice flour and use gluten-free versions of beef stock and beef base.

MAKE IT VEGETARIAN

Choose pre-made, plant-based meatballs from the freezer section of your local grocery store or make your own by creating a mixture of ⅓ ground cauliflower, ⅓ ground mushrooms and ⅓ ground garbanzo beans. For the sauce, swap beef base and stock with vegetarian versions. This sauce would pair well with portobello mushrooms or cauliflower steaks.

MAKE IT "FIT-FRIENDLY"

For the Swedish Meatballs, swap the brioche bread for a low-calorie bread, use skim or 1% milk instead of 2% or whole, and swap the Italian pork sausage for chicken sausage.
For the sauce, use low-calorie cream cheese (Neufchatel) and swap plain yogurt for the sour cream. Serve with a puree of celery root, cauliflower and potato.

MAKE IT BUDGET-FRIENDLY

Swap the brioche bread for a cheaper version of white bread and swap all or some of the sausage for ground beef. You can also swap the cream cheese or sour cream for each other (use all sour cream or all cream cheese) to save money if you have more of one of these items on hand.

MEATBALLS

Spicy Italian
Meatballs with Marinara

You may literally jump out of your chair when you taste these meatballs! The spice level is on fire – which is my favorite way to enjoy meatballs with sweet marinara sauce.

I confess, I typically double the amount of crushed red peppers when I'm making these meatballs at home. For this cookbook, however, I toned down the heat so more people could enjoy it.

But if you love a spicy meatball, start with the quantity called for, cook a bit, taste and keep adding more crushed red peppers until you feel the heat with your whole body! It should shake you a little with its' invigorating kick and exciting flavor.

For the Marinara sauce, I designed this version to be simple and quick to prepare while still sweet, bright and delicious, while keeping the meatballs the star of the show.

If you would like to try my traditional version of Marinara sauce (which requires several hours to make), visit the Members Only section of our website at www.frozenandfabulous.com and search for "Chef Gail's Traditional Italian Sausage Marinara Gravy." It is authentically made and well worth the time and effort.

But for a stress-free weeknight or make-ahead meal, you'll love this quick and easy version that pairs beautifully with these lively meatballs.

They also make an excellent "flavor bowl" when packaged as an individual serving with pasta, sauce, meatballs, and steamed vegetables. Our Frozen & Fabulous microwaveable bowls with vented lids (see Chapter 3: Packaging Options & Recommendations) will ensure even heating (from frozen) in the microwave, and the vent will allow steam to release so the pasta won't overcook.

I recommend keeping plenty of these spicy little flavor bombs in the freezer – it's the perfect way to bring a bit of excitement to your day!

INGREDIENTS

No of Servings				
4		**6**	**10**	**14**
qty | msmt (weight)		qty | msmt (weight)	qty | msmt (weight)	qty | msmt (weight)
	SPICY ITALIAN MEATBALLS			
1 LB (456g)	Angus Ground Beef (90/10 lean beef/fat ratio)	1 ½ LB (684g)	2 ½ LB (1140g)	3 ½ LB (1596g)
1 LB (456g)	Ground Italian Sweet Sausage	1 ½ LB (684g)	2 ½ LB (1140g)	3 ½ LB (1596g)
2 TBSP (1g)	Panko Bread Crumbs	3 TBSP (1g)	⅓ cup (2g)	½ cup (2g)
¼ cup (25g)	Grated Parmesan Cheese	½ cup (37g)	¾ cup (62g)	1 cup (87g)
4 fl oz (118mL)	Milk (Whole or 2%)	6 fl oz (177mL)	10 fl oz (296mL)	14 fl oz (414mL)
1 tsp (5mL)	Worcestershire Sauce	1 ½ tsp (8mL)	2 ½ tsp (13mL)	3 ½ tsp (18mL)
2 TBSP (59mL)	Olive Oil	3 TBSP (89mL)	⅓ cup (148mL)	½ cup (207mL)
1 each (226g)	Medium White or Yellow Onion, chopped into small squares (small dice cut)	1 ½ each (339g)	2 ½ each (565g)	3 ½ each (791g)
4 each (38g)	Garlic Cloves, minced	6 each (57g)	10 each (95g)	14 each (132g)
1 TBSP (1g)	Fresh Flat-Leaf Italian Parsley, finely chopped	1 ½ TBSP (1g)	2 ½ TBSP (2g)	3 ½ TBSP (2g)
1 each (43g)	Eggs, whisked with fork	2 each (65g)	3 each (108g)	4 each (151g)
2 tsp (5g)	Italian Seasoning (dried)	3 tsp (8g)	5 tsp (13g)	7 tsp (18g)
1 TBSP (3g)	Dried Basil Leaves	1 ½ TBSP (5g)	2 ½ TBSP (8g)	3 ½ TBSP (11g)
1 TBSP (3g)	Dried Oregano	1 ½ TBSP (5g)	2 ½ TBSP (8g)	3 ½ TBSP (11g)
⅛ tsp (3g)	Crushed Red Pepper Flakes * *Adjust "spicy heat" level by increasing or reducing this ingredient.	¼ tsp (4g)	⅓ tsp (7g)	½ tsp (10g)
1 ½ tsp (11g)	Salt	2 ¼ tsp (16g)	3 ¾ tsp (26g)	5 ¼ tsp (37g)
1 tsp (2g)	Black Pepper	1 ½ tsp (3g)	2 ½ tsp (5g)	3 ½ tsp (7g)
	MARINARA SAUCE			
1 TBSP (15mL)	Olive Oil	1 ½ TBSP (23mL)	2 ½ TBSP (38mL)	3 ½ TBSP (53mL)
1 each (28g)	Medium Shallot, whole, peeled and rough-chopped	1 ½ each (43g)	2 ½ each (71g)	3 ½ each (99g)
4 each (38g)	Garlic Cloves, peeled & smashed	6 each (57g)	10 each (95g)	14 each (132g)
2 fl oz (59mL)	Red Wine	3 fl oz (89mL)	5 fl oz (148mL)	7 fl oz (207mL)
2 (14.5 oz cans) (822g)	Fire-Roasted Diced Tomatoes, with juice	3 (14.5 oz cans) (1233g)	5 (14.5 oz cans) (2055g)	7 (14.5 oz cans) (2877g)
½ tsp (1g)	Dried Basil Leaves	¾ tsp (1g)	1 ¼ tsp (1g)	1 ¾ tsp (2g)
½ tsp (1g)	Dried Oregano	¾ tsp (1g)	1 ¼ tsp (1g)	1 ¾ tsp (2g)
⅛ tsp (3g)	Crushed Red Pepper Flakes or Crushed Red Pepper Flakes * *Adjust "spicy heat" level by increasing or reducing this ingredient	¼ tsp (4g)	½ tsp (7g)	¾ tsp (10g)
½ tsp (4g)	Salt	¾ tsp (5g)	1 ¼ tsp (9g)	1 ¾ tsp (12g)
¼ tsp (1g)	Black Pepper	½ tsp (1g)	¾ tsp (1g)	1 tsp (2g)
5 each (<1g)	Fresh Basil Leaves, whole	8 each (<1g)	13 each (<1g)	18 each (1g)
½ TBSP (8g)	Sugar (as needed)	¾ TBSP (12g)	1 ¼ TBSP (20g)	1 ¾ TBSP (28g)

Serving Size 8 oz   **Calories** 370   **Total Fat** 21g   **Total Carbohydrates** 18g   **Protein** 30g

The portion size shown is based on industry dietary standards and may be smaller than the portion size allowed for in recipe.

INSTRUCTIONS

Prepare Meatballs.
Preheat oven to 375°F (190°C).

Combine **all listed ingredients** for **Spicy Italian Meatballs** in a large mixing bowl. Mix well by hand or with a stand mixer.

Testing for Seasoning Levels.
Once all ingredients are incorporated, remove a small portion of the mixture (approximately 1 TBSP (14g)) and cook over medium heat in a small skillet. Once cooked (takes 1-2 minutes), taste, then adjust salt, pepper and crushed red pepper in the mixture as desired. Mix well, then continue testing for flavor by cooking 1 TBSP (14g) pieces until you are happy with the salt, pepper and seasoning levels – then the mixture is ready to form into meatballs.

Prepare to Bake Meatballs.
Place parchment or foil on a baking sheet and spray with non-stick pan spray. Form the mixture into 1-½" (4cm) round meatballs (1 oz (29g) each), then place on the baking sheet approximately ½" (1.3cm) apart.

Bake meatballs at 375°F (190°C) for 20 to 25 minutes or until internal temperature reaches 165°F (74°C) with a stem thermometer. Allow to rest 5 minutes before serving or chilling.

Prepare Marinara Sauce.
Place **olive oil** in a saucepan over MEDIUM heat. Sauté **shallots** until softened and beginning to brown, then add in **garlic**. Stir until garlic is softened and the pan is nearly dry, then add **red wine** and stir to deglaze the pan. Continue cooking over MEDIUM heat until the wine is reduced by 20%.

Add **fire-roasted diced tomatoes, dried basil and oregano, crushed red pepper flakes, salt and black pepper.**
Allow to simmer for 5 to 10 minutes, then use a hand immersion blender to break up the ingredients and release juices from the tomatoes. Blend until the mixture is thickened with no large chunks of tomato or shallots, but do not overmix. The sauce will not be completely smooth – it should have a rustic texture (blended, not pureed).

While simmering, bright orange bubbles or foam will rise to the top of the sauce. I call this "the bitters." Skim off the bitters with the edge of a spoon and discard.

> **MIS EN PLACE**
> 1. Chop onion, garlic and fresh parsley for meatballs.
> 2. Chop shallot, garlic and remove fresh basil leaves from stem for Marinara sauce.
> 3. Assemble remaining ingredients for meatballs and sauce.

While simmering, add **fresh basil leaves**, whole and uncut, to rest on top of the sauce. Do not stir in. (*Stirring in would break down the basil leaves too early – you will extract more flavor by letting them simply sit on top of the sauce.*)

Continue simmering until sauce is reduced by 20%.

Taste and adjust. If the sauce is still a little bitter or acidic, add in the **sugar** and cook for 1 to 2 minutes and taste again. Add additional sugar, salt, black pepper and crushed red pepper flakes according to your taste preference.

> **Note:** There are two ways to counteract the bitterness of the tomatoes: Adding sweetness (like sugar or honey) or "cooking it out" which just takes time. To speed up the process, add a bit of sugar at the end of the cooking process. Adding at the end will prevent over-sweetening but achieve the desired effect of removing bitterness.

Remove from heat.

MAKE IT NOW!

Serve fully cooked meatballs with warm Marinara sauce. Optional: Serve over cooked pasta.

MAKE IT A FREEZER MEAL

Option 1: Package Meatballs and Sauce Together.
Cool sauce and meatballs completely in the refrigerator.

Package portions of meatballs and sauce together in a resealable zippered bag with all air removed, a vacuum-sealable bag or in a microwave- and freezer-safe container. Garnish with freshly chopped parsley. Attach label *"Spicy Italian Meatballs in Marinara Sauce,"* place in freezer, and follow reheating instructions when ready to serve.

Option 2: Package Meatballs, Sauce and Side Dish Together.
This packaging style is perfect for single-serving grab-and-go meals, similar to those recipes found in *Chapter 7: Grab & Go Lunch Recipes*.

Cool sauce and meatballs completely in the refrigerator.

For Pasta as a Side: Prepare pasta by cooking in salted, boiling water until **almost** *al dente*. Pasta should be firm and almost fully cooked, but not all the way. Remove pasta from boiling water and reserve the water. Set aside to cool.

Choose a freezer- and microwave-safe container that will hold the desired portion sizes for time of service. Place cooled, par-cooked pasta in the bottom of the container, then add some of the cooled water used for boiling the pasta, and toss lightly. (Use 2 TBSP (30mL) of the starchy water for every 1 cup of par-cooked pasta.)

Push the pasta over to one side of the container, then place the Marinara Sauce on the other side. Place meatballs on top of the Marinara Sauce.

Garnish with freshly chopped parsley. Seal the container and apply the label, *"Spicy Italian Meatballs with Marinara & Pasta."* Follow reheating instructions when ready to serve.

Option 3: Package Meatballs and Sauce Separately.
Place cooled baking sheet in the freezer, making sure no meatballs are touching - this is the IQF method discussed in *Chapter 2: From Planning to Plate*. Allow to freeze for 30 to 45 minutes, or until each individual meatball is frozen. Transfer frozen meatballs into a resealable, zippered bag with all air removed. Attach label *"Spicy Italian Meatballs."*

Transfer sauce into a 2" (5cm) deep container, then place in refrigerator to cool completely. Once cooled, store in a resealable zippered bag with all air removed, a vacuum-seal-able bag, or in a microwave- and freezer- safe container. Attach label *"Marinara Sauce for Spicy Italian Meatballs"* and follow reheating instructions when ready to serve.

FREEZER LABELS

Find and print freezer meal labels for this dish at www.frozenandfabulous.com. (See also *"Chapter 13: Quick Guide to Online Tools."*)

SUGGESTED PAIRINGS

SIDE DISH PAIRINGS

- Pasta (*The best pastas to pair with this dish are spaghetti, bucatini, penne, tagliatelle and vermicelli.*)
- Steamed Broccoli with Lemon and Garlic
- Garlic Toast
- Brussel Sprouts with Balsamic Vinegar and/or Parmesan Cheese
- Bruschetta
- Caesar Salad
- Grilled Asparagus
- Balsamic-Marinated Tomatoes & Mushrooms

WINE AND/OR ALCOHOL PAIRINGS

- Italian Red Wine
- Chianti
- Valpolicella (Ripasso variety)
- Lambrusco
- Cabernet Sauvignon
- Merlot

ONLINE RESOURCES

Scan this QR code for a direct link to an instructional cooking video for this recipe on www.frozenandfabulous.com.

VARIATIONS

MAKE IT GLUTEN-FREE

For the meatballs, exchange Panko bread crumbs for gluten-free bread crumbs and choose a gluten-free version of Worcestershire sauce. The Marinara sauce is naturally gluten-free as written.

MAKE IT VEGETARIAN

Choose pre-made, plant-based meatballs from the freezer section of your local grocery store or make your own by creating a mixture of 1/3 ground cauliflower, 1/3 ground mushrooms and 1/3 ground garbanzo beans. The Marinara sauce is vegetarian as written.

MAKE IT "FIT-FRIENDLY"

For the meatballs, swap the sweet Italian sausage for chicken sausage. For the sauce, omit the sugar and cook longer to remove the bitterness from the tomatoes.

MAKE IT BUDGET-FRIENDLY

Swap the beef and sweet Italian sausage for a cheaper grade of ground beef; otherwise, this dish is already inexpensive to prepare.

Chapter 9:
DROP & GO SLOW COOKER RECIPES

Coming home to a hearty, satisfying meal is never easier than when you simply pull from the freezer in the morning, drop in the crockpot, and go about your day.

But crockpot meals are notoriously terrible for being mushy in texture. It's nearly impossible to layer in complexity of flavor, get caramelization on meat and vegetables, or bloom spices and aromatics using traditional methods. Crockpot meals are popular because they're easy. But delicious? Not usually.

Until now. In this chapter, I share several recipes easily prepared in the crockpot for quick and easy drop-and-go meals. However, the "secret" to making these dishes truly enjoyable – in fact, a gourmet meal experience – is in the techniques shared in the instructions. I'm going to show you how to layer in loads of flavor, texture and aromatics to make memorable, crave-able meals you'll truly love for the taste, not just the convenience.

DROP & GO PACKAGING METHOD

For all the recipes in this section, if you want to create a customized "drop and go" package that can go **from the freezer directly into your crockpot**, the package must be a size that will fit. Once frozen, you'll be forced to thaw before cooking if it is too big for your crockpot.

To avoid this problem, it's super easy **to "shape and freeze"** the packaged food so it will fit into your crockpot even when frozen solid.

INSTRUCTIONS:

1. Before filling the bag with food, spray the inside with non-stick spray.

2. Apply instruction labels to the outside of the bag.

3. Place filled, labeled bag of food on a baking sheet.

4. Form the bag into a size and shape that will fit into your crockpot. You can use bags of frozen vegetables to help "hold" the shape during the freezing process.

5. Freeze for 1 to 2 hours so it retains its shape. Multiple bags can be placed on the baking sheet – just keep them all formed into the size/shape needed.

6. Once frozen enough to hold the shape and size, remove the baking sheet and store and stack bags as usual in your freezer.

For a demonstration of this technique, please see our helpful "how-to" video, "Shape & Freeze" Storage Technique for Crockpot Cooking" at www.frozenandfabulous.com.

BEST CUTS OF MEAT FOR CROCK-POT AND SLOW-COOKING METHODS

Choosing the right cut of meat is essential for successful crock-pot or slow-cooking methods to achieve pleasant moisture, flavor and texture.

BEEF

Choose blade, chuck, rump, brisket, clod, neck, leg, shin or foreshank, middle ribs, silverside or round pot roast, skirt or flank steak.

Avoid fillet, tenderloin, or sirloin.

For veal cuts, shoulder and knuckle work well with slow cooking methods, but all other cuts are not well-suited since veal has a high water content.

CHICKEN & POULTRY

All cuts of chicken, including whole chickens, can be cooked in the slow cooker using a braising or stew method. Roasting is better achieved in the oven to ensure maximum moisture retention.

Turkey cuts, specifically joints, can work well in the slow cooker using a high-liquid cooking method.

Duck breast is a good option for slow cooking methods, but remove large pieces of fat before cooking in a crockpot. The fat will not render as well with this method of cooking.

> **A note from the chef:** Always save the duck fat. It has incredible flavor and can be used when cooking with other oils and fats.

Game birds (pheasant, quail, wild duck) are great options for slow-cooking and braising methods.

LAMB

The best cuts of lamb for slow-cooking are the shoulder, leg, shanks, neck, breast, and chump. For higher-fat cuts, trim off most of the extra fat before cooking in the crockpot.

PORK & PORK SAUSAGE

Cured cuts of pork (whole bacon, ham and gannon) will perform well in the crockpot, but if already sliced, add at the end of the cooking time. Crispy bacon, for example, is an excellent last-minute-topping to your crockpot meals to add texture and flavor; or sliced, cubed ham can be added to a stew or soup near the end of cooking time, just long enough to heat through but not overcook.

DROP & GO SLOW COOKER RECIPES

Chunky Chicken
& Corn Chili

What started as a healthier chili option for my family has become one of our favorite go-to recipes for everyday meals. It is rich with flavor, easy to prepare, and satisfying to eat.

Whenever I get a day to do nothing but sit in my jammies and watch movies, this is one of my favorite dishes to have on hand. It's comfort food without the guilt!

It's also great for high-protein, low-carb eating plans. To reduce carbs even more, swap the frozen corn for frozen peas – still delicious!

This dish can be prepared in a Dutch oven or crockpot – either way, it comes together quickly and easily.

I also recommend packaging a few as single servings to keep in the freezer. These make a perfect heat-and-serve grab-and-go lunch or dinner. Delicious and super convenient - this will heat perfectly from frozen in the microwave.

So grab the big spoon - this will be your new favorite!

INGREDIENTS

No of Servings		4-5 Qt Crock Pot		6+ Qt Crock Pot
2 Qt Crock Pot				
4		**6**	**10**	**14**
qty | msmt (weight)		qty | msmt (weight)	qty | msmt (weight)	qty | msmt (weight)
	CHUNKY CHICKEN CHILI			
2 tsp (10mL)	Olive Oil	1 TBSP (15mL)	1 2/3 TBSP (25mL)	2 1/3 TBSP (35mL)
1 each (226g)	Medium Sweet White Onion, chopped into small squares (small dice cut)	1 ½ each (339g)	2 ½ each (565g)	3 ½ each (791g)
6 each (33g)	Garlic Cloves, minced	9 each (50g)	15 each (83g)	21 each (116g)
1 TBSP (14g)	Butter (Salted)	2 TBSP (21g)	3 TBSP (35g)	4 TBSP (49g)
1 ½ TBSP (14g)	Dark Chili Powder	2 ¼ TBSP (20g)	3 ¾ TBSP (34g)	5 ¼ TBSP (47g)
1 tsp (2g)	Ground Cumin	1 ½ tsp (3g)	2 ½ tsp (5g)	3 ½ tsp (7g)
1 tsp (2g)	Ground Coriander	1 ½ tsp (4g)	2 ½ tsp (6g)	3 ½ tsp (8g)
1 tsp (3g)	Ground Cinnamon	1 ½ tsp (5g)	2 ½ tsp (8g)	3 ½ tsp (11g)
1 LB (456g)	Boneless Chicken Thighs, cut into 1" (2.5cm) pieces	1 ½ LB (684g)	2 ½ LB (1140g)	3 ½ LB (1596g)
1 (15-oz can) (425g)	Tomato Sauce	1 ½ (15-oz cans) (638g)	2 ½ (15-oz cans) (1063g)	3 ½ (15-oz cans) (1488g)
2 (15-oz cans) (850g)	Dark Red Kidney Beans, rinsed and drained	3 (15-oz cans) (1275g)	5 (15-oz cans) (2125g)	7 (15-oz cans) (2975g)
1 ½ tsp (2g)	Dried Oregano	2 ¼ tsp (2g)	3 ¾ tsp (4g)	5 ¼ tsp (5g)
2 cups (255g)	Frozen Sweet Corn (whole kernels)	3 cups (383g)	5 cups (638g)	7 cups (893g)
1 pinch (<1g)	Cayenne Pepper	2 pinches (<1g)	1/8 tsp (<1g)	¼ tsp (1g)
1 tsp (7g)	Salt	1 ½ tsp (11g)	2 ½ tsp (18g)	3 ½ tsp (25g)
½ tsp (1g)	Black Pepper	¾ tsp (2g)	1 ¼ tsp (3g)	1 ¾ tsp (4g)

NUTRITION FACTS:

Serving Size 8 oz   **Calories** 170   **Total Fat** 2.5g   **Total Carbohydrates** 16g   **Protein** 21g

The portion size shown is based on industry dietary standards and may be smaller than the portion size allowed for in recipe.

INSTRUCTIONS

Prepare Onions, Garlic and Bloom Spices.
Warm **olive oil** in skillet or Dutch oven over MEDIUM-HIGH heat. Add chopped **onions** and cook until translucent, then add in minced **garlic** and **butter**. Once the garlic is softened and butter is melted, add dried spices: **dark chile powder, cumin, coriander** and **cinnamon**. Cook until spices are "bloomed" and aromatic.

Toss the **chicken** pieces into the mixture until the pieces are coated and starting to cook (about 3 minutes). (Chicken pieces will be raw in the middle and partially cooked on the outside.)

MAKE IT NOW!

Crockpot Method
Set crockpot temperature to HIGH.

Place the onion, spices and chicken mixture into the crockpot, then add the **tomato sauce, oregano** and **kidney beans**. Stir well, then cover tightly.

Cook for 4 hours on HIGH. Add in frozen **corn, cayenne pepper, salt** and **black pepper**. Stir well, cover tightly, and cook an additional 30 minutes on HIGH.

Taste and adjust salt and pepper levels, if necessary, then serve with a garnish of sour cream (optional).

MIS EN PLACE

1. Chop onions and garlic.
2. Cut chicken into 1" (2.5cm) pieces
3. Assemble remaining ingredients

Stovetop Method
Add **tomato sauce, kidney beans** and **oregano** to the onion, spices and chicken mixture. Stir well, then continue cooking until chicken is cooked through and reaches an internal temperature of 165°F (74°C) with a stem thermometer.

Add the frozen **corn, cayenne pepper, salt** and **black pepper** and stir well. Taste and adjust salt and pepper levels if necessary. Serve with a garnish of sour cream (optional).

MAKE IT A "DROP & GO" CROCKPOT FREEZER MEAL

Add **tomato sauce, kidney beans** and **oregano** to the onion, spices and chicken mixture. Stir well, then remove from heat and transfer to a small container. Place in the refrigerator until it has cooled completely.

Once cooled, place in a resealable zippered bag or vacuum-sealable bag and apply the label *"Chunky Chicken Chili – Step 1."* Freeze into a shape that will fit inside your crockpot using the "drop & go method" instructions provided at the beginning of this chapter.

In a second resealable zippered bag or vacuum-sealable bag, place the frozen **corn, cayenne pepper, salt** and **black pepper**. Seal and apply the label *"Chunky Chicken Chili – Step 2."* Since these ingredients will thaw while the Step 1 ingredients are cooking, there is no reason to freeze this bag into a particular shape.

Place both bags into a larger single resealable zippered bag for storage in the freezer, then follow cooking instructions on labels when ready to serve.

FREEZER LABELS

Find and print freezer meal labels for this dish at www.frozenandfabulous.com. (See also *Chapter 13: Quick Guide to Online Tools.*)

SUGGESTED PAIRINGS

SIDE DISH PAIRINGS

- Cornbread with honey
- Mashed potatoes
- Seasonal mixed greens salad

WINE AND/OR ALCOHOL PAIRINGS

- Corona Beer
- Stella Artois Beer
- Alsace Riesling
- Dry German Riesling
- Cava Sparkling Wine

ONLINE RESOURCES

Scan this QR code for a direct link to an instructional cooking video for this recipe on www.frozenandfabulous.com.

VARIATIONS

MAKE IT GLUTEN-FREE	MAKE IT VEGETARIAN	MAKE IT "FIT-FRIENDLY"	MAKE IT BUDGET-FRIENDLY
This dish is naturally gluten-free when prepared as written.	Swap the chicken for dice-cut butternut squash, turnips, potatoes, or a medley of wild mushrooms and tofu marinated in diced tomatoes.	This dish is already very low in calories and high in protein. To reduce carbs, swap the frozen corn for frozen peas.	This dish is already very inexpensive to prepare, but to save even more purchase chicken in bulk or on sale.

DROP & GO SLOW COOKER RECIPES

Guinness Pot Roast with Gravy

An update on classic pot roast, the Guinness beer used to slow braise beef chuck roast brings a rich, deep flavor to the meat and gravy. Serve with mashed potatoes and corn, and you have a true "home-style" meal everyone will enjoy. Plus, the leftovers make yummy sandwiches when paired with thick buttered French bread.

When choosing your beef roast, I recommend using a bone-in chuck roast for the best flavor and because the bone marrow will add silkiness to the gravy. If you don't have bone-in, you can "beef up" the taste of the sauce by adding a bit more of the beef base according to your taste preference. If your sauce is missing depth of flavor, a little more base and a pinch of salt will usually get you there.

The carrots, celery and onions used during the braising process will be DISCARDED at the end of the cooking time. I realize you (or your momma or grandma) may have traditionally cooked these vegetables with the meat and served them as a side dish, or you may have seen countless recipes that call for this, but I don't recommend it.

Why? Because the flavor of the carrots, celery and onion will be extracted from the vegetables to flavor the meat and gravy during the long cooking process. By the time the meat is cooked, the vegetables are over-cooked and mushy. Bottom line: They did their job and now they're over it!

If you want to serve carrots, potatoes or any other vegetables as a side dish, here are my recommendations:

- For carrots, new or fingerling potatoes, or other small root vegetables: About an hour before the end of the cooking time remove the original onion, carrot and celery and replace them with fresh vegetables. Finish cooking, and the vegetables will be done along with the meat and still be tender and flavorful.

- For whole potatoes, add at the beginning of the cooking process. Ensure there is plenty of room in the pot so the roast can heat evenly, and add additional salt and liquid (1:1 beef stock/Guinness beer), as the potatoes will absorb these elements.

So enjoy! I hope this dish will become one of your "new classics" like it did for me.

INGREDIENTS

No of Servings 2 Qt Crock Pot 4 qty | msmt (weight)		4-5 Qt Crock Pot 6 qty | msmt (weight)	10 qty | msmt (weight)	6+ Qt Crock Pot 14 qty | msmt (weight)
CHEESECLOTH BAG FOR AROMATICS				
3 each (3g)	Fresh Rosemary, whole sprigs	4 each (4g)	7 each (7g)	10 each (10g)
3 each (2g)	Fresh Thyme, whole sprigs	4 each (3g)	7 each (5g)	10 each (7g)
3 each (8g)	Garlic Cloves, peeled & smashed	4 each (13g)	7 each (21g)	10 each (29g)
2 TBSP (18g)	Whole Peppercorns (black or a medley of black, white, pink and green)	3 TBSP (27g)	4 TBSP (45g)	5 TBSP (63g)
GUINNESS POT ROAST				
2 ½ LB (1140g)	Beef Chuck Roast (bone-in) *For larger roasts, cut into 2 to 3 LB pieces	3 ¾ LB (1710g)	6 ¼ LB (2850g)	8 ¾ LB (3990g)
1 TBSP (4g)	Kosher Salt	1 ½ TBSP (6g)	2 ½ TBSP (11g)	3 ½ TBSP (15g)
½ TBSP (3g)	Black Pepper	¾ TBSP (4g)	1 ¼ TBSP (6g)	1 ¾ TBSP (9g)
3 TBSP (45mL)	Olive Oil	5 TBSP (68mL)	8 TBSP (113mL)	11 TBSP (158mL)
ROUX FOR GRAVY				
1 TBSP (14g)	Butter (Salted)	2 TBSP (21g)	3 TBSP (35g)	4 TBSP (49g)
1 TBSP (10g)	All-Purpose Flour	2 TBSP (15g)	3 TBSP (25g)	4 TBSP (35g)
BRAISING INGREDIENTS				
1 ½ each (102g)	Carrots, medium-sized, sliced 2" (5cm) pieces	2 ½ each (153g)	4 each (255g)	5 ½ each (357g)
1 each (99g)	White or Yellow Onion, peeled & sliced into ½" (1.25cm) slices	1 ½ each (149g)	2 ½ each (248g)	3 ½ each (347g)
2 ribs (102g)	Celery, sliced into 1" (2.5cm) pieces	3 ribs (153g)	5 ribs (255g)	7 ribs (357g)
5 fl oz (148mL)	Beef Stock or Broth	8 fl oz (222mL)	13 fl oz (370mL)	18 fl oz (518mL)
8 fl oz (237mL)	Guinness Draught Beer	12 fl oz (355mL)	20 fl oz (591mL)	28 fl oz (828mL)
GUINNESS BEEF GRAVY				
as available	Reserved Pan Drippings, strained	as available	as available	as available
5 fl oz (148mL)	Beef Stock or Broth	8 fl oz (222mL)	13 fl oz (370mL)	18 fl oz (518mL)
8 fl oz (237mL)	Guinness Draught Beer	12 fl oz (355mL)	20 fl oz (591mL)	28 fl oz (828mL)
1 tsp (6g)	Beef Base (Chef Gail recommends "Better Than Bouillon Beef Base")	1 ½ tsp (9g)	2 ½ tsp (15g)	3 ½ tsp (21g)
1 tsp (1g)	Fresh Rosemary Leaves, finely chopped	1 ½ tsp (2g)	2 ½ tsp (3g)	3 ½ tsp (4g)
1 tsp (1g)	Fresh Thyme Leaves, finely chopped	1 ½ tsp (1g)	2 ½ tsp (2g)	3 ½ tsp (3g)
1 pinch (<1g)	Cayenne Pepper	2 pinches (<1g)	⅛ tsp (<1g)	¼ tsp (1g)
1 pinch (<1g)	Salt	2 pinches (<1g)	⅛ tsp (1g)	¼ tsp (1g)
1 pinch (<1g)	Black Pepper	2 pinches (<1g)	⅛ tsp (1g)	¼ tsp (1g)
2 tsp (<1g)	Fresh Flat-Leaf Italian Parsley, finely chopped, for garnish	1 TBSP (1g)	1 ½ TBSP (1g)	2 TBSP (2g)

NUTRITION FACTS:

Serving Size 8 oz   **Calories** 230   **Total Fat** 16g   **Total Carbohydrates** 1g   **Protein** 17g

The portion size shown is based on industry dietary standards and may be smaller than the portion size allowed for in recipe.

INSTRUCTIONS

Prepare Cheesecloth Cooking Bag for Aromatics.
Lay out a double layer of cheesecloth flat on the counter. Place the **rosemary, thyme, garlic** and **peppercorns** in the center, then pull up all four corners of the cheesecloth to create a bag. Tie into a secure knot or tie off with kitchen twine.

Sear the Roast.
Pat the **roast** dry with paper towels, then sprinkle generously on all sides with **kosher salt** and **black pepper**.

Heat **olive oil** in a cast-iron skillet over HIGH heat. When the oil is hot and shimmering, sear the roast on all sides for about 4-5 minutes per side. (For helpful tips on how to properly sear meat, see the link to our "how it's done" video at the end of this recipe.) Remove from heat and set aside.

Prepare Roux for Gravy.
In a small skillet, melt the **butter**, then whisk in the **flour** to create a roux. Cook while whisking until the mixture is dark brown and has a nutty aroma. Remove from heat and set aside until ready to prepare the gravy.

MAKE IT NOW!

Crockpot Method
Set crockpot temperature to HIGH.

Place the **carrots, onion** and **celery** on the bottom of the pot, then place the seared roast on top.

Pour the **beef stock** and **Guinness beer** over the top of the roast, making sure it is about 50% covered.

> **Note:** *If your pot is too big and the roast isn't at least 50% covered, add more liquids (equal parts Guinness beer and beef stock).*

Add in the **cheesecloth bag of aromatics**, making sure it is fully submerged in the liquid.

Cover tightly and cook on HIGH for 5 hours or on LOW for 8 hours. (If cooking on low, always start on HIGH for at least 30 minutes.)

About an hour before the cooking is finished for this step, set the ingredients listed under "Guinness Gravy" on the counter to come to room temperature.

MIS EN PLACE

1. Wrap rosemary, thyme, garlic and peppercorns in cheesecloth and tie up to make a bag.
2. If working with a larger roast, cut into 2 to 3 LB (912g to 1368g) pieces to ensure even cooking.
3. Chop celery, carrots, and onion.
4. Chop fresh rosemary, thyme and parsley for the gravy.
5. Assemble remaining ingredients.

Make the gravy.
Remove roast, onion, celery, carrots and bag of aromatics from the crockpot, leaving behind the liquids.

In the crockpot set to HIGH heat, bring the reserved liquids to boil. Whisk in the **cooked roux** until all lumps are gone and the roux is incorporated into the liquids.

> **Note:** *Some crockpots will not get hot enough to perform this step. If the liquids are not coming to a boil quickly enough, transfer to a saucepan and build the sauce on the stovetop.*

Add to the liquids: **Beef stock or broth, Guinness beer, beef base, rosemary, thyme, cayenne pepper, salt,** and **black pepper**. Whisk well.

Bring back to a boil, then return the roast to the crockpot.

Cover tightly and cook on LOW for 1 to 2 hours, or until meat is tender and pulls apart easily with a fork, and the gravy is thickened enough to coat the back of a spoon.

Inside the crockpot, or on a cutting board, use a fork and knife to break apart the beef roast into 2" (5cm) chunks. Taste and add salt and black pepper, if needed.

Taste the gravy and add cayenne pepper, salt and black pepper if needed.

It's ready to serve – just garnish with freshly chopped **parsley**.

Note: *The gravy should be thick enough to coat the back of a spoon. If it needs to be thickened after cooking, make more roux and whisk in, or create a slurry with 1 TBSP (14g) corn starch to ¼ cup (59mL) of cold water and add to the boiling gravy. With either method, allow the sauce to continue cooking for 5 minutes after adding the thickening mixture.*

CHEF NOTES: WHY A CHEESECLOTH BAG?

The reason to create the cheesecloth bag for these aromatics instead of cooking the individual ingredients along with the meat is because once the meat is cooked and all the flavoring elements discarded, you'll need to cut the meat into chunks.

The full-size rosemary leaves and peppercorns are wonderful for adding flavor but not pleasant to eat (peppercorns can break your teeth). Once the meat is cooked, these items are super annoying to find, pick and remove.

The cheesecloth bag solves this problem, while letting the ingredients do their job to flavor the dish.

If you don't have cheesecloth, then I recommend omitting or crushing the peppercorns and finely chopping the rosemary and thyme before adding to the meat. You can leave the garlic cloves whole and smashed as they will be easy to find when the roast is done and will transmit more flavor than if they were chopped or minced.

Oven & Stovetop Method
Preheat oven to 300°F (149°C).

Spray the bottom of a roasting pan and rack with non-stick spray. Place the **carrots, onion** and **celery** on the bottom of the pan, then place the **seared roast** on the roasting rack.

Pour the **beef stock** and **Guinness beer** over the top of the roast, making sure it is about 50% covered.

Note: *If your roasting pan is too big and the roast isn't at least 50% covered, add more liquids (equal parts Guinness beer and beef stock).*

Add in the **cheesecloth bag of aromatics**, making sure it is fully submerged in the liquid.

Cover tightly and cook at 300°F (149°C) for 3 hours or until meat is tender and parts easily with a fork. Depending on the size of the roast, cooking time could take up to 4-5 hours. You'll know it's done when the meat is fall-apart tender when pulled with a fork.

Remove roast from the pot and set on a cutting board. Cut into 2" (5cm) chunks. Taste and add salt and black pepper if needed. Cover with a tent of aluminum foil while finishing the gravy.

Make the gravy.
Strain the **pan liquids** into a skillet or saucepan, discarding the cooked onion, celery, carrots and bag of aromatics.

Bring the pan liquids to a boil over MEDIUM-HIGH heat, then whisk in the **cooked roux** until all lumps are gone and the roux is incorporated into the liquids.

Add to the liquids: **Beef stock or broth, Guinness beer, beef base, rosemary, thyme, cayenne pepper, salt,** and **black pepper.** Whisk well.

Reduce heat to LOW, then continue cooking until reduced by $1/3$ and sauce is thickened to the point it coats the back of a spoon.

Taste and add salt and black pepper if needed.

Toss the beef with gravy, reserving extra gravy to serve as a side sauce.

Garnish with freshly chopped **parsley**.

Note: *The gravy should be thick enough to coat the back of a spoon. If it needs to be thickened after reducing by one-third, make more roux and whisk in, or create a slurry with 1 TBSP (14g) corn starch to ¼ cup (59mL) cold water and add to the boiling gravy. With either method, allow the sauce to continue cooking for 5 minutes after adding the thickening mixture.*

MAKE IT A "DROP & GO" CROCKPOT FREEZER MEAL

Add the following items to resealable zippered or vacuum-sealed bags:

Bag #1:
Cheesecloth bag of aromatics
Seared, cooled roast
All the ingredients listed under "Braising Ingredients"
Apply label "*Guinness Pot Roast with Gravy – Step 1 of 2*"
Freeze into a shape that will fit inside your crockpot using the "drop & go method" instructions at the beginning of this chapter.

Bag #2:
Cooked, cooled Roux (individually packaged)
All the ingredients listed under "Guinness Gravy"
Apply label "*Guinness Pot Roast with Gravy – Step 2 of 2*"
(*This bag will have time to thaw before freezing on the day of service, so there's no need to freeze it into any particular shape.*)
Place both bags into a larger single resealable zippered bag for storage in the freezer. Follow cooking instructions on label on day of service.

FREEZER LABELS

Find and print freezer meal labels for this dish at www.frozenandfabulous.com. (See also "*Chapter 13: Quick Guide to Online Tools.*")

SUGGESTED PAIRINGS

SIDE DISH PAIRINGS
- Buttery Mashed Potatoes
- Roasted Carrots and Root Vegetables
- Roasted New Potatoes or Fingerling Potatoes with Rosemary-infused Butter
- Celery Root Puree

WINE AND/OR ALCOHOL PAIRINGS
- Guinness Draught Beer
- Cabernet
- Sauvignon
- Merlot
- Syrah
- Pinot Noir
- Zinfandel Red

ONLINE RESOURCES

Scan this QR code for a direct link to an instructional cooking video for this recipe on www.frozenandfabulous.com, along with this helpful "How It's Done" video."

- The "Shape & Freeze" Storage Technique for Crockpot Cooking

VARIATIONS

MAKE IT GLUTEN-FREE
Swap the all-purpose flour used in the roux for white rice flour and choose a gluten-free beer to replace the Guinness Draught Beer

MAKE IT VEGETARIAN
Sorry, my vegetarian friends – this dish is all about the beef!

MAKE IT "FIT-FRIENDLY"
To reduce calories, exchange the roux for a corn starch/cold water slurry to help thicken the gravy, and reduce portion size. Also, serve with plenty of roasted vegetables for an extra boost of healthy goodness.

MAKE IT BUDGET-FRIENDLY
Find beef on sale, then make a big batch! The cooked roast will easily reheat for sandwiches, or as an add-in to a cheesy pasta to yield several meals for the same cost. You can also swap the Guinness Draught Beer for a cheap, dark beer.

DROP & GO SLOW COOKER RECIPES

Carolina-Style BBQ
Pulled Pork

Tender, slow-cooked pork is married with a vinegar-based Carolina-style BBQ Sauce (inspired by my chef friend, Kay Conley) for the perfect balance of sweet and savory. It is absolutely divine! So simple to prepare, this dish is ideal for drop-and-go crockpot cooking convenience.

For an authentic Southern-style BBQ experience, serve this pork on toasted rolls or slider buns with a bit of coleslaw on top. The crunchy creaminess of the slaw is the perfect accent to the juicy pork and makes a memorable meal from the simplest of ingredients.

Cooking for a large group? This pulled pork is perfect for a DIY backyard catering – it's both delicious and affordable to make for a crowd. Place the cooked pork and sauce in a chafing dish to keep it hot, then let guests build their own pulled pork sandwiches by providing a variety of rolls, breads and condiments.

*You may also want to make a little extra of the **BBQ Dry Rub**, as you will find it useful in other recipes in this collection, including Bourbon Babyback Ribs. It's a vigorous spice blend that will add a delicious flavor profile to your own BBQ recipes, so keeping extra on hand will serve you well.*

Just add a bit of sweet tea and sunshine, and you'll have yourself a little slice of Southern any day of the week.

DROP & GO SLOW COOKER RECIPES

INGREDIENTS

No of Servings 2 Qt Crock Pot		4-5 Qt Crock Pot	6+ Qt Crock Pot	
4 qty | msmt (weight)		**6** qty | msmt (weight)	**10** qty | msmt (weight)	**14** qty | msmt (weight)
PORK				
2 ½ LB (1140g)	Boneless Pork Loin Roast	3 ¾ LB (1710g)	6 ¼ LB (2850g)	8 ¾ LB (3990g)
	* Pre-brine with **Overnight Brine for Pork** (see *Chapter 11: Meat Brines*)			
¼ cup (36g)	**Chef Gail's BBQ Dry Rub** (see Recipe in *Chapter 10: Spice Blends*)	½ cup (54g)	¾ cup (91g)	1 cup (127g)
SOUTHERN-STYLE BBQ SAUCE				
5 fl oz (148mL)	Apple Cider Vinegar	8 fl oz (222mL)	13 fl oz (370mL)	18 fl oz (518mL)
1 TBSP (15g)	Spicy Brown Mustard	1 ½ TBSP (23g)	2 ½ TBSP (38g)	3 ½ TBSP (53g)
½ cup (128g)	Ketchup	¾ cup (192g)	1 ¼ cup (320g)	1 ¾ cup (448g)
¼ cup (57g)	Brown Sugar, firmly packed	½ cup (86g)	¾ cup (143g)	1 cup (200g)
¼ cup (57g)	Sugar	½ cup (86g)	¾ cup (143g)	1 cup (200g)
3 each (17g)	Garlic Cloves, minced	5 each (25g)	8 each (41g)	11 each (58g)
3 TBSP (27g)	**Chef Gail's BBQ Dry Rub** (see Recipe in *Chapter 10: Spice Blends*)	4 ½ TBSP (41g)	½ cup (68g)	2/3 cup (95g)
½ tsp (5g)	Salt	¾ tsp (7g)	1 ¼ tsp (11g)	1 ¾ tsp (16g)
½ tsp (5g)	Black Pepper	¾ tsp (7g)	1 ¼ tsp (11g)	1 ¾ tsp (16g)

NUTRITION FACTS:

Serving Size 6 oz   **Calories** 380   **Total Fat** 12g   **Total Carbohydrates** 29g   **Protein** 40g

The portion size shown is based on industry dietary standards and may be smaller than the portion size allowed for in recipe.

INSTRUCTIONS

Brine Meat
Place **boneless pork loin roast** in **Overnight Brine for Pork** for 12 to 24 hours. Remove the pork loin from the brine. Brush away the aromatics and pat dry with a paper towel.

Prepare Pork for Braising
If you don't already have it on hand, prepare **Chef Gail's BBQ Dry Rub** and set it aside.

Cut pork loin roast into evenly sized pieces, approximately one pound (456g) each. Apply **BBQ Dry Rub** mixture to all sides of each piece of pork. Set aside for 30 minutes to let Rub absorb into the meat.

Prepare Sauce
Whisk together the **list of ingredients under "Southern-Style BBQ Sauce"** in a saucepan over MEDIUM heat. Bring to a boil, then reduce heat and simmer for 10 minutes or until thickened. The sauce should coat

the back of a spoon. Taste and adjust salt and black pepper as needed.

MAKE IT NOW!

Preheat oven to 300°F (149°C).

Wrap rubbed pork pieces tightly in aluminum foil, then place in a covered baking pan. Add an inch of water to the bottom of the baking pan and cover.

Roast for 3 hours, then remove from oven and carefully open a small area of aluminum foil to test meat for doneness.

Using two forks, try to pull the meat apart. If it pulls apart easily, it is done. If not, or if it feels a little tough, close up the foil and continue cooking another 45 to 60 minutes or until meat is very tender.

When meat is done, unwrap and remove the aluminum foil. Reserve the juices. Transfer the pork to a large bowl or baking dish and remove all the large pieces of fat.

Then begin pulling apart (shredding) the pork using two forks.

Once shredded, pour HALF of the reserved juices over the pork to moisten. Mix together, then add additional pan juices as needed to make the meat moistened but not too wet. Let stand 10 minutes.

Pour enough of the **BBQ Sauce** over the meat to coat well, stirring to ensure all pieces are covered. More sauce may be needed for the pork later once it has absorbed some of the initial amount of sauce so reserve any extra.

MAKE IT A PRE-COOKED DROP & GO CROCKPOT FREEZER MEAL

Prepare and cook the pork according to the "Make it Now!" instructions above.

Cool the pork thoroughly, then package in a zippered freezer bag or vacuum-sealed freezer bag and apply the label, "*Southern-Style Shredded Pork - fully cooked.*"

Package the leftover **BBQ Sauce** in a freezer-safe container, then apply label, "*BBQ Sauce for Southern-Style Shredded Pork.*"

Freeze into a shape that will fit inside your crockpot using the "drop & go method" instructions at the beginning of this chapter.

MAKE IT A RAW (UNCOOKED) DROP & GO CROCKPOT FREEZER MEAL

Place the uncooked pork pieces that were covered with **BBQ Dry Rub** into a zippered freezer bag or vacuum-sealed freezer bag and apply the label, "*Southern-Style Shredded Pork – uncooked.*"

Freeze into a shape that will fit in your crockpot using the "drop & go method" instructions outlined at the beginning of this chapter.

> ### MIS EN PLACE
> 1. A day ahead, brine the pork loin.
> 2. If you don't already have it on hand, make a batch of Chef Gail's BBQ Dry Rub and set aside.
> 3. Assemble remaining ingredients.

Place the cooled BBQ sauce into a bag or freezable container and apply the label, "*BBQ Sauce for Southern-Style Shredded Pork.*"

Place both the packaged pork and sauce in a single, larger resealable bag before freezing.

FREEZER LABELS

Find and print freezer meal labels for this dish at www.frozenandfabulous.com. (See also "*Chapter 13: Quick Guide to Online Tools.*")

SUGGESTED PAIRINGS

SIDE DISH PAIRINGS

- Slider Buns
- Cole Slaw
- Grilled Vegetables
- Baked beans
- Cornbread or Corn Cakes
- Potato Salad

WINE AND/OR ALCOHOL PAIRINGS

- Rosé wine
- Zinfandel
- Hard Lemonade
- Pale Ale or bright, citrusy beer options

ONLINE RESOURCES

Scan this QR code for a direct link to an instructional cooking video for this recipe on www.frozenandfabulous.com, along with this helpful "How It's Done" video."

- The "Shape & Freeze" Storage Technique for Crockpot Cooking

VARIATIONS

MAKE IT GLUTEN-FREE

This dish is naturally gluten-free. To serve as a sandwich, choose gluten-free rolls, sliders or bread.

MAKE IT VEGETARIAN

Use the BBQ Spice Rub on shredded zucchini or pulled jackfruit for a refreshing and flavorful vegetarian option.

MAKE IT "FIT-FRIENDLY"

This pork is delicious and low-calorie served on its' own with a light salad or on pita bread. Save even more calories by reducing the sugar in the sauce, and the amount of sauce mixed with the meat.

MAKE IT BUDGET-FRIENDLY

This dish is already very affordable. Choose pork roast when it goes on sale to save even more.

DROP & GO SLOW COOKER RECIPES

Andouille Sausage & Shrimp
Cajun Jambalaya

Legend has it, the first Mardi Gras parade was led by a masked man wearing a purple cape, green hat and waving a large golden spoon. And when you dive into this hearty bowl of Cajun Jambalaya, you'll know why New Orleans is still celebrating with the lively flavors of Andouille sausage, bell peppers, spicy shrimp and jumpin' Creole seasonings!

This recipe was developed for both slow cookers and stovetop cooking. By crockpot, this meal can be frozen, placed in the crockpot still frozen, and heated to perfection just in time for an exciting, memorable meal. By stovetop, this meal can be ready in just about an hour.

It is also a dish that reheats well so you can enjoy it now, set aside some fully-cooked servings in the refrigerator or freezer and enjoy with a quick heat-up in the microwave. The flavors only get better!

So put on your party hats, raise your spoon, and let's start cookin'!

INGREDIENTS

No of Servings 2 Qt Crock Pot		4-5 Qt Crock Pot		6+ Qt Crock Pot
4		6	10	14
qty | msmt (weight)		qty | msmt (weight)	qty | msmt (weight)	qty | msmt (weight)
ANDOUILLE SAUSAGE & SHRIMP JAMBALAYA				
2 TBSP (12g)	**Chef Gail's Creole Seasoning Spice Blend** (see Recipe in *Chapter 10: Spice Blends*)	3 TBSP (18g)	5 TBSP (31g)	7 TBSP (43g)
2 TBSP (24mL)	Olive Oil, divided	3 TBSP (35mL)	5 TBSP (59mL)	7 TBSP (83mL)
1 LB (28g)	Boneless Chicken Breasts or Thighs, cut into 1" (2.5cm) pieces	1 ½ LB (43g)	2 ½ LB (71g)	3 ½ LB (99g)
½ LB (228g)	Andouille Sausage Links, cut into ¼" (.6cm) coin-shaped pieces	¾ LB (342g)	1 ¼ LB (570g)	1 ¾ LB (798g)
½ LB (227g)	Raw Shrimp, peeled and deveined, tail-off	¾ LB (340g)	1 ¼ LB (567g)	1 ¾ LB (794g)
½ tsp (4g)	Salt, divided	¾ tsp (5g)	1 ¼ tsp (9g)	1 ¾ tsp (12g)
½ tsp (1g)	Black Pepper, divided	¾ tsp (2g)	1 ¼ tsp (3g)	1 ¾ tsp (4g)
½ each (113g)	Medium White or Yellow Onion, chopped into small dice	¾ each (170g)	1 ¼ each (283g)	1 ¾ each (396g)
1 each (91g)	Green Bell Peppers, de-seeded and cut into medium-sized squares (diced)	1 ½ each (136g)	2 ½ each (227g)	3 ½ each (318g)
1 rib (91g)	Celery, sliced into ¼" (.6cm) pieces	2 ribs (136g)	3 ribs (227g)	4 ribs (318g)
3 each (8g)	Garlic Cloves, minced	5 each (13g)	8 each (21g)	11 each (29g)
½ TBSP (7g)	Butter (Salted)	¾ TBSP (11g)	1 ¼ TBSP (18g)	1 ¾ TBSP (25g)
1 cup (181g)	Basmati Rice (white or brown)	1 ½ cups (272g)	2 ½ cups (454g)	3 ½ cups (635g)
2/3 (14.5 oz can) (272g)	Fire-Roasted Diced Tomatoes, with juice	1 (14.5 oz cans) (409g)	2 (14.5 oz cans) (681g)	2 ½ (14.5 oz cans) (953g)
½ TBSP (7mL)	Sriracha Sauce	¾ TBSP (11mL)	1 ¼ TBSP (18mL)	1 ¾ TBSP (25mL)
1 tsp (4mL)	Worcestershire Sauce	2 tsp (6mL)	3 tsp (10mL)	4 tsp (13mL)
16 fl oz (379mL)	Chicken Stock or Broth, divided	24 fl oz (568mL)	40 fl oz (946mL)	56 fl oz (1325mL)
2 each (0.3g)	Bay Leaves	3 each (0.4g)	5 each (0.7g)	7 each (0.9g)
1 each (11.0g)	Scallions (Green Onions), sliced thinly	1 ½ each (17mL)	2 ½ each (28mL)	3 ½ each (39mL)
2 tsp (<1g)	Fresh Flat-Leaf Italian Parsley, finely chopped, for garnish	1 TBSP (1g)	1 ½ TBSP (1g)	2 TBSP (2g)

NUTRITION FACTS:

Serving Size 8 oz   **Calories** 270   **Total Fat** 9g   **Total Carbohydrates** 24g   **Protein** 24g

The portion size shown is based on industry dietary standards and may be smaller than the portion size allowed for in recipe.

INSTRUCTIONS

If you don't already have it on hand, assemble **Chef Gail's Creole Seasoning Spice Blend** ingredients. Mix well with a fork or whisk to make sure all the spices are evenly distributed. There may be more than is needed for a single recipe, so place any extra in an airtight container, label it, and use this spice blend to add a bit of Cajun flavor to many of your everyday dishes.

MAKE IT NOW!

In a cast iron skillet, heat 1/3 of the **olive oil** over MEDIUM heat. Sear **chicken** pieces until golden, but do not fully cook. Remove chicken from pan and set aside uncovered in the refrigerator to cool.

In the same skillet, sear the **Andouille sausage** pieces until caramelized. Remove sausage from pan and set aside uncovered in the refrigerator to cool.

With 1/3 of the **olive oil**, bring the pan to MEDIUM-HIGH heat, then quickly sauté the **shrimp** for about 1 minute or until they are lightly browned on both sides. Do not fully cook. Sprinkle with a pinch of the **salt** and **black pepper**, then remove from pan and set aside, uncovered, in the refrigerator to cool.

In the same skillet, heat the remaining 1/3 of the **olive oil** over MEDIUM heat. Sweat the **onions, bell peppers** and **celery** until onions are translucent. Add in the **garlic** and cook til softened. Bell peppers and celery should be softened but still crunchy and not overly cooked.

Add **butter** and allow to melt. Then whisk in **Chef Gail's Creole Seasoning Spice Blend** and cook over MEDIUM-LOW heat until the spices "bloom" with fragrance (about 1 to 2 minutes).

Add in **Basmati rice** and stir together with the onion/peppers/celery/garlic mixture until the rice is slightly toasted. It will smell "nutty" when done (about 1 to 2 minutes). Be sure to continue stirring the rice so it will cook evenly.

Add **fire-roasted diced tomatoes with juice, Sriracha sauce, Worcestershire sauce,** HALF of the **Chicken Stock or Broth,** and **bay leaves.** Bring to a boil, then reduce heat, cover and cook until reduced by 20% (about 20 minutes). Add remaining **salt** and **black pepper.** Rice should be softened but slightly firm.

Add **par-cooked chicken** and **Andouille sausage** into the rice mixture, plus the remaining **chicken stock or broth.** Continue cooking until chicken is fully cooked through (reaches an internal temperature of 165°F (74°C) with a stem thermometer) and Basmati rice is fluffy (about 3-4 minutes). Add in **par-cooked shrimp** and continue cooking until shrimp are opaque (about 1-2 minutes).

Taste and adjust salt and pepper, if needed. Remove bay leaves.

Remove from heat. Garnish with freshly sliced **scallions**, chopped **Italian flat-leaf parsley** and serve.

Optional: Garnish with a dollop of sour cream.

MIS EN PLACE

1. If you don't already have it on hand, make a batch of Chef Gail's Creole Seasoning Spice Blend and set aside.
2. Cut chicken into 1"x1" (2.5cm x 2.5cm) pieces.
3. Cut Andouille Sausage into ½" (1.3cm) slices.
4. Chop onions.
5. De-seed and cut Green Bell Peppers into medium-sized dice.
6. Clean & cut celery ribs into ¼" (.6cm) slices.
7. Clean, peel and devein shrimp.
8. Just before serving, cut up fresh parsley to add as a garnish, or to stir into the jambalaya.

CHEF NOTES:

Why "bloom" the spices? It is an extra step in the process, but one that pays off big flavor dividends. By heating the spices in fat (butter or oil), it allows the flavors to fully release.

You have the option to just throw the spices into the dish and to skip the "blooming" process, but it will take away from the full flavor experience.

CHEF NOTES:

WEIGHING SHRIMP: If you are starting with unpeeled shrimp, you will want to have enough on hand to get the amount called for in the recipe after it is peeled, deveined and the tail removed. A good rule of thumb is to start with 1 LB (456g) if you want to have ¾ LB (342g) yield for the recipe. If you have a little more than the recipe calls for, it's okay to just throw it in. It doesn't have to be exact.

FROZEN SHRIMP: If you are starting with frozen shrimp here are a few tips:

If you are making this with the "Crock-Pot Method", wait to thaw, clean and devein the shrimp until the day you want to serve the dish. This prevents you from thawing, cleaning, then re-freezing the shrimp which could affect its texture and quality.

THAWING: To thaw frozen shrimp, place it in a colander and set under cold, running water. Toss the shrimp frequently to make sure all the pieces are getting thawed evenly.

Once thawed, clean the shrimp by removing the shell, vein and tail.

We also have a video demonstrating this technique - for a link, please see the Online Resources section of this recipe.

MAKE IT A "DROP & GO" CROCKPOT FREEZER MEAL

Cut raw **chicken** into 1" x 1" (2.5cm x 2.5cm) pieces. Sprinkle with **salt** and **black pepper** and place in a resealable freezer bag or cooking bag.

> **Note:** If you use a Cooking Bag, at the time of cooking you can place the Cooking Bag directly into your Crockpot without removing the contents. For this method, put the filled Cooking Bag inside of a resealable zippered bag before freezing.

Slice **Andouille sausage** links into ¼" (.6cm) coin-shaped pieces. Add to the freezer bag.

Dice the **onions** and **bell peppers**. Slice the **celery** into ¼" (.6cm) wide pieces. Mince the **garlic**. Toss with HALF of the **olive oil**, then add to the freezer bag.

In a small sauté pan, melt the **butter** over MEDIUM heat. Add **Chef Gail's Creole Seasoning Spice Blend** to the warmed butter and stir until the aroma starts to "bloom" or become very fragrant. Remove from heat, cool completely, then add to the freezer bag.

Add **fire-roasted diced tomatoes**, **Sriracha sauce**, **Worcestershire sauce**, **salt**, **black pepper**, **chicken stock or broth**, and **bay leaves** to the freezer bag. Seal the bag (removing as much air as possible), then MIX the contents thoroughly by manipulating the outside of the resealable bag.

Package **shrimp** separately.

<u>Thawed Shrimp:</u> Peel, clean, devein and remove tails. Place in a separate resealable freezer bag. Toss with the remaining HALF of **olive oil**, then seal tightly, removing as much air as possible.

<u>Frozen Shrimp:</u> Measure out the amount needed, but do not thaw or clean. Place frozen shrimp in a separate resealable freezer bag. You will clean, peel and devein on the day you serve the dish.

Measure out the **Basmati rice** and place it in a separate, resealable bag.

Place all resealable freezer bags into a larger resealable freezer bag so everything is together in a single bag, removing as much air as possible.

Apply label titled *"Andouille Sausage & Shrimp Jambalaya."*

Freeze into a shape that will fit in your crockpot using the "drop & go method" instructions outlined at the beginning of this chapter.

When ready to serve, follow the cooking instructions on the label.

FREEZER LABELS

Find and print freezer meal labels for this dish at www.frozenandfabulous.com. (See also *"Chapter 13: Quick Guide to Online Tools."*)

SUGGESTED PAIRINGS

SIDE DISH PAIRINGS

- Corn Bread
- Start with a bottled Ranch-style dressing, add **Chef Gail's Creole Seasoning Spice Blend** to your desired taste, and serve with a Seasonal Garden Salad
- Collard Greens

WINE AND/OR ALCOHOL PAIRINGS

- Rose and blush wines
- Sauvignon blanc
- Chardonnay
- Albarino
- Muscadet
- Smoked Beer (Black Cabin Smoked Ale, Holger Danske, Kohlminator German-Style Smoked Bock, Scruffy's Smoked Alt, Smoking Wood, or Wildfire Wheat)

ONLINE RESOURCES

Scan this QR code for a direct link to an instructional cooking video for this recipe on www.frozenandfabulous.com, along with this helpful "How It's Done" video.

- How to De-Shell, Clean and De-Vein Shrimp or Prawns
- How to Sear Meat

VARIATIONS

MAKE IT GLUTEN-FREE

To make this dish gluten-free, use gluten-free versions of Andouille sausage, chicken stock or broth, and Worcestershire sauce.

MAKE IT VEGETARIAN

Replace the chicken with firm tofu cut into 1" (2.5cm) squares, replace the Andouille sausage with sweet potatoes or yams, cut into 1" or 2" (2.5cm or 5cm) pieces, and omit the shrimp. Replace the chicken stock or broth with vegetarian broth. This makes a flavorful vegetarian dish with a great variety of textures.

MAKE IT "FIT-FRIENDLY"

Increase the amount of chicken breast, while decreasing or omitting the corresponding amount of Andouille sausage, for a lower-calorie version of this flavorful dish. Andouille sausage can also be exchanged for a spicy chicken sausage or dice-cut butternut squash to save calories and fat.

MAKE IT BUDGET-FRIENDLY

The Andouille Sausage and Shrimp are the most expensive ingredients in this dish. To save money, increase the amount of chicken breast, while decreasing or omitting the corresponding amount of Andouille sausage, and replace the shrimp with smoky ham.

Chapter 10: SPICE BLENDS

To make cooking come together more quickly, I generally prepare batches of my Spice Blends to use in recipes or everyday cooking. These Spice Blends will add a lot of flavor to your dishes and save a lot of time if you make up a larger batch and keep them on hand.

Storage: Once you've prepared a batch of a Spice Blend, store in a tightly sealed mason jar, spice jar, or any other vessel that will keep the spices airtight. If you store these blends properly, they will last up to a year and still be very aromatic.

You can also freeze spice blends to make them last longer. If you choose this method, I encourage you to use a plastic container (not a glass jar). Once a glass jar breaks in the freezer, the tiny shards can be very dangerous if consumed.

MIXING

For each of these Spice Blend recipes, whisk together the dry ingredients. If some spices are dried or hard, run the mixture through a mesh strainer to ensure an even blend.

MEASURING

I find it much easier to weigh spices for these blends than to use tablespoons or teaspoons. If you have a kitchen scale, I encourage you to try making the "16 oz (456g) by weight" batch to save a lot of time and get more precise results. Just remember to tare out the scale between each ingredient to ensure proper measuring. For more help using a kitchen scale, watch our helpful "how-to" video, *How to Speed Up Production with a Kitchen Scale.* For a link to this video, please see *Chapter 13: Quick Guide to Online Tools.*

CHEF GAIL'S BBQ DRY RUB

Batch Size				
½ Cup (79g)		1 Cup (158g)	3 Cups (472g)	16 oz (456g) (by weight)
BBQ DRY RUB				
3 TBSP (16g)	Smoked Paprika (Spanish)	⅓ cup (32g)	1 cup (97g)	3 oz (93g)
2 TBSP (16g)	Brown Sugar, firmly packed	¼ cup (32g)	¾ cup (97g)	3 oz (93g)
1 TBSP (16g)	Sugar	2 TBSP (32g)	⅓ cup (68g)	3 oz (93g)
½ TBSP (15g)	Dry Mustard Powder	1 TBSP (30g)	3 TBSP (9g)	3 oz (86g)
½ TBSP (4g)	Celery Salt	1 TBSP (8g)	3 TBSP (24g)	0.8 oz (23g)
½ TBSP (4g)	Garlic Powder	1 TBSP (8g)	3 TBSP (13g)	0.8 oz (23g)
½ TBSP (4g)	Onion Powder	1 TBSP (8g)	3 TBSP (15g)	0.8 oz (23g)
½ tsp (2g)	Kosher Salt	1 tsp (4g)	3 tsp (12g)	0.4 oz (10g)
½ tsp (1g)	Black Pepper	1 tsp (2g)	3 tsp (9g)	0.2 oz (5g)
¼ tsp (<1g)	Cayenne Pepper	½ tsp (1g)	1 2/3 tsp (2g)	0.1 oz (2g)

CHEF GAIL'S CHIPOTLE DRY RUB

Batch Size				
½ Cup (93g)		1 Cup (186g)	3 Cups (559g)	16 oz (456g) (by weight)
CHIPOTLE DRY RUB				
1 ½ TBSP (26g)	Brown Sugar	3 TBSP (52g)	2/3 cup (156g)	4.5 oz (126g)
1 ½ TBSP (13g)	Dried Chipotle Powder	3 TBSP (26g)	2/3 cup (78g)	2 oz (63g)
1 TBSP (14g)	Salt	2 TBSP (29g)	6 TBSP (86g)	2.5 oz (70g)
½ TBSP (4g)	Ancho Chile Powder	1 TBSP (9g)	3 TBSP (26g)	1 oz (21g)
½ TBSP (3g)	Sweet Paprika	1 TBSP (6g)	3 TBSP (17g)	0.5 oz (14g)
½ TBSP (16g)	Dry Mustard Powder	1 TBSP (32g)	3 TBSP (95g)	3 oz (77g)
½ TBSP (3g)	Ground Cumin	1 TBSP (6g)	3 TBSP (17g)	0.5 oz (14g)
½ TBSP (4g)	Ground Coriander or Dried Coriander Leaves	1 TBSP (7g)	3 TBSP (22g)	0.6 oz (18g)
½ TBSP (4g)	Garlic Powder	1 TBSP (9g)	3 TBSP (26g)	1 oz (21g)
½ TBSP (4g)	Onion Powder	1 TBSP (9g)	3 TBSP (26g)	1 oz (21g)
¼ TBSP (1g)	Dried Thyme	½ TBSP (1g)	1 ½ TBSP (4g)	0.1 oz (4g)
⅛ TBSP (1g)	Ground Cloves	¼ TBSP (2g)	¾ TBSP (6g)	0.2 oz (5g)

CHEF GAIL'S COFFEE RUB

Batch Size				
½ Cup (86g)		1 Cup (173g)	3 Cups (518g)	16 oz (456g) (by weight)
COFFEE RUB				
1 ½ TBSP (11g)	Espresso Powder or Dark Roast Coffee Beans, finely ground	3 TBSP (21g)	2/3 cup (64g)	2 oz (56g)
1 ½ TBSP (13g)	Ancho Chile Powder	3 TBSP (26g)	2/3 cup (77g)	2 oz (68g)
1 ½ TBSP (26g)	Dark Brown Sugar, firmly packed	3 TBSP (51g)	2/3 cup (154g)	5 oz (135g)
¾ TBSP (4g)	Smoked Paprika (Spanish)	1 ½ TBSP (9g)	4 ½ TBSP (26g)	0.8 oz (23g)
¾ TBSP (9g)	Kosher Salt	1 ½ TBSP (17g)	4 ½ TBSP (51g)	1.6 oz (45g)
1 tsp (2g)	Black Pepper	2 ⅛ tsp (4g)	6 ½ tsp (13g)	0.4 oz (11g)
1 tsp (3g)	Ground Coriander or Dried Coriander Leaves	2 ⅛ tsp (5g)	6 ½ tsp (16g)	0.5 oz (14g)
1 tsp (12g)	Dry Mustard Powder	2 ⅛ tsp (24g)	6 ½ tsp (71g)	2 oz (62g)
1 tsp (3g)	Dutch Process Cocoa Powder	2 ⅛ tsp (6g)	6 ½ tsp (19g)	0.6 oz (17g)
¾ tsp (2g)	Lemon Salt (or Lemon Pepper Seasoning Salt)	1 ½ tsp (4g)	4 ½ tsp (13g)	0.4 oz (11g)
½ tsp (2g)	Crushed Red Pepper Flakes	1 tsp (5g)	3 tsp (14g)	0.4 oz (12g)

This recipe calls for pure Lemon Salt, which is difficult to find sometimes. However, I really prefer it over the Lemon Pepper Seasoning blends so if you can find it or make it, you'll enjoy a better result. To make your own, just put salt and lemon zest (1 part lemon zest to 2 parts salt) into a mason jar, shake well and cover tightly. Store in the refrigerator for three weeks, then run the salt through a fine-mesh strainer to separate the zest from the salt. Label and keep it handy in your spice cupboard for a lovely way to brighten any dish.

CHEF GAIL'S CREOLE SEASONING SPICE BLEND

Batch Size				
½ Cup (49g)		1 Cup (98g)	3 Cups (293g)	16 oz (456g) (by weight)
CREOLE SEASONING				
1 TBSP (10g)	Garlic Powder	2 ¼ TBSP (20g)	6 2/3 TBSP (59g)	3 oz (91g)
1 TBSP (10g)	Onion Powder	2 ¼ TBSP (20g)	6 2/3 TBSP (59g)	3 oz (91g)
1 TBSP (7g)	Sweet Paprika	2 ¼ TBSP (13g)	6 2/3 TBSP (39g)	2 oz (61g)
2 1/3 tsp (2g)	Dried Thyme	4 ½ tsp (4g)	1 TBSP (13g)	1 oz (20g)
1 ¾ tsp (3g)	Black Pepper	3 ½ tsp (7g)	2/3 TBSP (20g)	1 oz (30g)
1 ¾ tsp (3g)	Cayenne Pepper	3 ½ tsp (7g)	2/3 TBSP (20g)	1 oz (30g)
1 ¾ tsp (2g)	Dried Basil	3 ½ tsp (3g)	2/3 TBSP (10g)	0.5 oz (15g)
1 ¾ tsp (2g)	Dried Oregano	3 ½ tsp (3g)	2/3 TBSP (10g)	0.5 oz (15g)
1 ¾ tsp (2g)	Dried Parsley	3 ½ tsp (3g)	2/3 TBSP (10g)	0.5 oz (15g)
1 ¾ tsp (8g)	Salt	3 ½ tsp (16g)	10 ½ tsp (49g)	2.7 oz (76g)
1 tsp (1g)	Optional: Dried Sassafras Leaves (or Gumbo File)	2 tsp (2g)	5 2/3 tsp (5g)	0.3 oz (8g)

Sassafras gives this spice blend an earthy, citrus flavor. A little goes a long way, but it can add nice depth to Southern-style recipes. It is a bit difficult to find in local stores sometimes, at least on the West coast of the country, so it's okay to leave it out of the recipe and still enjoy a very flavorful dish.

Also, if you find this spice blend too "hot" for your taste, you can reduce the Cayenne Pepper. If you want more heat, increase the Cayenne Pepper or add ½ tsp (2g) of Red Pepper Flakes to the ½ Cup batch size.

CHEF GAIL'S INDIAN BUTTER CHICKEN SPICE BLEND

Batch Size				
½ Cup (68g)		1 Cup (136g)	3 Cups (408g)	16 oz (456g) (by weight)
INDIAN BUTTER CHICKEN SPICE BLEND				
4 ½ TBSP (37g)	Butter Chicken Masala Spice Blend	2/3 cup (74g)	1 2/3 cups (223g)	9 oz (247g)
2 ¼ TBSP (19g)	Curry Meat Masala Spice Blend	4 ½ TBSP (37g)	1 cups (111g)	4 oz (124g)
1 TBSP (9g)	Turmeric	2 ¼ TBSP (19g)	½ cup (56g)	2 oz (62g)
1 tsp (3g)	Red Chile Powder	2 ¼ tsp (6g)	2 ¼ TBSP (19g)	1 oz (21g)

You can usually find these Masala spice blends in Indian markets or specialty stores. I prefer the Shan and MDH brands, which are commonly found in these markets. If you don't have a local source, there are many online sources to choose from, so read the reviews to help you decide on alternatives.

SPICE BLENDS

CHEF GAIL'S MEXICAN SPICE BLEND

Batch Size				
½ Cup (50g)		1 Cup (100g)	3 Cups (301g)	16 oz (456g) (by weight)
MEXICAN SPICE BLEND				
2 ¼ TBSP (12g)	Ground Cumin	4 ½ TBSP (25g)	1 cup (74g)	4 oz (113g)
2 ¼ TBSP (6g)	Dried Oregano (recommend Mexican Oregano if available)	4 ½ TBSP (12g)	1 cup (37g)	2 oz (57g)
1 TBSP (6g)	Sweet Paprika	2 TBSP (12g)	½ cup (37g)	2 oz (57g)
1 ½ TBSP (12g)	Ancho Chile Powder	3 TBSP (25g)	2/3 cup (74g)	4 oz (113g)
2 ¼ tsp (6g)	Garlic Powder	4 ½ tsp (12g)	4 ½ TBSP (37g)	2 oz (57g)
½ TBSP (3g)	Black Pepper	1 TBSP (6g)	3 ¼ TBSP (18g)	1 oz (28g)
2/3 tsp (3g)	Salt	1 ¼ tsp (6g)	4 tsp (18g)	1 oz (28g)
½ tsp (1g)	Cayenne Pepper	1 tsp (2g)	3 ¼ tsp (6g)	0.4 oz (11g)

CHEF GAIL'S SOUTHERN SPICE BLEND

Batch Size				
½ Cup (97g)		1 Cup (197g)	3 Cups (591g)	16 oz (456g) (by weight)
SOUTHERN SPICE BLEND				
2 TBSP (16g)	Garlic Salt	3 ¾ TBSP (31g)	¾ cup (94g)	2.5 oz (72g)
2 TBSP (57g)	Dry Mustard Powder	3 ¾ TBSP (115g)	¾ cup (344g)	9.3 oz (264g)
2 TBSP (10g)	Smoked Paprika (Spanish)	3 ¾ TBSP (21g)	¾ cup (63g)	2 oz (48g)
1 TBSP (8g)	Celery Salt	2 TBSP (16g)	1/3 cup (47g)	1 oz (36g)
1 TBSP (5g)	Black Pepper	2 TBSP (10g)	1/3 cup (31g)	1 oz (24g)
1 tsp (1g)	Ground Ginger	2 tsp (2g)	2 TBSP (5g)	0.1 oz (4g)
½ tsp (<1g)	Dried Oregano	1 tsp (1g)	1 TBSP (3g)	0.1 oz (2g)
½ tsp (<1g)	Dried Thyme	1 tsp (1g)	1 TBSP (3g)	0.1 oz (2g)
1/8 tsp (<1g)	Cayenne Pepper	¼ tsp (<1g)	¾ tsp (1g)	0.04 oz (1g)

Chapter 11:
MEAT BRINES

Placing meat (especially poultry, leaner cuts of pork and some types of seafood) into a Brine before preparing will dramatically improve moisture retention. I have included my most-used brines here, which are referenced in recipes throughout this cookbook.

ABOUT THE CHICKEN BRINE

I always – **100% of the time** – recommend putting **Chicken Breasts** into this quick-brine for 15 minutes before preparing the recipes.

Chicken breasts can be very dry, especially after freezing, but pre-brining in this mixture will give you **better moisture retention whether you're serving the same day as prepped or after 12 months of freezing**.

Chicken thighs hold moisture better than breasts, so quick-brining thighs isn't necessary.

This quick brine is simple and effective – I keep a gallon of it in the fridge so it's always ready to go whenever I'm making a chicken dish. It will last three months in the refrigerator, so it's a good idea to make a big batch.

Worried about the sugar? It is an essential tenderizing agent of the brine; however, only a tiny amount of sugar is actually absorbed by the chicken (<1g per serving).

ABOUT THE PORK BRINE

I always recommend putting **Pork Loin Roasts and Pork Chops** into this flavorful brine either overnight, or for a minimum of 4 hours, before preparing your recipes. Here is a good rule of thumb for optimal brining time based on the type of pork you are working with:

- Pork Chops – 8-12 hours
- Pork Loin Roast – 12 to 24 hours

These cuts of pork are very lean and therefore dry, especially after freezing. Pre-brining in this mixture is the best way to ensure **maximum moisture and flavor retention**, especially after freezing.

When it comes to **Pork Tenderloin**, I do not always pre-brine. I have found I can get a deliciously tender, flavorful result by rubbing with fresh herbs, searing HOT and finishing in the oven.

However, if I am already preparing other cuts of pork, I will go ahead and brine the tenderloin and I do notice an enhanced flavor and moisture level. If you want to brine the tenderloin, here is what I recommend for timing:

- Pork Tenderloin – 4-6 hours (do not exceed 12 hours)

Preparing this pork brine is simple and effective, and also works beautifully with chicken or seafood.

Don't skip the brown sugar, even if you're trying to make the dish healthier. It is an essential tenderizing agent of the brine; however, only a tiny amount is absorbed by the meat (<1g per serving).

WHEN NOT TO BRINE

It is not recommended to brine meats with a higher fat content, such as beef or lamb.

Even though many cuts of pork frequently have a fat cap (and you may think they therefore have a high fat content), the meat itself is typically very lean. Lean meats need help breaking down fibers in order to yield a more tender, juicy bite, which is why a brine will make such a difference in your finished product.

Quick Brine for Chicken Breast

INGREDIENTS

brine for 4 servings of chicken		brine for 6 servings of chicken	brine for 10 servings of chicken	brine for 14 servings of chicken
qty | msmt (weight)		qty | msmt (weight)	qty | msmt (weight)	qty | msmt (weight)
QUICK BRINE FOR CHICKEN BREASTs				
2 cups (473mL)	Cold Water	3 ½ cups (710mL)	5 cups (1183mL)	7 cups (1656g)
¼ cup (50g)	Sugar	½ cup (100g)	¾ cup (150g)	1 cup (200g)
2 ½ TBSP (35g)	Kosher Salt	¼ cup (58g)	½ cup (115g)	¾ cup (173g)

INSTRUCTIONS

Place **cold water, sugar** and **kosher salt** into a saucepan over MEDIUM heat.

Stir or whisk just until the salt and sugar are fully dissolved (about 3-5 minutes).

> **NOTE:** *The water does not need to boil – it just needs to get warm enough to dissolve the salt and sugar (water will be clear and there will be no gritty feel to it).*

OPTIONAL: Add sprigs of fresh herbs or lemon slices to the brine for added flavor.

Remove from the heat and allow to cool.

When ready to use, place chicken pieces in a shallow dish. Pour just enough brine over the chicken to fully cover.

Allow chicken to sit in the brine (on the counter) for **15 minutes** (no longer than 30 minutes). Then remove the chicken and discard the used brine. (Un-used brine can be frozen or refrigerated for up to 3 months.)

Prepare chicken for any recipe of your choosing.

Overnight Brine for Pork

INGREDIENTS

No of Servings				
4 qty | msmt (weight)		**6** qty | msmt (weight)	**10** qty | msmt (weight)	**14** qty | msmt (weight)
OVERNIGHT BRINE FOR PORK				
4 cups (946mL)	Water	6 cups (1420mL)	10 cups (2366mL)	14 cups (3312mL)
¼ cup (59mL)	Apple Cider Vinegar	½ cup (89mL)	¾ cup (148mL)	1 cup (207mL)
¼ cup (57g)	Brown Sugar, firmly packed	½ cup (86g)	¾ cup (143g)	1 cup (200g)
¼ cup (52g)	Kosher Salt	½ cup (78g)	¾ cup (130g)	1 cup (182g)
2 sprigs (1g)	Fresh Thyme	3 sprigs (2g)	5 sprigs (3g)	7 sprigs (4g)
1 sprig (1g)	Fresh Rosemary	2 sprigs (2g)	3 sprigs (3g)	4 sprigs (4g)
1 TBSP (6g)	Dried Orange or Tangerine Peel *1 TBSP of dried orange peel is equal to zest of 1 medium fresh orange. Dried works best for this recipe.	1 ½ TBSP (9g)	2 ½ TBSP (15g)	3 ½ TBSP (21g)
1 TBSP (9g)	Peppercorns, whole	1 ½ TBSP (14g)	2 ½ TBSP (23g)	3 ½ TBSP (32g)
1 tsp (4g)	Red Pepper Flakes	1 ½ tsp (6g)	2 ½ tsp (10g)	3 ½ tsp (14g)

INSTRUCTIONS

Place **cold water, apple cider vinegar, brown sugar** and **kosher salt** into a saucepan over MEDIUM heat.

Stir or whisk just until the salt and sugar are fully dissolved (about 3-5 minutes).

NOTE: *The water does not need to boil – it just needs to get warm enough to dissolve the salt and sugar (water will be clear and there will be no gritty feel to it).*

OPTIONAL: Add lemon slices or other aromatics to to the brine to match the flavor profile of your finished dish.

Remove from the heat and add in **fresh thyme, fresh rosemary, dried orange or tangerine peel, whole peppercorns**, and **red pepper flakes**.

Set aside to cool.

When cooled, place pork in a dish or vessel deep enough to allow the pork to be covered with the brine. Pour just enough brine over the pork to fully cover. Cover tightly with a lid or plastic wrap.

Place pork and brine in refrigerator for the recommended amount of time (see above "About the Brine" section). Then remove the pork and discard the used brine. (Un-used brine can be frozen or refrigerated for up to 3 months.)

Prepare pork for any recipe of your choosing.

Chapter 12:
TROUBLESHOOTING
How to Correct Mistakes

Oops! It happens – adding too much of one ingredient, not enough of another, or grabbing the wrong item by mistake can threaten to ruin a dish and make all your hard work for naught.

But for most mistakes, there is a way to fix the problem and create something tasty.

OVER-COOKED FOODS

MEATS

If meat is overcooked and dry, it can typically be remedied by adding a sauce to bring back moisture to the dish. Sometimes this means you're making a completely different dish (overcooked pot roast becomes pulled BBQ sandwiches or pot roast stew, for example).

Burnt meat is more difficult but can still be saved for stews or saucy dishes. Cut out as much of the burnt pieces as possible and work with what is left. Placing the overcooked meat into a vacuum-sealed bag with flavorful liquids (stock, fresh herbs, herb-infused oil/vinegar blends) can also help return moisture to the meat.

VEGETABLES

If vegetables are overcooked it will affect the texture of a dish. If severely overcooked, puree the vegetables to create a creamy soup or sauce.

If only slightly overcooked, prepare new vegetables and mix them all together. The properly cooked vegetables will provide texture to support the slightly overcooked ones.

SAUCES

Overcooked sauce will result in 1) not enough sauce for your finished dish because it over-reduced; or 2) the sauce will have a burnt flavor.

If the sauce is simply over-reduced, it's easy enough to add stock or liquids, reduce back down a bit, and end with a flavorful, rich sauce with plenty available for your recipe.

If the sauce is burnt, it is usually better to start over and discard the burned portion. The burnt smell will permeate the rest of your dish and cause the entire meal to taste "off."

CASSEROLES OR LAYERED DISHES

Overcooking casseroles or layered dishes will generally affect the texture of the dish, but the flavors will be okay. To incorporate texture, add a crunchy element (like a panko-butter crust) to the top of the dish, then sauté vegetables complementary to the dish's flavor profile. At the time of service, place the sauteed vegetables on the plate, top with the overcooked casserole, and it will improve the taste/texture experience of the overall dish. Generally, these additions will add sufficient texture that you won't notice the overcooked elements as much.

If you burn the casserole or layered dish, the best way to save it is to cut away the burnt edges and serve the unburned center pieces. Then treat the overcooked-but-edible section as recommended above by adding texture back to the dish.

BAKED GOODS OR DESSERTS

Over-baking will cause your baked goods and flour-based desserts to become very dry and lose texture.

For cakes and dessert breads (like banana bread), start by cutting away any dark (overly burnt) areas. Add moisture to the remainder by poking holes into the item and pouring flavored simple syrup over the top. Allow the baked item to absorb the liquid, then cover it all with delicious frosting and voila! Problem solved.

Overbaked cookies can be crumbled and turned into a flavorful topping or ingredient for other desserts. They can be especially tasty when added to a fudgy brownie and served with ice cream.

If you seriously burn the items, your best recourse is to dump and start over. The charred taste isn't likely to go away and can be very unpleasant.

OVER-SALTED FOODS

MEATS & VEGETABLES
Mix over-salted meats and vegetables with sauce, then marry with pasta or rice to distribute the saltiness throughout the new dish. You can also use over-salted meats and vegetables to create delicious stews, soups or casseroles, as the salt level will normalize once added to the larger volume of liquids and ingredients.

SAUCES, SOUPS, STEWS AND HIGH-LIQUID BRAISED DISHES
The easiest way to reduce salt in any dish with liquid is to add a whole, peeled potato and let it cook in the sauce or liquid for 15 to 20 minutes, or until the excess saltiness has been absorbed by the potato. Then remove the potato, and your dish should be back on track.

CASSEROLES OR LAYERED DISHES
Unfortunately, you're not likely to know that a casserole or layered dish is over-salted until you're sitting at the table and eating it. However, if you discover the over-saltiness during prep, de-compose the elements. Whichever element is over-salted, just mix with more ingredients of that kind to balance the salt level. Then re-layer the components back into the dish and finish preparations.

DESSERTS
Just like casseroles, you often won't realize a dessert or baked dish is over-salted until it's too late. Sometimes you can save the dish by adding a sweet element – buttercream frosting, ice cream, Chantilly cream, chocolate ganache – to balance the salt level.

If you discover the over-saltiness while the dish is still raw and in a batter state, simply double the recipe (omit the salt on the second batch), and it should balance out.

UNDER-SALTED FOODS

It's pretty easy to add more salt to most under-salted dishes; however, casseroles and baked goods can be a little trickier to fix.

CASSEROLES OR LAYERED DISHES
If you discover the lack of salt while still prepping the dish, try peeling back a few layers to add a bit of salt throughout the dish.

If it's fully cooked, don't try to fix an under-salt problem by salting the top of the casserole – it can create an overly salty bite. Just make sure you have salt on the table to add it at the time of service.

BAKED GOODS OR DESSERTS
The best way to bring more salt to a fully baked dessert item is to add a salty element on top or served on the side. For example, a crunchy nut brittle or salty caramel sauce can bring salt and flavor to the entire dish.

Have a problem that isn't covered here? Visit our website at www.frozenandfabulous.com for more troubleshooting ideas, or send me your questions via DM on Instagram @AskChefGail or through our website.

Chapter 13: QUICK GUIDE TO ONLINE TOOLS

See the beginning of this cookbook for your **exclusive access QR code** to the **Members-Only** section of the www.FrozenandFabulous.com website. This code will give you one full year of free access following the purchase of this cookbook. In this section of the website, you'll have access to valuable tools and resources to help you cook like a pro and create truly enjoyable freezer meals.

FREEZER MEAL LABELS

Every recipe in this cookbook refers to a Freezer Label with detailed cooking and/or reheating instructions for the dish and its' components.

You will find these labels online at www.frozenandfabulous.com where you can create and print labels as follows:

1. Copy and paste the information onto your favorite labels or software application;
2. Print the labels directly from our website. They have been formatted to print on Avery 5164 labels;
3. Order pre-printed labels that we will print and ship to you within 3 business days; or

Not convenient for you to visit the website? **Send us an email** to info@frozenandfabulous.com. Let us know which recipe labels you need and we will email you the labels for easy printing or cut-and-paste into your own document.

Find and print freezer meal labels for all recipes in this cookbook at www.frozenandfabulous.com.

QR CODES

Each recipe has a QR code that you can scan with your phone's camera. This will take you to a video showing a chef demonstration on how to prepare the dish, along with additional helpful tips.

Here is an example of a QR code you'll find included with each recipe:

If you don't already have a QR reader on your phone, you can obtain one for free – just go to the app store for your phone and search "free QR reader."

You can also search for the videos at www.frozenandfabulous.com in the Members-Only section and type the recipe name into the search bar.

"HOW IT'S DONE" VIDEOS

Throughout this cookbook, you'll see references to our "how-to" videos. All these helpful teaching videos are available in our Members-Only section of the frozenandfabulous.com website.

Here are a few examples:

- What is "Mis En Place?"
- How to Sear Meat
- What is "Au Sec?"
- How to Bloom Spices
- How to Sharpen a Chef Knife
- Knife Skills - Advanced
- Knife Skills - Basics
- How to Speed Up Production with a Kitchen Scale
- How to Calibrate Thermometers
- Preparing Top Round Beef Roast for Roulade
- Dry/Wet/Dry Breading Method
- Chef Gail's Secrets for Amazing Burgers

- How to Make Flavored Butters & Logs
- How to Butterfly-Cut a Chicken Breast
- How to Butterfly-Cut a Pork Loin Roast
- How to Split a Chicken Breast
- The "Breast Pocket" Stuffed Chicken Technique
- How to Grill Directly on Coals
- How to Create an Emulsion for Oil-based Marinades and Dressings
- How to Clean and Prepare Flank Steak for Cooking
- Cutting and Slicing Flank Steak
- How to Work with Fresh Ginger Root
- How to Grill-Mark Meat
- How to Clean Mushrooms
- How to Dice Cut an Onion
- How to Slice Scallions (Green Onions)
- How to Supreme an Orange
- How to Roulade-Cut a Pork Loin Roast
- How to Prep Pork Tenderloin for Cooking
- Preparing Ribs
- How to De-Shell, Clean and De-Vein Shrimp or Prawns
- Sous Vide Cooking Basics
- The "Shape & Freeze" Storage Technique for Crockpot Cooking

ONLINE SHOPPING GUIDE

Before you go shopping, grab our handy **Shopping Guide Tool** to quickly and easily create shopping lists. Our Shopping Guide will automatically pull ingredient lists from recipes you choose, combine amounts for ingredients used across multiple recipes, and sort them by "shopping category" to make it quicker to find the items across the store.

This tool is available in our Members-Only section of frozenandfabulous.com.

ONLINE BATCH & GROUP PRODUCTION PLANS

When preparing for your next group or batch cooking day, stop by our website first to use our very handy **Production Planning Tool**. This is an exclusive online tool available only in our Members-Only section and will make the preparation process so easy.

BATCH COOKING PLAN

Use our tool to create a **Batch Cooking Plan** that will:

- Combine ingredient "prep steps" across multiple recipes. For example, if you're going to cut onions for three of your five recipes, it's easier to cut them all at once. This tool will tell you how much to prep and then split the total amount to cover what is needed for each separate recipe.
- Categorize processes across all recipes. Our planning tool will categorize food prep, cooking, cooling and packaging processes across all your selected recipes to maximize efficiency.

GROUP COOKING PLAN

Our **Group Cooking Plan** does everything that the **Batch Cooking Plan** does; PLUS allows you to split up the work amongst everyone in the group.

Imagine: Your group shows up, each member receives a "to do" list, and everyone can happily get to work without stepping on each other's toes. These prep lists can be catered to each person's particular skill set, or by "prep station" if you have a limited supply of space, cutting boards, knives or other kitchen tools.

The key to keeping a group cooking day fun and relaxed is to be super organized, and this tool will help you get there.

EXTRA-LARGE BATCH RECIPES

The recipes in this cookbook provide instructions for small to large batch sizes, which can easily be halved or doubled to achieve targeted serving counts. But it's important to be aware of a couple of things when calculating for larger batch sizes.

Some ingredients do not extrapolate evenly. This is a challenge with most conversion calculators – they simply multiply the ingredients and call it done. However, when working with aromatics and binding elements, the multiplication factor will change across larger batch sizes.

When doubling or halving the batch size for a recipe in this cookbook, use the batch size that can most easily be halved or doubled. For example, if you want a batch of 28 servings, just double the 14-serving batch. If you're going to make 20 servings, just double the 10-serving batch.

QUICK GUIDE TO ONLINE TOOLS

When you need to build even larger batches, it is better to use the **Large Batch Recipe Converter Tool** found in the Members Only section of www.frozenand-fabulous.com. This tool was designed to provide proper extrapolation for all of my recipes, including new and exclusive creations you will find on the website.

BONUS RECIPES

I am constantly creating exciting new recipes and would love to share them with you. You can find these exclusive new recipes on our website in the Members Only section.

Chapter 14: RESOURCES

The following are valuable guides to make it easier to prep, plan and prepare the recipes in this cookbook.

INDEX OF INGREDIENTS

Alcohol, Beer, Guinness Draught
Guinness Pot Roast with Gravy

Alcohol, Cointreau (French Orange Liqueur)
Lamb Cutlets with Mint Orange Cointreau Sauce

Alcohol, Whiskey, Bourbon
Bourbon BBQ Babyback Ribs
Chipotle Roasted Leg of Lamb
Peanut Butter, Bourbon & Bacon Burgers
Pork Tenderloin with Bourbon Pear Sauce

Alcohol, Whiskey, Bourbon, Maple-Flavored
Peanut Butter, Bourbon & Bacon Burgers

Alcohol, Whiskey, Irish
Drunk Irishman's Shepherd's Pie

Alcohol, Wine, Red
Cherry-Stuffed Pork Loin with Black Cherry Chutney
Chicken Cacciatore with Basmati Rice
Spicy Italian Meatballs with Marinara
Tuscan-Style Horseradish-Crusted Beef Roulade with Roasted Red Peppers & Provolone

Alcohol, Wine, Sherry
Drunk Irishman's Shepherd's Pie

Alcohol, Wine, White
Blood Orange-Roasted Chicken
Chicken Ballotine with Rosemary Beurre Blanc Sauce
Lamb Cutlets with Mint Orange Cointreau Sauce
Prosciutto-Stuffed Chicken Breasts with Fig & Honey Sauce

Bacon
Chicken Ballotine with Rosemary Beurre Blanc Sauce
Peanut Butter, Bourbon & Bacon Burgers
Southern-Fried Bacon-Wrapped Chicken & Waffles

Base, Beef
Chipotle Roasted Leg of Lamb
Drunk Irishman's Shepherd's Pie
Swedish Meatballs with White Gravy
Tuscan-Style Horseradish-Crusted Beef Roulade with Roasted Red Peppers & Provolone

Base, Chicken
Blood Orange-Roasted Chicken
Chicken Cacciatore with Basmati Rice
Chicken Enchiladas
Lamb Cutlets with Mint Orange Cointreau Sauce
Pork Tenderloin with Bourbon Pear Sauce

Basil, Fresh
Prosciutto-Stuffed Chicken Breasts with Fig & Honey Sauce
Roasted Vegetable Lasagna (Vegetarian)
Spicy Italian Meatballs with Marinara
Spinach & Feta Stuffed Chicken with Pesto & Mediterranean Salsa

Beans, Kidney, Dark Red
Chunky Chicken & Corn Chili

Beef Base
Chipotle Roasted Leg of Lamb
Drunk Irishman's Shepherd's Pie
Swedish Meatballs with White Gravy
Tuscan-Style Horseradish-Crusted Beef Roulade with Roasted Red Peppers & Provolone

Beef Broth
Bourbon BBQ Babyback Ribs
Cantonese Braised Beef
Drunk Irishman's Shepherd's Pie
Guinness Pot Roast with Gravy
Swedish Meatballs with White Gravy

Beef Stock (cont.)
Tuscan-Style Horseradish-Crusted Beef Roulade with Roasted Red Peppers & Provolone

Beef Stock
Bourbon BBQ Babyback Ribs
Cantonese Braised Beef
Chipotle Roasted Leg of Lamb
Drunk Irishman's Shepherd's Pie
Guinness Pot Roast with Gravy
Swedish Meatballs with White Gravy
Tuscan-Style Horseradish-Crusted Beef Roulade with Roasted Red Peppers & Provolone

Beef, Angus Ground
Peanut Butter, Bourbon & Bacon Burgers
Spicy Italian Meatballs with Marinara
Swedish Meatballs with White Gravy

Beef, Brisket
Cantonese Braised Beef

Beef, Chuck Roast
Guinness Pot Roast with Gravy

Beef, Flank Steak
Latin Flank Steak with Spanish Rice & Bell Peppers in Chipotle Crema Sauce

Beef, Roast, Top Round
Tuscan-Style Horseradish-Crusted Beef Roulade with Roasted Red Peppers & Provolone

Beef, Steak, Flank
Latin Flank Steak with Spanish Rice & Bell Peppers in Chipotle Crema Sauce

Beef, Steaks
Coffee-Rubbed Steak with Coffee Butter

Beer, Guinness Draught
Guinness Pot Roast with Gravy

Bell Peppers, any color
Roasted Vegetable Lasagna (Vegetarian)

Bell Peppers, Green
Andouille Sausage & Shrimp Cajun Jambalaya
Chicken Cacciatore with Basmati Rice
Latin Flank Steak with Spanish Rice & Bell Peppers in Chipotle Crema Sauce
Roasted Vegetable Lasagna (Vegetarian)

Bell Peppers, Red
Roasted Vegetable Lasagna (Vegetarian)
Seafood-Stuffed Portobello Mushrooms
Tuscan-Style Horseradish-Crusted Beef Roulade with Roasted Red Peppers & Provolone

Bourbon Whiskey
Bourbon BBQ Babyback Ribs
Chipotle Roasted Leg of Lamb
Peanut Butter, Bourbon & Bacon Burgers

Pork Tenderloin with Bourbon Pear Sauce

Bourbon Whiskey, Maple-Flavored
Peanut Butter, Bourbon & Bacon Burgers

Bread Crumbs, Panko
Habanero, Turkey & Sausage Meatballs
Macadamia Nut-Crusted Halibut with Raspberry Sauce
Oven-Baked Parmesan Chicken
Spicy Italian Meatballs with Marinara
Tuscan-Style Horseradish-Crusted Beef Roulade with Roasted Red Peppers & Provolone

Bread, Brioche
Swedish Meatballs with White Gravy

Brine, Quick Brine for Chicken Breasts
Blood Orange-Roasted Chicken
Butter Chicken (a/k/a Indian Chicken Makhani)
Chicken Ballotine with Rosemary Beurre Blanc Sauce
Chicken Enchiladas
Cilantro-Grilled Chicken with Mango Salsa
Just Add Mayo: Curry Chicken Salad
Prosciutto-Stuffed Chicken Breasts with Fig & Honey Sauce
Spinach & Feta Stuffed Chicken with Pesto & Mediterranean Salsa

Broccoli Florets
Teriyaki Chicken with Rice & Broccoli

Broth, Beef
Bourbon BBQ Babyback Ribs
Cantonese Braised Beef
Drunk Irishman's Shepherd's Pie
Guinness Pot Roast with Gravy
Swedish Meatballs with White Gravy
Tuscan-Style Horseradish-Crusted Beef Roulade with Roasted Red Peppers & Provolone

Broth, Chicken
Andouille Sausage & Shrimp Cajun Jambalaya
Blood Orange-Roasted Chicken
Chicken Cacciatore with Basmati Rice
Chicken Enchiladas
Just Add Mayo: Curry Chicken Salad
Lamb Cutlets with Mint Orange Cointreau Sauce
Latin Flank Steak with Spanish Rice & Bell Peppers in Chipotle Crema Sauce
Pork Tenderloin with Bourbon Pear Sauce
Prosciutto-Stuffed Chicken Breasts with Fig & Honey Sauce

Broth, Lamb
Chipotle Roasted Leg of Lamb

Butter (Salted)
Andouille Sausage & Shrimp Cajun Jambalaya
Blood Orange-Roasted Chicken

RESOURCES

Butter Chicken (a/k/a Indian Chicken Makhani)
Cherry-Stuffed Pork Loin with Black Cherry Chutney
Chicken Ballotine with Rosemary Beurre Blanc Sauce
Chicken Cacciatore with Basmati Rice
Chipotle Roasted Leg of Lamb
Chunky Chicken & Corn Chili
Coffee-Rubbed Steak with Coffee Butter
Drunk Irishman's Shepherd's Pie
Guinness Pot Roast with Gravy
Lamb Cutlets with Mint Orange Cointreau Sauce
Latin Flank Steak with Spanish Rice & Bell Peppers in Chipotle Crema Sauce
Macadamia Nut-Crusted Halibut with Raspberry Sauce
Pork Tenderloin with Bourbon Pear Sauce
Prosciutto-Stuffed Chicken Breasts with Fig & Honey Sauce
Seafood-Stuffed Portobello Mushrooms
Swedish Meatballs with White Gravy
Teriyaki Chicken with Rice & Broccoli
Tuscan-Style Horseradish-Crusted Beef Roulade with Roasted Red Peppers & Provolone

Buttermilk
Oven-Baked Parmesan Chicken
Southern-Fried Bacon-Wrapped Chicken & Waffles

Capers, non-pareil
Spinach & Feta Stuffed Chicken with Pesto & Mediterranean Salsa

Carrots
Drunk Irishman's Shepherd's Pie
Guinness Pot Roast with Gravy
Just Add Mayo: Curry Chicken Salad
Seafood-Stuffed Portobello Mushrooms

Cashews
Just Add Mayo: Curry Chicken Salad

Cauliflower Florets
Chicken Enchiladas

Celery
Andouille Sausage & Shrimp Cajun Jambalaya
Drunk Irishman's Shepherd's Pie
Guinness Pot Roast with Gravy
Just Add Mayo: Curry Chicken Salad

Cheddar Cheese
Chicken Enchiladas
Peanut Butter, Bourbon & Bacon Burgers

Cheese, Cheddar
Chicken Enchiladas
Peanut Butter, Bourbon & Bacon Burgers

Cheese, Chevre
Habanero, Turkey & Sausage Meatballs
Prosciutto-Stuffed Chicken Breasts with Fig & Honey Sauce
Seafood-Stuffed Portobello Mushrooms

Cheese, Cream
Chicken Ballotine with Rosemary Beurre Blanc Sauce
Chicken Enchiladas
Swedish Meatballs with White Gravy
Tuscan-Style Horseradish-Crusted Beef Roulade with Roasted Red Peppers & Provolone

Cheese, Feta, crumbled
Spinach & Feta Stuffed Chicken with Pesto & Mediterranean Salsa

Cheese, Goat
Habanero, Turkey & Sausage Meatballs
Prosciutto-Stuffed Chicken Breasts with Fig & Honey Sauce
Seafood-Stuffed Portobello Mushrooms

Cheese, Mexican Cheese Blend
Chicken Enchiladas

Cheese, Mozzarella
Roasted Vegetable Lasagna (Vegetarian)

Cheese, Parmesan, Grated
Drunk Irishman's Shepherd's Pie
Habanero, Turkey & Sausage Meatballs
Oven-Baked Parmesan Chicken
Roasted Vegetable Lasagna (Vegetarian)
Seafood-Stuffed Portobello Mushrooms
Spicy Italian Meatballs with Marinara
Spinach & Feta Stuffed Chicken with Pesto & Mediterranean Salsa

Cheese, Parmesan, Shredded
Drunk Irishman's Shepherd's Pie

Cheese, Provolone
Tuscan-Style Horseradish-Crusted Beef Roulade with Roasted Red Peppers & Provolone

Cheese, Ricotta
Roasted Vegetable Lasagna (Vegetarian)

Cherries, Black (fresh or frozen)
Cherry-Stuffed Pork Loin with Black Cherry Chutney

Cherries, Dried Tart
Cherry-Stuffed Pork Loin with Black Cherry Chutney

Cherries, Red Tart, Canned
Cherry-Stuffed Pork Loin with Black Cherry Chutney

Chevre Goat Cheese
Habanero, Turkey & Sausage Meatballs
Prosciutto-Stuffed Chicken Breasts with Fig & Honey Sauce
Seafood-Stuffed Portobello Mushrooms

Chicken Base
- Blood Orange-Roasted Chicken
- Chicken Cacciatore with Basmati Rice
- Chicken Enchiladas
- Lamb Cutlets with Mint Orange Cointreau Sauce
- Pork Tenderloin with Bourbon Pear Sauce

Chicken Broth
- Andouille Sausage & Shrimp Cajun Jambalaya
- Blood Orange-Roasted Chicken
- Chicken Cacciatore with Basmati Rice
- Chicken Enchiladas
- Just Add Mayo: Curry Chicken Salad
- Lamb Cutlets with Mint Orange Cointreau Sauce
- Latin Flank Steak with Spanish Rice & Bell Peppers in Chipotle Crema Sauce
- Pork Tenderloin with Bourbon Pear Sauce
- Prosciutto-Stuffed Chicken Breasts with Fig & Honey Sauce

Chicken Stock
- Andouille Sausage & Shrimp Cajun Jambalaya
- Blood Orange-Roasted Chicken
- Chicken Cacciatore with Basmati Rice
- Chicken Enchiladas
- Just Add Mayo: Curry Chicken Salad
- Lamb Cutlets with Mint Orange Cointreau Sauce
- Latin Flank Steak with Spanish Rice & Bell Peppers in Chipotle Crema Sauce
- Pork Tenderloin with Bourbon Pear Sauce
- Prosciutto-Stuffed Chicken Breasts with Fig & Honey Sauce

Chicken, Breasts
- Andouille Sausage & Shrimp Cajun Jambalaya
- Blood Orange-Roasted Chicken
- Butter Chicken (a/k/a Indian Chicken Makhani)
- Chicken Ballotine with Rosemary Beurre Blanc Sauce
- Chicken Enchiladas
- Cilantro-Grilled Chicken with Mango Salsa
- Just Add Mayo: Curry Chicken Salad
- Prosciutto-Stuffed Chicken Breasts with Fig & Honey Sauce
- Spinach & Feta Stuffed Chicken with Pesto & Mediterranean Salsa

Chicken, Tenderloins
- Oven-Baked Parmesan Chicken

Chicken, Thighs
- Andouille Sausage & Shrimp Cajun Jambalaya
- Butter Chicken (a/k/a Indian Chicken Makhani)
- Chicken Ballotine with Rosemary Beurre Blanc Sauce
- Chicken Cacciatore with Basmati Rice
- Chunky Chicken & Corn Chili
- Drunk Irishman's Shepherd's Pie
- Oven-Baked Parmesan Chicken
- Southern-Fried Bacon-Wrapped Chicken & Waffles
- Teriyaki Chicken with Rice & Broccoli

Chiles, Chipotle Chiles in Adobo Sauce
- Chipotle Roasted Leg of Lamb
- Latin Flank Steak with Spanish Rice & Bell Peppers in Chipotle Crema Sauce

Chiles, Green (canned)
- Chicken Enchiladas
- Latin Flank Steak with Spanish Rice & Bell Peppers in Chipotle Crema Sauce

Chipotle Chiles in Adobo Sauce
- Chipotle Roasted Leg of Lamb
- Latin Flank Steak with Spanish Rice & Bell Peppers in Chipotle Crema Sauce

Chu Hou Paste
- Cantonese Braised Beef

Cilantro, Fresh
- Butter Chicken (a/k/a Indian Chicken Makhani)
- Chicken Enchiladas
- Cilantro-Grilled Chicken with Mango Salsa
- Latin Flank Steak with Spanish Rice & Bell Peppers in Chipotle Crema Sauce

Cocoa Powder, Dutch Process
- Chef Gail's Coffee Rub

Coconut Milk
- Butter Chicken (a/k/a Indian Chicken Makhani)
- Macadamia Nut-Crusted Halibut with Raspberry Sauce

Coffee Beans, Dark Roast, ground
- Chef Gail's Coffee Rub

Cointreau (French Orange Liqueur)
- Lamb Cutlets with Mint Orange Cointreau Sauce

Corn
- Chunky Chicken & Corn Chili

Corn Starch
- Blood Orange-Roasted Chicken
- Firecracker Salmon
- Oven-Baked Parmesan Chicken
- Teriyaki Chicken with Rice & Broccoli
- Tuscan-Style Horseradish-Crusted Beef Roulade with Roasted Red Peppers & Provolone

Cornmeal, Yellow
- Southern-Fried Bacon-Wrapped Chicken & Waffles

Cream Cheese
- Chicken Ballotine with Rosemary Beurre Blanc Sauce
- Chicken Enchiladas
- Swedish Meatballs with White Gravy
- Tuscan-Style Horseradish-Crusted Beef Roulade with Roasted Red Peppers & Provolone

Cream, Half & Half
- Butter Chicken (a/k/a Indian Chicken Makhani)

RESOURCES

Cream, Heavy Whipping
    Chicken Ballotine with Rosemary Beurre Blanc Sauce
    Peanut Butter, Bourbon & Bacon Burgers

Cream, Sour
    Chicken Ballotine with Rosemary Beurre Blanc Sauce
    Chicken Enchiladas
    Swedish Meatballs with White Gravy
    Tuscan-Style Horseradish-Crusted Beef Roulade with Roasted Red Peppers & Provolone

Cremini Mushrooms
    Chicken Cacciatore with Basmati Rice
    Tuscan-Style Horseradish-Crusted Beef Roulade with Roasted Red Peppers & Provolone

Daikon Radish
    Cantonese Braised Beef

Dijon Mustard
    Chicken Ballotine with Rosemary Beurre Blanc Sauce
    Prosciutto-Stuffed Chicken Breasts with Fig & Honey Sauce
    Tuscan-Style Horseradish-Crusted Beef Roulade with Roasted Red Peppers & Provolone

Dried Fruit, Cherries, Tart
    Cherry-Stuffed Pork Loin with Black Cherry Chutney

Dried Fruit, Figs
    Prosciutto-Stuffed Chicken Breasts with Fig & Honey Sauce

Dried Fruit, Orange
    Cantonese Braised Beef
    Overnight Brine for Pork

Dried Fruit, Pomegranate Arils
    Cherry-Stuffed Pork Loin with Black Cherry Chutney

Dried Fruit, Tangerine
    Cantonese Braised Beef
    Overnight Brine for Pork

Eggplant
    Roasted Vegetable Lasagna (Vegetarian)

Eggs
    Habanero, Turkey & Sausage Meatballs
    Macadamia Nut-Crusted Halibut with Raspberry Sauce
    Oven-Baked Parmesan Chicken
    Peanut Butter, Bourbon & Bacon Burgers
    Roasted Vegetable Lasagna (Vegetarian)
    Southern-Fried Bacon-Wrapped Chicken & Waffles
    Spicy Italian Meatballs with Marinara
    Swedish Meatballs with White Gravy

Espresso Powder
    Chef Gail's Coffee Rub

Feta Cheese, crumbled
    Spinach & Feta Stuffed Chicken with Pesto & Mediterranean Salsa

Fig Jam
    Prosciutto-Stuffed Chicken Breasts with Fig & Honey Sauce

Figs, Dried
    Prosciutto-Stuffed Chicken Breasts with Fig & Honey Sauce

Figs, Fresh
    Prosciutto-Stuffed Chicken Breasts with Fig & Honey Sauce

Fire-Roasted Diced Tomatoes
    Andouille Sausage & Shrimp Cajun Jambalaya
    Chicken Cacciatore with Basmati Rice
    Roasted Vegetable Lasagna (Vegetarian)
    Spicy Italian Meatballs with Marinara

Fish Sauce
    Peanut Butter, Bourbon & Bacon Burgers

Flank Steak
    Latin Flank Steak with Spanish Rice & Bell Peppers in Chipotle Crema Sauce

Flour, AP (all-purpose)
    Cantonese Braised Beef
    Drunk Irishman's Shepherd's Pie
    Guinness Pot Roast with Gravy
    Macadamia Nut-Crusted Halibut with Raspberry Sauce
    Oven-Baked Parmesan Chicken
    Prosciutto-Stuffed Chicken Breasts with Fig & Honey Sauce
    Swedish Meatballs with White Gravy
    Tuscan-Style Horseradish-Crusted Beef Roulade with Roasted Red Peppers & Provolone

Flour, Self-Rising
    Southern-Fried Bacon-Wrapped Chicken & Waffles

Frank's Red Hot Sauce (Original)
    Oven-Baked Parmesan Chicken
    Southern-Fried Bacon-Wrapped Chicken & Waffles

Garlic, Cloves or Minced
    Andouille Sausage & Shrimp Cajun Jambalaya
    Blood Orange-Roasted Chicken
    Bourbon BBQ Babyback Ribs
    Butter Chicken (a/k/a Indian Chicken Makhani)
    Cantonese Braised Beef
    Carolina-Style BBQ Pulled Pork
    Cherry-Stuffed Pork Loin with Black Cherry Chutney
    Chicken Ballotine with Rosemary Beurre Blanc Sauce
    Chicken Cacciatore with Basmati Rice
    Chicken Enchiladas
    Chipotle Roasted Leg of Lamb

Chunky Chicken & Corn Chili
Cilantro-Grilled Chicken with Mango Salsa
Drunk Irishman's Shepherd's Pie
Firecracker Salmon
Guinness Pot Roast with Gravy
Habanero, Turkey & Sausage Meatballs
Just Add Mayo: Curry Chicken Salad
Lamb Cutlets with Mint Orange Cointreau Sauce
Latin Flank Steak with Spanish Rice & Bell Peppers in Chipotle Crema Sauce
Peanut Butter, Bourbon & Bacon Burgers
Pork Tenderloin with Bourbon Pear Sauce
Prosciutto-Stuffed Chicken Breasts with Fig & Honey Sauce
Roasted Vegetable Lasagna (Vegetarian)
Seafood-Stuffed Portobello Mushrooms
Spicy Italian Meatballs with Marinara
Spinach & Feta Stuffed Chicken with Pesto & Mediterranean Salsa
Swedish Meatballs with White Gravy
Teriyaki Chicken with Rice & Broccoli
Tuscan-Style Horseradish-Crusted Beef Roulade with Roasted Red Peppers & Provolone

Ginger Root, Fresh
Butter Chicken (a/k/a Indian Chicken Makhani)
Cantonese Braised Beef
Firecracker Salmon
Teriyaki Chicken with Rice & Broccoli

Goat Cheese
Habanero, Turkey & Sausage Meatballs
Prosciutto-Stuffed Chicken Breasts with Fig & Honey Sauce
Seafood-Stuffed Portobello Mushrooms

Green Bell Peppers
Andouille Sausage & Shrimp Cajun Jambalaya
Chicken Cacciatore with Basmati Rice
Latin Flank Steak with Spanish Rice & Bell Peppers in Chipotle Crema Sauce
Roasted Vegetable Lasagna (Vegetarian)

Green Jalapeno Jelly
Peanut Butter, Bourbon & Bacon Burgers

Green Onion
Andouille Sausage & Shrimp Cajun Jambalaya
Cantonese Braised Beef
Firecracker Salmon
Teriyaki Chicken with Rice & Broccoli

Guinness Draught Beer
Guinness Pot Roast with Gravy

Habanero Peppers
Habanero, Turkey & Sausage Meatballs

Half & Half Cream
Butter Chicken (a/k/a Indian Chicken Makhani)

Halibut
Macadamia Nut-Crusted Halibut with Raspberry Sauce

Heavy Whipping Cream
Chicken Ballotine with Rosemary Beurre Blanc Sauce
Peanut Butter, Bourbon & Bacon Burgers

HERBS: Basil, Fresh
Prosciutto-Stuffed Chicken Breasts with Fig & Honey Sauce
Roasted Vegetable Lasagna (Vegetarian)
Spicy Italian Meatballs with Marinara
Spinach & Feta Stuffed Chicken with Pesto & Mediterranean Salsa

HERBS: Cilantro, Fresh
Butter Chicken (a/k/a Indian Chicken Makhani)
Chicken Enchiladas
Cilantro-Grilled Chicken with Mango Salsa
Latin Flank Steak with Spanish Rice & Bell Peppers in Chipotle Crema Sauce

HERBS: Mint, Fresh
Chipotle Roasted Leg of Lamb
Lamb Cutlets with Mint Orange Cointreau Sauce

HERBS: Oregano, Fresh
Habanero, Turkey & Sausage Meatballs
Roasted Vegetable Lasagna (Vegetarian)

HERBS: Parsley, Italian Flat-Leaf, Fresh
Andouille Sausage & Shrimp Cajun Jambalaya
Drunk Irishman's Shepherd's Pie
Guinness Pot Roast with Gravy
Lamb Cutlets with Mint Orange Cointreau Sauce
Macadamia Nut-Crusted Halibut with Raspberry Sauce
Prosciutto-Stuffed Chicken Breasts with Fig & Honey Sauce
Seafood-Stuffed Portobello Mushrooms
Spicy Italian Meatballs with Marinara
Spinach & Feta Stuffed Chicken with Pesto & Mediterranean Salsa
Swedish Meatballs with White Gravy
Tuscan-Style Horseradish-Crusted Beef Roulade with Roasted Red Peppers & Provolone

HERBS: Rosemary, Fresh
Cherry-Stuffed Pork Loin with Black Cherry Chutney
Chicken Ballotine with Rosemary Beurre Blanc Sauce
Drunk Irishman's Shepherd's Pie
Guinness Pot Roast with Gravy
Habanero, Turkey & Sausage Meatballs
Lamb Cutlets with Mint Orange Cointreau Sauce
Peanut Butter, Bourbon & Bacon Burgers
Pork Tenderloin with Bourbon Pear Sauce
Prosciutto-Stuffed Chicken Breasts with Fig & Honey Sauce

RESOURCES

Tuscan-Style Horseradish-Crusted Beef Roulade with Roasted Red Peppers & Provolone
Overnight Brine for Pork

HERBS: Thyme, Fresh
Blood Orange-Roasted Chicken
Guinness Pot Roast with Gravy
Lamb Cutlets with Mint Orange Cointreau Sauce
Tuscan-Style Horseradish-Crusted Beef Roulade with Roasted Red Peppers & Provolone

Hoisin Sauce
Cantonese Braised Beef

Honey
Blood Orange-Roasted Chicken
Cilantro-Grilled Chicken with Mango Salsa
Prosciutto-Stuffed Chicken Breasts with Fig & Honey Sauce

Horseradish, Prepared
Tuscan-Style Horseradish-Crusted Beef Roulade with Roasted Red Peppers & Provolone

Hot Sauce
Andouille Sausage & Shrimp Cajun Jambalaya

Hot Sauce, Frank's Red Hot Sauce (Original)
Oven-Baked Parmesan Chicken
Southern-Fried Bacon-Wrapped Chicken & Waffles

Irish Whiskey
Drunk Irishman's Shepherd's Pie

Italian Sausage, Ground
Drunk Irishman's Shepherd's Pie
Spicy Italian Meatballs with Marinara
Swedish Meatballs with White Gravy

Italian Sausage, Sweet, Ground
Spicy Italian Meatballs with Marinara

Jalapeno Peppers
Bourbon BBQ Babyback Ribs
Cilantro-Grilled Chicken with Mango Salsa
Latin Flank Steak with Spanish Rice & Bell Peppers in Chipotle Crema Sauce

Jam, Fig
Prosciutto-Stuffed Chicken Breasts with Fig & Honey Sauce

Jelly, Green Jalapeno
Peanut Butter, Bourbon & Bacon Burgers

Jelly, Jalapeno, Green
Peanut Butter, Bourbon & Bacon Burgers

Juice, Apple
Bourbon BBQ Babyback Ribs

Juice, Lemon
Spinach & Feta Stuffed Chicken with Pesto & Mediterranean Salsa

Juice, Lime
Chipotle Roasted Leg of Lamb
Cilantro-Grilled Chicken with Mango Salsa
Latin Flank Steak with Spanish Rice & Bell Peppers in Chipotle Crema Sauce

Juice, Orange
Lamb Cutlets with Mint Orange Cointreau Sauce

Juice, Orange, Mandarin
Lamb Cutlets with Mint Orange Cointreau Sauce

Ketchup
Bourbon BBQ Babyback Ribs
Carolina-Style BBQ Pulled Pork

Kidney Beans, Dark Red
Chunky Chicken & Corn Chili

Lamb Broth
Chipotle Roasted Leg of Lamb

Lamb Stock
Chipotle Roasted Leg of Lamb

Lamb, Cutlets
Lamb Cutlets with Mint Orange Cointreau Sauce

Lamb, Ground
Drunk Irishman's Shepherd's Pie

Lamb, Leg of Lamb Roast
Chipotle Roasted Leg of Lamb

Lemons/Lemon Zest
Cherry-Stuffed Pork Loin with Black Cherry Chutney
Just Add Mayo: Curry Chicken Salad
Pork Tenderloin with Bourbon Pear Sauce

Liqueur, Orange
Lamb Cutlets with Mint Orange Cointreau Sauce

Macadamia Nuts
Macadamia Nut-Crusted Halibut with Raspberry Sauce

Mango
Cilantro-Grilled Chicken with Mango Salsa

Maple Syrup
Peanut Butter, Bourbon & Bacon Burgers
Southern-Fried Bacon-Wrapped Chicken & Waffles

Mayonnaise
Just Add Mayo: Curry Chicken Salad

Mexican Cheese Blend
Chicken Enchiladas

Mexican Crema
    Latin Flank Steak with Spanish Rice & Bell Peppers in Chipotle Crema Sauce

Milk (Whole or 2%)
    Chicken Enchiladas
    Drunk Irishman's Shepherd's Pie
    Seafood-Stuffed Portobello Mushrooms
    Spicy Italian Meatballs with Marinara
    Swedish Meatballs with White Gravy

Milk, Coconut
    Butter Chicken (a/k/a Indian Chicken Makhani)
    Macadamia Nut-Crusted Halibut with Raspberry Sauce

Mint, Fresh
    Chipotle Roasted Leg of Lamb
    Lamb Cutlets with Mint Orange Cointreau Sauce

Mirin Sweet Rice Cooking Wine
    Just Add Mayo: Curry Chicken Salad

Mozzarella Cheese
    Roasted Vegetable Lasagna (Vegetarian)

Mushrooms, Cremini
    Chicken Cacciatore with Basmati Rice
    Tuscan-Style Horseradish-Crusted Beef Roulade with Roasted Red Peppers & Provolone

Mushrooms, Portobello
    Seafood-Stuffed Portobello Mushrooms

Mushrooms, White
    Chicken Cacciatore with Basmati Rice
    Tuscan-Style Horseradish-Crusted Beef Roulade with Roasted Red Peppers & Provolone

Mustard, Dijon
    Chicken Ballotine with Rosemary Beurre Blanc Sauce
    Prosciutto-Stuffed Chicken Breasts with Fig & Honey Sauce
    Tuscan-Style Horseradish-Crusted Beef Roulade with Roasted Red Peppers & Provolone

Mustard, Spicy Brown
    Bourbon BBQ Babyback Ribs
    Carolina-Style BBQ Pulled Pork

Nuts, Cashews
    Just Add Mayo: Curry Chicken Salad

Nuts, Macadamia
    Macadamia Nut-Crusted Halibut with Raspberry Sauce

Nuts, Pine
    Spinach & Feta Stuffed Chicken with Pesto & Mediterranean Salsa

Nuts, Pistachio
    Lamb Cutlets with Mint Orange Cointreau Sauce

Nuts, Walnuts
    Cherry-Stuffed Pork Loin with Black Cherry Chutney
    Prosciutto-Stuffed Chicken Breasts with Fig & Honey Sauce

Oil, Canola
    Cantonese Braised Beef
    Firecracker Salmon

Oil, Olive
    Andouille Sausage & Shrimp Cajun Jambalaya
    Blood Orange-Roasted Chicken
    Bourbon BBQ Babyback Ribs
    Butter Chicken (a/k/a Indian Chicken Makhani)
    Cherry-Stuffed Pork Loin with Black Cherry Chutney
    Chicken Ballotine with Rosemary Beurre Blanc Sauce
    Chicken Cacciatore with Basmati Rice
    Chicken Enchiladas
    Chipotle Roasted Leg of Lamb
    Chunky Chicken & Corn Chili
    Cilantro-Grilled Chicken with Mango Salsa
    Coffee-Rubbed Steak with Coffee Butter
    Drunk Irishman's Shepherd's Pie
    Guinness Pot Roast with Gravy
    Habanero, Turkey & Sausage Meatballs
    Lamb Cutlets with Mint Orange Cointreau Sauce
    Latin Flank Steak with Spanish Rice & Bell Peppers in Chipotle Crema Sauce
    Macadamia Nut-Crusted Halibut with Raspberry Sauce
    Pork Tenderloin with Bourbon Pear Sauce
    Prosciutto-Stuffed Chicken Breasts with Fig & Honey Sauce
    Roasted Vegetable Lasagna (Vegetarian)
    Seafood-Stuffed Portobello Mushrooms
    Spicy Italian Meatballs with Marinara
    Spinach & Feta Stuffed Chicken with Pesto & Mediterranean Salsa
    Swedish Meatballs with White Gravy
    Tuscan-Style Horseradish-Crusted Beef Roulade with Roasted Red Peppers & Provolone

Oil, Peanut
    Southern-Fried Bacon-Wrapped Chicken & Waffles

Oil, Sesame
    Firecracker Salmon
    Teriyaki Chicken with Rice & Broccoli

Oil, Vegetable
    Cantonese Braised Beef
    Firecracker Salmon

Olives, Italian Castelvetrano, Green
    Spinach & Feta Stuffed Chicken with Pesto & Mediterranean Salsa

RESOURCES

Onion, Green
- Andouille Sausage & Shrimp Cajun Jambalaya
- Cantonese Braised Beef
- Firecracker Salmon
- Teriyaki Chicken with Rice & Broccoli

Onion, Red
- Blood Orange-Roasted Chicken
- Cilantro-Grilled Chicken with Mango Salsa
- Just Add Mayo: Curry Chicken Salad
- Spinach & Feta Stuffed Chicken with Pesto & Mediterranean Salsa

Onion, White
- Andouille Sausage & Shrimp Cajun Jambalaya
- Bourbon BBQ Babyback Ribs
- Cherry-Stuffed Pork Loin with Black Cherry Chutney
- Chicken Enchiladas
- Chunky Chicken & Corn Chili
- Guinness Pot Roast with Gravy
- Habanero, Turkey & Sausage Meatballs
- Latin Flank Steak with Spanish Rice & Bell Peppers in Chipotle Crema Sauce
- Peanut Butter, Bourbon & Bacon Burgers
- Seafood-Stuffed Portobello Mushrooms
- Spicy Italian Meatballs with Marinara
- Swedish Meatballs with White Gravy

Onion, White, Sweet
- Bourbon BBQ Babyback Ribs
- Chunky Chicken & Corn Chili
- Peanut Butter, Bourbon & Bacon Burgers
- Seafood-Stuffed Portobello Mushrooms

Onion, Yellow
- Andouille Sausage & Shrimp Cajun Jambalaya
- Bourbon BBQ Babyback Ribs
- Butter Chicken (a/k/a Indian Chicken Makhani)
- Chicken Cacciatore with Basmati Rice
- Chunky Chicken & Corn Chili
- Guinness Pot Roast with Gravy
- Habanero, Turkey & Sausage Meatballs
- Peanut Butter, Bourbon & Bacon Burgers
- Seafood-Stuffed Portobello Mushrooms
- Spicy Italian Meatballs with Marinara

Orange Peel, Dried
- Cantonese Braised Beef

Oranges, Blood
- Blood Orange-Roasted Chicken

Oranges, Mandarin
- Lamb Cutlets with Mint Orange Cointreau Sauce

Oranges, Naval
- Lamb Cutlets with Mint Orange Cointreau Sauce

Oranges, Valencia
- Lamb Cutlets with Mint Orange Cointreau Sauce

Oregano, Fresh
- Habanero, Turkey & Sausage Meatballs
- Roasted Vegetable Lasagna (Vegetarian)

Oyster Sauce
- Cantonese Braised Beef

Panko Bread Crumbs
- Habanero, Turkey & Sausage Meatballs
- Macadamia Nut-Crusted Halibut with Raspberry Sauce
- Oven-Baked Parmesan Chicken
- Spicy Italian Meatballs with Marinara
- Tuscan-Style Horseradish-Crusted Beef Roulade with Roasted Red Peppers & Provolone

Parmesan Cheese, Grated
- Drunk Irishman's Shepherd's Pie
- Habanero, Turkey & Sausage Meatballs
- Oven-Baked Parmesan Chicken
- Roasted Vegetable Lasagna (Vegetarian)
- Seafood-Stuffed Portobello Mushrooms
- Spicy Italian Meatballs with Marinara
- Spinach & Feta Stuffed Chicken with Pesto & Mediterranean Salsa

Parmesan Cheese, Shredded
- Drunk Irishman's Shepherd's Pie

Parsley, Italian Flat-Leaf, Fresh
- Andouille Sausage & Shrimp Cajun Jambalaya
- Drunk Irishman's Shepherd's Pie
- Guinness Pot Roast with Gravy
- Lamb Cutlets with Mint Orange Cointreau Sauce
- Macadamia Nut-Crusted Halibut with Raspberry Sauce
- Prosciutto-Stuffed Chicken Breasts with Fig & Honey Sauce
- Seafood-Stuffed Portobello Mushrooms
- Spicy Italian Meatballs with Marinara
- Spinach & Feta Stuffed Chicken with Pesto & Mediterranean Salsa
- Swedish Meatballs with White Gravy
- Tuscan-Style Horseradish-Crusted Beef Roulade with Roasted Red Peppers & Provolone

Pasta, Lasagna Sheets
- Roasted Vegetable Lasagna (Vegetarian)

Peanut Butter, Creamy or Crunchy
- Peanut Butter, Bourbon & Bacon Burgers

Pear, Anjou
- Pork Tenderloin with Bourbon Pear Sauce

Pear, Bartlett
- Pork Tenderloin with Bourbon Pear Sauce

Pear, Bosc
- Pork Tenderloin with Bourbon Pear Sauce

Pears, Canned
    Pork Tenderloin with Bourbon Pear Sauce

Peas
    Drunk Irishman's Shepherd's Pie

Peppers, Bell, any color
    Roasted Vegetable Lasagna (Vegetarian)

Peppers, Bell, Green
    Andouille Sausage & Shrimp Cajun Jambalaya
    Chicken Cacciatore with Basmati Rice
    Latin Flank Steak with Spanish Rice & Bell Peppers in Chipotle Crema Sauce
    Roasted Vegetable Lasagna (Vegetarian)

Peppers, Bell, Red
    Roasted Vegetable Lasagna (Vegetarian)
    Seafood-Stuffed Portobello Mushrooms
    Tuscan-Style Horseradish-Crusted Beef Roulade with Roasted Red Peppers & Provolone

Peppers, Habanero
    Habanero, Turkey & Sausage Meatballs

Peppers, Jalapeno
    Bourbon BBQ Babyback Ribs
    Cilantro-Grilled Chicken with Mango Salsa
    Latin Flank Steak with Spanish Rice & Bell Peppers in Chipotle Crema Sauce

Pine Nuts
    Spinach & Feta Stuffed Chicken with Pesto & Mediterranean Salsa

Pistachio Nuts
    Lamb Cutlets with Mint Orange Cointreau Sauce

Pomegranate Arils, dried
    Cherry-Stuffed Pork Loin with Black Cherry Chutney

Popcorn Kernals
    Southern-Fried Bacon-Wrapped Chicken & Waffles

Pork Sausage, Ground
    Drunk Irishman's Shepherd's Pie
    Habanero, Turkey & Sausage Meatballs
    Spicy Italian Meatballs with Marinara
    Swedish Meatballs with White Gravy

Pork, Babyback Ribs
    Bourbon BBQ Babyback Ribs

Pork, Bacon
    Chicken Ballotine with Rosemary Beurre Blanc Sauce
    Peanut Butter, Bourbon & Bacon Burgers
    Southern-Fried Bacon-Wrapped Chicken & Waffles

Pork, Loin Roast, Boneless
    Carolina-Style BBQ Pulled Pork
    Cherry-Stuffed Pork Loin with Black Cherry Chutney

Pork, Prosciutto
    Prosciutto-Stuffed Chicken Breasts with Fig & Honey Sauce

Pork, Tenderloins
    Pork Tenderloin with Bourbon Pear Sauce

Portobello Mushrooms
    Seafood-Stuffed Portobello Mushrooms

Potatoes, Russet
    Cantonese Braised Beef
    Drunk Irishman's Shepherd's Pie

Prosciutto
    Chicken Ballotine with Rosemary Beurre Blanc Sauce
    Prosciutto-Stuffed Chicken Breasts with Fig & Honey Sauce

Provolone Cheese
    Tuscan-Style Horseradish-Crusted Beef Roulade with Roasted Red Peppers & Provolone

Radish, Daikon
    Cantonese Braised Beef

Raisins, Black
    Cherry-Stuffed Pork Loin with Black Cherry Chutney
    Just Add Mayo: Curry Chicken Salad

Raisins, Black or Golden
    Cherry-Stuffed Pork Loin with Black Cherry Chutney

Raisins, Golden
    Cherry-Stuffed Pork Loin with Black Cherry Chutney

Raspberries, Fresh or Frozen
    Macadamia Nut-Crusted Halibut with Raspberry Sauce

Raw Sugar
    Macadamia Nut-Crusted Halibut with Raspberry Sauce

Red Bell Peppers
    Roasted Vegetable Lasagna (Vegetarian)
    Seafood-Stuffed Portobello Mushrooms
    Tuscan-Style Horseradish-Crusted Beef Roulade with Roasted Red Peppers & Provolone

Red Wine
    Cherry-Stuffed Pork Loin with Black Cherry Chutney
    Chicken Cacciatore with Basmati Rice
    Spicy Italian Meatballs with Marinara
    Tuscan-Style Horseradish-Crusted Beef Roulade with Roasted Red Peppers & Provolone

Rice Wine
    Cantonese Braised Beef

Rice, Basmati
    Andouille Sausage & Shrimp Cajun Jambalaya
    Chicken Cacciatore with Basmati Rice

RESOURCES

    Latin Flank Steak with Spanish Rice & Bell Peppers in Chipotle Crema Sauce
    Teriyaki Chicken with Rice & Broccoli

Ricotta Cheese
    Roasted Vegetable Lasagna (Vegetarian)

Rock Sugar
    Cantonese Braised Beef

Rosemary, Fresh
    Cherry-Stuffed Pork Loin with Black Cherry Chutney
    Chicken Ballotine with Rosemary Beurre Blanc Sauce
    Drunk Irishman's Shepherd's Pie
    Guinness Pot Roast with Gravy
    Habanero, Turkey & Sausage Meatballs
    Lamb Cutlets with Mint Orange Cointreau Sauce
    Peanut Butter, Bourbon & Bacon Burgers
    Pork Tenderloin with Bourbon Pear Sauce
    Prosciutto-Stuffed Chicken Breasts with Fig & Honey Sauce
    Tuscan-Style Horseradish-Crusted Beef Roulade with Roasted Red Peppers & Provolone

Russet Potatoes
    Cantonese Braised Beef
    Drunk Irishman's Shepherd's Pie

Salmon
    Firecracker Salmon
    Glazed Salmon (multiple varieties)

Sausage, Andouille
    Andouille Sausage & Shrimp Cajun Jambalaya

Sausage, Chicken, Ground
    Drunk Irishman's Shepherd's Pie

Sausage, Italian, Ground
    Drunk Irishman's Shepherd's Pie
    Spicy Italian Meatballs with Marinara
    Swedish Meatballs with White Gravy

Sausage, Italian, Sweet
    Spicy Italian Meatballs with Marinara

Sausage, Pork, Ground
    Drunk Irishman's Shepherd's Pie
    Habanero, Turkey & Sausage Meatballs
    Spicy Italian Meatballs with Marinara
    Swedish Meatballs with White Gravy

Scallions
    Andouille Sausage & Shrimp Cajun Jambalaya
    Cantonese Braised Beef
    Firecracker Salmon
    Teriyaki Chicken with Rice & Broccoli

Scallops, Whole Bay
    Seafood-Stuffed Portobello Mushrooms

Sesame Seeds
    Teriyaki Chicken with Rice & Broccoli

Shallot
    Cantonese Braised Beef
    Chicken Ballotine with Rosemary Beurre Blanc Sauce
    Chipotle Roasted Leg of Lamb
    Drunk Irishman's Shepherd's Pie
    Lamb Cutlets with Mint Orange Cointreau Sauce
    Pork Tenderloin with Bourbon Pear Sauce
    Prosciutto-Stuffed Chicken Breasts with Fig & Honey Sauce
    Spicy Italian Meatballs with Marinara
    Tuscan-Style Horseradish-Crusted Beef Roulade with Roasted Red Peppers & Provolone

Shaozing Wine
    Cantonese Braised Beef

Sherry Wine
    Drunk Irishman's Shepherd's Pie

Shrimp
    Andouille Sausage & Shrimp Cajun Jambalaya
    Seafood-Stuffed Portobello Mushrooms

Soup Base, Beef
    Chipotle Roasted Leg of Lamb
    Drunk Irishman's Shepherd's Pie
    Swedish Meatballs with White Gravy
    Tuscan-Style Horseradish-Crusted Beef Roulade with Roasted Red Peppers & Provolone

Soup Base, Chicken
    Blood Orange-Roasted Chicken
    Chicken Cacciatore with Basmati Rice
    Chicken Enchiladas
    Lamb Cutlets with Mint Orange Cointreau Sauce
    Pork Tenderloin with Bourbon Pear Sauce

Sour Cream
    Chicken Ballotine with Rosemary Beurre Blanc Sauce
    Chicken Enchiladas
    Swedish Meatballs with White Gravy
    Tuscan-Style Horseradish-Crusted Beef Roulade with Roasted Red Peppers & Provolone

Soy Sauce
    Cantonese Braised Beef
    Firecracker Salmon
    Latin Flank Steak with Spanish Rice & Bell Peppers in Chipotle Crema Sauce
    Peanut Butter, Bourbon & Bacon Burgers
    Teriyaki Chicken with Rice & Broccoli

Soy Sauce, Dark
    Cantonese Braised Beef

SPICE BLEND: Chef Gail's BBQ Dry Rub
    Bourbon BBQ Babyback Ribs
    Carolina-Style BBQ Pulled Pork

SPICE BLEND: Chef Gail's Butter Chicken Masala
    Chef Gail's Indian Butter Chicken Spice Blend

SPICE BLEND: Chef Gail's Chipotle Dry Rub
    Chipotle Roasted Leg of Lamb

SPICE BLEND: Chef Gail's Coffee Dry Rub
    Coffee-Rubbed Steak with Coffee Butter

SPICE BLEND: Chef Gail's Creole Seasoning Spice Blend
    Andouille Sausage & Shrimp Cajun Jambalaya

SPICE BLEND: Chef Gail's Indian Butter Chicken Spice
    Butter Chicken (a/k/a Indian Chicken Makhani)
    Chef Gail's Indian Butter Chicken Spice Blend

SPICE BLEND: Chef Gail's Mexican Spice Blend
    Chicken Enchiladas
    Latin Flank Steak with Spanish Rice & Bell Peppers in Chipotle Crema Sauce

SPICE BLEND: Chef Gail's Southern Spice Blend
    Southern-Fried Bacon-Wrapped Chicken & Waffles

SPICE: Ancho Chile Powder
    Chef Gail's Chipotle Dry Rub
    Chef Gail's Coffee Rub
    Chef Gail's Mexican Spice Blend

SPICE: Basil Leaves, dried
    Chef Gail's Creole Seasoning Spice Blend
    Spicy Italian Meatballs with Marinara

SPICE: Bay Leaves
    Andouille Sausage & Shrimp Cajun Jambalaya
    Cantonese Braised Beef

SPICE: Cardamom Seeds, pods (black or green)
    Cantonese Braised Beef

SPICE: Cardamom Seeds, whole
    Cantonese Braised Beef

SPICE: Cassia Bark Sticks
    Cantonese Braised Beef

SPICE: Cayenne Pepper
    Chef Gail's BBQ Dry Rub
    Chef Gail's Creole Seasoning Spice Blend
    Chef Gail's Mexican Spice Blend
    Chef Gail's Southern Spice Blend
    Cherry-Stuffed Pork Loin with Black Cherry Chutney
    Chipotle Roasted Leg of Lamb
    Chunky Chicken & Corn Chili
    Cilantro-Grilled Chicken with Mango Salsa
    Drunk Irishman's Shepherd's Pie
    Firecracker Salmon
    Guinness Pot Roast with Gravy
    Just Add Mayo: Curry Chicken Salad
    Lamb Cutlets with Mint Orange Cointreau Sauce

    Oven-Baked Parmesan Chicken
    Peanut Butter, Bourbon & Bacon Burgers
    Pork Tenderloin with Bourbon Pear Sauce
    Tuscan-Style Horseradish-Crusted Beef Roulade with Roasted Red Peppers & Provolone

SPICE: Celery Salt
    Chef Gail's BBQ Dry Rub
    Chef Gail's Southern Spice Blend

SPICE: Chinese Five Spice
    Cantonese Braised Beef

SPICE: Chipotle Powder, dried
    Chef Gail's Chipotle Dry Rub

SPICE: Cinnamon Sticks
    Cantonese Braised Beef

SPICE: Cinnamon, Ground
    Cherry-Stuffed Pork Loin with Black Cherry Chutney
    Chunky Chicken & Corn Chili
    Drunk Irishman's Shepherd's Pie

SPICE: Cloves, Ground
    Chef Gail's Chipotle Dry Rub

SPICE: Coriander, Ground or Dried Leaves
    Chef Gail's Chipotle Dry Rub
    Chef Gail's Coffee Rub
    Cherry-Stuffed Pork Loin with Black Cherry Chutney
    Chunky Chicken & Corn Chili

SPICE: Cumin, Ground
    Chef Gail's Chipotle Dry Rub
    Chef Gail's Mexican Spice Blend
    Chunky Chicken & Corn Chili

SPICE: Curry Powder
    Just Add Mayo: Curry Chicken Salad

SPICE: Dark Chili Powder
    Chunky Chicken & Corn Chili
    Habanero, Turkey & Sausage Meatballs

SPICE: Dry Mustard Powder
    Chef Gail's BBQ Dry Rub
    Chef Gail's Chipotle Dry Rub
    Chef Gail's Coffee Rub
    Chef Gail's Southern Spice Blend

SPICE: Fenugreek Leaves, dried
    Butter Chicken (a/k/a Indian Chicken Makhani)

SPICE: Garlic Powder
    Chef Gail's BBQ Dry Rub
    Chef Gail's Chipotle Dry Rub
    Chef Gail's Creole Seasoning Spice Blend
    Chef Gail's Mexican Spice Blend

SPICE: Garlic Salt
    Chef Gail's Southern Spice Blend

RESOURCES

SPICE: Ginger, Ground
    Chef Gail's Southern Spice Blend

SPICE: Italian Seasoning, dried
    Chicken Cacciatore with Basmati Rice
    Habanero, Turkey & Sausage Meatballs
    Oven-Baked Parmesan Chicken
    Spicy Italian Meatballs with Marinara

SPICE: Kasoori Methi, dried
    Butter Chicken (a/k/a Indian Chicken Makhani)

SPICE: Lemon Salt
    Chef Gail's Coffee Rub

SPICE: Montreal Steak Seasoning (McCormick brand)
    Swedish Meatballs with White Gravy

SPICE: Nutmeg, Ground
    Drunk Irishman's Shepherd's Pie
    Swedish Meatballs with White Gravy

SPICE: Onion Powder
    Chef Gail's BBQ Dry Rub
    Chef Gail's Chipotle Dry Rub
    Chef Gail's Creole Seasoning Spice Blend

SPICE: Oregano Leaves, dried
    Chef Gail's Creole Seasoning Spice Blend
    Chef Gail's Mexican Spice Blend
    Chef Gail's Southern Spice Blend
    Chunky Chicken & Corn Chili
    Spicy Italian Meatballs with Marinara
    Spinach & Feta Stuffed Chicken with Pesto & Mediterranean Salsa

SPICE: Paprika, Smoked (Spanish)
    Chef Gail's BBQ Dry Rub
    Chef Gail's Coffee Rub
    Chef Gail's Southern Spice Blend
    Spinach & Feta Stuffed Chicken with Pesto & Mediterranean Salsa

SPICE: Paprika, Sweet
    Chef Gail's Chipotle Dry Rub
    Chef Gail's Creole Seasoning Spice Blend
    Chef Gail's Mexican Spice Blend

SPICE: Parsley Leaves, dried
    Chef Gail's Creole Seasoning Spice Blend

SPICE: Peppercorns
    Guinness Pot Roast with Gravy
    Overnight Brine for Pork

SPICE: Peppercorns, Szechuan
    Cantonese Braised Beef

SPICE: Peppercorns, White
    Cantonese Braised Beef

SPICE: Red Chili Powder

Chef Gail's Indian Butter Chicken Spice Blend

SPICE: Red Pepper Flakes
    Chef Gail's Coffee Rub
    Chicken Cacciatore with Basmati Rice
    Firecracker Salmon
    Seafood-Stuffed Portobello Mushrooms
    Spicy Italian Meatballs with Marinara
    Overnight Brine for Pork

SPICE: Sassafras Leaves, dried
    Chef Gail's Creole Seasoning Spice Blend

SPICE: Star Anise
    Cantonese Braised Beef

SPICE: Thyme, dried
    Chef Gail's Chipotle Dry Rub
    Chef Gail's Creole Seasoning Spice Blend
    Chef Gail's Southern Spice Blend

SPICE: Turmeric
    Chef Gail's Indian Butter Chicken Spice Blend

Spinach Leaves, Fresh
    Prosciutto-Stuffed Chicken Breasts with Fig & Honey Sauce
    Spinach & Feta Stuffed Chicken with Pesto & Mediterranean Salsa
    Tuscan-Style Horseradish-Crusted Beef Roulade with Roasted Red Peppers & Provolone

Squash, Yellow
    Roasted Vegetable Lasagna (Vegetarian)

Sriracha Sauce
    Andouille Sausage & Shrimp Cajun Jambalaya

Stock, Beef
    Bourbon BBQ Babyback Ribs
    Cantonese Braised Beef
    Chipotle Roasted Leg of Lamb
    Drunk Irishman's Shepherd's Pie
    Guinness Pot Roast with Gravy
    Swedish Meatballs with White Gravy
    Tuscan-Style Horseradish-Crusted Beef Roulade with Roasted Red Peppers & Provolone

Stock, Chicken
    Andouille Sausage & Shrimp Cajun Jambalaya
    Blood Orange-Roasted Chicken
    Chicken Cacciatore with Basmati Rice
    Chicken Enchiladas
    Just Add Mayo: Curry Chicken Salad
    Lamb Cutlets with Mint Orange Cointreau Sauce
    Latin Flank Steak with Spanish Rice & Bell Peppers in Chipotle Crema Sauce
    Pork Tenderloin with Bourbon Pear Sauce

Prosciutto-Stuffed Chicken Breasts with Fig & Honey Sauce

Stock, Lamb
Chipotle Roasted Leg of Lamb

Sugar
Carolina-Style BBQ Pulled Pork
Chef Gail's BBQ Dry Rub
Cherry-Stuffed Pork Loin with Black Cherry Chutney
Chicken Cacciatore with Basmati Rice
Chicken Enchiladas
Lamb Cutlets with Mint Orange Cointreau Sauce
Latin Flank Steak with Spanish Rice & Bell Peppers in Chipotle Crema Sauce
Pork Tenderloin with Bourbon Pear Sauce
Quick Brine for Chicken Breasts
Spicy Italian Meatballs with Marinara
Teriyaki Chicken with Rice & Broccoli

Sugar, Brown
Carolina-Style BBQ Pulled Pork
Chef Gail's BBQ Dry Rub
Chef Gail's Chipotle Dry Rub
Firecracker Salmon
Teriyaki Chicken with Rice & Broccoli
Overnight Brine for Pork

Sugar, Dark Brown
Bourbon BBQ Babyback Ribs
Chef Gail's Coffee Rub

Sugar, Raw Sugar
Macadamia Nut-Crusted Halibut with Raspberry Sauce

Sugar, Rock
Cantonese Braised Beef

Sugar, Turbinado
Cantonese Braised Beef
Macadamia Nut-Crusted Halibut with Raspberry Sauce

Sun-Dried Tomatoes
Tuscan-Style Horseradish-Crusted Beef Roulade with Roasted Red Peppers & Provolone

Syrup, Maple
Peanut Butter, Bourbon & Bacon Burgers
Southern-Fried Bacon-Wrapped Chicken & Waffles

Tangerine Peel, Dried
Cantonese Braised Beef

Thyme, Fresh
Blood Orange-Roasted Chicken
Guinness Pot Roast with Gravy
Lamb Cutlets with Mint Orange Cointreau Sauce
Tuscan-Style Horseradish-Crusted Beef Roulade with Roasted Red Peppers & Provolone

Overnight Brine for Pork

Tomato Paste
Bourbon BBQ Babyback Ribs
Butter Chicken (a/k/a Indian Chicken Makhani)
Chicken Cacciatore with Basmati Rice
Chicken Enchiladas
Drunk Irishman's Shepherd's Pie

Tomato Puree
Chicken Enchiladas

Tomato Sauce
Chunky Chicken & Corn Chili
Latin Flank Steak with Spanish Rice & Bell Peppers in Chipotle Crema Sauce

Tomatoes, Diced, Fire-Roasted
Andouille Sausage & Shrimp Cajun Jambalaya
Chicken Cacciatore with Basmati Rice
Roasted Vegetable Lasagna (Vegetarian)
Spicy Italian Meatballs with Marinara

Tomatoes, Diced, Small-Diced
Spinach & Feta Stuffed Chicken with Pesto & Mediterranean Salsa

Tomatoes, Sun-Dried
Tuscan-Style Horseradish-Crusted Beef Roulade with Roasted Red Peppers & Provolone

Tortillas, Flour or Corn
Chicken Enchiladas

Turbinado Sugar
Cantonese Braised Beef
Macadamia Nut-Crusted Halibut with Raspberry Sauce

Turkey, Ground
Habanero, Turkey & Sausage Meatballs

Turnips
Cantonese Braised Beef

Vinegar, Apple Cider
Bourbon BBQ Babyback Ribs
Carolina-Style BBQ Pulled Pork
Chicken Enchiladas
Overnight Brine for Pork

Vinegar, Balsamic
Cherry-Stuffed Pork Loin with Black Cherry Chutney
Firecracker Salmon
Prosciutto-Stuffed Chicken Breasts with Fig & Honey Sauce
Tuscan-Style Horseradish-Crusted Beef Roulade with Roasted Red Peppers & Provolone

Vinegar, Balsamic, White
Lamb Cutlets with Mint Orange Cointreau Sauce

Vinegar, Red Wine
    Spinach & Feta Stuffed Chicken with Pesto & Mediterranean Salsa

Vinegar, Rice
    Teriyaki Chicken with Rice & Broccoli

Vinegar, White Wine
    Chicken Ballotine with Rosemary Beurre Blanc Sauce
    Pork Tenderloin with Bourbon Pear Sauce

Waffles, Belgium
    Southern-Fried Bacon-Wrapped Chicken & Waffles

Walnuts
    Cherry-Stuffed Pork Loin with Black Cherry Chutney
    Prosciutto-Stuffed Chicken Breasts with Fig & Honey Sauce

Whiskey, Bourbon
    Bourbon BBQ Babyback Ribs
    Chipotle Roasted Leg of Lamb
    Peanut Butter, Bourbon & Bacon Burgers
    Pork Tenderloin with Bourbon Pear Sauce

Whiskey, Bourbon, Maple-Flavored
    Peanut Butter, Bourbon & Bacon Burgers

Whiskey, Irish
    Drunk Irishman's Shepherd's Pie

White Balsamic Vinegar
    Lamb Cutlets with Mint Orange Cointreau Sauce

White Mushrooms
    Chicken Cacciatore with Basmati Rice
    Tuscan-Style Horseradish-Crusted Beef Roulade with Roasted Red Peppers & Provolone

White Wine
    Blood Orange-Roasted Chicken
    Chicken Ballotine with Rosemary Beurre Blanc Sauce
    Lamb Cutlets with Mint Orange Cointreau Sauce
    Prosciutto-Stuffed Chicken Breasts with Fig & Honey Sauce

Wine, Red
    Cherry-Stuffed Pork Loin with Black Cherry Chutney
    Chicken Cacciatore with Basmati Rice
    Spicy Italian Meatballs with Marinara
    Tuscan-Style Horseradish-Crusted Beef Roulade with Roasted Red Peppers & Provolone

Wine, Rice
    Cantonese Braised Beef

Wine, Shaozing
    Cantonese Braised Beef

Wine, Sherry
    Drunk Irishman's Shepherd's Pie

Wine, White
    Blood Orange-Roasted Chicken
    Chicken Ballotine with Rosemary Beurre Blanc Sauce
    Lamb Cutlets with Mint Orange Cointreau Sauce
    Prosciutto-Stuffed Chicken Breasts with Fig & Honey Sauce

Worcestershire Sauce
    Andouille Sausage & Shrimp Cajun Jambalaya
    Bourbon BBQ Babyback Ribs
    Chicken Enchiladas
    Peanut Butter, Bourbon & Bacon Burgers
    Spicy Italian Meatballs with Marinara
    Swedish Meatballs with White Gravy

Zucchini
    Roasted Vegetable Lasagna (Vegetarian)

INDEX OF RECIPE MIX & MATCH COMPONENTS

Marinades
- Cilantro Marinade 108
- Firecracker Marinade 53
- Latin Flank Steak Marinade 37
- Teriyaki Chicken & Marinade 43
- Tuscan-Style Marinade 67

Proteins
- Bacon Burger Patties 77
- Grilled Lamb Cutlets 116
- Guinness Pot Roast 188
- Pork Tenderloin 125, 127
- Seafood Stuffing 142
- Shepherd's Pie Filling 154

Rice Dishes
- Basmati Rice 33, 43
- Spanish Rice 37

Salsas & Chutneys
- Black Cherry Chutney 127
- Cherry & Walnut Stuffing 127
- Mango Salsa 108
- Mediterranean Salsa 98

Sauces & Glazes
- Blood Orange Glaze 49
- Bourbon BBQ Sauce 136
- Bourbon Pear Sauce 132
- Chipotle Crema Sauce 37
- Chipotle Pan Sauce 120
- Coffee Butter 73
- Enchilada Sauce 163
- Fig & Honey Sauce 83
- Firecracker Glaze 53
- Guinness Beef Gravy 188
- Makhani Sauce 88
- Marinara Sauce
- Mediterranean Salsa 98
- Mint Orange Cointreau Sauce 176
- Peanut Butter, Bourbon & Jalapeno Sauce 77
- Pesto Sauce 98
- Raspberry Sauce 146
- Red Wine Demi-Glace 68
- Rosemary Beurre Blanc Sauce 92
- Southern-Style BBQ Sauce 193
- Teriyaki Chicken & Marinade/Sauce 43
- White Gravy 171

Side Dishes
- Basmati Rice 33, 46
- Grilled Mandarin Oranges 116
- Mashed potatoes 154
- Sauteed Bell Peppers 37
- Seafood Stuffing 142
- Spanish Rice 37

RESOURCES

EQUIVALENCY & MEASUREMENT GUIDE

DRY MEASUREMENT EQUIVALENTS

tsp (teaspoon)	TBSP (Table-spoon)	cup (fraction)	cup (decimal)
3	1	1/16	0.06
6	2	1/8	0.13
9	3	3/16	0.19
12	4	1/4	0.25
16	5 TBSP + 1 tsp	1/3	0.33
24	8	1/2	0.50
32	10 TBSP + 2 tsp	2/3	0.66
36	12	34	0.75
48	16	1	1.00

Dash or pinch = less than 1/8 teaspoon

1 CUP CONVERSIONS - DRY & LIQUID

cups	TBSP	tsp	fl oz / oz	g	mL
1	16	48	8	227	240
3/4	12	36	6	170	180
2/3	10 + 2/3	32	5	142	158
1/2	8	24	4	113	120
1/3	5 + 1/3	16	3	85	79
1/4	4	12	2	57	60
1/8	2	6	1	28	30
1/16	1	3	1/2	14	15

1 CUP QUICK REFERENCE

1 cup =	48 tsp
	16 TBSP
	227 grams
	8 fluid ounces (fl oz)
	1/2 pint
	1/4 quart
	1/16 gallon
	240 mL
	1 cup BUTTER = 2 sticks = 16 TBSP = 8 ounces = 1/2 pound = 227 grams

LIQUID MEASUREMENT EQUIVALENTS

fl oz	tsp	TBSP	cup	pint	quart	gallon	metric
1 fl oz	6	2	1/8	1/16	1/32	1/128	30mL
2 fl oz	12	4	1/4	1/8	1/16	1/64	60mL
4 fl oz	24	8	1/2	1/4	1/8	1/32	120mL
8 fl oz	48	16	1	1/2	1/4	1/16	240mL
16 fl oz	96	32	2	1	1/2	1/8	480mL
32 fl oz	192	64	4	2	1	1/4	.95 liters
64 fl oz	384	128	8	4	2	1/2	1.9 liters
128 fl oz	768	256	16	8	4	1	3.8 liters

COMMON US TO METRIC EQUIVALENTS

1 oz	= 28g
1 fl oz	= 30mL
1 cup	= 228g
1 fl cup	= 237mL
1 pound	= 456g
1000g / 1kg	= 35 oz = 2.2 pounds

1 POUND QUICK REFERENCE

1 pound =	16 ounces
	2 cups
	32 TBSP
	96 tsp
	454 grams
	.45 kilograms

COMMON METRIC TO US EQUIVALENTS

1g	= .035 oz
100g	= 3.5 oz
228g	= 8 oz = 1 cup
454g	= 2 cups = 1 pound
500g	= 1.1 lb
1000g / 1kg	= 35 oz = 2.2 pounds
1mL	= .03 fl oz
15mL	= .5 fl oz = 1 TBSP
100mL	= 3.38 fl oz
237mL	= 8 fl oz = 1 fl cup
500mL	= 17 fl oz
950mL	= 32 fl oz = 1 quart
3787mL	= 128 fl oz = 1 gallon

EGG EQUIVALENTS QUICK REFERENCE

Recipe calls for:	Extra-Large	Medium	Small	Liquid Eggs	Metric
1 egg	1	1	2	3 TBSP	45 mL
2 eggs	2	2	3	1/3 cup	90 mL
3 eggs	3	4	4	1/2 cup	135 mL
4 eggs	3	5	6	3/4 cup	180 mL
5 eggs	4	6	7	1 cup	225 mL
6 eggs	5	7	8	1-1/4 cup	270 mL

TEMPERATURE GUIDE FOR COOKING MEATS AND FISH

Temperatures shown should always be taken with an instant-read stem thermometer or meat thermometer. To ensure your thermometer is reading temperatures accurately, calibrate often (at least once per month or before a batch cooking session).

For instructions on how to calibrate thermometers, please watch the *"How to Calibrate Stem Thermometers"* instructional video (*see Chapter 13: Quick Guide to Online Tools*).

BEEF
GROUND BEEF

160°F
(71°C)
Ground Beef

BEEF ROASTS & STEAKS

120°F	130°F	140°F	150°F	160°F
(49°C)	(54°C)	(60°C)	(65°C)	(71°C)
Rare	Medium-Rare	Medium	Medium-Well	Well Done

CHICKEN / POULTRY

165°F	165°F
(74°C)	(74°C)
All Poultry	Ground Poultry

LAMB
GROUND LAMB

160°F
(71°C)
Ground Lamb

LAMB ROASTS & STEAKS

120°F	130°F	140°F	150°F	160°F
(49°C)	(54°C)	(60°C)	(65°C)	(71°C)
Rare	Medium-Rare	Medium	Medium-Well	Well Done

PORK
GROUND PORK

160°F
(71°C)
Ground Pork

PORK LOINS, ROASTS & STEAKS

145°F	160°F
(63°C)	(71°C)
Medium	Well Done

FISH

145°F
(63°C)
Fish will be opaque and will flake easily with a fork

"The temperatures listed above represent the Author's opinion and best practices at time of this printing. Temperature safety guidelines are subject to change. For the most current cooking temperature recommendations, consult the USDA website.

Questions?

Reach out to Chef Gail with any questions you may have:

 *@askchefgail*
info@frozenandfabulous.com

*To stay in touch, and receive exciting new recipes and cooking tips, subscribe to
Chef Gail's newsletter at
www.frozenandfabulous.com*